CW01648231

'A one-stop shop for students and scholars of the eighteenth century interested in the history of girlhood.'

Elaine Chalus, *University of Liverpool*

'Deborah Simonton draws on her extensive research in lesser-known archives to offer a comprehensive overview of a life-stage which is often overlooked. The wealth of material makes it a valuable resource for both students and educators.'

Alison Duncan, *freelance historian*

'[This book] provides a comprehensive and current overview of the experience of girlhood in eighteenth-century Europe. A must read for students and scholars of early modern social history.'

Katie Barclay, *Macquarie University*

GIRLHOOD IN EIGHTEENTH-CENTURY BRITAIN

This book draws on a wide range of sources to provide the first comprehensive account of the experience of eighteenth-century working girlhood across all regions of Britain, examining the lifecycle stage of growing up for the middling and lower classes as they worked and prepared for a life of work.

Studies of history have often tended to slide over the distinct history of girls in its focus on women's history, merging their stories into broader narratives. This volume continues the more recent historical reclamation of girls and girlhood as a useful analytical tool, while also specifically addressing the lacunae in histories of eighteenth-century working girls. Examining the role of home, schools and apprenticeships in girls' upbringing, it considers how mobility shaped their trajectories. Furthermore, it examines sociability, love, sex and the 'misfortunes' they might encounter. An underpinning message is the active role that girls played in shaping their own destinies using whatever tools were at their disposal.

Written in an accessible style and bridging gaps in the literature, this volume is a valuable resource for university courses in the history of childhood and women's studies/history.

Deborah Simonton is Associate Professor of British History, *emerita*, University of Southern Denmark; Visiting Professor, University of Turku; and Fellow of the Royal Historical Society. She is co-editor of the *Routledge History of Loneliness* (2023), and author of *Gender in the European Town* (2023).

Consider, my dear girl, that you have no portions, and endeavour to supply the deficiencies of fortune by mind.

Eliza Heywood, *Present for a Servant Maid* (1743), 41.

GIRLHOOD IN EIGHTEENTH-CENTURY BRITAIN

The Working Girl

Deborah Simonton

Routledge
Taylor & Francis Group
LONDON AND NEW YORK

Designed cover image: *The Watercress Girl* (oil on canvas). Zoffany, Johann (1733–1810) / German.
Private Collection. © Bonhams, London, UK / Bridgeman Images.

First published 2026
by Routledge
4 Park Square, Milton Park, Abingdon, Oxon OX14 4RN

and by Routledge
605 Third Avenue, New York, NY 10158

Routledge is an imprint of the Taylor & Francis Group, an informa business

British Library Cataloguing-in-Publication Data
A catalogue record for this book is available from the British Library

ISBN: 978-1-032-53464-0 (hbk)
ISBN: 978-1-032-53465-7 (pbk)
ISBN: 978-1-003-41216-8 (ebk)

DOI: 10.4324/9781003412168

Typeset in Sabon
by Apex CoVantage, LLC

CONTENTS

FIGURES

IMAGES

TABLES

ACKNOWLEDGEMENTS

This volume is the culmination of sporadic work over some fifty years and over that time so many people have kindly provided advice, documents, ideas and sources that are too many to remember or name. Parts of this began as a thesis under the supervision of Ludmilla Jordanova, examined by Leonore Davidoff and John Rule. I thank them for their guidance and advice all those many years ago. When considering how to publish the material, especially Chapter 5, I am grateful for the conversation with Helen Berry and Patrick Wallis. I am also grateful to Patrick for sharing his unpublished manuscript with me; so very generous. Some of this material was published in different forms across the years and most of this is noted in the bibliography, but Maxine Berg, Hugh Cunningham and Jacques Le Carré were instrumental in encouraging me to do so. Over the years sections were presented at a number or conferences, especially ESSHC and EAUH, and I appreciate the comments made during these discussions.

Essex and Staffordshire County Archives and Aberdeen City Archives, Aberdeen University Archives and Local Studies at Aberdeen City Library were important sources for much of the original research and I thank especially Janet Nelson, at Staffordshire then Essex, and colleagues in Aberdeen. Elizabeth-Anne Haldane and Silvija Banic at the V&A were prompt and helpful when I asked about the definition of the mysterious word 'slesy' which flummoxed us all. Similarly, Lucy Lead of the V&A Wedgwood collection provided the text of Ann Keeling's hiring agreement because my notes were remarkably vague. Chris Speller, Headmaster of King Edward's School, and his assistant, David Kendrick-White, were enthusiastic in proving a good image of the Romford Charity Girl statue, which sits in the foyer of the school, the successor of the charity school included here. Becky Geller of

Haverhill Public Library helped with the Bennet Family papers in their collection and Derek Heideman for transcriptions on the Old Sturbridge Village site.

Fundamental to this project were my colleagues and friends who egged me on, read bits, discussed images and other bits and pieces. I am grateful to them for being there: Elaine Chalus, Katie Barclay, Nina Javette Koefoed, Marjo Kaartinen, Anne Montenach, Janine Lanza. My deep gratitude goes to Jennifer Morrow of Routledge for clearing up my messes in the manuscript to make this a better book and to Chelsea Jackman of Apex for a sensitive and sympathetic copyediting. As ever, I appreciate the support of (and dinners with) Eve Setch of Routledge—we go a long way back now. And everlasting gratitude to David Hastie who tolerates me and tries to protect me from myself, and to our two wonderful girlies, Cally and Clio.

INTRODUCTION

Prelude: two working girlhoods

Elizabeth Palmer was born in Wootten Wawen in June of 1768, with only her mother, also Elizabeth, noted in the registers. She was later recorded as from Henley in Arden, 5 km away. At ten, Solihull parish placed her as an apprentice to Joseph Chamberlain of Lapworth, a farmer. She was described as a 'singlewoman', often code for an orphan. She stayed two months and then went to Kidderminster to live with her 'father in law', possibly a stepfather, or her unnamed father, where she stayed for three years. She went back to Solihull when she was thirteen, about 1781, but no reason was given for her leaving him. Solihull parish then removed her to Lapworth, presumably because officials thought they no longer had responsibility for her. In 1783, the Lapworth parish officer took her to Northfield because her master, Mr Chamberlain, was on poor relief in the parish, and as such, he and his parish were responsible for her. He agreed to her serving another farmer, George Davenport, for a year with a wage of 25s, thus removing her from Solihull parish responsibility. She then disappears from poor law records. However, in 1784, in Birmingham St Martin parish, Elizabeth Palmer 'of this parish' married William Yates also of the parish. He signed while she made a mark.[1] Thus despite an erratic youth, she may well have entered into adulthood with some security.

Tradesmen's daughters also worked. Sarah Hurst of Horsham, Sussex, (1736–1808) was recorded in the register when she was baptised at St. Mary's parish church on 4 May 1736 as 'the base-born daughter of Mary Tasker', though certainly Richard Hurst, a local tailor, was her father, and her parents married in November that year. Tailoring was in the family since both her

DOI: 10.4324/9781003412168-1

IMAGE 0.1 Prince Hoare, 1755–1834, Head of a Young Girl, 1780. Graphite, red chalk and black chalk on medium, slightly textured, cream laid paper, Yale Center for British Art, Paul Mellon Collection, B1977.14.5050.

grandfather and an uncle were tailors. Despite modest means, she was well educated, and at ease in polite society. But hers was a working girlhood. Home and work were the same place, and she expected to help with chores around the house as well as assisting in the tailoring business, which occupied her during the day. Sarah worked for her father by keeping accounts, writing letters to suppliers or clients and serving in the shop. She also cut out farm labourers' smocks and sailors' jackets and sewed ladies' clothes. She worked six days a week and she often commented on its incessant character. 'Wednesday, 26 September 1759. Work very hard fancying the pattern of my apron, but am often interrupted by people in the shop. Allmost wish I did not love work so well, yet it passes away many hours that I shou'd probably employ by tormenting myself about what hangs like a heavy load at my Heart (her love interest).' 'Wednesday, 16 April 1760. Extreamly busy in the shop with various sorts of customers & work, business is certainly the finest thing in the world for depressed spirits.' 'Thursday, 27 November 1760. Fair Day, a great many people in the shop, am fatigu'd with waiting on them.' She also travelled to London to buy stock at London warehouses and tried to smooth over disagreements that occurred between her father and his brother, Robert, in their partnership. On a visit to London in November 1761, Sarah carried a large sum of money to invest in 'the Stocks' (Consolidated Bank Stocks) sewn into her stays for safe keeping. She had close friends with whom she spent her spare time, often playing cards; she visited other places in England on holidays. She also visited local dignitaries, attended theatre and was a regular churchgoer.

At age sixteen she met and fell in love with Henry Smith, a marine who served in the Seven Years War (1756–1763). He was thirteen years older and theirs was largely a private courtship, often by correspondence since he was away for most of it, while his merchant family did not approve of his liaison with the daughter of a tradesman. There is some indication that her father also wanted to keep her working in the shop and that he, like her future in-laws, had concerns about finding the dowry. When they married in 1762 it was a private wedding, and the pages of her diary were cut out, leaving a blank in her story. Ultimately the dowry was sorted, and they remained married until his death; she returned to Horsham as a widow, living in Causeway House, Horsham, gifted to her by her brother.[2]

Thus, Sarah Hurst had quite a different girlhood from Elizabeth Palmer. Because she kept a diary for part of her girlhood, we also get glimpses into what mattered to her, her feelings and experiences. We hear her voice, and we see the life of Sarah in a way that we don't see many of the working girls this book discusses. Her experience reinforces one of the key themes of this volume: that girls worked during their girlhoods and were not only from the labouring orders, but also from the middling families, like tradesmen's. Like many others whose stories help shape this volume, this feature helps nuance and illustrate the lives of girls who worked, played, loved and dealt with what life threw at them.

Girlhood as lifecycle

The lifecycle stage identified with girlhood is fraught with complexities and multi-layered views of what the stages of life before adulthood consisted and how they were demarcated. Similarly, milestones by which we measure lifecycle are not consistent over time and place. Our world is frequently shaped by age-bound identities, many created by influences outside girls, like schools, churches and legislation. Such markers were far more nebulous for the eighteenth century, although Hugh Cunningham notes that 'in the eighteenth-century birthdays were increasingly recognised and celebrated as signs of progress through the life course'.[3] Society nevertheless had an awareness of the life course, which shaped how boys and girls were perceived. Likewise, they had a common-sense view of girlhood. This stage was seen as formative and was a time when girls engaged in the process of earning, learning and becoming adults. It was a transitional period, characterised as semi-dependent in contrast to the complete dependence of infancy and the relative independence of adulthood. Girls and their parents understood that girlhood was a period when they began to separate from the family and go into school, apprenticeship, service or work. It was when they internalised adult roles and came into adult rights. It was also when they explored their sexuality, when they played and socialised with others like themselves. They sometimes struggled as they were buffeted by storms that girlhood brought them and developed strategies for coping. Many showed great resilience; others were not so lucky. Girlhood was multifaceted. Some girls spent years at home, like Hurst, but many spent these years in the homes of others as Palmer did. Throughout the early modern period, children were sent to homes other than their families' for work, service and training and for the acquisition of manners and patterns of behaviour. Marriage commonly marked the end of girlhood, and the skills, knowledge, customs and dowries they had acquired were necessary prerequisites to set them up as married women. While parental attitudes and agendas often shaped the outlines of girlhood, girls themselves had a hand in making decisions about how they traversed these years. They often hired themselves out, especially servants who were highly mobile and were prepared to move jobs to suit themselves. So, while girlhood had significance within the social constructions of eighteenth-century Britain and Europe, it also had meaning for the girls themselves.

Studying girls

Girls and girlhood have often been merged into other histories, rather than recognising them as having a distinct history of their own. As women's history developed in the latter quarter of the twentieth century, it subsumed girls under the heading of woman, as 'young women', and they disappeared as an identifiable lifecycle stage. With the growth of women's studies, the term 'girl' was eschewed for its often demeaning use; referring to women as 'girls' was a way to undermine and diminish them, so avoiding the term became a means to assert women's rights and their positions in society, contemporarily and historically. Contemporary girlhood studies began to reclaim the term 'girl' and especially girlhood from the 1980s. The writing of women's history was slower to reclaim girls, although 'single' women featured prominently in Joan Scott and Louise Tilly's *Women, Work and Family* in 1978, most of whom fit the description of girl, while Amy Froide's research on single women recognised the importance of young singletons.[4] Broad surveys, like Merry Wiesner's *Women and Gender in Early Modern Europe*, Heide Wunder's *He is the Sun and She is the Moon* and Sheilagh Ogilvie's *A Bitter Living*, contextualise girls' experience, but do not give detailed recognition to it.[5] Certainly most histories of women pay some attention to childhood and to 'young women'. The largest body of research on eighteenth-century girls comprises educational histories although most focus on middling girls and rarely examine girlhood as a period or stage in itself. The wide literature on service—domestic, rural and industrial—similarly are about the lifecycle stage while not always marking it.

The context is further complicated by youth and childhood studies which frequently do not distinguish between girls and boys, in which neutral terms like 'children' or 'scholars' are employed. For example, Philippe Ariès's landmark study *Centuries of Childhood* uses the term 'pupils' and grants girls a precious few sentences.[6] However, surveys by Hugh Cunningham, Colin Heywood, Anthony Fletcher and Peter Stearns disaggregate girls and boys to some extent as does Ivy Pinchbeck and Margaret Hewitt's classic *Children in English Society*, although their story is the overview of childhood.[7] Fletcher, in particular, sought to gender the history of childhood, and while not surprisingly dominated by the better sorts, his *Growing Up in England: The Experience of Childhood, 1600–1914* stands apart from the others. Anna French's edited collection *Early Modern Childhood: An Introduction* represents newer literature on gendered childhood, with a sensitive approach to the differences between girls' and boys' childhoods. Historical approaches to girls as daughters, children, servants, apprentices and workers have been shaped by fashions in history, so the idea of girlhood was less likely to infuse older studies. However, recent collections, like Paula Fass's *Routledge History of Childhood in the Western World*, far more often contrasts girls' and boy's experiences. Nevertheless, often the story told is simply male and none of these discuss girlhood explicitly.

More recently there has been an upsurge in interest in female youth, or girlhood, which recognised that contemporary girls' experience differed significantly from boys'. The field expanded rapidly in the early years of the twenty-first century with the creation of journals, like *Girlhood Studies: An Interdisciplinary Journal* and the *Journal of Childhood and Youth* in 2008. *Girlhood Studies* aimed to both set up and challenge the need for girlhood studies and examine the relationship between girlhood studies, women's, boyhood and masculinity studies.[8] Several monographs and edited collections complemented this development, claiming a place for girlhood studies in the canon. Notable among these is Claudia Mitchell and Carrie Rentschler's *Girlhood and the Politics of Place*, which 'approach[es] place as an especially productive and enabling concept in the field of girlhood studies, one that provides needed specificity to the very meaning of *girl*'. Their volume speaks to the ways girls 'struggle to assert their rights to territory and autonomous spaces'.[9] An important contribution is that girlhood studies is increasingly a multi-sited and transnational field, a feature exemplified by Jennifer Helgren and Colleen A. Vasconcellos's *Girlhood: A Global History*, placing girls within their national settings within a global project. It critically explores history of girlhood in international and transnational contexts to ask new questions and reframe old ones with new insights.[10] Thus, girlhood studies have increasingly recognised that the experience of the western world and especially a Eurocentric lens radically misses the experience of vast numbers of girls in other cultures and regions. Studies also expanded interest into non-white studies, acknowledging that middle-class white experience certainly did not represent the life cycles of black and ethnic minority girls, and especially those from other cultures. The significance of this research and the ensuing discussions cannot be underestimated. It coincided with the declaration of 11 October as the International Day of the Girl Child by the United Nations in 2012.

This interest in girls also provoked studies exploring national and regional identities. Arguing that most research has embraced either Anglo-American contexts or the global South, *Nordic Girlhoods: New Perspectives and Outlooks* makes the case for in-depth studies of specific areas and focuses on 'how different Nordic girlhoods and young femininities—some idealized and internationally known, others more invisible and degraded—are imagined, produced, and negotiated through different societal and cultural norms'.[11] This expanding research reflects the increase in consideration of girls' roles and behaviour and their singular visibility in modern popular culture. As a result, these histories are explicitly tied to the contemporary world and the meanings of female adolescence, while girls before the rise of modern feminism tended to be left out of the story. Edited collections on girlhood often began with the twentieth century, sometimes the middle of the nineteenth. For example, *Girlhood: A Global History* has one chapter dealing with the eighteenth and nineteenth centuries, attempting to look beyond the tendency of the present-mindedness of contemporary popular culture; the rest of those mentioned earlier begin mid- to late nineteenth century, and are contemporary. So, while a historical girlhood has gradually developed, bringing girls into focus in their own right, most remain tied to contemporary girls, adolescence and the 'girl problem'.

The eighteenth century, often seen as a watershed between the early modern and modern world, however, was largely under-researched until recently. In 2005, a small group of researchers recognised the lacuna and included chapters on the seventeenth and eighteenth centuries in *Secret Gardens and Satanic Mills: Placing European Girls in European History, 1750–1960*.[12] With a firmly European focus, it embraced a range of themes from education and work, leisure, to girls in trouble and building identities. As Mary-Jo Maynes explained, 'taking girls into account pushes us toward a revision of many aspects of modern European history'.[13] A pioneering and wide-ranging collection, it stood almost alone. Ten years later, a panel on the history of the girl at the Congress of the International Committee of Historians held in Jinan, China, returned to the issue, leading to the slightly eclectic volume, *A History of the Girl: Formation, Education and Identity*. While it concentrates on upbringing, education and work, it also reaches out to embrace a global story. Nevertheless, the bulk of the resultant volume remains centred on the nineteenth and twentieth centuries, though with Mary O'Dowd's useful discussion of girls in eighteenth-century Ireland.[14] In 2018, Elizabeth Cohen and Margaret Reeves edited a collection specifically on *Early Modern Female Youth*.[15] With a broad European spread, it examines perceptions and meanings of girlhood, education, training and sexual behaviour. As each chapter considers a specific place and case study, they contribute to generating a picture of girls and girlhood from the sixteenth to early eighteenth century. However, the term 'female youth' positions the male as the norm and the female as the other; this is the key reason for using a term like girlhood in this volume, which speaks directly to girls' experience and the formation of identity. An exception is French's collection, mentioned earlier, which is not only 'early modern' but also includes substantial research on the eighteenth century in its analyses.

Gender, class and race

The central thesis of Catherine Hall and Leonore Davidoff's *Family Fortunes: Men and Women of the English Middle Class, 1780–1850* rests on the assumption that gender and class always operate together, and that consciousness of class always takes a gendered form. Their identification of a tension between class aspirations and feminine identity corresponds with the ways in which gender was constructed for girls through schooling, apprenticeship and informal systems through which culture was transmitted. Thus, class and gender are intertwined in the ways that girlhood is constructed. While girls who worked are often perceived as coming from the plebeian orders, a significant cohort were from the middling orders. As Froide says:

> Never-married women whose fathers were craftsmen, tradesmen, or professionals often found they needed to support themselves. Some of these women had parents who provided them with an education or training to ensure that they would be able to maintain themselves if need be. Other women pursued training or skills on their own or later in life.[16]

Recovering girls' own voices is highly problematic for this period. Because so few describe their own experiences, historians struggle to see them as actors in their own lives, and 'the sources documenting the history of childhood and youth are at best scattered, often sketchy and inconsistent'.[17] As Peter Earle said:

> [T]he chief witness, the child, is rarely heard at all and parents too are normally silent about their relationships with their children. One is left with a few hints from diarists and autobiographers, a few vignettes providing

> glimpses of children at home, at school or at play, a large number of complaints about the bad behaviour of the children of the poor, and a whole library of moralistic and didactic literature telling readers what children and childrearing should be like but not necessarily what they were like.[18]

Girls were recorded in administrative records, like apprenticeship records, school minute books and early censuses, but the material is often opaque and projects a passive image of girls. Also, these texts which give us glimpses of girls' life stories are mediated, like the Settlement Examinations used frequently in this volume, which were written by adults. These are invaluable for the insights they provide, while at the same time they are often formulaic and relate to the demands of the poor law system. Court cases may illuminate the lives of girls lower down the scale, but they present a snapshot, and girls are less well represented than boys in these records. They also do not reflect the 'normative' girl because they involve the exceptional, though careful reading can open doors into their lives.

Memoirs and autobiographies, suggesting recollections of lived experience, also were often produced by the adult narrator, not the child or girl. A tantalising few autobiographical materials do exist, and an important feature is that not all were poor or illiterate—though many were. Rarely, however, do we hear girls' own voices, since the voice of the girl is mediated in these cases by adults and officials, so that 'much of the history of girlhood is necessarily, because of the nature of the sources, not the history of girls but rather of the ways in which adults tried to shape young women through laws, schools, apprenticeship, sermons, advice, and other means'.[19]

In scholarship, elite and middling girls often get more attention simply because there is more information and accessible material. Diaries and letters are far more plentiful for them, several of whom were articulate recounters of their youth. Yet, several of these girls were also 'working girls' often as authors, but not exclusively so. Thus, Elizabeth Ham, daughter of a struggling farmer, gave an account of going to a variety of and considerable number of schools, of a less-than-stable family life and feeling unwanted. Anne Taylor Gilbert described how she and her sisters worked with their mother keeping house and learned engraving with their father and his apprentices.[20] Sarah Hurst described her work in the family tailoring business. Such middling accounts provide indicative insights to girlhood.

Most historians of the eighteenth century use the language of the period which refers to 'orders' and 'ranks', and most eschew a concept of 'class' as inappropriate to the period. However, this is not an unchallenged view, much of the debate centring on what is meant by 'class' in the first place.[21] The term 'class' did not appear in contemporary language until the nineteenth century, while 'class consciousness in the sense of recognising the collective interest of a "working class" as opposed to a "capitalist class", and expressed in terms of the ideologies which both form and develop from that consciousness, are inappropriate to the analysis of eighteenth-century society'.[22] Yet, if class is 'a *historical* category . . . derived from the observation of the social process over time', a case can be made for using the term predating the nineteenth century but exerting 'caution against any tendency to read back subsequent notions of class'.[23] Contemporary perceptions of 'place' in eighteenth-century society manifest cultural ideals in a variety of practices which define the social relations between what E. P. Thompson refers to as patrician society and plebeian culture. Plebeian culture of the eighteenth century was in many respects articulate in its resistance to the ideas and institutions of the ruling classes, while tracts which promulgated a particular form of behaviour for different groups of people partly articulated a tension between classes which marked relations at the end of the eighteenth century.

Contemporary writers referred to the lower orders or middling orders because eighteenth-century society did not perceive monolithic or homogenised classes, but several echelons. Both Gregory King's and Patrick Colquhoun's listings of society based on income lend weight to this assertion as does Defoe's ranking of society into seven groups, according to consumption.[24] Within each level, there were minute gradations which were important to people throughout the century in creating status differentiation and defining one's place in society. As society changed, these distinctions were continually reworked. Defoe was at great pains to distinguish tradesmen from manufacturers and artisans on the one hand and pedlars on the other.[25] Amongst the poor, society distinguished between the deserving poor and paupers, poor honest labourers and those reliant upon parish relief. For example, educationalist Catharine Cappe separated 'orphan children of worthy respectable parents reduced by misfortune and the distressed offspring of those who may always have filled the lowest stations'.[26] In this way, these girls came from not only the labouring orders or the poor but also from the middling folk, like Ann and Mary Hogarth, sisters of artist William Hogarth, both of whom became milliners like their mother; or Ann Buchanan from an established gentry family of Clackmannanshire. Such blurring of class distinctions is a reminder that work encompassed a wide range of occupations from the casual and menial tasks supporting eighteenth-century life, to highly skilled women in medicine, business and fashion trades. Earning a living was often the motivation for girls, and family support was not necessarily available, nor was it always desirable. Girls could and did make choices when opportunities allowed.

Because this volume focuses on Britain, race and ethnicity play a smaller role than they would in a global volume. Yet, a growing black community in Europe was feature of the century, with slaves brought directly from Africa and others who came to Europe, and especially Britain, via the West Indies.[27] In Britain, Lord Mansfield estimated the population of Indians and blacks at

15,000 in 1772. In most cases, this was not a voluntary migration and had already begun to cause anxiety in the metropole. Additionally, free blacks arrived, often with masters and mistresses or as soldiers and sailors. Singular individuals like Samuel Johnson's manservant, Francis Barber, worked and lived in bourgeois, aristocratic, royal and elite houses, or Mansfield's niece, Dido Elizabeth Belle, born of a slave mother and a British naval officer, was raised as a gentlewoman. Others became educated and notable authors like Olaudah Equiano and Ignatius Sancho in Britain. A tension with people of colour as 'others' formed early. The Mansfield judgement (1772), though intended to protect free blacks in Britain from enslavement, was only partly successful. At the same time, the black community itself manifested concern about the 'continuing plight of the Black poor in Britain'.[28] Many members of the black communities were integrated into the labouring classes often as servants. Options tended to be limited, and many were members of the menial poor, including prostitutes, but others made it into entertainment worlds, like Irish singer Rachel Baptiste who sang in Ireland and Britain from 1750 and continued to do so after her marriage in 1758.[29]

Eighteenth-century girlhood

This book complements and enriches existing studies on modern girlhood and adolescence described previously by examining the lives of girls and the cultural meanings associated with them in the eighteenth century. It looks at the range of their experiences across the years we associate with adolescence, while clearly acknowledging the significant differences not only in experience but also in the ways girlhood was conceived, its purposes and options. It focuses on girls who worked to counter the larger literature on middling girls' education and family life and pulls them from the shadows of children's history. It explores the positives of this experience offsetting the often negative images associated with children's lives in poorer families.

This history focuses on the experience of British girls, drawing attention to comparisons and contrasts. Its focus is on the *working girl*—that is, girls who worked—so that most are from below the middling sort, girls who are often side-lined in historical studies or subsumed under the term children. At the same time, it acknowledges that some girls from the middling orders also worked and trained for work, and this volume explores how and why they became working girls. It draws on a body of primary research and a variety of British archives as well as building on existing studies to create a comprehensive account of girls' experience of becoming adults. Thus, as a blend of original research and synthesis it provides a wide-ranging story of the experiences of growing up in the eighteenth century.

It opens by examining the idea of girlhood within eighteenth-century society, exploring both contemporary perceptions and historians' interpretations.

It then places female childhood in the context of the lifecycle. The remainder of the volume is organised thematically beginning with learning and training opportunities and then working. These necessarily overlap since, for example, service and apprenticeship embraced both activities. Many girls were remarkably mobile and this theme threads through several chapters. The discussion then broadens out to explore girls' relationship to money including earning, spending, saving and even credit relations. Life was not all work however, and girls' social life, leisure and associational activities further expanded their lives. These activities then led to a fuller discussion of sex, intimacy, courtship and choices for adulthood. Life in the eighteenth century carried with it a number of pitfalls, and so we turn to look at 'when it all goes wrong', including poverty, illness and the implications of broken promises and potentially pregnancy. Girls were not passive in the process of their girlhood and so in addition to the range of decision-making in the previous chapters, the volume explores how they coped with misfortune—or not. The story concludes by looking briefly at the end of girlhood, and finishes by arguing that girls were active in shaping the course of their girlhood, utilising the opportunities and options they had at hand and working within social, economic and legal systems.

How do we know?

Historians deploy a wide range of sources in their work, and in the case of girls, we are often looking for hidden voices.[30] Historical evidence comes in a variety of different forms, and the range of materials employed by historians has expanded, especially because women's and gender historians have exploited new sources or approached well-known sources with a new eye and new questions. Primary sources are in one sense the 'raw material' of history. They are the closest we will come to the past; they are the 'original traces' of the people we want to know and understand. But they are not the history itself. They are laden with potential but must be read, understood and contextualised to realise their possibilities. They are also limited in that one source only tells one story—and probably part of one at that. So they have to be read together and situated in context. They also have to be interrogated. A key source for girls' lives is observer's testimonies, everything from tracts and conduct books to observations from lawyers, travellers, commentators and more. Clearly these are written from specific perspectives, often moralistic or campaigning for change, but they can provide detailed insights to the circumstances of girls' lives. There is a mythical notion that sources give us historical 'truth', but not so. People are notoriously poor witnesses even when they intend to be or assume they are being reliable. And consciously or unconsciously, writers and other producers of evidence were steeped in their own 'baggage' of class, gender and values, and their texts must be read with a critical mind. Thus Sarah Trimmer, Catharine Cappe, Arthur Young and Daniel Defoe were useful in developing this book, but they have to be understood in their own context, and Young and Defoe for example were not necessarily interested in girls' lives—girls were a by-product and a key example of looking for hidden lives. Newspapers, like the *Aberdeen Journal*, and magazines fall into the slightly grey area of sources. They are a key form of historical artefact and are usually treated as primary sources. And, logically, they need to be treated with the same sort of scepticism and critical mind as any other text. For example, the editors of the *Aberdeen Journal*, James Chalmers, Sr and Jr, father and son, were Hanoverians, which shaped much of the content of the paper, but had less effect on their reportage of women's indiscretions and their sometimes not-so-subtle attitudes to women.

The most obvious kind of source is the array of documents concerning legal, domestic or business matters, produced for a practical purpose at the time, not with historians in mind, such as legal deeds, apprenticeship indentures, school minute books or codes of law. Many local and national administrative records from parish records to census materials fall into this category. A frequent source used here is the English settlement and bastardy exams generated from *The Act of Settlement and Removal* (1662) which established the need to prove entitlement to poor relief by the issuing of Settlement Certificates. The certificates proved which parish a family belonged to and therefore which parish had the legal responsibility to provide poor relief if needed. This was not always their place of birth since girls could achieve a settlement by working for a year, serving an apprenticeship or marrying. In this book we shall see that even officials could be unclear about a girl's place of settlement, which entitled her to poor relief; those applying for settlement were not always paupers. The exam was an interview to determine where a person's place of settlement was. Criminal records, like those of the Old Bailey, also provide insight to girls' lives, both as victims and the accused. Although they were factual on one level, thus operating within the constraints of the law, the testimony was coloured by individual perspectives. Also, they are limited in showing only one side of girls' lives, and like settlement exams, they are inclined to capture the darker sides of their experience, whether for crimes, including infanticide, or as victims of rape and abuse. Yet careful interrogation again helps reveal details and snippets of girls' experiences.

There are also personal documents that were intended to be private, such as letters or diaries, like Sarah Hurst's. Letters nominally were between the author and the recipient, but secretaries and friends also assisted in writing, and letters were often shared in close circles. In any case, the author almost inevitably shaped the content for her audience, and if she knew it might be read by others, this would also influence what she wrote as well as its tone. Similarly, memoirs might have been nominally private—written for family members. Yet, some of these were intended for publication or the author imagined that they might be published, and for example, it is probable that the memoirs of the *Friends' Library* were intended for publication. The study of material culture has enlisted the help of fabric, patterns, design, dresses, hats and gloves, pottery, porcelain, silverware, tables, chairs—and these are useful in understanding the spending patterns of girls.

Because this book is partly synthetic, it also draws on the myriad studies which exist on specific aspects of female experience, not all of it explicitly focused on girls but which enables us to build a holistic sense of their lives. Thus, demographic material, studies of all forms of apprenticeship, literacy, family life, schools, childhood, singletons and women more broadly, marriage and sexuality help to construct a view of the lives and experience of girls who worked for a living. In this way, this range of sources and topics creates a well-rounded picture of these girls' lives, restoring their visibility, understanding their lives and their agency and vulnerabilities in eighteenth-century Britain.

Notes

1 BDRO 14. Birth and marriage records from Ancestry.
2 Hurst, *The Diaries of Sarah Hurst*; 'Hurst's Progress—A Horsham Tailor's Daughter and her World': text for website, Horsham Museum.
3 Cunningham, *Children and Childhood*, 24.
4 Tilly and Scott, *Women, Work and Family*; Bennett and Froide, *Singlewomen in the European Past*; Froide, *Never Married: Singlewomen in Early Modern England.*
5 Wiesner, *Women and Gender in Early Modern Europe*; Wunder, *He is the Sun, She is the Moon*; Ogilvie, *A Bitter Living: Women, Markets, and Social Capital in Early Modern Germany.*
6 Ariès, *Centuries of Childhood.* For an overview of the historiography of childhood see Heywood, *Childhood in Modern Europe*, 1–11.
7 Pinchbeck and Hewitt, *Children in English Society*; Heywood, *Childhood in Modern Europe*; Cunningham, *Children and Childhood*; Stearns, *Childhood in World History.*
8 Mitchell, Reid-Walsh and Kirk, 'Editorial'.
9 Mitchell and Rentschler, *Girlhood and the Politics of Place.*
10 Helgren and Vasconcellos, *Girlhood: A Global History*, 1.
11 Formark, Mulari and Voipio, *Nordic Girlhoods: New Perspectives and Outlooks*, 2.
12 Benninghaus, Maynes and Söland, *Secret Gardens, Satanic Mills.*
13 Maynes, 'Age as a Category of Historical Analysis', 115; see also Maynes, 'Age as a Category of Historical Analysis', 14.
14 O'Dowd and Purvis, *A History of the Girl.*
15 Cohen and Reeves, *The Youth of Early Modern Women.*
16 Froide, *Never Married*, 90.
17 Maynes, 'Age as a Category', 117.
18 Earle, *A City Full of People, 1650–1750*, 20.
19 Maynes, 'Girlhood in Modern European History', 24I.
20 Ham, *Elizabeth Ham, by herself*; Gilbert, *Autobiography*; Hurst, *The Diaries of Sarah Hurst.*

21 Much of the debate stems from Perkin's description of a latent working class in *The Origins of Modern English Society, 1780–1880*, and from the work of Thompson including *The Making of the English Working Class*; 'Time, Work Discipline and Industrial Capitalism'; 'The Moral Economy of the English Crowd'; 'Patrician Society, Plebeian Culture'; and 'Eighteenth-Century English Society: Class Struggle Without Class?'
22 Rule, *Experience of Labour*, 208.
23 Thompson, 'Eighteenth-Century Society', 147–8.
24 Reprinted in George, *England in Transition*, 150–5; Defoe, *Review*, 142.
25 Defoe, *The Complete English Tradesman*, 2.
26 Cappe, *Observations on Charity Schools*, 21.
27 Fryer, *Staying Power: The History of Black People in Britain*, especially chapter 4.
28 Ramdin, *Remaining British: 500 Years of Black and Asian History in Britain*, 15.
29 Fryer, *Staying Power*, 75–6, 79–88.
30 This discussion draws on Simonton, Introduction, *Women in European Culture and Society*.

1

DEFINING GIRLHOOD

Ages and stages

Girls composed a significant portion of eighteenth-century European society (Image 1.1). Drawing on data from E. A. Wrigley and Roger Schofield, in 1700, girls aged to fifteen made up 32.1 per cent of the female population and if we include those up to twenty-four, who were likely to be still single, they composed 48.7 per cent. With rapid population rise in the eighteenth century, girls became an even higher portion of the population so that those aged fifteen and under in 1800 had risen to 36.8 per cent and those aged up to twenty-four had become the majority of females at 54.9 per cent. At the same time, the average age of single English women marrying was about 25.8 years. In 1700 it was 26, but it dropped afterwards and by 1775 it was about 23.7 years with a slight fall after 1775.[1]

The sort of records used by English demographers were unreliable in Scotland, due to poor recording and because of destruction of registers during the Jacobite risings. However, using deponents at the High Court of Justiciary between 1660 and 1770, Rab Houston suggests that 26.6 years was the average age of marriage, with the youngest females married at 18. Furthermore, he argues that the age remained stable to the 1810s. At the same time 11 per cent of those aged over 50 described themselves as single, higher than the English figures, but lower than earlier estimates. His unpublished research on Edinburgh suggests a lower age at first marriage there, while the evidence for the Highlands is 'ambivalent'. Illustrating how variable such estimates may be, he also notes that anecdotal evidence from visitors and clergy in the Highlands suggested a much lower age at marriage, but a partial reconstitution study of Laggan in Inverness-shire showed a normal marriage age for

DOI: 10.4324/9781003412168-2

IMAGE 1.1 Charles Howard Hodges, 1764–1837, The Cottage Girl, 1794. Mezzotint on medium, slightly textured, cream laid paper, Yale Center for British Art, Paul Mellon Fund, B1970.3.491.

women of twenty-six to twenty-eight. He also argues that between 20 and 25 per cent of Highland women remained unmarried in their mid-forties.[2]

Thus, girls frequently experienced a lengthy period between puberty and marriage, and they also constituted an important proportion of society. With the relatively late age of marriage, and the mean duration of a marriage of about twenty years, most females spent at least half their life not married, and easily a third or more as a 'juvenile', or a girl. So, when we study 'women' we should remember that most of them were children, adolescents and young single women. This pattern had important implications for how girlhood was constructed, and the uses to which it was put. Working girls in the eighteenth century travelled several routes to adulthood, and sprinkled throughout records and historical accounts are a myriad of tales about these young women's experiences.

The language of age and the practice of 'rites of passage' from one lifecycle stage to another are variable and contextualised in the culture and time in which they are situated. There are several issues involved. Historians have primarily been interested in understanding childhood, and most historiography is focused on what childhood meant and the ages that bracketed it. There is however a further historiography, less copious but important which focused on defining and understanding youth—sometimes adolescence. And this leads to two further issues. Firstly, the language of youth or adolescence is complicated. While often 'youth' continues to be used as a term for the period between childhood and adulthood, in modern times it is often elided with or replaced by 'adolescence'. Even then it is often split into two periods of the early teen years, i.e., adolescence, and a later period described as youth. This raises the obvious point that most historians have been considering male youth, with girls as an aside. For example, in Mary Abbott's otherwise excellent chapter on lifecycle, she comments 'Boys went into the workshop and the fields, and girls stayed indoors', and gives almost no other discussion of girl's experience before marriage.[3] The discussion of youth and girlhood also requires a better understanding of the locations in which this period took place, and thus historians have also attempted to discover when children left home and what levels of dependence, or semi-dependence, they operated under. These are the issues that this chapter examines in order to arrive at an understanding of the concept of girlhood in the eighteenth century.

Since at least Egyptian times, societies have divided the human life into stages, from the riddle of the sphinx adopted by Sophocles in the story of *Oedipus* to the modern day. The ladder of life as a depiction of the lifecycle was as common in the eighteenth century as wall calendars are today. The ladder ascends then descends, each rung representing a stage in the lifecycle. These stages and terminology varied in meaning and in number and are blunt stages which are relatively meaningless without an understanding of their context. Four stages became common before the eighteenth century referencing infancy, childhood, maturity and old age, although applying various terms to each stage. These were often depicted in 'ladders of life', such as one by John Amos Comenius in *Orbis sensualium pictus* (1659) with the seven ages of man showing both men and women and representing infancy, followed by childhood, or youth, then maturity, old age and decrepitude.[4] Significantly, only in infancy is gender not distinguished in this woodcut. In the early years of the nineteenth century (c. 1810), a French representation of the stages of life comprised eleven annotated stages largely based on decades, in which age two was the age of puerility, age ten drew no comment, but twenty was the age of youth. Ages thirty, forty and fifty were categorised as ages of virility, discretion and maturity, and the remaining stages marked increasing decline to imbecility at one hundred. This depiction also clearly aligned the stages to a male rather than female lifecycle. Unfortunately, a British one from the eighteenth century remains to be discovered. One from the United States in 1835 described the *female* life course in eight stages, marking infancy at one, two stages at twelve and eighteen which could compose girlhood, then thirty

IMAGE 1.2 The life and age of woman, stages of woman's life from the infancy to the brink of the grave. 1835. [Barre, Mass.: A. Alden] Photograph. https://www.loc.gov/item/2006686268/.

when she is 'at her intellectual and physical peak', then fifty, seventy-five and ninety marking decline to the 'brink of the grave'. Notably this is one of the few which does not show a woman in a wedding dress, but the caption remarks 'the virtuous woman is a crown to her husband'. A common ladder depicted the child, the adolescent girl, betrothed maiden, bride, mother and grandmother, fixing females in society and culture based on their 'biological imperative' and their reproductive cycle. Thus, in practice, these representations are about constructing stages of life and defining normative ideas about age and gender, rather than measuring experience.

The ambiguity about age during the eighteenth century, before the *Births and Deaths Registration Act* (1836) and despite church records, meant there was little reliability about ages. Court records, settlement exams, apprenticeship indentures and school records often only approximated a person's age. As Sarah Toulalan notes, they recorded, for example, 'a Young Girl about Nine years of Age'; 'a small Child of about 9 years of Age'; 'an Infant of the age of eight years'; 'an Infant of 17 years of Age'; 'a Virgin of the age of

Ten years'; 'Spinster, of 11 Years of Age'.[5] Individuals also described themselves as 'about ten years of age' or like Mary Hyde, who requested settlement, 'on her oath says that she is about 35 years of age'.[6] And yet, as Cunningham noted, birthdays and knowledge of them was becoming more accurate so that when Mary Matthews was raped in October of 1770, her mother testified 'I am mother to the child that has been abused; she was ten years old the fifth of October.'[7] Abbott shows how birthdays, as chronological markers, were festive occasions shared with family and friends among the middling orders. For example, Abigail Gawthern of Nottingham noted biological milestones in her children's lives in her diary: 'Eliza, born 8 June 1788, "had eight teeth before she was nine months old"; and Anna, born 22 January 1784, "began to run alone" on 9 June 1785. Frank's "first partridges," shot when he was sixteen, marked the crossing of a social threshold on the way to full adult male status.'[8] So, while we discuss ages as markers of stages of life, for the eighteenth-century world, the meanings of those stages were significant, and socio-economic factors contributed to shaping rites of passage and the understandings of life stages. Eighteenth-century society strongly believed that 'years do not make up our ages, it is our vigour and temperament that distinguishes them', and that progression was contingent on a variety of legal, intellectual, financial, social, sexual and physical factors.[9] The next section, therefore, examines these stages of life with the explicit purpose of understanding what the years before a nominal 'adulthood' comprised and how they were understood in the eighteenth century.

Childhood

To understand girlhood, we need to be clearer about how childhood and girlhood were connected. On the one hand, girlhood could encompass all the years before adulthood, but also the two stages are usually seen as comprising at least two periods, sometimes three. Ariès, in his seminal study *Centuries of Childhood* (*L'enfant et la vie familiale sous l'ancien régime*), argued that preindustrial worlds made no distinction between childhood and other phases of the lifecycle: they expressed an 'ambiguity between childhood and adolescence on the one hand and the category known as youth on the other. People had no idea of what we call adolescence, and the idea was a long time in taking shape.'[10] Cunningham indicates that 'in nearly all societies people have differed quite substantially in their thinking on the age at which childhood ends', while John Gillis regarded the language of age in preindustrial Europe as 'hopelessly vague', noting that children as young as six and as old as thirty were described as children.[11] Females were frequently termed girls long into their thirties if still working as servants and unmarried.

By the seventeenth century, the first years of life more clearly looked like what we understand as childhood; nevertheless, there is no clear agreement among historians as to what ages this described: Heide Wunder identifies childhood as the period between birth and age fourteen; Cunningham, 'anyone under fifteen'; Joseph Kett describes age ten as the nominal end of childhood in eighteenth-century America; Mary O'Dowd draws on late nineteenth-century work by psychologists, medical doctors and anthropologists to assign nine or ten as the end of childhood; and today the International Labor Organization uses age fifteen to determine child labour.[12] This underlines the point that the rationale and description of childhood, and indeed youth and adulthood, are slippery, dependent on cultural considerations and not on fixed biological ages. Ariès claimed that 'Nobody would have thought of seeing the end of childhood in puberty', and Sarah Toulalan points out that 'Equating the end of childhood with bodily markers such as sexual maturation or puberty, or with social developmental stages such as entering paid employment, are no less problematic.'[13] The split between childhood and girlhood is often marked by the reference to gender as we saw earlier, when children were regularly presented as asexual, but became gendered beings from around age seven.

All these variables notwithstanding, historians and contemporary commentators tended to see the years to age seven as 'infancy', a time when children were at home, dependent and under the care and control of women. This applied to both boys and girls, and their treatment was often quite similar. Seven was seen as the age when children became teachable; it was also the age when boys tended to move into fathers' control and influence, while girls stayed with mothers. Across Europe it was commonly used as the age to begin school attendance, and when elite boys got tutors.

Yet childhood could be more complex. As we shall see, living in a settled parental home was not the experience of all children, and many were orphaned or abandoned, or lived in an unsettled family situation, often with one parent. Also, numbers of children were sent to other families, for upbringing, nurture or simple sustenance, sometimes to kin or to poor law service, apprenticeship or foundling homes. This is discussed further in Chapter 2, but emphasises the point that childhood was not necessarily a stable home-based experience. Even so, it could also effectively last longer, since schools accepted children at varying ages as did apprenticeship.

The concept of childhood was tied up with dependence, a feature recognised by the parish practice of sending poor children to other homes to relieve the burden on families that struggled. The link between childhood and dependence also explains how terminology reflected those in a state of dependence who often were far older than a nominal child. Words like 'sons', 'varlets' and 'boys', and indeed 'daughters', 'maids', 'lasses' and 'girls' underlined the significance of dependence. 'One would leave childhood only by leaving the state of dependence, or at least the lower degrees of dependence.'[14] The age at which this occurred was complicated and depended on family circumstances. Both boys and girls in labouring families might stay at home, probably contributing financially or at least providing labour to the household. If the family were able to send a daughter to school, she might stay until she finished, or she might stay home until leaving for work or apprenticeship. For example, a 1778 list of 'the labouring persons in the parish of Terling, Essex' records sixteen *children* over fourteen living at home (of 192 children), ranging in age from fifteen to thirty-three, a young man living with a widowed mother.[15] Therefore, childhood was an idea and not a fixed state of being, and thus this book also assigns the boundary between childhood and girlhood flexibly reflecting reality.

Youth and girlhood

The period of girlhood is even more amorphous, and various historians define it differently. Jennifer Higginbotham argues that 'For girlhood to become a distinctly gendered life stage, childhood first had to be disassociated from femininity and femaleness in general'.[16] The importance of gender is central to understanding girls and girlhood, because it shaped the context in which they operated and how they and others understood normative behaviour and opportunities. Gillis argued that this stage represented a very long transition period, lasting from the point that the child first became somewhat independent of his or her family, usually about seven or eight, to the point of complete independence.[17] Eighteenth-century society recognised youth or girlhood as a period during which the essential transmission of culture as well as training in the knowledge and skills needed to make a living and become a member of society took place. It coincides with the period when children learned the values, beliefs and roles that underwrote the social system in which they participated. It was also a period in which society recognised the maturing of the body, sexual urges and 'a moment of passion'; a gradual development of maturity 'by the physical body and in the growing ability to make rational decisions'.[18] It was when girls were expected to gather the prerequisites for marriage and adulthood, which meant that the period was flexible and could be influenced by economic shifts, politics and wars, in addition to biological and familial factors and customs. For working boys, the journey to manhood meant leaving mothers' direct care, often going to school, working or studying with fathers; commonly from about fourteen they might have gone to apprenticeships or service or continued working. Many of the markers of male youth were institutional whereas girls' markers were more personal and indeed domestic. Girls started a similar journey to womanhood; however, often they remained close to mothers, mirroring their activities and learning many of the 'womanly' skills girls would need as adults.

Thus, youth followed childhood, with another dividing line around fourteen—coinciding not accidentally with the 'traditional' age of apprenticeship and finishing at twenty-one, when boys (and apprentices explicitly) became 'men'. It also reflected the tendency of many children to go into service at fourteen, and poor law officials tended not to allow families with children over fourteen to receive poor relief. For example, *An Account of the Poor in Terling*, 1801, shows no boys over fourteen and only four girls, one of whom was thirty-six and an 'idiot'.[19] Notably, like the ladders of life, the timing around youth was predicated on the male life cycle as the norm, thus universalising male worlds, while less often reflecting girls' experiences. When girlhood was conceptualised, the period usually was configured as maidenhood and as the automatic precursor to marriage and motherhood. It was less associated with age than with family relationships, sexual chastity and potentially menarche. 'In the early modern prescriptive literature for young women, the emphasis on marriage generated a triad of categories—maids, wives, or widows—that obscured adolescence as a distinct intermediate stage on the path to adulthood.'[20] In the eighteenth century, Caroline Lennox claimed menstruation was an essential characteristic of 'becoming a woman'.[21] Cohen and Reeves, concurred noting that 'with the onset of sexual maturity the body was a central locus of change', and 'outside of learned medical literature, menarche did not attract much attention before the eighteenth century.'[22] Historians now largely think that menarche arrived around age fourteen, maybe fifteen, thus placing it as the age corresponding to many girls leaving school and going to service. While this remains problematic, as Toulalan said, the coincidence of menarche with other markers around fourteen as a second stage of girlhood is noteworthy. Thus, girlhood was defined in association with the female body and not with work, intelligence or individual identity.

A constant reference in this lifecycle stage is that of service, portrayed as a period to build up the financial wherewithal to set up house. As such it was central to the way youth or girlhood was traversed. However, this interpretation, while largely accurate, is also problematic. What happened when service did not end with marriage, or when a woman remained single well into adulthood? Indeed, in Danish the words maid and girl were interchangeable, *pige*, and in German, *Mädchen* also described the stage, the role and indeed the biological understanding as virgin. French distinguishes the terms more, but girl and maiden are *fille* and *jeune fille*, somewhat confusing the issue. English similarly has a conundrum with a range of terms used, as this study shows, including girl, maid, maiden, lassie, miss and spinster also tied up with work as spinners or servants. To clarify, ages did not define girlhood: social practices did.

Law, custom and girlhood

Girls' legal status varied by where they lived as well as by their age, position in society and gender. Where they lived mattered, because law was not the same across the British Isles, and community practices and local regulations could also make a difference. Legal regulation was usually determined by two key factors: responsibilities and relationships to parents, elders and guardians, and property, and thus control of marriage. Girls were also bound by laws associated with poor law, settlement regulations and contractual relationships related to service, apprenticeship and employment. There was little protective legislation at the time, although apprenticeship legislation provided routes for a child to complain about treatment—nonetheless a supporter was almost always necessary for success—and in 1780, law stipulated that masters should abide by the contractual terms. Other laws gave recourse for masters and mistresses to deal with runaways. Each of these issues is examined more closely in the chapters that follow.

Law and custom in both England and Scotland required parents to maintain, protect and educate their children while children owed parents subjection and obedience during the period of minority, and honour and reverence afterward.[23] Both William Blackstone and John Erskine wrote of the child and parent as male, although Erskine's discussion of the laws of Scotland was sympathetic to the situation of daughters and widowed mothers to a greater degree than Blackstone's *Commentaries on the Laws of England.* The main impact of their treatises is, however, concerned with regulating property, and thus marriage, which had less purchase for working families. English common law maintained 'a very great and tender consideration . . . especially for Minors' and expected age to be taken into account when convicting, but 'failed to distinguish fully between children and adults until the mid-nineteenth century.'[24]

Legal and civil authorities as well as society at large could not agree on what the 'age of majority' and the beginning of adulthood was. Law regimes often referred to twenty-one as the age of maturity, when a person could inherit on his or her own, and male apprenticeship designated twenty-one as the point when a boy became a man on completion. In Britain, legal scholars of the period were concerned about the age of discretion, distinguishing between infancy as 'an Age of Impotence, Weakness and Disability' when children were considered incapable of managing their 'Concerns with Discretion and for their better profit and Advantage'.[25] Thus jurists were concerned to establish what the age of discretion was, and help to identify what contemporary society thought of as girlhood. William Blackstone, writing on England, explicitly named twenty-one as the age of discretion:

> [T]he legal power of a father,—for a mother, as such, is entitled to no power, but only to reverence and respect; . . . over the persons of his children ceases at the age of twenty-one: for they are then enfranchised by arriving at years of discretion, or that point which the law has established, as some must necessarily be established, when the empire of the father, or other guardian, gives place to the empire of reason.[26]

John Erskine says in Scotland, 'the compelling power of a father over his issue lasts only until they arrive at a *perfect age* [my italics]; and that they are from that period their own masters in every respect.' Furthermore, he says 'as soon as the children can subsist by their own labour or industry' his obligation to support them ceases, and he can charge them board if they remain at home.[27] The sixteenth-century English Statute of Artificers, 1563, said children aged ten to twenty-four could be apprenticed to husbandry or other trades.[28] The earlier Poor Law of 1536 provided parish officials with the authority to put 'single' children aged between five and fourteen with masters of husbandry or other crafts or labours. They were to be taught so that they could support themselves as adults.[29] The Elizabethan poor laws extended parish apprenticeship to children whose parents the overseers of the poor thought unable to maintain them. Boys could be apprenticed to age twenty-four whilst girls were initially released at eighteen, but the age was raised to twenty-one in 1597.[30] The terminal age was reduced for London boys in 1767 and for all others in 1777 to twenty-one years old.[31]

Most historians of childhood emphasise the fluidity in how girlhood and adulthood could be conceived depending on circumstances. The 'age of discretion' when person became responsible for his or her own behaviour varied considerably in contemporary thought, and law often varied from custom and practice. For example, as Beatrice Gottlieb notes:

> The age of fourteen was far from a rigid boundary. Maturity of a sort . . . came as early as nine in seventeenth-century England and New England, according to some lawyers' handbooks, which said that nine was the 'age of discretion', the age at which a person could be held responsible for such offenses as slander. This later rose to fourteen and even sixteen before 1800.[32]

Contemporary Matthew Hale argued that incapacities, including infancy, are not excuses for civil offences such as trespass and batteries, but in 'cases of crimes and misdemeanours . . . the law in some cases, and under certain temperaments take notice of these defects, and in respect of them relaxeth the severity of their punishments.'[33] He defined the age of discretion as fourteen.

Even so, age itself was no clear marker, and even entering into a range of adult responsibilities and roles was no guarantee of real autonomy either. Independence is culturally determined, so what adulthood means is as malleable as any other life course stage. Although a girl could get pregnant in her teens, she hardly became an adult, even if she were theoretically self-supporting. Since manhood might be described as completion of apprenticeship and reaching age twenty-one, most young men were not completely independent at this point, remaining under control of a master if they were artisans. As Blackstone and Erskine noted, fathers' control and influence could continue well into what we might think of as adulthood. Returning to the example of service, women in their thirties might remain both single and in service and thus also subservient to the vagaries of another. Although marriage was often seen as the point of adulthood for young women, in the eighteenth century, it was more common in their mid-twenties, not at twenty-one. Even so, they were legally dependent on a male, usually moving from fathers to husbands. Single women found it difficult to be regarded as adults and could be passed to brothers or other kin once their father had died, unless she could establish financial and legal independence, and even this could be tenuous.[34]

Notably the period between childhood and adulthood was frequently divided into two, adolescence and youth, recognising that the early teen was physically and mentally less capable than the later teen. As Sarah Goldsmith says, 'the age at which adolescence ended and youth began was variously set at eighteen, twenty-one or twenty-five, whereas youth could end at twenty-five, twenty-eight or thirty-five.' So, the legal age of majority ranged from twenty-one to twenty-four, and custom and practice tended to identify childhood, or girlhood, as lasting well into their twenties, until marriage. Thus, this book follows this and many of the girls discussed are aged up to twenty-four as long as they remained unmarried.[35] Certainly many servants remained single longer, often marrying in their thirties, and up to 25 per cent of females never married in Britain, although they might have become mothers.

Girlhood and gender

Girls' constraints and opportunities were more likely to be affected by views of the feminine and of female obligations and responsibilities, and in most cases, these were situated in domestic and familial concerns. In 1777, in *Essays on Various Subjects*, Hannah More explicitly posited the private world of the female and the public world of the male, linking these to physical differences. For women,

> Greater delicacy evidently implies greater fragility; and this weakness, natural and moral, clearly points out the necessity of a superior degree of caution, retirement and reserve. . . . MEN, on the contrary are formed for the more public exhibitions of the great theatre of human life. Like the stronger and more substantial wares, they derive no injury, and lose no polish by being always exposed, and engaged in the constant commerce of the world. It is their proper element.[36]

More clearly saw the female in relation to men, family and domestic pursuits, referring to

> the man whose happiness she is one day to make, whose family she is to govern, and whose children she is to educate . . . he will seek for her in the bosom of retirement, in the practice of every domestic virtue . . . to embellish the narrow but charming circle of family delights.[37]

Yet she differed subtly from many male commentators in demonstrating greater concern for the development of self. Whereas they tended to see men and women only in relational terms, she argued for educating women for self-regulation, contributing to the well-being of others and the dignity of Christian teaching. Her construction of a domestic female image was significant because of her potential for influencing working-class women through philanthropy amongst them and her authorship of the *Cheap Repository Tracts*.

However, the cultural and economic nexus of working-class life meant that the child-oriented, domesticated female was an alien image. Robert Acklom Ingram recognised this essential difference, so while formulating his proposals for schools of industry for girls from working families in a similar 'domestic' language, and promoting domestic comforts as a key aim of their education, he also framed his advice for girls who needed to work:

> To secure them effectually from immorality and error, we must teach them to respect their own characters, by first, indeed, respecting them ourselves, and conferring on them an essential value. . . . it must be our endeavour to render them more desirable in the marriage state for their ability to assist in the maintenance and education of a family, and to add to the mass of domestic comforts by economy and cleanliness. . . . In the first place, the kind of institution, that is desired for training up poor girls, is not a mere spinning school. The process of education ought to be a proper pattern, or model, of the business of life. Their employment and duty in life will probably be to discharge the several offices at first of menial servants, and afterwards of wives and mothers . . . as well as to assist in the maintenance of a family by some species of profitable industry.[38]

Bourgeois ideals at all levels of personal relationships can be seen to be divergent from plebeian culture. Likewise, the construction of emotion took alternative forms: 'Among the eighteenth-century plebs . . . the compatibility of individual affection and collective solidarity was an ideal worth struggling for.'[39] John Gillis argued that 'in the face of greater need to control the labour of children, parental control appeared to be lessening. Sex and age relations had become simultaneously more equal and more problematic.'[40] Similarly, the construction of female identity within the plebeian orders was shaped by factors which diverged from middle-class experience and culture. Within the family or household unit, the woman's power and strength rested on her management of the household and the importance of her labour. Relations between husbands and wives were characterised by interdependence, by a partnership involving pursuit of a common goal.[41] Yet, cooperation in economic matters and clandestine marriage only partly defined gender relations. While it is important to see the plebeian orders as active in shaping their own life experience, middle-class ideology and structural changes in the economy altered the kind of education and work available to women. Eighteenth-century Britain was a patriarchal society in which men held all the overt political power and in which law and custom recognised the subordination of women to men. At the same time there is evidence that the Pauline dogma, 'Wives submit yourselves unto your own husbands as unto the Lord,' was less likely to be construed in an absolute sense than in previous centuries.

Traversing girlhood

The routes and patterns of girls' experience were varied—as were boys', of course. An important marker in the course of girlhood was the act of leaving home. At the same time, it was not necessarily a one-off episode, and it was common for girls and boys to leave for short periods and then return home, such as those going to farm service or periodic work away from home. It was common in Scotland for girls to travel from the highlands to the lowlands for farm work like the soft fruit industries in the Carse of Gowrie, living in bothies, and then return to homes when the season ended. These experiences gave girls increasing freedom and responsibilities, and loosened ties to home. The details of this experience are discussed later, but here we want to understand the pattern and potential for being at home or leaving.

Children normally lived in their familial home for at least the first ten to fifteen years of their lives. Richard Wall and Ann Kussmaul suggest the end of the range, i.e. fifteen, while half of parish apprentices were indentured before they reached the age of ten. Keith Snell argued that male farm servants in the East of England went to work on average at 14.8 years, and to apprenticeships at 14.2.[42] Peter Laslett was cagey about when children left home, only saying 'any time after the age of ten', while Gottlieb similarly says children under seven rarely left home while leaving between seven and fourteen was common.[43] Yet, Wall's research showed that in eighteenth-century England, between a half and three quarters of fifteen- to nineteen-year-old boys and girls were living at home; 'there was no sudden rush . . . to leave the parental home.'[44] In Cardington, 1782, more children aged ten to fourteen remained in households headed by males (86 per cent) than in households headed by widows, but the proportion reversed so that more children between sixteen and twenty-nine remained in widows' households (44 per cent) than in men's (35 per cent). In all households, girls over fifteen were more likely to remain at home (48 per cent) than boys (11 per cent). Also, less than half remained at home in families of tradesmen (46 per cent) and labourers (36 per cent).[45] In Terling in 1778, twice as many girls over fourteen remained at home than boys did.[46] While limited examples, these are indicative of the likely patterns, especially in rural English communities in the second half of the century. Clearly there were several routes between birth and adulthood. Figure 1.1 illustrates typical life cycle routes for working children, which approximate the more common points of change. All routes posed possibilities for girls, which the following chapters develop, yet probably most girls from labouring families followed a pattern of spending their early and formative years and much of their early working life in the familial home. Some would have left home by fourteen, going into farm or domestic service, parish or trade

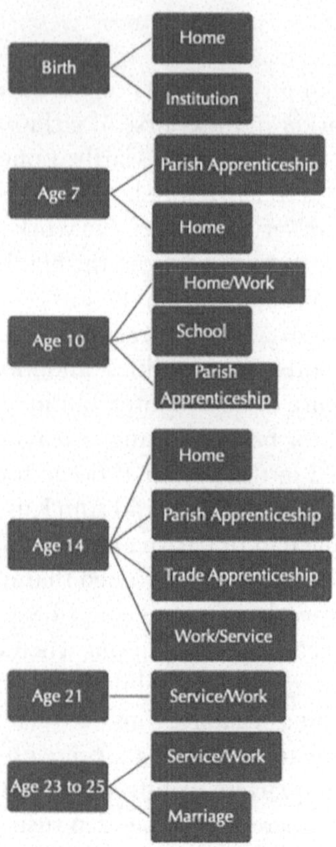

FIGURE 1.1 Typical Lifecycle Routes, ca. 1780

apprenticeship or non-apprenticed work. But still one third to a half probably remained at home until marriage and emphasises the contribution which the home made to girls' upbringing.

The balance of children at home depended on skills needed in the household. Those girls who stayed at home were usually needed, helping with younger children, supporting mothers, or adding skills like cloth working for household industry, and families would prefer to use their own children's labour than hire outsiders. Children would be sent to others' homes to work when they needed to hire in labour with a specific skill to balance the consumer-labour needs of the household. It is useful to remember that in Britain, the household consisted mainly of a nuclear family, together with servants, who could have been kin. Girls followed many routes, but service was the mainstay of this period, whether in parental homes or the homes of others, as apprentices, contracted servants or employees. Wall argued that three quarters of children aged between fifteen and twenty-four could be servants, with a length of service between twelve and twenty years.[47] Although service was usually described—and used—as a lifecycle stage, it also could extend far beyond what we would normally consider girlhood.[48]

Other considerations could lead to a girl leaving home. Disruptions in the family itself, perhaps abuse by a parent or even sibling, could be the trigger for leaving. In 1734, Elizabeth Hewit described leaving home because of abuse by her stepmother and her father who took no care of her.[49] Alan Macfarlane suggested that incestuous temptations could also be a factor with puberty acting as a trigger for leaving home:

> [W]e might well have expected that such [delay in marrying] would lead to sexual competition within families. Incestuous temptations, however, would be minimized by the virtual absence of more than two co-residing adults of the same family. Another source of tension, the changes in patterns of authority as the children approached adulthood, would also be diminished.[50]

Kussmaul nuances this view, however, suggesting that an apparent motive of avoiding incest, based on the age at which farm servants left home, may have been no more than a reflection of the age of the youngest servants that farmers would have been willing to hire.[51] Evidence from Essex records used later in this volume similarly suggest the opportunity for employment was significant and drew girls away from home.

Conclusion

Because of the character of our evidence, it is difficult if not impossible to see how power dynamics operated in making decisions about how girlhood was enacted. Families could keep children at home, send them elsewhere for work including forms of service, arrange apprenticeships, even negotiate with parish officials to place them out. They could send them to school if one was available or affordable. Many families employed several strategies, sequentially or sporadically, or depending on the birth order and gender of the child. Power tended to rest with parents, mainly fathers, but mothers also had a significant role to play with girls, and some of a mother's power was in shaping decisions about daughters. Gillis noted that it was common for a mother to apprentice her daughter to herself as a way of bonding her closer.

Girls' experiences covered the period from birth to adulthood, with potentially numerous stages and routes in between. While there is no regular pattern to this trajectory, the period was divided into a several commonly understood periods. Infancy or childhood usually lasted between seven and ten years of age, when girls were most dependent, and most likely to be living in a familial home. This was not necessarily so, however: parents' deaths, abandonment and poverty could mean she was placed with others or in an institution like a foundling home or workhouse. Girlhood, covering the remaining years to adulthood, that is from about seven upwards, was a long period of transition in which she learned many of the skills, knowledge and social values that would create the kind of adult she became. These years could also encompass perhaps two stepping stones: the period before fourteen was often still spent at home, though as we have seen this was not straightforward, while from about fourteen, girls usually moved into apprenticeships, service and work. These stages and the experiences of girls form the basis of the remainder of this volume. It begins with childhood, a period of experiences more often shared with boys, and one which was often spent under mothers' care and control. It then examines the options, opportunities and difficulties which shaped girlhood. It concludes with a closer study of what the end of girlhood looked like. In this way, the book creates a broad portrait of girls' lives, enhancing their presence in the eighteenth-century world, uncovering their lives, agency and risks.

Notes

1 Wrigley and Schofield, *Population History of England,* 122, 534, and Wrigley et al., *English Population History from Family Reconstitution*, 131.
2 Houston, 'Age at Marriage of Scottish Women', 65 and 'The Demographic Regime', 19–20. Flinn, *Scottish Population History*, 276–8.
3 Abbott, 'Life Cycle'.
4 See Higginbotham, *Fair Maids and Golden Girls,* 189.
5 Toulalan, '"Unripe" Bodies: Children and Sex in Early Modern England', 134.
6 Chelsea Settlement and Bastardy Examinations, No. 307.
7 *OBP*, 5 December 1770, reference t17701205–39.
8 Abbott, 'Life Cycle', 111.

9 Neale, *Practical Essays and Remarks on that Species of Consumption Incident to Youth*, 31.
10 Ariès, *Centuries of Childhood*, 27.
11 Cunningham, *Children and Childhood*, 17; Gillis, *Youth and History*, 1.
12 Wunder, *He is the Sun, She is the Moon*, 27; Kett, 'The Stages of Life', 181.
13 Toulalan, '"Unripe" Bodies', 133.
14 Aries, *Centuries of Childhood*, 26: see also Gillis, *Youth and History*, 2.
15 ERO, D/DRa E16.
16 Higginbotham, *Fair Maids*, 186.
17 Gillis, *Youth and History*, 2.
18 Barclay, *Caritas*, 70–1.
19 ERO, D/P 299/12/3.
20 Cohen and Reeves, *Youth of Early Modern Women*, 12.
21 Cited in Tillyard, *Aristocrats: Caroline, Emily, Louisa and Sarah Lennox, 1750–1832*, 229.
22 Cohen and Reeves, *Youth of Early Modern Women*, 20–1.
23 Blackstone, *Commentaries on the Laws of England*, 446; Erskine, *An Institute of the Law of Scotland*, 156–8.
24 Bullock, *Child Testimony and the Legal Definition of Childhood*, 20.
25 *The Infants Lawyers*, 12–3.
26 Blackstone, *Commentaries*, 442.
27 Erskine, *An Institute of the Law of Scotland*, 158.
28 Eliz. I, c.4.
29 27 Henry VIII, c.25.
30 14 Eliz. I, c.5 (1572); 39 Eliz. I, c.3 (1597); 43 Eliz. I, c.2 (1601).
31 7 Geo. III, c.39 and 18 Geo. III, c.47.
32 Gottlieb, *The Family in the Western World*, 155.
33 Hale, *Historia Placitorum Coronae, the History of the Pleas of the Crown*, 159.
34 See Gottlieb, *Family in the Western World*, 156.
35 Goldsmith, 'Imagining Youth', 41.
36 More, *Essays on Various Subjects*, 4–5.
37 More, *Essays on Various Subjects*, 135.
38 Ingram, *Essay on the Importance of Schools of Industry*, 25, 37.
39 Gillis, 'Affective Individualism and the English Poor', 127.
40 Gillis, 'Resort to Common Law Marriage in England and Wales, 1700–1850', 10.
41 Gillis, 'Resort to Common Law Marriage in England and Wales, 1700–1850', 10.
42 Wall, 'Age at Leaving Home', 190–9; Kussmaul, *Servants in Husbandry*, 70–2; Snell, *Annals of the Labouring Poor*, 323.
43 Laslett, *The World We Have Lost*, 15; Gottlieb, *Family in the Western World*, 155.
44 Wall, 'Age at Leaving Home', 190–1.
45 Wall, 'Age at Leaving Home', 194, 195, 198.
46 ERO, D/DRa E16.
47 Wall, 'Age at Leaving Home', 182.
48 Simonton, 'Birds of Passage', 2–11.
49 *OBP Ordinary of Newgate's Account*, July 1734 (OA17340709; *OBP*, April 1734 (t17340424–55).
50 Macfarlane, *The Family Life of Ralph Josselin*, 205.
51 Kussmaul, *Servants in Husbandry*, 77.

2

THE CHILD

The idea of the child

New attitudes towards children were important features of the Enlightenment construction of the model family. Certainly, these views did not spring fully formed from the heads of eighteenth-century philosophers and had a longer pre-history, while their application and understanding was erratic and conflicted. Yet the idea of a period of childhood became a distinct feature in the Enlightenment canon, and central to understanding girlhood. From the Reformation, a concern with the spiritual welfare of the individual contributed to a growing interest in childhood and its role as a formative stage in personality development accompanied by tangible physical changes in their treatment and position in the family. Increasing privacy and comfort, an interest in the individual and a holistic rather than strictly spiritual approach to life shaped far-reaching changes in how people thought about children. It became acceptable, indeed desirable, to invest emotional energy in children and to mould their moral character. By 1800, the child emerged as a fragile creature to be safeguarded and reformed.

John Locke characterised the mind at birth as blank, innocent, a *tabula rasa*, which experience furnished with ideas, intellect and character: 'We have reason to conclude, that great Care is to be had of the forming Children's Minds, and giving them that seasoning early, which shall influence their Lives always after.' The child's special capacities and needs should shape the process of learning, since 'The right Way to teach them Those things is, to give them a liking and Inclination to what you propose to them to be learn'd.'[1] He also warned against overindulgence or fondness, wishing to instil obedience and parental respect in children. In contrast, Jean-Jacques Rousseau

DOI: 10.4324/9781003412168-3

argued that children were born good. In *Émile*, he promulgated a child, 'born sensitive' and 'capable of learning, but knowing nothing, perceiving nothing', corrupted by the world. Central to *Émile* was the necessity of preserving children's original perfect innocent natures by controlling education and environment through the 'gift of education': 'as soon as the child begins to take notice, what is shown him must be carefully chosen.'[2]

The model of familial relations underwent significant changes triggered by these Enlightenment ideas, and economic change complemented them in ways that influenced how families made decisions about the management of their household economies and the deployment of family members. Social expectations meant that parents were increasingly expected to take a role in bringing up children in ways that were qualitatively and quantitatively different. Importantly, these values were most readily adopted by the middling orders, which also reacted more readily to newer ideas of how motherhood was constructed and understood. They invested in their children by purchasing goods and services designed expressly for them, and through inheritance strategies, managed their economies to preserve the family for posterity. Children's 'value' shifted. A leading characteristic of the idea of childhood was the creation of a privatised family group in which the socialisation and protection of the young gained primacy. As a corollary, family relationships became more affectionate so that the older style of formality between parents and children was superseded by a more loving attitude. The ideal suggests that children were more likely to be found in their own home, not another household, and the concept of 'home' gained meaning. The family gained pre-eminence as a formative force in the child's character, so that 'the family ceased to be simply an institution for the transmission of a name and an estate—it assumed a moral and spiritual function, it moulded bodies and souls.'[3] At the heart of this archetype was the mother-child relationship. 'Children came to fulfil an emotional and sentimental role within the family, as opposed to a financial role, and this required intensive parental and especially maternal involvement with children.'[4] Cunningham argued this was the emergence of a *middle-class view* of childhood, so that 'by the middle of the nineteenth century an ideology of childhood had become a powerful force in middle-class Europe and America.' However, the 'move towards a more child-oriented society was challenged at every stage, and never completed. Both in attitudes . . . and behaviour . . . we are confronted at every turn by ambivalence and contradictions.'[5] A key divergence was conceptualisation of children of the labouring orders. Society believed their children should work and not be allowed to be idle. William Hogarth's series of etchings, *Industry and Idleness*, captured these ideas explicitly with the good industrious apprentice succeeding, becoming Lord Mayor of London, while the idle apprentice went from bad to worse and was hanged at Tyburn. This trope especially permeated didactic literature and sermons aimed at the labouring classes. Such discourses were not limited to the first seven years of life, and therefore also impacted on the girlhood of the working orders.

The experiences and expectations of poor, artisan or labouring girls were significantly different from those of middle- and upper-class girls. The idea of home and its enclosing character did not yet have meaning for cottagers', artisans' and labourers' families in the eighteenth century since poverty and labour demands precluded the widespread adoption of child-centred attitudes. Social relationships were often influenced by the economic and labour requirements of household enterprise so that children's needs were not necessarily the central concern. They may have been more of a handicap than an advantage. At the same time, 'children's work at an early age and their freedom of movement in the neighbourhood involved a degree of independence which was incompatible with middle-class conceptions of childhood.'[6] Additionally, the labouring home was hardly the middle-class haven. Members moved in and out for work, and mothers rarely were full-time homemakers, since they, like children, needed to bring in money.

Even though the reality of plebeian life created alternative preconditions for women, many commentators drew on their own largely middle-class experiences and expectations to promote many of the same values universally. Thus in 1787, Sarah Trimmer pled for the poor woman unable to use her own feminine skills and forced to work in the fields:

> Instead of sitting down in peace and quietness in her own neat apartment, surrounded by playful innocents, she finds in the fields or gardens a set of reprobates, who shock her ears with oaths, blasphemies and indecency. Her mind is filled with anxiety for her children's safety; she is not at liberty to return home to prepare a comfortable dinner, nay not even a supper for her husband.[7]

Similarly, Locke's views of childhood were transcribed into a recipe for poor children. Dr James Talbot, in *The Christian Schoolmaster*, acknowledged the susceptibility of the child's mind: 'As to the Business of Instruction, it must be consider'd, that the Minds of Children, like blank Paper, or smooth wax, are equally capable of any Impression: . . . and Susceptible only of such Notions, as it receives from others, by the Means of the Outward Senses.'[8] Talbot was primarily concerned with moulding an obedient, subservient Christian poor population. Consequently, he declared,

> all Children should be Inured betimes to Submission and Obedience; Childhood being properly a state of Subjection to the Will of those that are more capable to Govern and Direct us than we our Selves . . . They must likewise be admonished to order themselves lowly and reverently, (i.e. humbly and respectfully) to all their Betters, in Age, Degree, Wisdom or Goodness.[9]

Richard Acklom Ingram explicitly directed his thinking to the girls of the labouring orders. He felt too much industrial work and division of labour had caused women to forget household skills they had previously known. As a result, they had become 'helpless and torpid in all aspects of domestic arrangements'.[10] Central to his concerns was preparation for household concerns and 'such occupations as have a tendency to generate a sedate and orderly deportment'.[11] His proposed schools of industry were a means of reasserting this 'traditional' knowledge and female function. Thus, education for labouring girls aimed to train them as either domestic servants or good wives, emphasising industry, frugality, diligence and good management. While it is important to see the plebian orders as active in shaping their own life experience, middle-class ideology and structural changes in the economy altered the context of childhood even for labouring children.

Family and the child

Children were born into families of various sizes. They could be orphaned at birth or before they reached adulthood. When she was twenty-seven, Londoner Ann Way explained:

> I have heard and believe that my father and mothers names were Thomas and Dorothy Way and that they lived over against St Andrews Church in Holbourn and that I was born there and that they dyed in my infancy and that by the care of my aunt Sarah Pauling I was nursed.[12]

Similarly, Mary Saxby, born in Hollowell, whose mother died after the birth of a second child, recounted:

> I was born in London, in the year 1738. My mother dying when I was very young, and my father going into the army, I was exposed to distress, even in my infancy. I was continually removed from the charge of one relation to that of another; in consequence, I verily believe, chiefly of my own perverse temper; which, because I had no parent, scorned to be under the controul [sic] of any of my friends, even at that early period.[13]

Obviously, children could be stillborn and sometimes were illegitimate or victims of infanticide or abandonment or born to single mothers.

Contrary to the perception that preindustrial families were burdened with hordes of children, they were in fact modest in size, though it varied by social status. The mean number of live births per English woman hovered under seven across the century and women could expect a couple of years to elapse between births of live children. With relatively late marriage, and because women did not have large numbers of children in quick succession, with gaps of two or three years common, completed families did not tend to be large.[14]

Couples usually delayed having children until they were 'set up', and there is evidence that during periods of hardship, they delayed childbearing until better times. Also, marriage and conceptions followed a seasonal pattern, linked to hiring contracts and the rhythm of work, including harvest dates. It was common for couples to set up house after harvests since they received wages then, often their full annual wages, especially in rural areas. Better living conditions amongst middling and upper orders, lower age at marriage and different childrearing practices led to a propensity for larger families. Also, mothers who relied on wet nurses, primarily among elite families, tended to have more children than those who did not. Living and working conditions could limit the number of pregnancies and live births among plebeian women. Completed family size, according to Wrigley and Schofield's calculations, ranged from 5.14 in the first half century, rising to 5.61 in the second half, while they note that not all births were necessarily recorded.[15] Peter Laslett estimated the numbers of children present in households by social status as:

Gentlemen	2.94
Clergy	3.53
Yeoman	2.76
Husbandmen	3.10
Tradesmen and craftsmen	2.90
Labourers	2.70
Paupers	2.34
Others	2.31[16]

These figures reflect the high incidence of infant and child mortality common in the eighteenth century. In Britain, the simple family household prevailed, that is, a family composed mainly of parents and their children. Research on mobility, mortality and remarriage has demonstrated how complex such a simple family unit could be. With high population turnover, most households may well have been hybrid families of parents, step- and foster children and their own offspring, at some time.[17]

Dependent on class and locality, children had a 15 to 30 per cent chance of dying in their first year, and approximately one in ten died before they reached ten years of age; only about 50 per cent survived until adulthood. Justus Möser commented in 1786 that is was 'an unfailing law of nature that fifty percent of children must perish before their tenth year'.[18] Data from London suggest that child mortality rose so that at mid-century, nearly two thirds of children, rich or poor, died before their fifth birthday, while in Aberdeen around half died before their fourteenth birthday.[19] Children, especially younger ones, were particularly susceptible to disease, chiefly digestive maladies, like roundworm and the notorious 'summer diarrhoea' from contaminated water as well as from simple malnutrition, especially among those being weaned. They also fell to epidemics like smallpox, measles and diphtheria, none of which had cures. In Aberdeen in 1660–61, 198 children died of smallpox, in a town of less than 8,000. Children's best chances were basic good health and nutrition—and luck. Eighteenth-century demographic changes are complex and highly contested by historians; however, modest, subtle changes took place in infant mortality over the century. A decline in epidemics and summer diarrhoea, due to better cleanliness linked to the increased accessibility of cottons replacing wool and some medical improvements including better midwifery practices, created a healthier prognosis. Dietary improvements resulting from fewer harvest failures, better harvests at the beginning of the century, better transportation and the increased use of potatoes led to a better-fed and healthier population which was also more disease-resistant. These features specifically contributed to lower infant mortality, but better maternal health also meant fewer stillbirths, and more full-term and healthier births.[20]

While there has been a burgeoning literature on sibling relations, balancing the weighty studies of marriage, family and childhood, virtually all focus on the elite and middling sorts.[21] This is understandable simply because of the paucity of material on plebeian lives that reveals these relations. While inheritance issues may have influenced sibling relations among older children of the upper orders, such considerations were usually irrelevant to the experiences of the plebeian child. Several factors came into play however, including family size, birth order, birth intervals and gender, but as Amy Harris notes, siblings 'encountered powerful reminders that they were equals—that they should share and share alike'.[22] Daily practice, and indeed law, treated them as peers, though gender and age remained aspects distinguishing childhood relations. And certainly, they spent their childhoods together. Siblings tended to be close in age, and Jane Humphries suggests her diarists described families of about six children per family. Since families were mobile in search of work, siblings were a constant.[23] They shared time and space, they ate the same food, 'enjoying the same entertainments, praying the same prayers, learning the same lessons'. Their persistent proximity meant they played together, shared beds and clothing and looked out for one another; they shared an easy familiarity, as Elizabeth Ham recorded. Siblings also 'cared for one another when ill and mourned the loss of a brother or sister', a common experience given the high infant and childhood mortality.[24] Losing a sibling during childhood has rarely been studied, but it must have had an impact. Even when children were abandoned or sent to workhouses or nurses, they often went in sibling groups. Thus:

> On 20 November 1716, for example, the Vestry [of St Clement Danes, London], ordered that a cow keeper in Islington be paid four shillings per

> week to keep three orphan siblings aged seven, five and 18 months . . . in 1803 siblings Susannah and Joseph Cooper, who had been suffering from smallpox in the workhouse, were ordered to go to Nurse Pluckrose's 'as soon as they are sufficiently recovered', [while] Elizabeth and William Mills, aged seven and five, were sent to two different nurses together before being cared for by their mother in town with the support of the parish.[25]

This is not to say sibling relations were always harmonious, and conflict as well as harmony shaped these experiences. Nevertheless, siblings had a special bond, one that would have taken priority over friendship. As Barclay argues, there was an emphasis on developing these familial bonds during childhood which was 'evidence of the ways that the child was imagined as having the capacity to produce and represent the affective bonds of family'.[26]

Love and care

The long-standing debate about whether or not parents loved their children has surely now been put to rest. No doubt they did love and care for them.

IMAGE 2.1 George Romney, 1734–1802, Learning to Walk, undated. Brown ink over graphite on medium slightly textured cream laid paper, Yale Center for British Art, Paul Mellon Collection, B1977.14.5464.

Family relations were in transition as suggested by Enlightenment ideology, and some ideas certainly spread to the labouring orders, even if balanced by the realities of their working lives. We have very few images and commentaries on working-class life and attitudes toward and treatment of children (see Image 2.1). As we have seen, infant and child death was frequent, and certainly families often gave the same name to succeeding children. But this may represent connecting family ties, or even a memorial to the child. It may have been simple stoicism and acceptance of a fact of life. It was not implicitly a lack of affection. If childcare practices seemed less child-centred than today, they reflected the reality of society and living situations. The modern world similarly manifests a range of attitudes with homeless children, child labour and child abuse, contrasted with high standards of care and attention, sometimes leading to over-protection. Maternal care in the past similarly shows an array of attitudes, but also several actualities within which families had to function. We should beware of modern subjective notions of bad and good mothering since accepted wisdom varies considerably by culture, country, custom and class. As indicated earlier, the bourgeois model of childcare and the idea of the child operated differently in the plebeian classes. Children were valued for themselves, for their economic contribution and for posterity. If they did not receive the level of attention that today's world asks, it does not mean that families did not care for them. The character of emotionality was measured differently, and priorities were, in some ways, far more basic. Men's authority over the household was shifting from 'an overt, authoritarian form to a covert version that brought out companionship and tenderness. The latter did not, however, diminish male authority. This was a change in emotional style, not substance', but one which reflected the shifting family values and children's position in it.[27] The familial model had some resonance for working families, and Joanne Bailey notes 'The question is not whether families suddenly fell in love with each other but why they chose to portray themselves in a particular way . . . [which] was conceptualized as tenderness, physical and emotional ministering to children, moral guidance of offspring, and personal self-sacrifice.' And she confirms 'that there was broad consensus that love was the foundation of . . . parent-child relationships'.[28] Furthermore, the household was the prime site of socialisation, transmitting social and cultural norms, including gender roles. Mothers were primary carers in the early years, but as children grew, boys tended to spend more time with fathers and girls with mothers, and both parents had a role in deciding the future of children, when there were options. In this context however, Katie Barclay reminds us that patterns of love and care might take different forms for different groups of children, especially those not born legitimate, orphaned or abandoned.[29]

The early years of life were the period of maximum dependency when children were less able to look after themselves. In busy working families, young children could be left to their own devices so that accident and neglect were factors in child mortality. Swaddling was used to restrict and protect children and to keep them warm and covered; parents believed it helped limbs grow straight. However, the practice was in decline and far less prevalent by the end of the century. As children became more active, mothers used walkers to prevent crawling and to encourage leg strength and leading strings on clothes to keep them from wandering off. In urban and rural households, cottage industries were a factor, with numerous hazards facing the young child. Children up to seven in all ranks were put in care of whoever was available to look after them—servants, apprentices, siblings or neighbours—but often children were unsupervised.

Certainly, caring for children was not all-absorbing and reflected the realities of the economic and labour needs of the household. Children were not the central focus, and their youth meant they were often a negative drain on the family, so that the number of deserted children in times of distress suggests that they were frequently most expendable. Many mothers, and fathers for that matter, worked so hard they had little time for childcare, although some mothers reduced their work time to create time for children. In households in which getting a living took precedence, women developed strategies to balance other responsibilities, such as childcare or housecleaning. They also took advantage of services, paying washerwomen and hiring servants to help with children or household tasks, possibly a seamstress for mending. With workshops and households often juxtaposed, mothers frequently moved between roles, and indeed tasks were not discrete in any meaningful sense. The need for labour may have affected decision-making and the structure of the household, but it does not rule out the importance of emotion in shaping the way strategies for survival were derived. Mothers believed that babies needed food and warmth; then they needed restraint. Restrictions were practical considerations given the danger of many households, but restraint was also psychological. Concern over wildness and animal-like behaviour, like crawling, was a factor. Cleanliness was not as important, though it gained in prominence as the century wore on. Babies were less likely to smell if they only consumed mother's milk, and mothers knew not to allow them to lie in wet or dirty hay. By the standards of the day, they kept them clean.

Wet nursing is often cited as evidence of lower standards of care. Far less common in Britain than in France, it was the only option for mothers whose own milk was inadequate or who were ill and unable to nurse. It was primarily urban women who employed wet nurses in order to concentrate on their role in a shop. Often mothers placed town children with rural nurses, believing that the country was healthier, but also when the working day did not allow her to nurse. However, Rousseau and other *philosophes* began to use wet nursing and swaddling as a critique of mothering: 'Since mothers have despised their first duty and refused to nurse their own children, they have had to be entrusted to hired nurses . . . having got rid of their babies [they] devote themselves gaily to the pleasures of the town.'[30] Real shifts took place in mothering practices, but with less impact on the labouring family. An increase in childcare manuals demonstrated tensions between clerics and medical men, who saw women as wedded to superstitious old-fashioned practices and holding out against new ideas and theories of childcare. For example, in 1748 William Cadogan, honorary medical attendant at the London Foundling Hospital, argued: 'I see at last the Preservation of Children become the Care of Men of Sense . . . In my Opinion, this business has been too long fatally left to the Management of Women, who cannot be supposed to have proper Knowledge to fit them for such a task.'[31] The more doctors emphasised that children's progress depended on the love and active care of their mother, the greater were mothers' feelings of guilt and failure.

Wall suggested that the perceived inferior status of girls could mean that they were more vulnerable to conscious or unconscious negligence, although he intimates that a variety of demographic changes in pre-industrial England may have been a factor. He discounts abandonment and wet nursing as differential treatment of children in England. While the historiography suggests girls being less well fed than boys, and women less than men, Wall remained unconvinced since no substantial data confirms it. Lifestyle however is more suggestive since girls died more frequently from scalds and burns associated with household duties. Sarah Stephenson for example, born 1738, commented in her biography: 'When I was about six years of age, I had a narrow escape of being burned to death, by falling on the fire when no one else was in the room.'[32] Barbara Hanawalt cites fourteenth-century statistics to show that at the early age of two or three more girls (27 per cent) than boys (14 per cent) died because of accidents with pots and scalding liquids in Bedfordshire. In contrast, 44 per cent of girls and 64 per cent of boys died outside the home in bodies of water.[33] Data from the nineteenth century show a clear differential in girls' deaths over boys' from scalds and burns. Wall argues that neglect, and misfortune due to culturally determined styles of dress, including hairstyle, were important influences on the health of girls in late nineteenth century England. In pre-industrial England, he argued that undervaluation of a girl emerged when a family had one or two daughters and at least one son past the age of five. Children being weaned might also be most at risk, since they began to place pressure on food supplies and yet were not capable of earning sufficiently to earn their keep. He recognised that his conjectures were based on limited examples but noted consistently higher female than male infant mortality after birth rank five, that is, after families had already burdened themselves with several children. Thus, 'on occasion the neglect of the female child is at least a strong possibility. A considerable amount of additional work still must be done before it could be said to be proven but the link between higher female than male infant mortality and high birth rank is certainly suggestive.'[34]

Abandonment

Not all children had the 'luxury' of a family, but we should remember that foundlings and orphans were not the same thing, although some charities took in 'fatherless' children, not specifying whether they were also 'motherless'. Barclay also argues that most illegitimate children probably were not abandoned or murdered, but incorporated into families, perhaps differently than those born within wedlock.[35] Orphans were among the most vulnerable even when taken in by kin, since they put pressure on the new family and did not necessarily 'belong'. The trope of the cruel stepmother has some foundation in fact, as Hewit's case showed (Chapter 1). Abandonment was not necessarily an indication of lack of care, and often represented the desire to provide a better life for the child than the parents could offer at that point in life. This section is focused on the child, and further discussion of girls who abandoned children, especially babies, forms a part of Chapter 9, in which the troubles of the girl rather than the child shape the discussion.

Children were abandoned for a variety of reasons. More common in larger towns, it was nevertheless a feature of early childhood for many. Richard Adair found only twenty-seven foundlings in eighteenth-century rural parishes, while in Wales only a small fraction of illegitimate children was abandoned.[36] Rural communities remained close enough that anonymity was less likely but in towns, many people had migrated without support systems. Women could be especially vulnerable to unwanted pregnancies and destitution in the metropolises, and it was common for pregnant single women to migrate to towns to gain anonymity. Some towns like Aberdeen were vigilant about pursuing cases of abandonment (along with infanticide) often with little sympathy for the mother. On 16 September 1765, the *Aberdeen Journal* reported:

> On Saturday morning was found the body of a male infant lying covered with some turf and grass . . . it had no cloaths on and seemed to be about three weeks old when exposed in this shocking and inhumane manner.[37]

In contrast, the story of Charlotte Dionis is a positive account of how children could fare in the system. Probably born in 1761, she appeared in the records of St Dionis Backchurch, London, when she was a sickly baby of a few months old. A pauper wet nurse was arranged for her in the workhouse, and three other paupers were paid to stand godparents for her on 1 January 1762. Captain Wiliam Wyld, under-church warden, passed her to the care of a parish nurse, Ann Collop, at Chigwell Row in Essex, who regularly acted as a dry nurse for the parish. Charlotte was transferred back and forth frequently because of her health, since she regularly had 'fits' exacerbating the demands on those caring for her. The parish was most assiduous in her care, insisting she was 'to have all proper assistance', and it laid out substantial sums for her transport, care and subsistence. She stayed with the Collops for most of her first nineteen years, with occasional visits to the pauper farm at Rose Lane, Spitalfields, for dedicated nursing, so probably developed a close bond with them. The parish attempted to put her out to service when she was sixteen, though there were difficulties placing her, probably due to her health. She disappeared from the parish records at the time of a potential placement as a servant, and her subsequent history is unknown.[38]

By 1700, abandonment of infants was an increasing social problem; as many as 1,000 were left on the streets to fend for themselves every year in London alone.[39] A response to the perceived increase in abandoned children was the creation or renovation of foundling societies. There was a long tradition of 'hospitals' in London, like Christ's Hospital, and others were created across Britain. For example, the Aberdeen Poor's Hospital, was created in 1741,

> for the reception of such idle and strolling vagrants as should be found in the town, and the poor inhabitants, who had no visible way of earning their bread; also for the boys and girls, the children of poor inhabitants, and for destitute orphans who had no relation to care for them.[40]

Numbers are extremely difficult to ascertain, except when an institution kept records. One of the best sources are the records of the London Foundling Hospital, where 18,539 abandoned children were received between its founding in 1741 and 1799. While altruism was a factor, especially in the early years, the development of the Foundling Hospital illustrated that orphans became a question of national importance as concern grew over the loss of potential 'cannon fodder' in this century of successive wars. While it operated a selective entry system from 1741, during the Seven Years War, the government funded a 'general reception', providing direct financial aid on the condition that selective admission would end.[41] History has tended to suggest that more girls than boys were abandoned, yet Alysa Levene's study shows that the sex ratio of children admitted was almost exactly the same as the sex ratio at birth, 106 boys to 100 girls, between 1741 and 1799. Valerie Fildes's study of the foundling hospital for 1560–1790s indicated that the only fifty-year period in which the percentage of girls exceeded that of boys was the second half of the seventeenth century.[42] Levene argued:

> The lack of gender preference suggests that parents using the hospital were faced with extreme poverty or hardship such that a baby had to be

> abandoned regardless of its longer-term earning potential. Alternatively, unmarried mothers may have realised that the hospital offered to preserve their sexual honour or their employment prospects.[43]

Some children also went into workhouses when parents could not afford to keep them, and Levene shows that often they entered as groups of siblings.[44] Some families even swapped children back and forth.

Most parents were driven by distress to abandon children, and inability to afford to care for them was the most common reason parents brought children to the hospital. Single mothers usually abandoned a child reluctantly, but economic circumstances coupled with stigma meant that for many it was the only route (see Chapter 9). Not all were bastards. Evans found that 9 per cent of petitioners were married and 4 per cent widowed, the result of poverty and an inability to keep them. In 1763, with her husband enlisting for America and concerned to be able to support herself and a four-month old child, Mary Evans said 'The Family in which she lived some years before she married would gladly take her again as a servant but the incumbrance of her child prevents her entering into that or any other method of getting her bread. Fathers' occupations were given in 40 per cent of petitions for admission, some still apprentices, testifying that abandonment was not solely a mother's problem.[45] They may have hoped to reclaim them, but meagre records, their own vulnerability and the likelihood of children succumbing to illnesses rife in these institutions, even the better ones, meant reunion was unlikely. The notes and memorials submitted with them show that many wished to retrieve children when times were better. For example, 'Florella Burney Born june the 19: 1,758: In the Parish off St. Anns SoHo. Not Baptize'd, pray Let porticulare care be take'en off this child, As it will be call'd for Again.'[46] However, it was mainly a forlorn hope: many died in infancy, and fewer than 200 were reclaimed alive, by the mid-nineteenth century, usually by mothers.[47]

Work

Families anticipated that all members would contribute to the household economy in a variety of ways, and even young children were drawn into contributing, varying, of course, by their age, sex, ability and position in the household. Young children's tasks also depended on what work the family did. People recognised children as net consumers in their first years of life, up to between five and seven years old. Young children needed feeding, clothing, housing and tending, so that families not only lost some of their mothers' work, but also there was a greater drain on family resources. Although children might start to contribute towards family sustenance early on, the strain of rearing younger siblings might mean that it was not until the eighteenth year of a marriage that a family would be in net profit from its children.[48]

Infancy was the time when children were least likely to be put to work. As they grew, and as more children were born into the household, they began to assist families, gradually taking on small undemanding tasks around age six or seven. They tended younger siblings, ran errands, carried messages and picked stones from fields (see Image 2.2). Parents also expected them to take more responsibility for themselves. Their work was intermittent. From perhaps five or six, girls were expected to assist mothers by performing simple but necessary tasks, which grew more complex as they grew older, more able and more experienced. Rural girls helped with cooking, cleaning, looking after the barnyard, candlemaking and foraging for firewood; boys assisted fathers in the fields, planting or mending fences. When they could be pressed into work varied depending on the family occupation, with evidence suggesting that in crafts and domestic industry they contributed earlier and more

IMAGE 2.2 Thomas Gainsborough, 1727–1788, Studies of Girls Carrying Faggots, ca. 1780. Black chalk and stumping, heightened with white chalk on medium, slightly textured, cream laid paper inset into a sheet of moderately thick, slightly textured, cream paper, Yale Center for British Art, Paul Mellon Collection, B1977.14.6067.

effectively than in agriculture, because the same level of strength was not required. With proto-industries, industrial work for children increased, and they assisted from a young age, with regular work possible as early as six. Textiles were the classic proto-industries, especially woollens, in which children helped clean and card wool. Industries were not seasonal, so children, like adults, were deployed as required. The division of labour employed children of all ages, usually at ancillary tasks until old enough to take on adult jobs. It offered a regularity of work not found in agriculture.

One point to remember is that children's relation to the family was never solely dependent on economic considerations, and decision-making was not necessarily rational. The family-balancing act went beyond production and consumption and took in a range of variables such as labour, leisure and marital and industrial activities as well as love, affection and intimacy. Considerations, such as transmission of culture, played a part. Increasing reliance on wages changed family relationships and affected plebeian responses linked to culture, custom and control. The need for labour affected decision-making but emotion also played a role in shaping the way strategies for survival were derived. Finally, we should not forget that many families did not feel they were making 'choices'. Often, they did what they had to do.

Play

If work was seen as a natural and expected part of childhood, nevertheless, play was inevitable and increasingly valued. Pleasure became more appreciated as an educational practice, as Locke wrote: 'The right Way to teach them Those things is, to give them a liking and Inclination to what you propose to them to be learn'd.'[49] Rousseau added to this trend with the emphasis on the 'natural child', for whom play was seen as a part of learning: 'for what games do they play in which I cannot find material for instruction for them? And even if I could not do so, so long as they are amusing themselves harmlessly and passing the time pleasantly, their progress in learning is not yet of such great importance.'[50] Notably, Rousseau neglected to mention play and amusement in his chapter on Sophie. Gradually, society valued a more sensitive and gentler approach to childhood, and while this was contested, especially for the labouring orders, it marked a significant shift in attitudes. John Plumb charted this shift in the commercialisation of education with new, more accessible and enticing teaching and reading materials, like John Newberry's *Pretty Little Pock-Book* which were part of a more child-centred approach to upbringing. The extent to which this percolated to the labouring classes is debateable and, in a world where children could be seen as 'wild creatures' and where childhood was increasingly inscribed as a period for preparing the child for the adult world, play could be regarded suspiciously.

Nonetheless, young children were rarely fully employed and had time on their hands for much of their childhood. Diarists and autobiographers seldom mention play and leisure time, and our knowledge of labouring children is even sparser, but tangential evidence exists. They accompanied parents on errands, often left to their own devices. For example, at the Old Bailey in April 1790, in a case investigating theft of clothing from a child, her father, Thomas Bailey, testified,

> I sell physical herbs and flowers in Covent-garden-market. I have a young child, about two years and a half old: her name is Elizabeth Bailey. On the 12th of April instant, as near as I can guess, about six in the afternoon, the child was playing about the Strand; it ran all about the market; it pays its visits all round; about half an hour after Mrs. Johnson and Mr. Ashmore brought the child, and asked me if it was mine; I had not missed it.[51]

Court cases of stolen children's clothing clearly show that children were permitted to play. In 1771, in care of a servant, Elizabeth Minton, aged five, was allowed to play in the street, and Jane Carpenter, age six, was playing in Spittle Square—both were stripped of their clothes whilst playing. More seriously, Elizabeth Sharpe was sexually assaulted as she was 'was playing with some peas, tossing them up upon the bed, as she sat in the room playing with her doll'.[52] A painting from the *London Cries* by Paul Sandby shows a young girl accompanying her parents as they buy from a fishmonger (Image 2.3). She is shown with a doll in one hand while petting a dog with the other. Such young children, as we have seen, had few tasks and often were left to fend for themselves. Their lives in villages, farms and towns would have provided opportunities and space to loiter, play and spend time with other children. For many, their logical playmates were siblings with whom they were in constant proximity, especially youngest children, whom older siblings might have been minding. They also mixed with children from their neighbourhoods and villages, and some of their tasks, fetching water, picking stones or gathering firewood, were done collectively, often loitering along the way. Theirs was not a closed world. As Thomas Bailey's testimony suggests, they had far more physical freedom to wander off and entertain themselves. Samuel Bamford (1788–1872) from near Manchester explained 'in summer days, we spent much of our time out of doors, digging holes in the sand, . . . wading up the stream, maybe laying hold of a trout now and then.'[53] They also were present on market and fair days. Mary Capper, later a member of the Friends, said that in childhood she 'was fond of active play; outdoing all my companions at ball, jumping, sliding, etc.'.[54]

Evidence from foundling and workhouse records also shows that play and leisure were seen as useful and important, despite a persistent image of drudgery and destitution. Bamford described playing ball and catch with

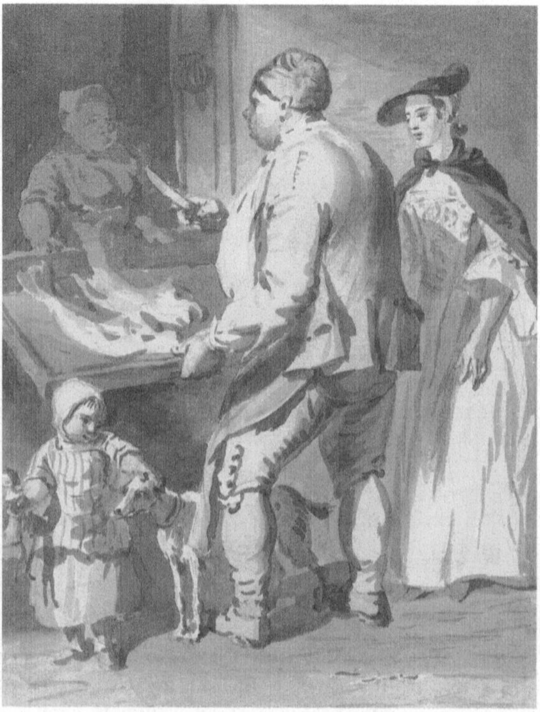

IMAGE 2.3 Paul Sandby, 1731–1809, London Cries: A Fishmonger, ca. 1759. Watercolour and graphite on medium, slightly textured, cream laid paper, Yale Center for British Art, Paul Mellon Collection, B1975.3.210.

the workhouse children. Levene suggests that there was an assumption that children should have time for recreation; if the records refer to older children, then it is even more likely that younger ones had the space to play. She points out:

> The 1708 account of the London Workhouse in Bishopsgate Street stated that it kept its children busy from 7am to 6pm, spinning wool and flax, but there was a break from noon to one for dinner and play as well as further breaks for reading and writing. . . . This is seen elsewhere too: St Andrew Holborn made provision for leisure time in the early decades of the century, stating that the children 'are not permitted to play until they have finished their Task'.[55]

Children invented games, climbed trees, investigated the worlds around them and played with toys. As Plumb chronicled, there was an explosion of toys available for children, many meant to be educational, but also for pleasure. Whilst most aimed at the more affluent and middling sorts, there is no doubt that poorer children played with toys as well. These may have been simple homemade ones, carved by family members, dolls made by mothers and aunties, tops, balls and hoops. Some toys were also available cheaply and could have been purchased throughout the social scale. In Scotland, Stuart Campbell pointed out a shipment of dolls worked out at 5d. per doll and 'it is a challenge to assert that such objects were available only to those of a certain class'.[56] Evans also points to the fact that the lottery approach to placing children in foundling homes reflected peoples' familiarity with games of chance and dice which they had played from childhood.[57]

Conclusion

Were children happy? As the notion of happiness entered social thought, e.g. 'life, liberty and happiness' and a term repeated throughout *Émile*, Peter Stearns points out that the idea 'did not immediately spill over into common advice about children or childhood'.[58] This is not to say children were not happy, nor that parents and others did not make them happy from time to time. Joy and pleasure were certainly part of the young child's experience. In many respects the concern over happiness is a modern construct. Stearns says 'What is clear is that happiness and childhood were not assumed regularly to coexist, that happiness was not seen as an adult or parental obligation, and that childhood was not viewed as a particularly happy period in the span of human life—until quite recently.'[59] The moralising tenor of society, even under Enlightenment principles, the belief in controlling noxious tendencies in children and the use of fear as a force for discipline remained very present. The exigencies of working people's lives left less room for worrying about happiness, and though it might have grown as a social value, it remained on the level of an ideal. The early years of the girl were embedded in this world view. Their practical experience was lived in families, communities and sometimes institutions where work was valued, subsistence mattered and love and affection, while it certainly existed, was not expressed in the same way it would be in the modern world. Getting to the next stage of life was more important. That next stage encompassed education, training and work which are dealt with in the following chapters.

Notes

1 Locke, *Some Thoughts Concerning Education*, §32, §72.
2 Rousseau, *Émile*, 6, 7, 28, 30.
3 Stone, *The Family, Sex and Marriage in England*, 412–5; Ariès, *Centuries of Childhood*, 390–1, 396–9.
4 Abrams, 'At Home in the Family', 33.

5 Cunningham, *Childhood in Western Society*, 30, 46.
6 Guttormsson, 'Parent-Child Relations', 270.
7 Trimmer, *The Oeconomy of Charity*, 66.
8 Talbot, *The Christian Schoolmaster*, 24.
9 Talbot, *The Christian Schoolmaster*, 41.
10 Ingram, *Schools of Industry*, 6.
11 Ingram, *Schools of Industry*, 15.
12 Earle, *City Full of People*, 188–9.
13 Saxby, *Memoirs of a Female Vagrant*, 1–2.
14 Coster, *Family and Kinship in England*, 1.
15 Wrigley and Schofield, *English Population History . . . Summary Results*, Table 12.
16 Laslett, 'Mean Household Size in England Since the Sixteenth Century', 154.
17 Laslett, *Family Life and Illicit Love in Earlier Generations*, 43.
18 Möser, *Anwalt des Vaterlands*, 327.
19 Razzell and Spence, 'The History of Infant, Child and Adult Mortality in London', 271–92; Dennison, Ditchburn and Lynch, *Aberdeen before 1800*, 117.
20 There is an ongoing debate about whether increased fertility or decreased mortality was more significant. For example, Wrigley and Schofield posited that two thirds or more of the acceleration in population growth during the 'long' eighteenth century was due to the rise in fertility and only one third or less to improved mortality, while Peter Razzell argued growth of population in eighteenth-century England was primarily due to a fall in mortality. Wrigley and Schofield, *English Population History*, Wrigley et al., *English Population History from Family Reconstitution;* Razzell, 'The Growth of Population in Eighteenth-century England'.
21 For a discussion of the literature, see Harris's introduction to *Siblinghood and Social Relations*, and Calvi and Blutrach-Jelín, 'Sibling Relations in Family History'; see also Davidoff, *Thicker than Water: Siblings and their Relations*.
22 Harris, *Siblinghood and Social Relations*, 9.
23 Humphries, *Childhood and Child Labour*, 126–7.
24 Harris, *Siblinghood and Social Relations*, 28.
25 Levene, *Childhood of the Poor*, 49, 85, 99.
26 Barclay, 'The Early Modern Family', 28.
27 Bailey, 'Family Relationships', 16.
28 Bailey, 'Family Relationships', 21, 24–6, 2. See also Barclay, *Caritas*, chapter 2.
29 Barclay, 'Love, Care and the Illegitimate Child'.
30 Rousseau, *Emile*, 11.
31 Cadogan, *An Essay upon Nursing and the Management of Children*, 1.
32 Stephenson, *Life of Sarah Stephenson*.
33 Hanawalt, 'Childrearing among the Lower Classes of Late Medieval England', 16.
34 Wall, 'Inferring Differential Neglect of Females from Mortality Data', 138–9.
35 Barclay, 'Love, Care and the Illegitimate Child', 112.
36 Adair, *Courtship, Illegitimacy and Marriage*, 34–5; Muir, 'Courtship, Sex and Poverty', 65.
37 *AJ*, 16 September 1765.
38 *LL* Charlotte Dionis, b. 1761, compiled by Deirdre Palk.
39 Levene, *Childcare, Health and Mortality*, 3.
40 Sinclair, OSA, XV, 190.
41 Andrew, *Philanthropy and Police*, 57–64.
42 Fildes, *Women as Mothers in Pre-Industrial England*, 150.
43 Levene, *Childcare, Health and Mortality*, 17.
44 Levene, *Children of the Poor*, 98–9.
45 Evans, *Unfortunate Objects*, 117.

46 Styles, *Threads of Feeling*, 17.
47 Levine, *Childcare, Health and Mortality*, 18, 33–5.
48 Smith, 'Some issues Concerning Families and their Property in rural England', 71.
49 Locke, *Some Thoughts Concerning Education*, §72.
50 Rousseau, *Émile*, 112.
51 *OBP*, 24 April 1790, t17900424-69.
52 Payne, *Children of the Poor in London*, 270, 271, quote 288.
53 Bamford, *Autobiography of Samuel Bamford*, vol. 1, n18.
54 Capper, 'A Memoir of Mary Capper', *FF.*
55 Levene, *Childhood of the Poor*, 125.
56 Campbell, 'Work and Play', 52.
57 Evans, 'Unfortunate Objects', 134.
58 Stearns, 'Defining Happy Childhoods', 168.
59 Stearns, 'Defining Happy Childhoods'.

3

UPBRINGING AND IDEOLOGY

Transitions

Girls moved from childhood to girlhood in a series of gradations, but nominally the 'girl' emerged around age seven as she left 'infancy' behind. From now on her world and experience would be profoundly shaped by gendered assumptions, ideas and practices. Her learning, training, work, behaviour and opportunities would reflect the gendered world of girlhood. Importantly, however, while she operated within nominal constraints, she also had options and choices. Some decisions may have been shared with parents or guardians, but she also had spaces in which to contribute to shaping her future. Circumstances may have operated to limit her choices, or defeat them altogether, but other times she had chances to forge her own destiny. Her voice in making these choices is muted, but even in testimonies we hear her contributing to the discourse in how she shaped her story.

This is also the point in which 'upbringing' begins to take a primary role in how girlhood was understood and traversed. The home remained an important site of what girls learned in the process of becoming an adult, many for extended periods of time, and a variety of patterns described girls' experience of learning. The kind of upbringing they had was partly conditional on the kind and shape of the family, its location, i.e., urban or rural, poor or middling, agricultural, artisanal or commercial. This chapter describes some of the routes, opportunities and profiles of upbringing, or learning for life. It begins with the home, which was a normative influence for most girls, which reflected domestic circumstances, the need for labour and the demography of the household. The community in which she and the family were situated was also a factor in learning about adult roles. The chapter then turns

DOI: 10.4324/9781003412168-4

educational ideology and the debates about whether girls needed formal education and literacy or not. Despite resistance to popular education, demands in favour of educating the labouring orders came from many quarters, but the intentions which lay behind those demands varied widely. They ranged from anxiety about the impact of social and economic change and a fear of encouraging sedition, to the importance of teaching Christian values, the desire to improve the manners and morality of society and the intention to keep the lower orders in their place.

Home and community

Many girls learned what they needed to know at home, in the homes of others or in the wider community, and we have tangential glimpses into this world (Image 3.1). The role of the family during the formative years is widely accepted today as a crucial factor in socialisation and transmitting culture. It was also true of eighteenth-century life and was accepted as true. Since the Renaissance, the idea that the home should be a space of learning was increasingly prized, and the Reformation and Counter-Reformation further

IMAGE 3.1 Francis Wheatley, 1747–1801, Morning, 1799. Oil on canvas, Yale Center for British Art, Paul Mellon Collection, B1977.14.120.

instilled the importance of family and home as a space for learning. Parents were expected to teach their children, and the head of the household was expected to instruct servants living there. Middle-class adoption of Lockean ideas of children's understanding further testifies to their belief that the influence of the home was crucial.[1] Similarly, Enlightenment ideology promoted the mother as the key influence on and the 'natural' educators of children, a view widely adopted by the middling orders. Mothers were responsible for bringing up children according to Christian values and virtues, and since they had the care of children at a critical time, 'the soundness or folly of our minds are not less owing to those first tempers and ways of thinking, which we receive from the love, tenderness, authority and constant conversation of mothers.' Likewise, the mother's demeanour and example were held to account for the effect they had on her children.[2] Both ideologically and practically mothers were responsible for daughters, with a particular responsibility for education of girls in the eyes of contemporaries. This was due to their commonality of sex and to the implications of female character for the whole of society. Thus, many tracts on children's education were addressed to mothers, and were not exclusively for the middling orders. Rousseau specifically admonished writers to 'Address your treatises on education to the women, for not only are they able to watch over it more closely than men, not only is their influence always predominant in education, its success concerns them more nearly.'[3]

Drawing on their own experience and expectations, the middling orders, in turn, promulgated these views for the consumption of the plebeian orders. John Moir, for example, claimed lessons were 'not wholly framed for young women in superior stations'.[4] Despite the distinct differences between the realities of middling and plebeian life, such views were constantly transmitted to working girls and their families through contact with employers, ministers, schools, schoolbooks and teachers. How deeply they were internalised is open to speculation. While ideology may not have dictated action, the importance of socialisation during the early years of a child's life was widely recognised. Girlhood was seen as formative and the home, however defined, had a significant role to play in shaping the influences of that period. Since most girls remained in their familial home until fourteen or fifteen, or even later, home could be crucial. Christina de Bellaigue, among others, argues for the 'longevity of the home for providing a vital educational culture that did not depend on formal schooling', and challenges the artificial distinction between learning in the home and institutional instruction.[5]

As part of their normal daily working, most mothers or other females in the household would have transmitted to younger ones the skills and knowledge which they believed girls should know. Within domestic industry and farming households, children's and women's work were intertwined, as was

IMAGE 3.2 John Faber the Younger, ca. 1695–1756, The Housewife's Employment, undated. Mezzotint on medium, moderately textured, cream laid paper, Yale Center for British Art, Paul Mellon Fund, B1970.3.875.

the upbringing of the children with women's domestic and productive role (Image 3.2). Historians widely associate the supervision and training of children with the usual course of activities undertaken by mothers in performance of their other responsibilities. William Radcliffe, inventor of the dressing frame, remembered how 'My mother taught me [while too young to weave] to earn my bread by carding and spinning cotton, winding linen or cotton weft for my father and elder brothers at the loom, until I became of sufficient age and strength for my father to put me into a loom.'[6] Similarly girls were expected to assist mothers by performing simple but necessary tasks. As they grew older, more able and more experienced, the tasks could grow more complex under the supervision of a mother. It was a virtual apprenticeship to becoming a woman, learning the domestic, agricultural or technical skills she would need in adulthood. Women passed on to girls work practices as well as the understanding of strategies necessary for organising working and living. It was the nature of female work and knowledge, their proximity and relationships to the young, and the trends in domestic organisation which operated to create networks of women which related directly to their importance in passing on skills, knowledge and cultural values to girls. In this way, girls' roles, knowledge and status were transmitted through home-based instruction and emulation of the other women in the household.

Although there is tangible evidence of the role of schooling and training, the substantiation for home-based education is much more speculative. Nevertheless, circumstantial and suggestive evidence allows some insight into the part played by the home in working girls' formative years. Records and commentary are scant, and even when women wrote accounts of their lives, they tended to describe academic education or religious inspiration rather than general formative influences. Nicholas Hans found a high incidence of home education in his study of women in the *Dictionary of National Biography*, with over half educated there. Middle-class girls accounted for only 36 per cent of his sample but they represented 70 per cent of those educated at home, and family members taught 60 per cent of them.[7] Hans's study is suggestive, but its parameters do not speak to the experience of most girls and especially those of the plebeian orders. Nevertheless, other indicative evidence from diaries and autobiographies allows some insight into the part played by the home in working girls' formative years. Many authors were middling and probably more literate than most women, while others came from artisan families.[8] They tended to chronicle learning to read and write, followed in many cases by other subjects commonly taught at schools. But they described numerous experiences including physical exercise, learning 'the first lessons of parental obedience', being 'educated . . . in industry' or being 'brought up strictly in . . . religion'. Other references were vaguer, crediting parents or mothers with 'tenderness and solicitude for . . . [my] best welfare'. Quaker Ruth Follows wrote only that 'my dear parents taught me, both by example and precept, to live a sober and godly life'[9] (Image 3.3). These examples demonstrate that mothers, sometimes other women and female networks, were important influences on girls' upbringing. Women remained the strongest influence even for those women whose mothers died while they were young. Margaret Lucas was taken in hand by her uncle's housekeeper until sent to school about age twelve or thirteen. Sarah Grubb, whose mother died before she was five, praised her stepmother whom her father married when she was about ten, for her 'care and regard' and wrote that she was instrumental in the 'watchful and religious education' she received (Image 3.3).[10]

While the experience and situation of girls in labouring families were different in many respects from middling girls, there are good reasons for expecting home to play a vital role for girls further down the social scale. It was a natural development of the living and working patterns of the labouring classes, and other learning influences were situated in the domestic setting. When a literate member of the household could, they often read to others. John Smarte, a donor to a charity school, wrote when children 'can read

IMAGE 3.3 John Eginton, active 1763–1800, The Affectionate Daughter, 1792. Stipple engraving, printed in colour on moderately thick, moderately textured, cream wove paper, Yale Center for British Art, Paul Mellon Collection, B1977.14.14504.

in the bibles . . . they read them at home before their parents at least 3 tymes in the weeks'.[11] Similarly, when one child attended school, he or she might teach others in the household. And many schools were not far removed from a home-like setting. Most dames' schools were held in a woman's home, and frequently autobiographers credited them with teaching children to read; they were not necessarily mere babysitting services. In other schools, girls were expected to make clothing for the pupils and assist with the cleaning and cooking, and often lived in. Many girls were surely taught similar things in their own home by parents, siblings, relatives or servants in the household. Mothers were often limited by time and knowledge from teaching literate skills, but some were clearly able to do so. Amelia Bristow described how Mary Allen,

> though extremely fond of her child, did not evince her affection by mistaken and pernicious indulgence, but brought her up in the strictest habits

> of industry and cleanliness. She also early taught her to work at her needle, and to read a little, in which latter part [her husband] James assisted, but the utmost extent of their united book knowledge was very small; they could read their Bible, or a plain tract, but writing they were entirely ignorant of.[12]

As the century progressed, with indications of a higher level of literacy, more mothers could have taught reading. One diarist was taught by her sister, two others by their aunts; two by servants; two by friends, all female, in addition to those taught by mothers, stepmothers or governesses or at schools run by women. Ann Taylor recorded,

> In that little back parlour we were taught the formal rudiments, and in the garden and elsewhere, constantly under the eye of our parents, we fell in with more than is always included in the catalogue of school learning at so much per quarter. Books were a staple commodity in the house. From my mother's habit of reading aloud at breakfast and at tea, we were always picking up something; to every conversation we were auditors, and, I think, quiet ones, for, having no nursery, the parlour would have been intolerable otherwise. . . . Of course my dear mother, with health never strong, and all the needlework of the household on her hands, could not undertake our entire instruction. Reading, the Needle, and the Catechism, we were taught by her, and as my father was constantly engraving at the high desk in the same room, it was easy for him to superintend the rest. . . . The precise hours allotted to our instruction I now forget, but they were regular, and regularly kept.[13]

This may have been unusual but is a good indication of the possibilities, especially in the literate middling orders, from which many working women came. The home was always the site for some instruction and mothers frequently were a key part of this, especially for girls.

In a largely rural society, oral tradition retained an important place. For most people in villages and towns, their understanding of the world was still local, and their knowledge of the way things were done rested on verbal communication and established custom. In some cases, such activities were relatively formalised, as in the *spinnstüben* of Germany, in which one member might read aloud to the others. In Scotland, gatherings, literally ceilidhs, were a chance to share warmth, spin, knit, repair fishing nets and share information, songs and ballads. In such a way knowledge was also conveyed. The same was true of some workshops.

In rural society women's activities linked them to each other. For example, childbirth was exclusively a female activity amongst the lower orders of society, with midwives, 'wise women' or simply other women grouping together to help one another, sharing knowledge of the process. Women's participation in popular politics emanated from their collective experiences in managing strategies for household provision. Thus, women established and maintained their own communication links and networks. In conceptualising female upbringing in the household context, the oral tradition plays a central role. It was via the women around them that many girls were taught the work practices they would need and the roles they would fill as adults, thus forging another link in the female network. It is not clear whether the ideology of women's role and responsibility for daughters' upbringing had permeated the working classes, but their day-to-day experiences operated to create a female network of education and upbringing. Limiting understanding of girls' education to schooling, or even to schooling and apprenticeship, is to ignore the fact that many girls received their most formative education in other less formal but equally recognisable ways.

Ideology and education

The ideological context of the eighteenth-century world dictated the form and access of working girls to formal education. The attitudes of officials, subscribers, trustees, visitors or donors shaped educational provision, as did their views on the natural destinations for girls and boys, which was distinctly different, and whether girls needed to be educated anyway. Inflected by philosophical views, ideas about girl's education for both middling and working orders was complex and shifted across the century. From a period of keen interest at the beginning of the century with organisations like the Society for Promoting Christian Knowledge (SPCK) and local initiatives, a distinct slump from c. 1730 followed. However, a resurgence in educational interest in the last half of the century was a response to new social problems arising out of economic and demographic changes. In part these changes focused attention on the poor because of both their increasing number and their consolidation in new industrial areas. At the same time, the occupational controls of guilds and apprenticeship seemed to loosen, because many workers lay outside that structure, time-honoured occupations declined, and new ones rose to take their place. This situation created uncertainty about status and heightened a concern for maintaining social distinctions and a concern for social stability.

Not surprisingly education was an important vehicle of social elevation and emulation; this was an age when progress and improvement animated society's views of social development. The longstanding and essential argument against teaching children of the working orders was precisely that it would provide them an avenue of social advancement. Any form of education other than work could encourage them to forget their place in society or actively aspire beyond it and thus make them unfit for the station in life for which they were intended. It would divert them from habits of industry and from actively engaging in useful labour, leaving them disqualified from labour as adults. The result would be a class of unemployable semi-literates who would disrupt society through their discontent. A classic view was that of Bernard Mandeville who was sceptical of the civility taught in schools and who in 1723 argued,

> Those who spend a great part of their youth in learning to read, write and cypher, expect (and not unjustly) to be employed where those qualifications may be of use to them. Going to school, in comparison to working, is idleness; and the longer boys continue in this easy sort of life, the more unfit they will be, when grown up, for downright labour, both as to strength and inclination. Men who are to remain and end their days in a laborious, tiresome, and painful station of life, the sooner they are put upon it at first, the more patiently they will submit to it for ever after.[14]

Further, he argued schooling would make them unfit for their station in life, and they would become dissatisfied and socially irresponsible. This concern extended to girls as well. For example, in 1759, John Burton claimed it was folly for parents to send their daughters to schools

> with others of a higher class, whose fortunes or probable station in life, will enable them to appear in a superior style of living. The consequence to the former is often fatal; because the ideas they have imbibed are not compatible, with that humble rank, or perhaps employment, to which they are born.[15]

Such an education made girls idle and fit for nothing. Others, however, saw education as valuable in creating respectful and obliging wives and mothers.

Gender was an important feature of the ideology of schooling, of course. Concepts of woman's nature and her relative place in society clearly distinguished girls' education from that of boys. The perceived need to educate the female sex was the direct consequence of ideas about the nature of women, and their position and role in society. Advice literature firmly established that the correct province for women was home and family, so their education should 'rivet their young and ardent attentions wholly on domestic concerns', so that they provided the right atmosphere for bringing up children.[16] Female duty to husband, children and home appreciably inflected the purposes of education. It was characterised as education for virtue, to make woman a suitable companion to man and to give her children the right early start in life. Tract literature contained two basic assumptions about working girls' destiny: firstly, there was a specific female character, and secondly, many would become servants, wives and mothers. Thus, it was seen as essential to develop them in ways appropriate to their future, and to bring about an improvement in manners and morals for the benefit of society. As Cappe explained, 'cultivation of social and pious affections, gentleness of temper and resignation to the will of God [were] as important to the female character in the lowest as well as the highest forms of life.'[17] Although the economic circumstances of most middling and working females separated their goals in a pronounced fashion, labouring girls' education reflected bourgeois perceptions of women's domestic responsibilities and the upbringing of children.

However, the importance of making women pleasing to men and a desire for upward social mobility led to the growth of accomplishments among middling girls' education, overshadowing 'useful' housewifery skills. As Priscilla Wakefield claimed, 'in the education of females, the same view actuates every rank: an advantageous settlement in marriage is the universal prize, for which parents of all classes enter their daughters upon the lists.'[18] Such a fashionable education served little practical purpose; indeed its main function was to present a girl in the best light in the marriage market and to make her a suitable ornament in marriage. Even so, for some girls, even this schooling could prove useful if they had to fall back on a career as a teacher or governess. For girls from lower down the hierarchy, that kind of occupation would be an advance in social status. In the last quarter of the century, powerful criticisms were raised against accomplishments as a caricature of appropriate female education. Notably Mary Wollstonecraft and Hannah More, opposites in the political firmament, both condemned 'this phrenzy of accomplishments', with More criticising female education because it was geared exclusively for the transient period of youth and beauty. 'We educate them for a crowd, forgetting they live at home, for the world and not for themselves, for show and not for use, for time and not eternity.'[19] Wollstonecraft found common ground here complaining that 'the cultivation of the understanding is always subordinate to the acquirement of some corporal accomplishment.'[20]

It was acknowledged that some middling girls would need to make a living, and many day schools in villages and towns taught skills to prepare them to be self-supporting. Erasmus Darwin wrote of the Misses Parker who were 'themselves educated for the purpose of educating others'.[21] Similarly, when Hannah Robertson in Aberdeen advertised her evening school for 'Young ladies and others' for learning cookery and pastry, she sought also to teach 'some young Women, in order to qualify them for Service in Gentlemen's Families'.[22] The range of day schools in particular appealed to middling families and were well placed to provide the skills such girls might need, perhaps preparing them for apprenticeships or a place as teachers themselves.

The crucial class difference in education was the recognition that plebian girls *had* to support themselves. Thus, the other prong of the argument in favour of sending poor girls to school was that education should train them to provide their own living. Most educationalists would have agreed with Ingram that

> Their employment and duty in life will probably be to discharge the several offices at first of menial servants, and afterwards of wives and mothers, with the fear of God before their eyes; as well as to assist in the maintenance of a family by some species of profitable industry. Let their education, therefore be calculated to impress them with a sense of religious obligation as also to prepare them for the various employments of the stations they are expected to occupy, as far as is practicable in a school.[23]

Yet he limited the 'species of profitable industry' to 'such occupations as have a tendency to generate a sedate and orderly deportment'.[24] Wakefield too advised 'useful occupations . . . without destroying the peculiar characteristic of the sex'.[25] Throughout the literature, schools were advised to teach religion and domestic arts to provide the skills for domestic service and for the natural female positions of wife, mother and 'homemaker'.[26] Proponents argued that instruction in reading, catechism, manners and some form of work would teach the children their place in society and make them more devout, modest and industrious. Prescriptive schooling would create better servants and more civilised and duly subservient labourers. However much social mobility was a middle-class expectation, it was not to be part of education for the masses. At the same time, those on both sides of the debate wished the 'inferior orders' to internalise middle-class values such as sobriety, modesty, diligence and thrift.[27] In this way education was intended to also overcome the 'bad' parenting that many commentators perceived, not trusting the family upbringing to meet the needs of society and especially of girls. While social mobility and social stability were central to the debate about working girls' education, plebeians were not impervious to the desire for social advancement, so that when they could afford the small fees charged by the variety of day schools available, often they did so. Against the portrayal of aspiration and achievement for one's children is the image of the reluctant poor parent unwilling to send his or her children to school, sending them to labour instead. A flurry of interest and educational charitable foundations and donations at the beginning of the century was a response to these attitudes, revived at mid-century, when the debate was renewed. Frequent concurrence that 'there are Reasons of *Civil Policy*, as well as *Religion*' to teach the poor is ample evidence of the concern with which the problem was regarded.[28]

During the last quarter of the century, increasing radicalism and the need to counter seditious ideas and wrong thinking amongst the labouring sectors of the population compounded these insecurities. This period coincided with renewed fears for social order which were awakened by radical ideas and publications, and ultimately by the two revolutions. For some, radicalism always posed a threat. But for others, like Edmund Burke, sympathy with American revolutionaries turned to aversion during the French Revolution. With the reaction which set in, the need to counter subversion, seditious ideas and wrong thinking amongst the labouring sectors of the population became even more critical. Blackstone argued in 1765 that a child with no education would 'lead a life useless to others and shameful to himself'. He believed compulsory education was the only safeguard of freedom and democracy.[29] In 1776 as the American colonies revolted, Adam Smith advocated mass instruction as an integral part of his broadly liberal approach, but he also foreshadowed the anxiety tied up in British responses to the French Revolution: 'The more [the poor] are instructed the less liable they are to the delusions of enthusiasm and superstition, which among ignorant nations frequently occasion the most dreadful disorders.'[30] Thomas Paine claimed that popular education would reduce the number of poor, because their abilities, by the aid of education, would be greater thus enabling them to provide for themselves.[31] Despite this apparently moderate view, it was precisely writers like Paine who stirred the concern and fear of the established conservative sectors of society. Concern about the security of the social system led people to turn to education as a preventative measure, creating the impetus for renewed efforts to educate the working orders. By the end of the century this view had shifted the discourse so that in 1798, although Thomas Malthus argued against progressives with his belief that population exercised unremitting pressure on society's resources, like others, he saw education and literacy as bulwarks against sedition: '[O]n this subject I agree most cordially with Adam Smith in thinking that an instructed and well-informed people would be much less likely to be led away by inflammatory writings, and much better able to detect the false declamation of interested and ambitious demagogues, than an ignorant people.'[32] For none of these authors was national education the central issue, but the frequency with which the subject occurred, and the general concern with 'right ideas', indicate how much education was the key to the realisation of many political theories. Sarah Trimmer could now claim that in the face of the threat of France, 'no less than the safety of the nation probably depends upon the education of those children who are now growing up to maturity.'[33]

The revival of the debate was the signal for a new approach to schooling. Instead of suppression through ignorance, the teaching of 'right ideas' took hold. According to John Chapman, to instil the 'Awe of Authority, they are tutored and governed by discreet Rules and Methods in their whole Behaviour'.[34] Providing models of manners and behaviour would teach the poor to behave more decently, losing their rough and uncontrollable ways. For girls, the female school 'visitor', trustee or occasional teacher was a key element. Trimmer addressed *Oeconomy of Charity* (1787) to 'ladies of rank and fortune' and those of 'the middling stations of life' to whom she pointed out 'the great advantages that would probably arise to society from their taking a more active part than it is at the present usual for them to take, in the management of Sunday Schools and the personal distribution of voluntary benefactions'.[35] She argued that the divide between the classes 'as if they came from different regions of the world' resulted from a lack of education and the good example of their betters.

Demand for literacy

The Brougham Commission (1816–1819) frequently commented that, 'The poor would thankfully receive the means of education,' 'The poor are desirous of having the means of education,' or not infrequently, 'The poor are without the means of instruction and are very desirous of them.'[36] While the structure of educational provision might make it seem that schooling was forced on working people, evidence suggests there was a demand, and that a number of social, cultural and economic factors fostered this. Social mobility was one factor. Evidence of a growing literate culture further indicates a need for and interest in the ability to read if not write, while commercial opportunities could foster a demand for numeracy and accounting skills. The growth of a reading public in Britain is illustrated by the increase in book ownership, large print runs of popular titles and an increase in the numbers of newspapers, almanacs, chapbooks, novels and pamphlets. For example, in 55 provincial towns, 140 new newspapers appeared between 1700 and 1760. The number of stamped newspapers rose from 7.3 million in 1750, to 11 million in 1756 and reaching 17 million in 1793 despite rises in stamp duty in 1757, 1776 and 1789 increasing their cost. Popular novels sold well: Fielding's *Joseph Andrews* (1742) sold 6,500 copies in thirteen months, and his *Amelia* (1751) sold out its first edition of 5,000 in a week. Importantly, the novel-reading public had access to far more individual titles, and circulating libraries made even more available. Thus, there was more reading material at a variety of ranges of reading ability.[37] While cost mattered, newspapers were posted at printing offices and available in clubs and coffeehouses. After the duty rise in 1757, the weekly country newspaper still cost only 2½d each. With workers' earnings from 1s to 2s per day, and a housemaid earning from about 2s a week, the purchase of a newspaper was 'within the reach of most pockets'.[38] Further, legal and commercial developments put pressure on people to read. As R.A. Houston argued, written documents and the law fixed and guaranteed the rights of ordinary people, so there was a defensive as well as offensive need to read.[39] Commonly reading and frequently writing and arithmetic were required for children put out as apprentices, especially in urban crafts. In Wales, farmer John Robert stated in his will that his son, David, and both daughters, Sarah and Hannah, were to 'receive some schooling after his death' while another farmer, Gilfach Roderick provided in his will that his daughter Mary should receive two years of schooling.[40] Furthermore, there was an emergent market for primers, alphabets and writing manuals stressing 'abridged methods' and 'quick and easy' learning.[41] Learning to read involved both the motive to do so and the opportunity.

British schools sprang from a genuine popular interest in learning to read and write, and schools were responsive to parental wishes because of their reliance on fees.[42] Since different lessons were often available from different teachers, parents moved children around to get those they valued. David Vincent and Thomas Laqueur were convinced there was a clear demand by working people.[43] Potentially there was a power and prestige in being able to read, and write, and perhaps also a vague unease and awareness of the disadvantages of being poor and powerless. Indeed for women it was a chance to gain some modicum of independence.[44] A decline in the oral tradition was more likely in urban areas where the prevalence of the written word, combined with the demands of trade and commerce, put a higher premium on literacy. Thus, the need for literacy was concentrated amongst the trading classes and within larger trading centres. These trends created a dichotomy between the urban and rural woman, between the commercial and the labouring woman, between the middling and plebeian woman. The diffusion of literacy was class-, occupation- and gender-specific in various degrees. The relationship between schooling and literacy is not necessarily causal or direct and evidence in Chapter 4 suggests that schooling may have contracted during the century while literacy levels rose, a factor explained by the impact of the range of informal mechanisms including home and community.

A primary problem facing historians is arriving at a satisfactory definition of literacy. The phasing of schooling meant that far more children were taught to read than to write. But the historian has only indirect and imprecise measures of reading ability such as evaluating the outpourings of printing presses. The only direct measurement of historical literacy is to count signatures, such as those on the marriage register after 1754 in England, or in Scotland, where Houston relied on court depositions and tax records.[45] Obviously signatures hinge on sustained writing ability, which was achieved by fewer than the number who could read. Thus, counting signatures necessarily underestimates readers but also overestimates true literates who could use the written word as a means of communication.[46] R.D. Anderson notes that 'the degree of this underestimate was not constant, but depended on educational practices, and on where a society stood in the long transition from partial to total literacy.'[47] Thus 'any change in the numbers capable of signing their names may be taken to indicate a parallel but not necessarily proportionate change in the numbers able to read.'[48] Instead we do not know and may never know the precise relationship between the ability to sign one's name and true literacy.

TABLE 3.1 Percentage of Occupational Illiteracy of Scottish and English Female Deponents by Work and Type of Residence, 1640–1770

Occupation	*England*			*Scotland*		
	City	*Town*	*Village*	*City*	*Town*	*Village*
Craft and trade	60	74	81	60	63	96
Servant	78	73	87	93	84	92

Source: adapted from Houston, 'Age at Marriage of Scottish Women', 61.

Roger Schofield's national sample shows female illiteracy declining from about 76 per cent to 66 per cent by 1800.[49] Comparing Scotland and England, Houston estimated illiteracy levels at 81 per cent in both Scotland and England.[50] He argued that Scottish girls in trades were likely to be 72 per cent illiterate, while servants were worse at 84 per cent. However, the significant differences between town and country are important. He found that over the period 1680–1750 that English and Scottish town girls in trades were 60 per cent illiterate, while servants ranged from 78 to 92 per cent illiterate, depending on where they lived (Table 3.1).[51]

Although the data is imperfect, learning to read and write were increasingly common acquisitions, representing a gradual improvement in the diffusion of literacy in eighteenth-century Britain. Generally, women were less literate than men across Europe, but social strata demonstrated significant differences. Geographic location played a significant role in that there were vast disparities even within a small region, as well as profound regional differences and an urban/rural divide in that towns generally had superior literacy. Yet the rapid inward urban migration at the end of the century tended to depress literacy levels in manufacturing towns in northern England, the central belt of Scotland.[52]

Conclusion

Girls experienced a form of upbringing usually based at home among mothers, perhaps servants and kin. Clearly those without parents may have been scooped up by kin, and even those who were abandoned still probably experienced an upbringing intended to prepare them for a life of work. Values, expectations, skills and the transmission of culture and behavioural norms was an integral part of bringing up girls. Eighteenth-century ideology accentuated the period of childhood and heightened the emphasis on early formation of character. As a corollary, the child's upbringing gained in importance during the century, and that upbringing was placed ideally within the parental home. So early girlhood education, at least, became seen as a family responsibility, and in conjunction with the evolution of female domestic ideology, mothers became primarily responsible for childcare and nurture. Women's and girls' work, their shared tasks and the emulation of mothers were important parts of a girl's upbringing, especially since large numbers remained at home until around fourteen and many stayed for their whole girlhood. At the same time, there was always concern that parents, especially poor parents, were incapable of meeting these obligations satisfactorily, and a growing urge to use schools to transmit values, behaviour and appropriate ideas about girls' place in society. Though educating poor children served a positive good, it was not appropriate to train them in a way which would raise their ideas above the very lowest occupations. Furthermore, especially in the latter half of the century, teaching girls to read—the right sorts of things—gained in importance. Social stability underpinned the debates on girls' upbringing and how they were be taught. Yet, girls and their families increasingly saw a value in the forms of education on offer, and there is good evidence that they too demanded education for girls, as the following chapters show.

Notes

1 See also Cohen, 'The Pedagogy of Conversation in the Home', 447.
2 Horne, *Reflections on . . . Forming the Female Character by Education*, 8. See also Wray, *The Ladies Library*, vol. 1, 59; Chapman, *Ends and Uses of Charity Schools*, 15; Brown, *Sermons on Various Subjects*, 4–12 and *On the Female Character and Education*, 18.
3 Rousseau, *Émile*, 5n.
4 Moir, *Female Tuition*, preface.
5 de Bellaigue, 'Home Education 1750–1900', 422.
6 Radcliffe, *Origin of the New System of Manufacture*, 10.
7 Hans, *New Trends in Education*, 195.
8 See Simonton, 'Education and Training', Appendix 6.1.
9 Capper, 'Memoir of Mary Capper', 2; Fox, 'Memoir of Mrs. Eliza Fox', 6; Lucas, 'Account of the Convincement', 170; Grubb, 'Some Account of the Life', 256. See Simonton, 'Education and Training', 267–72.
10 Lucas, 'Account of the Convincement', 179; Grubb, 'Account of the Life', 256.
11 Quoted Houston, *Literacy in Early Modern Europe*, 93.
12 [Bristow], *Faithful Servant*. The author claimed this was a true narrative, but there is some doubt.
13 Gilbert, *Autobiography*, 38–9.
14 Mandeville, 'An Essay on Charity and Charity Schools', 329–30.
15 Burton, *Lectures on Female Education*, I, 28.
16 Moir, *Female Tuition*, 49; see also Brown, *Female Character*, 8, Horne, *Reflections on Female Character*, 7–10, Kenrick, *Whole Duty of Woman*, 16.
17 Cappe, *Observations on Charity Schools*, 31.
18 Wakefield, *Reflections on the Female Sex*, 29.
19 More, *Strictures on Female Education*, 74, quote 72.
20 Wollstonecraft, *Vindication*, 105; see also 145–51.
21 Darwin, *A Plan for the Conduct of Female Education*, 'Apology'.
22 *AJ*, 16 January 1759.
23 Ingram, *Schools of Industry*, 37.

24 Ingram, *Schools of Industry*, 15.
25 Wakefield, *Reflections on the Female Sex*, 8–9.
26 Ingram, *Schools of Industry*, 6.
27 Trimmer, *Oeconomy of Charity*, 4.
28 Burton, *Religious Education of Poor Children*, 30.
29 Blackstone, *Commentaries*, Book 1, 450.
30 Smith, *Wealth of Nations*, vol. 2, 788.
31 Paine, *Rights of Man*, 1791.
32 Malthus, *An Essay on Population*, vol. 2, 213.
33 Trimmer, *Oeconomy of Charity* 10.
34 Chapman, *Ends and Uses of Charity Schools*, 19.
35 Trimmer, *Oeconomy of Charity*, 1–2. Cappe similarly encouraged 'Ladies of the middle ranks of life to patronize' charity schools, Cappe, *An Account of Charity Schools*, v.
36 For example, *Reports*, Beaumont, Belchamp and Benfleet in Essex.
37 Schofield, 'Dimensions of Illiteracy', 445–54; Altick, *English Common Reader*, 30–41, 48–50; Laqueur, 'Cultural Origins', 263–5; Webb, *Working Class Reader*, 23–45, but note his reference to the 'hearing public', 34; Ashton, *Chapbooks of the Eighteenth Century*, and Neuberg, *Popular Education*, 115–26; on newspapers see Cranfield, *Development of the Provincial Newspaper*, 175–6; Kelly, *Adult Education*, 83–5.
38 Cranfield, *Provincial Newspaper*, 188.
39 Houston, *Literacy in Early Modern Europe*, 102.
40 Lane, *Apprenticeship*, 215.
41 Maynes, *Schooling in Western Europe*, 11.
42 Maynes, *Schooling in Western Europe*, 26.
43 See Vincent, *Literacy and Popular Culture*, 54, and Laqueur, *Working-class Demand*, 192, 202–3.
44 Houston, *Literacy in Early Modern Europe*, 102.
45 See Schofield, 'The Measurement of Literacy', Houston, *Literacy in Early Modern Europe,* chapter 6 and Vincent, *Literacy and Popular Culture*, Introduction.
46 Stone, 'Literacy and Education in England', 98.
47 Anderson, *Education and the Scottish People*, 16. Nineteenth-century studies indicate that those claiming a basic reading ability were twice the number who could sign, but the proportion able to sign corresponded to the proportion who could read fluently; Webb, *Working Class Reader*, 17, Cressy, 'Levels of Illiteracy in England', 2; Schofield, 'Measurement of Literacy', 323–4.
48 Stone, 'Literacy and Education', 98.
49 Schofield, 'Dimensions of Illiteracy', 445–54.
50 Houston, *Scottish Literacy and the Scottish Identity*, 57.
51 Houston, 'Age at Marriage of Scottish Women', 61, 62.
52 Houston, *Literacy in Early Modern Europe*, 135, 137, 145.

4

SCHOOLING THE GIRLS

Introduction

There is a common assumption that schooling was an insignificant part of working girls' lives in the eighteenth century. For many this would have been the case, but this supposition underestimates the numbers who did get at least a modicum of school learning, while for others it was substantial. It is important also to remember the scope of working girlhood: it ranged from the very poor to the lower echelons of the middling orders. Girls' education has long interested historians with a wide range of approaches and 'fresh nodes of departure'—the emerging methodological approaches in histories of women's education that run alongside 'more prolonged conduits of inquiry' has led to diverse approaches and interests.[1] Interest in girls' schooling was especially prominent in the 1970s and 1980s, when it was also tied to the intense interest in literacy and its acquisition. Middling girls' educative influences, boarding school education and the pedagogies informing learning have had a long trajectory. Indeed, as with the history of girlhood, much of this has been embedded in feminist inquiry and has led to in-depth interest in intellectual learning, occupational change and a concern with women's role in society. Thus, women's educational history tends to focus on the period from the late eighteenth century, issues of public policy and the formalisation of state education. Pedagogy was important in eighteenth-century schooling, of course, and shaped who and what was taught. However, the practicalities of working girls' schooling—gender, schools, numbers, attendance and diffusion—have largely been left behind. These are some of the questions that form the basis for this chapter. The chapter begins with identifying school provision, its types and locations; it continues by examining the sex ratio

DOI: 10.4324/9781003412168-5

in schools, the curriculum and aspects of length of time spent in school and how long it lasted. It finishes with a snapshot of the location and geography of schools. Much of the discussion is based on a study of schools in Staffordshire and Essex, which provide statistical data on schooling these girls. This quantitative approach has the advantage of providing a visual map of girls' schooling and allows us to 'see' the context and opportunities for the working girl of the eighteenth century.

Provision of schools

Schools peppered the landscape from private, parish, village and town or burgh schools to charity, industry, circulating, Sunday and dame schools. Girls often shared schools with boys, and in Britain, they comprised four basic forms: 1) private ventures from dame schools and a variety of day schools to the middle-class boarding school. In these attendance depended upon ability to pay and willingness to do so (Image 4.1); 2) parish, town or village schools, usually funded by a variety of means by local authorities and benefactors, available to any children of the village or town, sometimes with fees, or with fees for specific lessons; 3) charity schools, including schools of industry, where uniforms and education were nominally free, funded by donations and subscribers; and 4) from the 1780s, Sunday schools, also nominally free, but sometimes charging a modest sum. In Wales, from 1763, the circulating schools initiated by Griffith Jones, who recognised the problems of teaching Welsh-speaking children in English, supplied another option. In contrast the Society in Scotland for Propagating Christian Knowledge 'was part of a general national strategy of integrating the highlands into a united Scotland and bringing them the benefits of lowland, English-speaking culture. This seemed especially urgent after 1745, when the secular authorities sought to combine the restoration of political order with economic development.'[2] Across England and Wales, the SPCK (founded 1698) established 'charity schools' which aimed to provide religious teaching to the poor, based on their Anglican catechism. In Ireland, girls also had access to legally established schools, such as those of the Incorporated Society for Promoting English Protestant Schools in Ireland, called Charter schools, as well as endowed schools similar to those in England and Scotland. If this seems relatively straightforward, it was anything but. Although national policy seemed to be a driver, Houston notes that England never had anything but the vaguest central government policy on education, and in Wales, Scotland and Ireland, there were no significant developments in state control. He argues that the funds were not available nor was the coercive power to implement reforms.[3]

Schools usually were not buildings of fixed location, and the term may simply have meant a teacher was available. Likewise, two schools in a village often meant one for girls and one for boys, even if foundation and administration were concurrent. The establishment of these schools also varied from those funded by the parish and ratepayers, those privately endowed, those funded by charities and those funded by subscriptions, in addition to those charging a fee for teaching some or all subjects. And a school could be several of these at the same time. For private schools, the life of the school coincided with the life or interest of the teacher. At the same time, that teacher might take paying pupils alongside children paid for by subscribers or the town. Often several distinct charities were applied toward one school, that is the schooling provided by a single teacher, instead of separate foundations. Local authorities could also fund schools or contribute to places in existing schools. A survey by the SPCK to identify the existing parochial schools in Scotland mid-century reveals some of this ambiguity:

> 'I don't think there is one parochial school properly so called within the bounds of this presbytery,' wrote the minister of Walls, Shetland, 'that is, a school with a legal standing salary. But in my parish I have several little schools in different corners. . .'. 'No parochial school properly so called, but there are five schools maintained by different heritors etc. and those at a much higher stent than what the law requires,' reported . . . Kilcalmonell and Kilberry in Kintyre. . . . [The reply from the clerk to the presbytery of Aberlour exemplifies the position adopted by the third group]: I can assure the Society that every parish in this presbytery has a parochial school, though some of them are very poorly endowed, and few of them have the minimum of legal salary.'[4]

The SPCK (and SSPCK) were often credited with creating the 'charity school', but charitable schools with a variety of funding mechanisms predated and ran parallel to their efforts.[5] Industry schools similarly operated within and independent of SPCK efforts. The Brougham Commission, *Reports on the Education of the Lower Orders* (1816–19), catalogued educational provision across England and Wales in the early nineteenth century, and showed a wide range of schools available, including numerous day schools across the landscape. These returns also chronicled the numerous Sunday schools which were sometimes the only free schooling available. With regard to girls' schooling, the *Reports* broadly confirmed that provision was erratic, but many communities were reasonably well-provided while others had no school.

The chance to go to a school, or the kind of school, was determined by several factors. These included social status, cost of a school including opportunity cost, age and gender. It also depended quite simply where schools were located. A girl's schooling opportunities were determined by her family's financial well-being and their interest in educating her. If able and willing to pay a modest sum for education, girls had access to many village and dame schools on much the same terms as boys, and sometimes to a grammar school or boys' schoolmaster for certain lessons. Plumb suggested that some families in the broad artisanal range did purchase schooling, made possible by the sheer number of small day schools.[6] Free places financed by charity were available to girls, though with strings attached.

Sarah Trimmer proposed a hierarchy of schools based on which children should be admitted:

> Charity Schools were for the first degree of the lower orders, in which a comprehensive plan of tuition would qualify them as teachers in charity supported schools, as apprentices to common trades and as domestic servants in respectable families.
>
> Day Schools of Industry mixed labour and learning and were best for those to be afterward employed in manufacturers and other inferior offices in life, including common servants.
>
> Sunday schools provided religious instruction appropriate to all degrees of the poor and suitable instruction for those who could not be spared during the week from the plough or other labours contributing to the family support.

She wished this last group would acquire a little writing and accounts but not at Sunday school.[7] Notably, she did not refer to parochial schools.

Some charity and Sunday school foundations restricted access to the poorest children, while others specifically excluded pauper children. In Essex, Romford Charity School dismissed children if they went into the workhouse. At Chelmsford, however, the master of the workhouse paid the Charity School to instruct children in his care, and at Ashdon, the overseers of the poor paid for three pupils each quarter. At the same time, tradespeople's children attended the Chelmsford Charity School.[8] In Newcastle, the parish charity schools catered exclusively for poorer children, although previously charity schools had catered for a more mixed clientele.[9] Often children were considered for admission to charitable foundations only on the recommendation of a subscriber or a trustee who sponsored them. Therefore, a child had to come to the favourable attention of such a person to gain admission. Though both charity and Sunday schools were aimed at the poor, they missed the neediest while attracting traders' children. Particularly in a parish without an inexpensive private school, more prosperous parents may have taken advantage of the charity school to educate their children. In Scotland, by way of contrast, most of the benefits and educational endowments were for the 'corporate' poor, drawing a distinction with the children of middling ranks. But unlike England few of the endowments were for day schools. Instead, towns often created 'hospitals' for needy children, where they were boarded, fed, clothed and educated. Two such were founded for girls in Edinburgh by bequests from Mary Erskine: the Merchant Maiden (1696) and Trades Maiden (1704). But other bursaries were provided to enable worthy children to have places in the existing town schools.[10] In Aberdeen, mortifications, or bequests, were applied to the employment of teachers, like Margaret Buchanan who was appointed under Mr Gerrard's mortification in 1797.[11] Girls were most likely to get access to parish schools when there were not enough boys to guarantee an adequate income for the master.[12] Industry schools were a particular option for poor girls, explicitly to promote industriousness, in addition to taught lessons. They aimed to provide a vocational option as well as, often, to help pay for the school through the girls' work. Providing such an education was also a route to avoiding poverty which ultimately cost the community.

Parochial or town day schools were important options for girls, and these would have appealed to families of the resident middling orders, especially families in which girls might have to provide for themselves or contribute to family income. Literacy and numeracy were valued, and these day schools also provided practical accomplishments and useful subjects including needlework, or in the case of Robertson's school, cookery classes. Elizabeth Ham attended several schools of a wide variety with gaps between them, and she was astonished at the poor quality of her teachers' abilities. Her schools varied from an evening writing school to a boarding school with an extra dancing master, but most were unpretentious day schools, of the village or dame variety, with a curriculum typical of charity schools (Image 4.1). Similarly, Quaker Margaret Lucas attended several schools or took occasional lessons.[13] Earle concluded that daughters of 'honest' London parents went to school, and most had a pretty good or decent and commendable education, and daughters of 'creditable parents' did little better. Further he argued that 'virtually all children, both boys and girls whose parents were in the artisan class and above had been to school, often for several years and that formal education was by no means unknown to the sons of poor parents if not their daughters.'[14] Like most towns, Newcastle offered a range of schools, listing thirty-two masters of non-grammar schools in 1746, but Barbara Crosbie adds that certainly not all school provision was noted in the visitation report. The first trade directory in 1778 recorded twenty-seven schoolmasters and one boarding school for girls. Nevertheless, newspaper adverts suggest there were still others. In Wickham, south of the Tyne, the charity school took thirty-six children, but the master also offered lessons for a fee.[15] Across Scotland, burghs tried to regulate schooling, partly to ensure qualifications, but also to ensure moral rectitude and Protestant conviction, and issued licenses to approved teachers, to the disadvantage of many private teachers. On 17 April 1769, the Aberdeen magistrates inserted a notice in the *Aberdeen Journal* 'to inform the public that Eleonora Grant, [schoolmistress] has always behaved herself to merit the countenance of the Magistrates, and . . . is to

IMAGE 4.1 Elias Martin, 1739–1818, Reading Lesson at a Dame School, undated. Graphite, pen and ink, and watercolour on moderately thick, slightly textured, cream wove paper, Yale Center for British Art, Paul Mellon Collection, B1986.29.442.

receive a public encouragement from the Town'.[16] The previous week, the Town Council appointed Miss Elizabeth Mitchell of Edinburgh as sewing mistress, noting that 'she has behaved herself decently and with a fair and unblemished character'.[17] The Council built a house for Grant when she was appointed in 1758 and granted her an annuity when she retired, then spent a great deal of time and energy in replacing her, appointing Mitchell in her place, having dutifully advertised for the replacement and then evaluated her credentials.[18] In larger towns, local acts made attendance compulsory, and sometimes included girls, and occasionally girls were sent to the music school for rudimentary skills.[19]

Most girls of the working orders would have been able to attend only modest private schools or free ones, including a charity school if there was one. The only avenue open to most pauper girls was the workhouse or Sunday school. In 1806, Colquhoun suggested half the population was earning £55pa or less, including artisans, labourers and lesser freeholders in addition to paupers who had £20pa including relief.[20] Whether any of those could have afforded to pay for schooling depended very much on local circumstances and individual prosperity. Cunningham, for instance, estimated that

20 per cent of the population could not afford to pay. Even small fees were a strong disincentive to sending children to school for the majority on low income since sending children to school involved an opportunity cost. While at school, a child did not work but continued to consume and remained a draw on family resources. When labour was seasonal, such as farming, the opportunity for children to attend school was more likely than in work which children were expected to perform continuously. The first stages of the industrial revolution with its opportunities for employing children throughout the year would have increased the opportunity cost of education significantly for families in regions affected by changing work patterns. Cost explicitly affected girls, since boys often had priority, and so a brother might have gone to school when a sister stayed home to work.

Gender and opportunity

Gender further inflected a girl's opportunity to attend school depending on the number of school places available to her and the length of time trustees allowed her to stay. Most towns and larger villages had schools which plebeian children could attend; however, founders and subscribers tended to favour boys over girls and provided places for girls less frequently than for boys. On average there were about nine schools for boys for every eight for girls in Essex and Staffordshire, and most charity schools consistently provided fewer places for girls than boys with the ratio of between 1.5 to 2 boys admitted to every girl. Boys outnumbered girls about seven to two in Staffordshire and three to two in Essex. The overwhelming tendency was to give preferential treatment to boys in admissions policies and practices.[21] Crosbie found a similar ratio in Newcastle charity schools in St Nicholas and All Saints where forty boys and twenty girls were taught in each parish.[22] Devon, which had some seventy schools, shows the variations that abounded. At Richards's School at Silverton, the master received over £90 a year from rents and hired a woman assistant to help teaching some seventy boys, but no girls. Walkhampton originally only allowed boys in 1719, but its generous endowment meant that the original register of twenty-five boys was raised in 1785 to thirty boys and ten girls. Tamerton, founded in 1734, allowed twenty boys 'and no more'; in 1810 however, it raised the roll to include seventeen girls. Thus, girls were largely an afterthought.[23] In rural Aberdeenshire, four boys were taught for every girl, and three to one in Shetland, while in Lanfyllan, Monmouthshire in Wales, the master was paid to teach twenty boys and ten girls.[24]

An archival examination of Essex and Staffordshire brings the picture into greater relief. The schools of six parishes illustrate the types and varieties of schools attended by the poor: Ashdon, Chelmsford, Romford and Witham in Essex and Penkridge and Wolverhampton in Staffordshire (Table 4.1). Great

TABLE 4.1 Proportion of Pupil Places by Sex

County	*Boys*	*Girls*	*Ratio of Boys to Girls*	*No. of Boys and Girls*
Staffordshire	78%	22%	3.5	715
Essex	61%	39%	1.6	843
Total	69%	31%	2.2	1,558

Sources: Compiled from Charities Commission, *Reports*, Staffordshire and Essex, and ERO and SRO school records.

Yeldham Industry School (for girls) gives a unique insight into one form of girls' education. It was a small residential school in which girls alternated between spells as domestic servants for the mistress with periods of learning, reading, writing, and religion. These parishes were chosen primarily because of the quantity and quality of information from a variety of sources. The main sources are trustees' account and minute books which do not lend themselves easily to quantitative analysis. The records were not kept for the purposes of historians, but to record meetings and decisions. Administration was relatively *ad hoc*, and the quality of the records depended very much on the ability, vigour and consistency of the recorders. All included admissions and discharges, though sometimes erratically.[25]

In Chelmsford, which had a charity school from 1713, fifty places were available to boys and twenty to girls. In practice it never took more than thirty boys and twenty girls, and was rarely full, with twenty-five boys and fifteen girls enrolled on a regular basis between 1718–1773. In a town of 3,755 people in 1801, this school was the main form of schooling for working children. Romford, smaller than Chelmsford, had a charity school for sixty-five children which included twenty places for girls, although by the end of the century it was taking sixty boys and thirty girls. In Wolverhampton, a similar pattern emerged (Image 4.2). With 13,000 people in 1801, it was one of the largest towns of Britain comprising several townships and chapelries. It brought together most of the types of schooling available, but the charity school mirrored those in Essex. While it provided up to ninety places, it was usually under-attended, probably because substantial work was available for both boys and girls. In 1746 it enrolled thirty-two boys and twenty-six girls—a drop of ten girls from the previous year. The highest number ever recorded in the minute book was eighty-nine pupils in 1723–24.[26] Some parishes, like Pelsall in Staffordshire, did create equal number of places for girls and boys, six each in this case, but the trend was clearly to privilege places for boys.

The Charity Commissioners' Reports and parish records for Essex and Staffordshire indicate the age of admission to thirty-eight schools and the age of discharge from thirty-four during the century. Most charity schools admitted children at seven or eight years of age, although nearly a third admitted

IMAGE 4.2 Statue of Girl at Romford Charity School, Now St Edwards Primary. Photo by David Kendrick-White. With permission of the Headteacher, Christopher Speller.

them younger. They tended to discharge children at fourteen, regardless of sex. There is little divergence by sex from this pattern, although practices varied by school. Wolverhampton admitted girls a year younger than boys, while Romford after 1768 discharged boys two years younger, at twelve. This marks a clear recognition of stages in the lives of both boys and girls, which maps onto the nominal starting ages for apprenticeship and service.

Teaching and learning

The curriculum was shaped by ideas about what working girls needed and ought to know and resulted in careful limitation of the programme with prescriptive schooling to create obedient, well-behaved, deferential Christians while providing 'useful' education. Thus, reading and religion dominated girls' schooling, often complemented by writing and arithmetic. The scientific, technical and economic changes taking place could heighten their need for the 3Rs, and if such knowledge became fundamental to girls' ability to relate to society, then all three skills passed from being desirable to being useful, from moral improvement to social improvement. The emphasis on reading and religion had a subtext as well, in that in Wales and Scotland, English was not the first language of many rural children. Thus, the desire to regularise English was also part of the agenda for homogenising the nation.

Virtually all schools taught reading and spelling—even industry and spinning schools, including Catholic ones, such as those in Ireland. This practice reflected the desire for all children to be able to read the Bible and understand the principles of religion. This was most apparent in Sunday schools which emerged at the end of the century, many of which taught only reading and religion since trustees sometimes perceived writing and arithmetic as too secular and unsuitable subjects for the Sabbath. For example, at Coggeshall, Essex, rules stipulated as follows: 'The religious observation of the Christian Sabbath being an essential object with the Society . . . the exercise of the scholars on that day shall be restricted to reading in the Old and new [sic] Testament and to spelling as a preparation for it.'[27] Girls in Lanfyllan, Wales, were taught catechism and to spin and sew, while boys could learn reading, writing and accounts, though in Bedwas, Monmouthshire, charity girls could learn 'reading, writing, sewing, needlework and any other useful science'.[28] The content of reading lessons was religious or moral, while religious lessons appeared more frequently in girls' education than boys and especially in Essex schools. This emphasis concurs with the strictures on educating servants and the future wives and mothers of the labouring classes.

Accounts, arithmetic or 'ciphering' became common for both sexes by the end of the century, although girls learned these less frequently than boys. Though 40 per cent of Essex and Staffordshire schools offered writing to girls, the percentage dropped significantly for arithmetic (Table 4.2). Again, the widest variance was in Essex where nearly three quarters of the schools taught boys writing and nearly one half taught them accounts. The dip in teaching arithmetic in Essex is explained by a larger number of single-sex schools where it was more likely to be left off the girls' curriculum. Gender difference was an important criterion in making educational provision. While for boys the established pattern was reading, writing and arithmetic, for girls it was reading, religious instruction and needlework or similar vocational training. Importantly, however, a sizeable proportion of girls at charity schools obtained more academic schooling than these averages indicate; a quarter received instruction in arithmetic and 40 per cent in writing.

Another reaction to critics of education for the poor and to the social mobility debate was the introduction of work-related skills. There were many advantages: work could be shown to critics as a positive way to inculcate proper 'industrious' attitudes; it might help to support schools dependent upon voluntary contributions; and it improved the chance of regular attendance if girls were allowed some small income from their work. At Wolverhampton, the trustees were adamant that the girls should keep their earnings from doing 'work' for the boys, and parents were not permitted access to this

TABLE 4.2 Subjects by Sex of Pupil Taught in Charitable Foundations in Eighteenth-Century Essex and Staffordshire

County/Sex	*Number of Schools by Sex*	*Proportion of Schools Teaching*					*Total No. of Schools*
		Reading	*Religion*	*Writing*	*Arithmetic*	*Work*	
Staffordshire							
Boys	84	95%	39%	52%	46%	2%	90
Girls	74	91	38	41	30	24	
Essex							
Boys	50	98	44	72	48	2	58
Girls	43	95	58	42	19	42	
Both							
Boys	134	96	41	60	47	2	148
Girls	117	92	45	41	26	31	

Sources: As for Table 4.1.

money.[29] However, except in unique circumstances, early eighteenth-century attempts failed to bring in income, but at the end of the century, industrial schools and work in the curriculum gained traction. Trimmer was certain that a modest form of education—reading, enough writing for the common purposes of life and an industrial occupation—would suit poor children for their appropriate station. As the Chester girls' working schools' pamphlet explained, whereas some may have doubted the need to teach the poor to read, none doubted the urgent necessity of teaching them to work. Hannah More likewise advocated a 'limited and strict plan', including work to fit them for service and excluding writing.[30] A variation on the theme, Ingram proposed opening industry schools for 'children of every class. . . . In short it is desired, that the lower classes should regard the admission of their children into the school of industry, as an advancement in respectability, in lieu of a degradation to the level of the poor-house.'[31] These views were widespread and rationalist writers like Catharine Cappe and Mary Wollstonecraft promoted work at schools as a natural part of their training. Wollstonecraft advocated plain sewing, mantuamaking and millinery.[32] Nevertheless, industrial training was not to overwhelm the main purposes of schooling, which was a good religious education, and the 'process of education ought to be a proper pattern, or model of the business of life'.[33] Numerous spinning and industry schools for girls were established, evidence that benefactors and educationalists alike recognised the value of useful knowledge to these girls. The Chester working school was set up in 1787 to train girls who were increasingly found to be 'unskilled in the common and most useful arts of life and plainly disqualified for domestic service and most other offices'. The scheme established four-day schools, each teaching a different brand of needlework, rotating the girls, so that after four years and of age to go into service, they would be capable of such work. A similar rotation applied at the Grey Coat School associated with Cappe in York; her spinning school included vocational training as did her plan for a school to train house servants and nursery maids.[34] At Tamworth in Staffordshire and Great Yeldham in Essex, two small industry schools taught girls to read and sew, and by implication, religion and good manners. At Gosfield School of Industry (Essex) the work consisted of sewing, spinning and strawplaiting.[35] Charity schools set both paid work and occupational training more frequently for girls than for boys. For example, at Chelmsford 'from time to time', boys were set such work as the trustees saw fit, such as picking stones or cleaning the town, but it did not have the urgency that it did in girls' schools. Trimmer made this distinction in *The Charity Spelling Book*, admonishing girls to follow the appropriate strictures to 'get a good place' while boys were simply to use school to improve themselves (Image 4.3).[36]

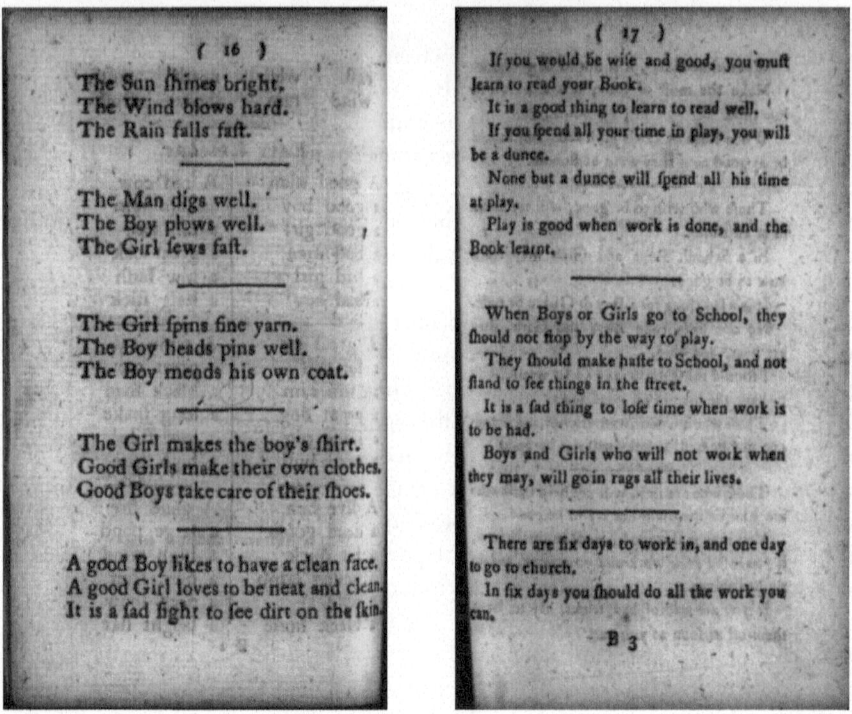

(16)

The Sun ſhines bright.
The Wind blows hard.
The Rain falls faſt.

The Man digs well.
The Boy plows well.
The Girl ſews faſt.

The Girl ſpins fine yarn.
The Boy heads pins well.
The Boy mends his own coat.

The Girl makes the boy's ſhirt.
Good Girls make their own clothes.
Good Boys take care of their ſhoes.

A good Boy likes to have a clean face.
A good Girl loves to be neat and clean.
It is a ſad ſight to ſee dirt on the ſkin.

(17)

If you would be wiſe and good, you muſt learn to read your Book.

It is a good thing to learn to read well.

If you ſpend all your time in play, you will be a dunce.

None but a dunce will ſpend all his time at play.

Play is good when work is done, and the Book learnt.

When Boys or Girls go to School, they ſhould not ſtop by the way to play.

They ſhould make haſte to School, and not ſtand to ſee things in the ſtreet.

It is a ſad thing to loſe time when work is to be had.

Boys and Girls who will not work when they may, will go in rags all their lives.

There are ſix days to work in, and one day to go to church.

In ſix days you ſhould do all the work you can.

B 3

IMAGE 4.3 Sarah Trimmer's Spelling Book, part 1, pages 16 and 17, 5th edition, 1799.

Providing girls with the knowledge and the opportunity to attain a place in service was tacitly accepted. In 1799, 'The Committee of a Congregational Union for Promoting the Knowledge of the Gospel' declared its intention to teach 'lads going to daily labour and young women in service' to read.[37] It also is consistent with the numbers of Essex girls who turned to domestic service upon leaving school since the agricultural composition of the county and its proximity to London meant it was a common route. This was less true in Staffordshire where most of the population lived in two industrial areas, the Potteries and the Black Country where industry provided a wider range of options for girls. At Romford and Chelmsford (Essex), the declared purpose was to teach girls reading, knitting, sewing and all other requisites to make them good servants, while Wolverhampton did not allow some girls to leave until they gained a place. In June 1724 Mary Lande left to go into service with Madam Vernons of Hilton. In another instance, Abraham Dudley's daughter Elizabeth was not allowed to enter the school in February 1729/30, until her elder sister had gone into service. She was admitted a few weeks later.[38] Because skill in textile and clothing occupations was a viable economic asset for girls and young women, the emphasis on work for girls was not misplaced. Education was not only to teach poor girls their station in life; it was geared to providing them with a particular type of knowledge leading to an explicit kind of adult job.

Spinning schools were a feature of Scottish girls' schooling because of the industrial need for textile production, especially linen. The SSPCK gained a patent for instructing 'husbandry and housewifery . . . trade and manufacture', accordingly creating schools to teach spinning, knitting, sewing and weaving. From 1769, having received a legacy of £2,000 to be spent on technical instruction, the society set up further schools, bought necessary equipment and paid mistresses to teach girls to spin and manufacture stockings. This scheme met only with limited success due, apparently, to the distances involved, poor travelling conditions and Highland women's resistance to instruction. Nevertheless, by 1783 there were more than twenty spinning schools in the Highlands.[39] The Aberdeen school which employed Betty Mitchell was also primarily a spinning school. The need for spinners was felt by the British Linen Company which regularly promoted schools to teach spinning:

> 10 October 1746 . . . If you have spinners we will send you a woman for ten days to teach your spinners.
>
> 19 May 1748 . . . enclosed . . . a letter to Mr Reid which you see will procure you a spinning mistress, or the opportunity of teaching one there, as you shall like best.[40]

This impetus suggests the importance that industrial skills had and the impact they could have on educational provision. The standard curriculum varied little over the century continuing to reflect the primary concerns with religion and work.

The working girl from the middling orders often learned lessons not so very different. Reading, writing and religion were constants. Similarly, needlework was a common part of their schooling. Earle depicted one daughter from 'creditable' parents, who

> went to school when I was at a proper age to one Mrs Banks . . . where I learned to work at my needle and likewise to dance. I continued there about two years. After I came from that school, I went to Poor Jury-Lane by Aldgate where I learned all sorts of plainwork and continued there about three years. The last school I went to was to one Mr Busking, facing Creed-church in Leadenhall-street, writing master and I continued with him some considerable time.[41]

Earle suggests she learned to cast accounts. Ciphering or accounts were regarded as important aspects of these girls' schooling.

> Give particular attention to your ciphering, and to acquire such a competent knowledge in this useful art, as is proper for a woman. I say for a woman; for it is not necessary that she would understand it so perfectly as a man; . . . You ought, however, I think to be a complete mistress of the four simple rules of arithmetic, the rule of proportion, and a plain method of bookkeeping, together with some knowledge of fractions vulgar and decimal.[42]

Obviously, such skills could help with housekeeping, but also, to work in businesses, as Sarah Hurst did. Commonly, wives of artisans and shopkeepers were expected to assist in family businesses, often dealing with orders and accounts, and as Defoe wrote, to 'become mistresses of the managing part of it'.[43] Those girls whose families could pay for education had wider options and they did 'shop around' to get the lessons they wanted and a more advanced education.

Anne Hazzard, daughter of a tailor, was sent to boarding school in Sussex where she learned French, dancing and music. These girls could expect an education which echoed the accomplishments of their 'betters', but at the same time, many studied in the village, parish or town schools which were less likely to offer a significantly different education from good charity schools. Ann Fisher, author of *A New Grammar*, 1745, intended her grammar for the 'Private Instruction of young ladies and gentlemen' and for 'the Use of publick schools'. A yeoman's daughter, she then set up a school at the end of Denton Chair in Newcastle, where she taught 'READING, according to the best Spelling-books and Grammars extant, WRITING, fine and plain SEWING'. Crosbie notes that 'when she advertised her school for young ladies for a second time in 1750 a much more confident emphasis was placed upon the teaching of English grammar, suggesting her methods had proved effective.'[44] Importantly this school for young ladies offered a similar curriculum for girls as most other schools. Perhaps it was more intensive and better taught, but nevertheless the curriculum varied little.

Attendance and duration of schooling

How long a girl spent in school and how consistently she attended were significant factors in how much she could have learned and how much her schooling could have set her up for her future. Virtually no schools of this period kept what we would understand as attendance records, but there is tangential evidence that it could be very sporadic and frequently seasonal. This is true across social strata. School minutes books regularly noted that girls should be reprimanded for not attending, even expelled for not doing so. At Wolverhampton, their charity clothing was to be taken away for poor attendance until the situation was resolved, and on 25 September 1725, the trustees decreed that 'the school be constantly attended at the hours appointed.'[45] On 4 July 1727 they decided 'that for the future any Charity girl that is absent from Church or School for the 1st time shall be admonished, for the 2nd shall be chastised & for the 3rd shall be expelled the school.' They also excused absence from time to time and on 2 October 1729, Elizabeth Hodson was pardoned for being absent.[46] Between July 1728 and October 1731, there were at least nine admonitions recorded about poor attendance, with no reason except a reference to parents sending children 'a leasing' or 'gleaning'.

A common feature was temporary absence for harvesting, or going 'a leasing', hop picking in Essex or in Aberdeenshire to take a 'tattie holiday' when potatoes needed uplifting, though many schools gave time off for this. This is the origin of the autumn school holidays across Britain, still called tattie holidays in Aberdeenshire. At Chelmsford, on 5 March 1746, Martha Springer and four boys were released to help their parents in the hop grounds.[47] Broadly speaking, attendance was probably more regular in towns than in the countryside, although temporary hardship could factor. The energy with which schools strove to get children to attend reflected parental decisions, taking them out, needing them to help in earning or finding other reasons to keep them away. But the children themselves could be culpable. Keith Thomas reports Welsh children telling their parents that school holidays were five weeks, not a month, to avoid going back.[48] Of more significance in agricultural areas, where farming could demand labour incessantly across the summer, winter attendance was often greater. Sinclair reported that in

Scottish schools at the end of the century summer attendance was two thirds to three quarters of winter attendance.[49] In contrast, however, are the large numbers of girls rewarded for their regular attendance and for staying their 'full time'. At the day schools studied in Essex and Staffordshire, 36 per cent of girls stayed their full time, being given a leaving book, and often keeping their clothes, thus being rewarded for good attendance. A further 15 per cent went to service or apprenticeship and were similarly rewarded.[50]

How long these girls stayed at school is of particular importance, since girls staying on for substantial periods of time could have achieved a reasonable reading standard as well as knowledge of writing and arithmetic. The phased learning pattern of teaching reading followed by writing also suggests that more girls might have been able to read than to write, thus underrating their functional literacy. Evidence suggests that most girls left school to go to work, and often service. Therefore, schooling often was girls' major, and perhaps sole, formal educational experience. This could encourage them to stay on longer, for as much preparation as possible before entering another's home. Spending longer in school could also produce girls who learned more or who consolidated their knowledge and skill. Also, of course, the slightly older girl, better able to read and perhaps write, more skilled in needlework and potentially more polished in her manner, may have obtained a better place in service than her younger less-educated counterpart. The minute books frequently record parents appearing to thank the school for their daughters' education when they leave. This seems to have been genuine and testifies to their interest in and appreciation of the opportunity that school opened for their daughters.

Examining the regulation ages at entry and leaving school, a child could have spent seven or eight years at school. However, few stayed this long. A variety of accounts suggest that anything from half a year to four was relatively normal. Houston cited three years as a normal maximum in towns, as did Cipolla. Many schools limited the length of schooling to three or four years, in any case. Tamerton (Devon) only allowed two years for each child.[51] Of those at Cupar burgh school in Scotland between 1774 and 1788, half were in school for a year or less. Only a fifth stayed for more than three years, and many of these missed one or more 'quarter', and girls attended very sporadically.[52]

Turning to the Essex and Staffordshire schools, their school records indicate an average duration of attendance of over three and a half years. This was a significant length of time for children to spend at such a school. Reading took twelve months to teach and writing and arithmetic another three to four years so that pupils at these schools could have gained a good foundation in reading, and possibly in writing and arithmetic.[53] Many children appeared in records only once, when admitted or discharged, but not both; the records are sometimes vague as to what the entry means; and some children were

TABLE 4.3 Average Length of Attendance at Day Schools by Sex

School	*Period of Data*	*Girls*		*Boys*		*No. of Cases*	*Overall Average*
		No.	*Ave.*	*No.*	*Ave.*		
Chelmsford CS	1716–99	23	3.08	29	3.09	52	3.09
Romford CS	1762–99	149	4.10	329	3.32	478	3.56
Essex Total		172	3.96	358	3.30	530	3.51
Penkridge CS	1779–98	3	3.17	8	3.00	11	3.05
Wolverhampton CS	1714–99	123	4.12	220	3.83	343	3.81
Staffs. Total		126	4.10	228	3.80	354	3.91
Both counties		308	3.89	586	3.49	884	3.67

Sources: ERO, D/Q 8/1, T/A 461, D/Q 24/1A, D/Q 24/2; SRO, D260/M/F/120, D1157/1/5/1.

still on the roll when the record ended. Using the records of admission and demission, table 4.3 shows the average attendance at four charity schools, including tiny Penkridge which illustrates that even in small villages, solid attendance was possible. Romford Charity School Minute Books are exceptional in documenting a very high proportion of admissions and discharges, usually giving the reason for leaving. The trustees seemed to fill vacancies immediately indicating a probable demand for places, and the data include three quarters of all children admitted from 1762, so that the average is likely to be reasonably accurate. On average children stayed some three and a half years, significant enough to provide them with the ability to read, and possibly to improve their position relative to their peers.

Wolverhampton also reported lengthy periods of attendance for their pupils, averaging 3.81 years. Yet, the trustees did not record dismissals regularly. The range of reported lengths of attendance was quite wide (one month to eight years eight months), but 71 per cent stayed three years or more. Less than 10 per cent were reported as leaving before the first year was up. The contrast is even stronger for the period 1750–97, when three quarters stayed for three and a half years or more, but only 2.5 per cent were reported as leaving after less than one year. A distinctive feature is that girls tended to stay longer than boys. At Romford, Wolverhampton and Penkridge, the trend was clear. Girls remained between three and ten months longer on average than boys and some girls stayed as long as between six and nearly nine years (Table 4.4) At Romford 61 per cent, Wolverhampton 53 per cent and Chelmsford 39 per cent of girls stayed at least four years and a third stayed three years at Penkridge. Additionally, the individual students enrolled longest were girls who stayed six to nine months longer than boys in

TABLE 4.4 Longest-Staying Pupils Recorded at Day Schools

	Girls	*Boys*
Chelmsford	6.0 years	5.0 years
Romford	7.5	6.7
Penkridge	3.7	3.7
Wolverhampton	8.7	7.0

Sources: as Table 4.3.

TABLE 4.5 Reasons Given for Leaving School, Sample Charity Schools

School	*Sex*	*At Leaving Age*	*Taken by Parents*	*Service*	*Apprentice*	*Work*
Romford Charity School	Boys	58%	11%	10%	3%	6%
	Girls	41	10	32	2	-
Chelmsford Charity School	Boys	16	26	-	23	3
	Girls	10	28	20	-	-
Wolverhampton	Boys	23	27	-	25	-
	Girls	43	18	3	4	-

Source: Simonton, 'Education and Training', 158. The remainder were spread between other reasons for leaving, including death.

the same school; more girls than boys stayed four years or more in the three larger schools.

Why and how girls left school were coloured by variations in school practices and by circumstances in the local community and family wishes. Recorded discharges show that by far the largest proportion of children stayed their 'full time' or to the maximum age which the schools allowed (Table 4.5). But at Chelmsford, children were far more likely to leave early, for service, absence, expulsion or removal by parents. At Wolverhampton, girls were far more likely to stay full time than boys. The next largest group was taken out by their parents, usually without the trustees' consent, before they completed the period allowed. These are distinct from those recorded as going to work, but it is reasonable to suggest that the family required their labour either contributing directly or working for wages. Again, at Wolverhampton, parents took more boys away early than girls, suggesting the girls had fewer opportunities in the metal trades, like smithing and toymaking, and as apprentices than boys. The same number left for service or apprenticeship as were taken away by their parents but comprising a slightly higher proportion of girls than boys. At Romford a much higher proportion of girls left school for service than boys, while at Chelmsford a clear sexual differentiation meant girls went to service and boys to apprenticeship. Clearly service was more likely to be a girl's destination upon leaving school and reflected notions of girls' place in life as wives, mothers and destined for domestic life. Those who went to charity school and then into service or apprenticeship were placed out by parents, by the school or by a charity, often attached to the school, not as parish apprentices. Wolverhampton records frequently referred to mothers finding their daughters a place. For example, on 12 June 1735, Hannah Perry's mother found her a place, and there were similar examples in October of the same year.[54]

A clear goal for schools was to prepare children for lives of useful work, obedience and respect. While features of the local labour market contributed, the reasons also lie in what awaited children upon leaving school. Boys usually could find work younger than girls, partly because there was a wider range of jobs that people expected boys to fill. Girls more frequently went into service, in which standards of feminine behaviour were more highly valued, especially if a girl entered a middling home. Thus, a school education, which could improve literacy and provide a veneer of 'finish', offered them a better chance of a good place and was thus occupationally important. The value of work skills to girls is clear from schools' policies and the curriculum which regularly included 'work' in their schooling, usually needlework and sometimes housewifery skills, echoing tract literature. As the century went on, the demand for female servants rose and at Romford Charity School, for example, the number and percentage of girls going into service on leaving increased, from 23 per cent in 1764–73 to 45 per cent between 1793–99.[55] Service, as we shall see, also had the potential for learning and training, and many of those in Sunday schools were servants hoping to improve themselves (Image 4.4). Not all girls had a chance of schooling, of course, due to a lack of a school or requirements of families for their labour or income or indeed being of lesser priority than a brother's schooling. At the same time, most schools were small and catered for a limited number of children, with girls usually given fewer opportunities than boys. Charity schools may have been a superior kind of school catering for a particular group of children, so that three years or more in school was true for a select portion of plebeian girls.

Geography and demography

Geography was clearly important to girls' access to schooling, and coverage was variable. Broadly, towns were better served than villages, and rural districts, especially those remote from built-up areas, were especially poorly served. English surveys suggested that between 30 and 60 per cent of dioceses had a school of some sort.[56] In 1724, the SPCK listed 14 schools containing 318 pupils in Staffordshire and 31 schools with 604 pupils in Essex; in

IMAGE 4.4 Maria Spilsbury, 1777–1820, A Sunday School, 1803. Oil on canvas, Yale Center for British Art, Paul Mellon Fund, B2024.3.

1759 the figures remained the same for Staffordshire while 37 schools and 676 pupils were reported for Essex.[57] The Brougham Commission reported a far larger number and type of school than the SPCK: 724 schools in Staffordshire and 639 in Essex.[58] Because Brougham included endowed grammar and fee-paying schools as well as monitorial schools, these inflate the number of schools and most girls would not have access to either due to gender or cost. Scotland, Ireland and Wales were some of least urbanised areas of Europe, although by 1800 a quarter of the Scottish population lived in towns. The distance and terrain, however, meant that availability and access to schools was far less proliferous. In Scotland, where law compelled parishes to provide schools by 1633, there were 800 schools, and at the beginning of the century all parishes in the most densely settled and developed lowlands had a parish school, and sometimes more than one.[59] Don Withrington argued that the Highlands were well catered for, often by combinations of parish schools and those established by lairds.[60] It is unclear how much access girls had, and the returns of the OSA consistently refer to 'children', not boys and girls. These returns, however, illustrate the difficulties of these parts of Britain. At

Strathdon, seventy kilometres east of Aberdeen, the minister reported that the school is 'seldom throng', i.e. full, because of the terrain: jills, burns and rivers; also a dearth of servants meant that children were required frequently to herd animals. There was an SSPCK school, and since it was located at the furthest point from the parish school, it was 'highly' useful. The teacher went between Kindyside and Curgarff alternately to teach children and they were hopeful of another teacher to take over Curgarff, since the children are 'not only at a great distance from the parish school, but are quite out of the reach of any other school, at any season'.[61] A similar story was told for Ireland: 'The state of education in the mountain regions is much more backward than any other part of Ireland that I am acquainted with; in the remote and sequestered glens, the inhabitants, being only a few and scattered, and unable to employ teachers, are indeed in a very degrading state of ignorance.'[62] Thus, distance and the patchy geography of school provision was another a factor in determining girls' access to schooling. As we have seen, larger towns like Wolverhampton, Colchester and Chelmsford as well as Aberdeen, Glasgow and Edinburgh, Dublin and Cardiff, offered much more likely opportunities.

The growth of population over the century, and indeed new work opportunities for children, had an impact on their chances to go to school. Many schools changed over the period, and sometimes the records were chaotic. For example, Chelmsford recorded reorganisations in 1746 and 1788, and recordkeeping improved after 1773. In 1776, the Colchester minute book closed with a plan setting the charity on a sounder footing and was absorbed into the new national school in the nineteenth century.[63] The registers sometimes shrank and ballooned for no specific reason. However, if we compare the population of the community with the size of the schools we arrive at an idea of the impact of urban population growth, which was rapid in the second half of the century. This demonstrates what proportion of working girls could have gone to the local charity school. Table 4.6 is based on four examples, Penkridge, Romford, Chelmsford and Wolverhampton which had

TABLE 4.6 Educational Opportunity for Girls in Selected Charity Schools

School	*Date of Data*	*Penetration*
Chelmsford	1740–49	22.90%
	1790–99	17.96
Penkridge	1779–1801	20.95
Wolverhampton	1729	11.72
	1716–99	6.6
Romford	1762	22.78
	1790–99	14.35
	1762–99	13.30

good record sets and allow comparison across time. The average 'penetration' of charity day schools in these communities at the end of the century intimates that approximately a fifth of the age group attended them. This assessment considers the fact that the number of places was fixed, that population rose over the century, and takes the length of average attendance into account.[64] Some of these parishes also had fee-charging schools of varying size and quality, but there are no records which allow them to be considered. This data may underestimate the extent of schooling, but not necessarily the schooling of working girls. About 20 per cent of girls had access to free schools at mid-century but declined significantly by 1801. Wolverhampton, however, stands out with a significantly lower average of 6.6 per cent across the century, also declining from 1729. Population rise would have accounted for much of the decay because the schools did not keep up with the increasing number of girls by natural growth and urban in-migration. The difference between Wolverhampton and the other large schools in Essex was mainly a response to work opportunities for girls. In Essex, the woollen industry had declined, and other evidence shows that service became increasingly important for them while Wolverhampton, situated in the Black Country, had plenty of work for child labourers. The town also grew rapidly in the second half of the century, further undercutting educational provision. Educational opportunity depended very much upon local variation, the period from which the figures are taken and gender.

Romford provides an interesting highlight to the relationship between the level of penetration of a charity school and literacy data. While literacy rates for both Essex and Staffordshire were lower than the national average for both men and women, Romford women were more literate than their national counterparts, while the opposite was true of the men. Over time, whereas the national data, particularly for women, show a slight improvement in literacy, the Romford data tend to show a decline, especially for men, and particularly for those educated from 1770, since the Charity School reduced the school leaving age for boys from fourteen to twelve years old.[65]

Conclusion

The gender difference in attitudes to social mobility suggests a tension with class. For girls, ideology was formulated around a domestic and 'non-working' image of woman so that the middle class viewed only certain kinds of work as appropriate for labouring women. Yet it was recognised they would have to contribute to family income. So, their education had to be suitable to their station since an 'inappropriate' education would disqualify a girl for work. The boundary between 'working' women and 'leisured' genteel females was one the middle classes were keen to maintain despite imposing their own behavioural values on plebeian women. The largest proportion of domestic servants were girls, who were in closest contact with their employers, so that it was necessary to maintain distance between them and the women of the family.

Access to schools was more restricted for girls than boys since usually fewer places were kept for them, but girls took advantage of the opportunities where they were offered. Over a third of those who could be traced were recorded as having stayed their 'full time' in school, taking full advantage of the opportunity. While the school records indicate that parents removed children, we have no idea of the internal family dynamic. The fact that girls' attendance was more regular and lasted longer than boys suggests that both the girls and their families were pro-active in this situation. If service were the primary route for girls, and a great deal of evidence supports this, then the additional years at school were a viable investment.

Improvement for girls meant better behaviour, cleanliness and the feminine attributes of submission and humility, not enhanced work opportunities or autonomy. Yet in improving those girls, in providing them with the manners and norms which the middling orders expected and which set them apart from the rest of the lower orders, they gave them a 'leg up' on the social ladder. The children of agricultural labourers and servants together with the children of small farmers were the chief source of supply of servants. Once having obtained a place, opportunities existed for rising within the servant hierarchy and using it for social ascent.

Notes

1 Gleadle, 'The Imagined Communities of Women's History', 524–40.
2 Anderson, *Education and the Scottish People*, 10.
3 Houston, *Scottish Literacy and the Scottish Identity*, 46, 47.
4 Withrington, 'The S.P.C.K. and Highland Schools', 92.
5 For example, see Jones, *The Charity School Movement* and Simon, 'Was there a Charity School Movement?'.
6 Plumb, 'New World of Children', 71–4.
7 Trimmer, *Reflections on Education*, 11–2.
8 ERO, T/A 461; D/Q 24/2, D/P 18/2/2.
9 Crosbie, *Age Relations and Cultural Change,* 57–8.
10 Moore, 'Urban Schooling in Seventeenth and Eighteenth-century Scotland', 87.
11 ACA, *Council, Baillie and Guild Registers*, vol. 67, 161.
12 O'Sullivan, *Ascendancy: Women and Elementary Education*, 116.
13 Ham, *Elizabeth Ham*, 42; Lucas, 'Account of the Convincement', 180.
14 Earle, *City Full of People*, 35.
15 Crosbie, *Age Relations and Cultural Change*, 53–4.
16 *AJ*, 17 April 1769.
17 ACA, *Council, Baillie and Guild Registers*, vol. 63, 123.
18 ACA, *Council, Baillie and Guild Registers*, vol. 62, 217, 250; vol. 63, 123.
19 Moore, 'Urban Schooling in Seventeenth and Eighteenth-century Scotland', 82.
20 Colquhoun, reprinted in George, *England in Transition*, 150–5.
21 See Simonton, 'Education and Training', Appendix 3.4.

22 Crosbie, *Age Relations and Cultural Change*, 56.
23 Sellman, *Devon Village* Schools, 13–14.
24 Moore, *Education and Learning*, 113; White, 'Women, Religion and Education in Eighteenth-century Wales', 215.
25 The original study is in Simonton, *Education and Training*.
26 Commission to Enquire Concerning Charities, *Reports* 4, 349–60; 5, 569–70, 588–9, 594–7; 32, pt. 1, 585–95, 731–41. PP, 1816, *Abstract of Answers and Returns of Charitable Donations. . .*, 1, 351–90, 466–76, 1787; 2, 1117–60, and PP, 1819, *Report from the Select Committee on the Education of the Lower Orders . . .* (Brougham), 1816–9; 3, 245, 250, 268; 4, 870; SPCK, *Account* (1724). ERO, D/P 18/3/75B, D/P 18/2/2, D/P 18/3/75, D/P 18/12/4, D/P 18/12/3, D/P 18/11/3D/Q 8/1; D/Q 8/3; T/A 461; D/AEM 2/4; D/Q 24/1A'; D/Q 24/2; SRO, D1157/1/5/1. Population figures from PP, *Population Returns*, 1801, vol. 2, *Abstract of Returns*.
27 ERO, D/NC 1/9.
28 White, 'Women, Religion and Education', 216.
29 SRO, D1157/1/5/1, 10 May 1720.
30 Trimmer, *Reflections on Education*, 11, 13, 23–4; Anon., *Working-Schools in Chester*, 4.
31 Ingram, *Schools of Industry*, 3739.
32 Cappe, *Account of Charity Schools*, 1–3; Wollstonecraft, *Vindication*, 287.
33 Ingram, *Schools of Industry*, 31.
34 Anon., *Working Schools in Chester*, 4–5; Cappe, *Observations on Charity Schools*, 13, 58–61 and *Account of Charity Schools*, iii.
35 SRO, D204/1; ERO, D/P 275/28/2; *Chelmsford Chronicle*, 5 November 1790; Brown, *Essex at Work*, 139.
36 ERO, D/Q 8/3; Trimmer, *Charity Spelling Book*, pt. 1, 115.
37 ERO, D/NC 9/1, 50.
38 SRO, 1157/1/5/1. There may have been three daughters, the unnamed daughter admitted November 1727/28, Mary admitted in April 1728/29 and Elizabeth, unless Mary and the unnamed daughter are the same.
39 Cameron, 'Female Birthing Customs and Beliefs', 118.
40 Durie, *The British Linen Company*, 29, 36.
41 Earle, *City Full of People*, 35.
42 Anon., *The Polite Lady*.
43 Defoe, *Complete English Tradesman*, 353.
44 Crosbie, *Age Relations and Cultural Change*, 60.
45 SRO, 1157/1/5/1.
46 SRO, 1157/1/5/1.
47 ERO T7A 461.
48 Thomas, 'Children in Early Modern England', 66–7.
49 Sinclair, OSA, vol. V, 81; Schofield, 'Dimensions of Illiteracy', 452.
50 Simonton, *Education and Training*, 156–9.
51 Houston, *Literacy in Early Modern Europe*, 54; Cipolla, *Literacy and Development in the West*, 32–4; Sellman, *Devon Village* Schools, 13–4.
52 Martin, *Cupar*, 127–9.
53 Schofield, 'The Measurement of Literacy in Preindustrial England', 317.
54 SRO, D1157/1/5/1.
55 ERO. D/Q 24/1A and D/Q 24/2.
56 Lawson and Silver, *Social History of Education in England*, 215.
57 SPCK, *Account* (1724, 1759).
58 PP, 1818, *Education of the Lower Orders*, 11, 250.

59 Moore, 'Urban Schooling', 81; Houston, *Scottish Literacy and the Scottish Identity*, 43, 49–50.
60 Withrington, 'The S.P.C.K. and Highland Schools'.
61 OSA, XIV, 705n.
62 James McParlan, *Statistical Survey of the Country of Donegal.*
63 ERO, T/A 613; D/Q 8/3; T/A 461; D/Q 8/1.
64 The term 'Penetration of schooling' was created to assess how many children could have gone to school over time and to allow comparison between boys and girls. It is defined as the proportion of children reaching fifteen who could have been to school and includes duration of attendance as a variable. Therefore, penetration of schooling considers the size of the male and female student population, the size of the age group likely to be in school (i.e. 5–14) and the average length of time spent in school. For the original study, see Simonton, *Education and Training*, 163–9 and Appendix 4.2. The original included other schools which have been omitted from this discussion and the original calculations included boys who had better access across all schools.
65 Simonton, *Education and Training*, 184–5.

5

TRAINING THE GIRLS

Routes to training

For some girls, the next stage was training for work. Although some had had informal instruction, learning work skills often was the first step upon leaving home. This chapter focuses on the role of apprenticeship in the lives of girls looking to gain a skill in preparation for work. It opens by explaining apprenticeship as a system and comparing it structurally with service, moving on to explain the forms of apprenticeship and their roles in society. The processes and characteristics of the main forms, private, charity and parish, are discussed separately, with a case study of milliner and mantuamakers' apprenticeships, which were significant for girls apprenticed by their families. Girls were remarkably mobile in the century, and the analysis of geographic mobility compares their trajectories, by forms of apprenticeship and also in relation to boys' experience. The chapter concludes by examining what apprenticeship might mean to girls and what their experiences looked like. The other main route for girls in their middle girlhood was service, which forms part of Chapter 6.

Histories of apprenticeship have, notoriously, tended to ignore girls, with a few significant exceptions. The classic work on apprenticeship by O.J. Dunlop and R.D. Denman, *English Apprenticeship and Child Labour*, devoted a substantial chapter to girls, apprenticeship and labour. More recent exemplary studies by Amy Erickson and Laura Gowing bring the focus on girls' experience into the discussion. However, John Rule's study of eighteenth-century apprentices by-passed them completely. Maarten Prak and Patrick Wallis's studies have also concentrated almost exclusively on boys, though Wallis turned to including girls in *The Market for Skill*. It is noticeable that much

DOI: 10.4324/9781003412168-6

of the recent work on apprenticeship focuses on the seventeenth century, like Wallis's and Gowing's. Katrina Honeyman's study of parish apprenticeship also incorporated girls, though much of the book deals with the nineteenth century. For the eighteenth century, Joan Lane integrated girls in her study of English apprenticeship, 1600–1914, with its concentration on Warwickshire, and Keith Snell has a chapter in *Annals of the Labouring Poor*, mainly dealing with the first half of the century. My own work focuses on the eighteenth century and much of this chapter is based on it.[1] Thus, study of female apprenticeship in the eighteenth century is patchy, and reflects the widespread perception that apprenticeship was intended for boys.

Apprenticeship and service were linked in many people's eyes as logical routes after school and a natural means of providing social values and behaviour. However, the two forms were structurally distinct.[2] Apprenticeship tied master and apprentice with a written contract, an indenture, to a certain term of years and conditions. In contrast, servants engaged in verbal or tacit contracts, typically of one year. Additionally, apprentices, their parents or guardians paid a master/mistress for training while servants were paid for working, and they could save to set up on their own in a way apprentices could not. But apprenticeship embraced patterns, which ranged from the highly structured and regulated to the relatively unstructured. Compare, for example, the guild apprentice with the farm labourer's daughter put to housewifery, or sometimes to 'that trade he now useth'. Parallel to apprenticeship were other forms which were educationally informal. Their primary purpose was not to educate but to create workers. Thus, service and the industrial workplace provided training, both explicitly and implicitly, while creating more skilled workers. Employers intended this education to develop the working ability of the employee. Nevertheless, it was a constituent part of the education available to the eighteenth-century girl.

A further issue is the blurring of the term service. Because apprenticeship was associated with boys, as school records showed, service was usually associated with girls although the jobs they did could be virtually identical. Similarly, the impression that apprenticeship was almost exclusively male is given credence by records like those of guilds and corporations, which did not actively encourage female involvement, while frequently prohibiting it. At the same time, apprenticeship often was another way for girls to enter entering service. It is worth remembering that only a small proportion of children of either sex underwent indentured apprenticeship. Many gained experience and 'training' through annual hirings as servants. Settlement examinations from Harborne in Staffordshire and Northfield illustrate how apprenticeship could become a series of hirings or how a hiring could turn into apprenticeship.[3] The line between formal and informal modes of training was very thin indeed.

The apprenticeship system

Apprenticeship as a system of training applied to girls as well as boys, and a variety of systems existed by the eighteenth century, based on the guild model and practices, but diverging from it in purpose and emphasis. Apprenticeship records of indentures were kept by a variety of institutions including central and parish administration, charities, corporations and guilds, and private firms and individuals (Image 5.1). The three most typical forms were private craft or trade apprenticeships, charity apprenticeships and parish apprenticeships. Private apprenticeships most clearly resembled the guild model in that training was undertaken by a master in exchange for a premium and a specified term of service by the child, nominally seven years. Those emanating from private charity adhered to similar conditions and terms, but the premium was paid by a charity and the trades and premiums tended toward the more modest end of the scale. Poor law officials arranged the details and paid any premium for parish apprentices, often putting out children with more regard for the

IMAGE 5.1 Indenture placing Elizabeth Richardson into the service of Jane Horam, England, 1769 January 4. Yale Center for British Art, Paul Mellon Fund, LC4096.G7 I63 1769 Box.

rates than for the child. Thus, the conditions and purposes of the system could and did vary widely. They were also recorded and taxed differently. Parish apprenticeships had existed since Tudor times as a way of relieving parishes of children whom they would otherwise have to support. Thus, the system was local with recording left to individual parishes, sometimes no fee was paid to a master or mistress, on other occasions a nominal fee of £5 was paid. Charity apprentices were also managed on a local basis, often attached to schools or other institutions, like the London Foundling Home or Aberdeen Poor's Hospital. The subtle difference was that the charity child might find an apprenticeship in a 'good' trade which was less likely for parish children. These could resemble either private apprenticeships or parish ones, depending on how they were managed. Both these forms of apprenticeship were not liable to taxation, being seen as public charity. However, from 1710 to 1811, a stamp duty was imposed on private apprenticeships which were taxed as part of a need for national income, especially for Queen Anne's wars, and it was conveniently left in place for a century. The duty was payable by the master or mistress at six pence on the pound for those premiums up to £50 and one shilling on the pound for those over £50. When the master refused, the parents or apprentice paid the duty to avoid prosecution and to ensure a legal apprenticeship for the child. Recording practices were also variable with gaps in the information, notably in the second half century when parents' names and residence largely disappeared.

The organisation of the apprenticeship system derived from guild practices, and as such it also closely aligned to an idealised male rite of passage from boy to man. Nominally a boy was to be apprenticed at fourteen, for seven years, completing his apprenticeship with his 'masterpiece' at twenty-one and becoming a 'man'. This did not, however, mean he was independent, many becoming journeymen and never reaching mastership. But the system clearly replicated a gendered route to adulthood, one which was also used for training girls, or relieving the parish, but with quite different outcomes for many of them. The terms of the *Statute of Artificers* (1563) applied equally to both sexes and frequently it was invoked to restrain unapprenticed women from practicing a trade. Craftsmen often regarded the employment of women as a means of introducing untrained cheap labour. However, traditionally guilds allowed wives and daughters of members to work in a trade and to continue as full guild members after husbands' or fathers' deaths, though not always permitted to take apprentices themselves. Some women gained their trading position because contemporaries accepted seven years' experience as equivalent to apprenticeship. Indeed, many apprentice mistresses did not appear to have been indentured themselves. Like many girls, they may have worked in family or milliners' shops to gain the skills and experience needed to set up their own shop. Additionally, some work, which was seen as traditionally female, usually did not take apprentices. Such a case is spinning, a common female occupation employing most Essex women in the 1740s, although girls were apprenticed to weavers, perhaps as spinners or as weavers. This was especially apparent in the Essex towns of Bocking and Braintree which sat at the heart of the baymaking industry (woollen cloth manufacture), in which large numbers of boys and girls were distributed by parishes to masters requiring child labour.

Though girls constituted a significant portion of apprentices, their opportunities were more limited than boys', reflecting women's position legally and economically. Women's apprenticeship did not carry with it the rights and privileges of men nor was their work regarded the same way. They were concentrated in parish apprenticeship and in less prosperous trades; but so were many boys. The main divergence was in professions and lucrative, prestigious occupations which largely excluded girls. They were less likely to be apprenticed privately, and in contrast made up a more significant proportion of parish apprentices. The trades to which girls were indentured privately were nominally female trades, which is logical if that was the most realistic option for an occupation as an adult.

As Gowing noted, for the seventeenth century, 'The path of trained apprenticeship for young women featured almost nowhere in printed literature, in advice to girls, in ballads or in plays. But it was a well-established route to independent work' both in London and around the country.[4] Eighteenth-century trades guides did include it, like Campbell and Collyer's for London. And this chapter confirms its importance for girls' training. Girls went to trades throughout the economy in their apprenticeship journey and clearly were regarded as able to do heavy and unpleasant work. From 1750, 46 per cent of girl apprentices in Essex and Staffordshire went to services, mainly housewifery, while 40 per cent worked in the textile trades. Agriculture took some 17 per cent but the remaining occupational groups took very few girls despite their importance to the economy (Figure 5.1). This overview

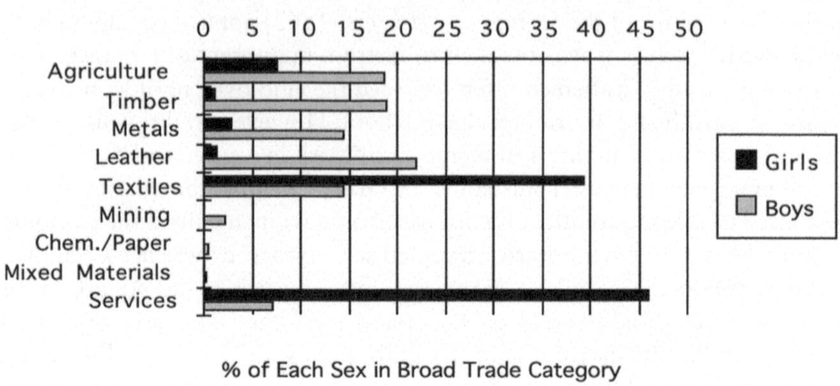

FIGURE 5.1 Distribution of Trades by Sex, 1750–99, Essex and Staffordshire

is skewed partly by the large number of parish apprentices compared to privately indentured girls. While this pattern indicates that society saw certain areas of work as more appropriate for girls and women, and that others were difficult for them to enter, the presence of girls across the spectrum underlines the extent of their activities.

Girls made up 9 per cent of apprentices in Essex and Staffordshire during the last half of the century (Figures 5.2 and 5.3). They accounted for just over 4 per cent of private apprentices recorded at the Inland Revenue while they composed only about 3 per cent of charity apprentices. In the first half of the century, privately apprenticed girls composed about 5 per cent in Wiltshire and 3 per cent in Sussex.[5] They were almost invisible in Kingston-upon-Thames; in Scotland, none were found. Charities more

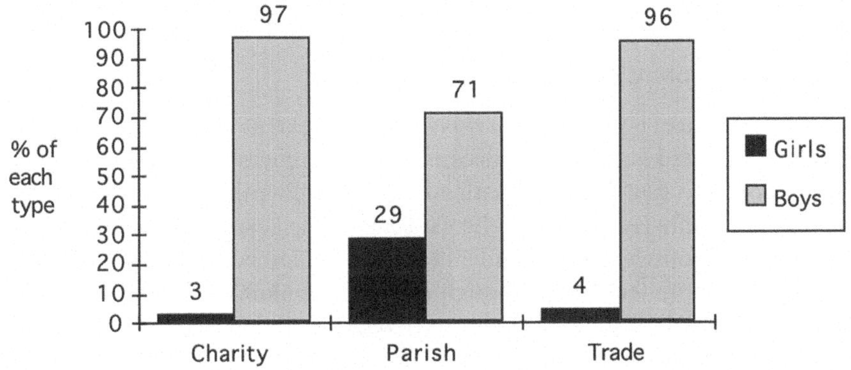

FIGURE 5.2 Apprentices as a Proportion of Types of Indentures, Staffordshire and Essex, 1750–1799.

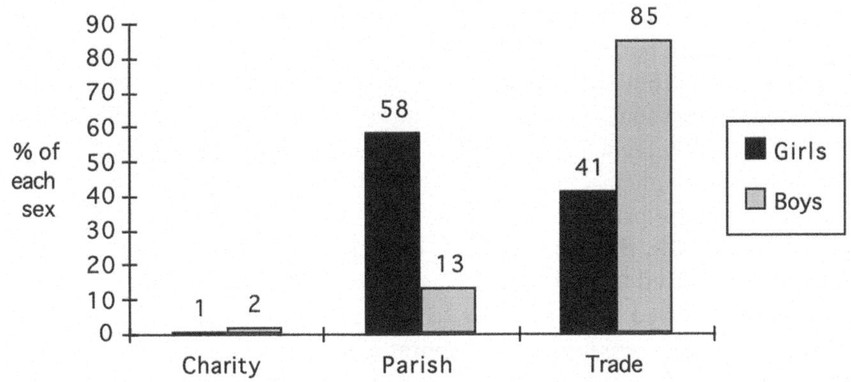

FIGURE 5.3 Apprentices as a Proportion of Their Sex by Type of Indenture, Staffordshire and Essex, 1750–1799.

commonly apprenticed only boys, replicating social ideas about boys having jobs and girls becoming servants, wives, mothers and casual workers. However, some like Rawlett's Trust in Staffordshire had both a boys' and girls' arm. Parish indentures showed a strikingly different pattern since almost a third of pauper apprentices in Staffordshire and Essex were girls, confirmed by Snell who showed girls represented 34 per cent of eighteenth-century parish apprentices in southern English counties. Also, 58 per cent of all female apprentices were put out by the parish rather than by their parents compared to about an eighth of boys.[6] Some girls went to apprenticeships that were not recorded 'properly', such as a list from Staffordshire intended for the Inland Revenue, but never sent, or girls in Scotland who appear to have had apprenticeships but were left out of guild or city records. Thus, apprenticeship was a part of many girls' lives, but was highly dependent on who she was, where she lived and what aspirations or hopes the family may have had.

The private apprentice

The records are not comprehensive, so the extent to which girls are under-represented is unknown. Because the tax records were created for the purpose of collecting duty, and with administrative weaknesses in the system, successful circumvention was to be expected.[7] The cost of the premium and tax may have outweighed the advantages to be gained in status and adult position for some families. Although average premiums were not very high and many menial, low-status trades were registered, the perceived obligation to register may have been taken more seriously as one moved up the social scale. The likelihood of under-registration was greater for girls since certain advantages were not in fact obtainable. They usually could not gain the freedom of a corporation, nor did apprenticeship necessarily enhance their trading or political position as it did with boys. They were largely restricted from guilds and the advantages of a collective work group, and women often were seen by men not as trading partners but as threats to their position or as simply assistants. Since they had less to gain from the formalities of indenturing, their families may have been less interested in fulfilling the obligations. In contrast, many French guildswomen strongly supported the corporate system, which gave them concrete economic benefits and better legal rights, and they used the privileges and structures to protect their trade. In towns with female guilds, they gained a corporate identity and a notion of female honour that derived from the female nature of their trades and the independence that it allowed them to enjoy.[8] Like in England, they resisted tailors' attempts to bring them into their corporations. Nevertheless, as we shall see, in certain trades like millinery and mantuamaking British female apprentices abounded. J-Jean Hecht in fact argued that it was common to apprentice girls to these trades as preparation for domestic service.[9]

Girls and their parents would be looking for a 'good' placement if they were paying, and it is clear from individual records that private apprentices were frequently from middling families or at least aspiring working families. Drawing on records from Bedfordshire, Essex, Staffordshire, Sussex and Wiltshire, we see daughters of saddlers, yeomen, carpenters, clothiers, gentlemen and parish clerks. Often parents' identity is not known since from the 1750s it was rarely recorded. There is also some synergy with the kinds of trades that girls went to; for example, Hannah Carde, a deceased husbandman's daughter, went to a local yeoman for eight years, while Edith Gore, daughter of a deceased yeoman, went to another farmer locally with no fee. This last was registered, potentially operating as fosterage and giving her some legal security. Several girls followed trades closely associated with their families, like Hester Gardner, daughter of a clothworker who went to Mary Cox, a widowed tailoress in Warminster, for five years in 1716, and Dinah Flower, daughter of a clothier of Winsley, Wiltshire, who went to a milliner of Devizes for five years. Frequently, one parent had died, often the father, so that apprenticing a daughter could help relieve the family burden but also give some chance of a trade and future for the girl. These were not parish children, but families looking for the best way to juggle their needs and opportunities.

Two features marked out private apprenticeships for girls: they tended to have shorter terms of service than boys, and especially shorter than parish girls; and their premiums tended to be smaller than boys'. Girls apprenticed by their families tended to serve on average four or five years. Only 5.4 per cent of their male peers served four years or less. The county data in Table 5.1 shows how little apprenticeship terms varied in several English counties. Averages are difficult, however, because counties varied in their practices. A girl in Wiltshire in the first half of the century was more likely to serve the 'traditional' seven-year term which matched boys' experience; but this was also true in Staffordshire, in the second half of the century. On the other hand, in the second half century parents in Essex only occasionally sent their daughters for seven years, and these girls had the shortest average of any in the sample counties. Probably local traditions shaped these decisions, but periods of service were also trade-specific. In Staffordshire, dominated by the metal trades, girls were apprenticed longer than boys on average, and in some ways their time as apprentices would have not been much different from some parish apprentices. Many girls at the lower end of the social ladder, whose parents or a benefactor could pay for an apprenticeship did so, and they are found in housewifery, agriculture, menial metal and textile trades as well as in crafts with good prospects. In those agricultural, textile and metal trades in which girls were best represented, i.e. husbandry, locksmithing, bucklemaking and weaving, their premiums were low, averaging £2 to £5. Terms tended to exceed seven years, while the skill needed for the trade was minimal suggesting that they were cheap labour.

TABLE 5.1 Girls as Private Apprentices in Five English Counties

County	*Dates*	*Average Term (years)*	*Mean Term (years)*	*Average Premium (£)*	*Mean Premium (£)*	*% Over £10*	*% Over €30*
Bedfordshire	1711–1720	3.44	4	£9.76	£8.00	61.1%	0.0%
Essex	1710/11; 1750–99	4.02	3	£19.27	£15.60	61.2%	27.1%
Staffordshire	1710/11; 1750–99	5.25	4	£9.95	£5.00	26.9%	10.5%
Sussex	1710–52	5.36	5	£14.45	£10.00	69.1%	9.3%
Wiltshire	1710–60	6.04	7	£9.03	£8.00	47.2%	3.2%
Overall average				£12.73			

Source: Dale, *Wiltshire Apprentices and their Masters*, Simonton, *Education and Training*, Rice, *Sussex Apprentices. Jenkinson, 'Apprenticeships, 1711–31; Jenkinson, List of Bedfordshire Apprentices, PRO, ERO and SRO apprenticeship records Essex and Staffordshire Records per bibliography. BDRO. 61/7/8. Harborne Parish Apprenticeship Indentures.*
Note: Currency is decimalised for calculation purposes

Short terms held throughout private female apprenticeship, not just in trades with good premiums, and while some girls certainly did serve seven years, it was far more common that they did not. Thus, girls were not following the 'traditional' guild model which carried with it certain prestige and rights. Also, girls apprenticed for short terms were available for work up to two years earlier than boys. While they were able to earn sooner than boys, perhaps saving for a dowry, their ultimate prospects both financially and socially may have been diminished. They could gain a respectable occupation, and the largest of this group were milliners' and mantuamakers' apprentices. A few also served terms more like parish apprenticeships, 'to age 21', especially if one or both parents had died.

Girls' premiums, or fees paid for training, also tended to be lower than boys', averaging £12.73 for girls and £18 for boys. For the first half of the century, the rural counties of Bedfordshire and Wiltshire showed lower averages, as did Staffordshire in the second half. Sussex, although also rural, sent several girls to London, and the average premiums were higher. In contrast, Essex girls seldom went to London, despite its closeness, but higher premiums were the result of a dominance of high-class milliners, especially in Colchester. Overall, a wider range of premiums existed for boys whilst on a trade-by-trade basis girls' premiums were regularly lower, averaging two thirds of boys'. Girls paid more than boys in only four of the most common occupations and dominated in mantuamaking and millinery. They were closest in tailoring in which girls' premiums averaged five sixths of boys', especially when a husband and wife worked together as a tailor and milliner or mantuamaker. Families also paid high premiums to send daughters to a variety of prestigious trades. Since the records give the master or mistresses' trade it is less clear what training the girl received, but a number went to other clothing trades like mercery, haberdashery and drapery. In the 1780s, girls began to appear as apprentices to schoolmistresses, matching the premiums and terms of milliners and mantuamakers, suggesting a new and growing opportunity for girls of middling families looking for an occupation.

Milliners and mantuamakers

One of the best opportunities for an occupation and a recognised status came from millinery and mantuamaking. The importance of these trades to girls is also demonstrated in the studies of Erickson and Gowing, on London needle trades. In Bedfordshire, Staffordshire and Sussex over half of girls were apprenticed to a mantuamaker or milliner; in Essex 72.9 per cent, but in Wiltshire only 37.2 per cent (Table 5.2). Such dominance shows us how important these two trades were to girls hoping for a *métier*, reflecting the real potential a working girl had for a sound working possibility in adulthood. The prestige of these trades becomes clear when we see that only five parish girls in Essex and Staffordshire went to mantuamaking and one to millinery between 1750 and 1799.

There were differences between these two trades, reflected in their terms and premiums. Girls had twice as many opportunities to go to a mantuamaker while milliners took only a third of private apprenticeships in the five counties. Milliners were far more exclusive, and they also expected higher premiums, with average fees of £27.45, and a median of about £25.00. A few

TABLE 5.2 Milliners' and Mantuamakers' Apprentices in Five English Counties

Milliners and Mantuamakers	*Dates*	*Average Term (years)*	*Median Term (years)*	*Average Premium (£)*	*Median Premium (£)*	*% Over €10*	*% Over £ 30*
Bedfordshire	1711–1720	3.70	4	£11.50	£8.00	61.1%	0.0%
Essex	1710/11; 1750–99	3.38	3	£22.49	£20.00	84.0%	37.2%
Staffordshire	1710/11; 1750–99	4.54	4	£13.47	£10.00	42.1%	17.8%
Sussex	1710–52	5.00	5	£15.80	£12.00	57.7%	14.8%
Wiltshire	1710–60	5.53	6	£12.67	£10.10	66.3%	7.2%
Total				£11.55	£10.00		

Source: Per Table 5.1.

paid less than £10, but Mary Paget paid Mary Gibbon £90 in 1773. Mantua-making training was available to a girl for as little as £1.00 like Mary Howell of Lewes, Sussex, in 1714. The terms expected of an apprentice also showed the same discrepancy with milliners offering terms of four years on average, while mantuamakers kept girls for four and a half years. In comparison with boys, these premiums are significant since few families paid such high premiums for boys; 85 per cent of all male premiums were less than £25, while 70 per cent of masters or mistresses received less than £15.[10]

Apprenticeship mattered most for girls when they were acquiring a *profession*, and those in towns like Colchester, Chelmsford, Devizes, Chichester, Lewes, Wolverhampton, Bath and Stafford clustered in the needleworking trades, especially mantuamaking and millinery. These towns and other county towns as well as London drew girls to them, and sometimes to specific well-known milliners, like Mary Gibbon, whose renowned millinery shop in Bath was held in high esteem and closely associated with fashion, probably benefitting from her working alongside her brother Thomas Gainsborough. A completed apprenticeship enhanced a girl's chances of good employment in the more exclusive and high-status trades in England, trades at the junction with luxury and fashion. Apprenticeship data, newspaper advertisements and insurance records show clearly that these needle trades offered the prospect a genuine occupation and good future for some girls.[11] Hogarth's mother and both sisters, Mary and Ann, became milliners (Image 5.2). Fifty-six per cent of private English apprentice mistresses were mantuamakers and milliners, showing that it was important for the status of the trade to conduct business utilising a well-understood mode of training. Amy Erickson's study of milliners and their apprentices in the London guilds similarly shows that the millinery business could be an attractive, respectable and prosperous career choice for women.[12] With apprenticeships, the high-status sewing trades could create barriers and mimic the exclusion rights of male guilds and trades, like tailors. They could argue that they too had a *métier*, and that what they offered to customers was of a different order than simple domestic sewing. They could claim the cachet of a profession.

Guides for apprentices and their parents echoed the significance of these trades to girls' futures. Millinery was seen as a prestige occupation and was recommended to girls of 'good family'. It was skilled and offered scope, attracting those with capital and some social standing. Robert Campbell's *The London Tradesman* (1747), a guide for parents on apprenticeship, was damning of the profession, but he acknowledged that women needed knowledge of fashion and that 'they make vast profits on every article they deal in'.[13] He thought a woman could begin business with capital ranging from £100–£1,000, but he stressed the need for parents to be able to provide adequately for their daughters since despite 'vast profits' made by mistresses, they 'yet give but poor, mean Wages to every Person they employ under them'.[14]

IMAGE 5.2 Trade card of Mary and Ann Hogarth, the old Frock Shop, William Hogarth, ca. 1730. Gift of Bella C. Landauer. The Metropolitan Museum of Art, 26.28.166. www.metmuseum.org.

For the top end of the trade and well-capitalised employers, it could be a good business enterprise, but for the less fortunate and especially employees, prospects were much less optimistic. In 1761, Joseph Collyer was more charitable in advising parents. He claimed that girls with the right qualities of gentility and literacy, and with some 'fancy and imagination', will 'hardly fail of procuring, in this branch of business, a comfortable and genteel support; I know of none fitter for the daughters of numerous families, where the parents live handsomely, yet have no fortunes to leave their children'.[15] The later *Book of Trades* declared 'In the milliner taste and fancy are required, with a quickness in discerning, imitating, and improving upon the various fashions, which are perpetually changing among the higher circles.' 'The business of a MILLINER, and the articles which she makes up for sale, are very well displayed in the plate' (Image 5.3).[16] She is fashionably if modestly dressed and with her wares properly displayed. Good profits could be made by those with the ability and finance to establish themselves once their apprenticeship was complete.

IMAGE 5.3 Milliner, *The book of trades, or, Library of the useful arts*. Part III, Vol 2, 45, Tabart and Co. 1806.

In contrast, and corresponding to their lower apprenticeship premiums, mantuamakers usually operated with under £100 capital, and were known for paying poor wages. Premiums varied considerably for their apprentices from £2 to £31, illustrating the range within the occupation. According to Campbell, their journeywomen 'may make shift with great Sobriety and Oeconomy to live upon their Allowance; but their Want of Prudence, and general Poverty, has brought the business into small Reputation.'[17] He warned that the pay was frequently so low as to make prostitution their alternative form of employment.

Millinery and mantuamaking could be closely aligned, and a milliner's shop almost always had mantuamakers working for them. In 1777, Lucia Reeve advertised saying their mantuamaker had 'informed herself of all the latest alterations' in London.[18] Their entries in the duty records also show variation in how they described themselves. Ann and Hannah Prior listed themselves as 'mercers', 'milliners', 'milliners and mercers' and 'milliners, etc.' Mary Gibbon designated herself as a mantuamaker, then milliner and mantuamaker and finally as a milliner. Girls' training was also variable, possibly in keeping with how much their family paid for their training, but perhaps just serendipity, or depending on their ability and potential. Nevertheless, milliners' and mantuamakers' apprentices obtained training and a trade through apprenticeship in a way in which many girls probably did not. Also, these girls conceivably expected to learn the polish and ways of a social class into which they might hope to marry. The apprenticeship of girls to mercers and drapers suggests this likelihood even more forcefully. It could have been a form of 'finishing' like boys who were apprenticed to gentlemen for similar sums and terms. This characteristic of female apprenticeship is also a clear reminder of the social class distinctions represented within apprenticeship. Even these more prestigious apprenticeships were not a monolithic form of training with a single function.

Reading between the lines of the indenture records, certainly some girls went to proven milliners, many with long-running firms, like Frances Heberden in Chichester, Lucia Reeves or Ann and Hannah Prior in Colchester, Mary Gibbon in Colchester then Bath, Phoebe Moreton or Dorothy Anslow, in Wolverhampton, amongst others. Others went to smaller firms but could have gained a solid training and start in the occupation. A much larger group were apprenticed to mantuamakers, and almost any small town had a dressmaker to attend to regular needs of the community. But the records are opaque. Many had a chance to be taught useful skills, and even those who went to housewifery could be in a setting where they learned useful skills, ones that could be deployed on marriage or in another workshop. This was most likely for privately apprenticed girls, and the continuities shown by milliners' apprentices, like the Woods and Reeves, or Mary Bettesworth, a successful milliner who trained with Frances Heberden of Chichester, supports this. Notably, despite an assumption that women did not appear in apprenticeship indentures, and that their husbands formally took the girls for training, women did appear both in partnerships and as mistresses on their own. Often the apparent partnership was no such thing: Mary Gibbon was sometimes listed with her husband, a minister; he never appeared alone, and she did after his death.

There is no doubt that there was a 'dark side' to the profession, recognised by advice books. Campbell was an explicit and outspoken critic, and while historians acknowledge his misogyny, he did reflect a frequent perception of milliners. Firstly, he argues that men targeted young girls in milliners' shops.

> The vast Resort of young Beaus and Rakes to Milliner's [sic] exposes young Creatures to many Temptations, and insensibly debauches their morals before they are capable of Vice. . . . if he chances to meet in her Shop any thing that has the Appearance of Youth, and the simple Behaviour of undesigning Innocence, he immediately accosts the young Sempstress

> with all the Raillery he is Master of, talks loosely, and thinks himself most witty, when he has cracked some obscene Jest upon the young Creature.[19]

He claims the mistress must accept this because she wants his business and will instruct the apprentice to admit this behaviour. Blaming men, he also criticises the lack of protection and a climate damaging to a girl's innocence: 'I am far from charging all Milliners with the Crime of Connivance at the Ruin of their Apprentices, but fatal experience must convince the Public, that nine out of ten of the young Creatures . . . are ruined and undone.' But he then turns the argument around saying that she becomes accustomed to this sort of conversation, and 'I am persuaded, more than half have been debauched of them that have been bred Milliners, and have been debauched in their Houses.'[20] He claimed that the dangers were so 'manifest' that parents should not apprentice their daughters to milliners. Since this runs counter to much of the accepted practice and understanding and against the view that millinery was a good and appropriate profession even for middle-class girls, it is hard to take this as fact. It was, instead, part of a larger discourse against workingwomen and girls of any class. But less strident than Campbell, Collyer pointed out, 'in this, as in almost all shop-keeping businesses, they will be exposed to the attempts of designing men; many of whom glory in one of the most shameful acts of baseness, that of betraying to ruin heedless and unwary innocence.' He warned girls about joining in with the 'young spark who makes loose allusions or impudent jests.[21]

In many respects this was a realistic warning, because young men did frequent these shops, maybe to purchase presents or even something for themselves, 'since the beau and fine gentleman has his Solitairs or Stock, his Watch or Canestring from the pretty Milliner.'[22] Women in seasonal urban trades were vulnerable since they were subject to periods of slack employment and low wages, and they had a narrower range of options than men in similar seasonal trades. Thus, in millinery advertisements, 'women negotiated most carefully between the competing claims to skill, reputation, fashion and price'.[23] Their adverts reflected gentility in the way they positioned the work and its location. The subtext to these accounts was that not all young women became successful high-street milliners. Mantuamakers were especially vulnerable because their trade covered a wider gamut and because many were working-class seamstresses. While it was a good business enterprise for the able and well-capitalised employer, prospects were much less promising for less fortunate employees.

The parish apprentice

Parish apprenticeship played an important role in many working girls' lives. For poor girls whose parents claimed poor relief, there were few options since parishes tended to put them to pauper apprenticeships. The extensive data from Essex and Staffordshire shows that almost a third of parish apprentices were girls. And 58 per cent of girls who had an identifiable apprenticeship were sent out by parishes. Because parish apprenticeship had been adopted to relieve parishes from the burden of supporting pauper children and orphans, vocational training was less overtly a part of their period of service. Nevertheless, most parish indentures carried the stipulation: 'That the said [Master/Mistress] the said Apprentice in the Art of [trade] which s/he now useth shall teach and Instruct or Cause to be taught and Instructed in the best way and Manner that s/he can.' Furthermore, the master or mistress undertook to feed, clothe and monitor her and guaranteed not to prevent her becoming chargeable to the parish. Thus, the overseers of the poor apprenticed Sarah Osbourne from Harborne, in 1781:

> a poor child of the said parish, Apprentice to Mark Pearsall of the County of Warwick Bucklechapemaker with him to dwell and serve from the Day of the Date of these Presents, until the said Apprentice shall accomplish her full age of twenty-one years . . . During all which Term the said apprentice her Master faithfully shall serve in all lawful Business, according to her Power, Wit, and Ability; and honestly, orderly, and obediently in all things demean hand behave herself towards her said <master and all his during the said Term. And the said Mark Pearsall for himself, his Executors and Administrators doth Covenant and Grant, to and with the said Overseers and Churchwardens . . . That the said Mark Pearsall in his trade of housewifery and chapefiling and polishing shall teach and Instruct or cause to be taught and instructed in the best way and manner that he can. And shall and will during the Term aforsesaid, find, provide and allow unto the said Apprentice, meet, competent Meat, Drink and Apparel, Lodging, Washing, and all other Things, necessary and fit for an Apprentice. And also shall and will provide for the said Apprentice, that she be not in any way a Charge to the said Parish, or the parishioners of the same; but of and from all Charge shall and will save the said Parish and Parishioners harmless and indemnify during said Term.[24]

Sometimes the Master or Mistress also had to provide the child with a suit of clothes on completion of her indenture. This formulation was so common that a form was printed for the purpose, and therefore the wording across a county and indeed across the country was virtually identical. The importance of the duty of care is shown in the order for Susannah Holbrook of Hackney,

> aged ten years a poor Child of this parish be forthwith bound apprentice to Joseph French of the parish of Saint Mary Overes in the County of Surry pin maker and that M^{r}. John Davis the Churchwarden do pay forty shillings with her and Six shillings towards provideing some Clothes for her she being almost naked and having had the meazles since she hath been upon liveing with him.[25]

The parish apprentice's experience usually began at a younger age and lasted longer than private apprenticeships and most were put out between seven and nine; only 6 per cent were indentured at fourteen. Half went to parish apprenticeships before they reached ten. Girls were commonly apprenticed until age twenty-one, though sometimes the indenture was cancelled if she married before completion of the contract—presumably placing responsibility on her husband for her support. Even some private apprentices were placed under these terms as well, while about 6 per cent of parish apprentices served terms like the private model. Thus, parish girls commonly could serve eleven years, far longer than privately apprenticed girls. Each model of apprenticeship thus construed different purposes and results, reinforcing perceptions of adult gender roles and the persistence of social difference. Certainly, the early age of indenturing could imply the use of cheap labour, although they probably began their apprenticeship as a liability. They were too young to work well and frequently spoiled materials. However, they were far more useful at the end of their lengthy terms, particularly if little skill were involved. Such young apprentices also reflected the parsimonious desire to remove children from the rates, which was very much in keeping with the general administration of the poor laws since officials tended not to allow families with children over fourteen to receive relief.

Girls had a limited repertoire of choices since three quarters of pauper girls were apprenticed to housewifery. About 10 per cent went to agricultural work, often 'husbandry', while a further 12 per cent went into textile work (Figure 5.4).[26] This reflects, in part, the rural character of the two counties and England as a whole. Pauper boys had a wider range of opportunities than girls, being spread more evenly throughout the trades. The difference from private apprenticeship is not simply that parish apprentices were put to poor

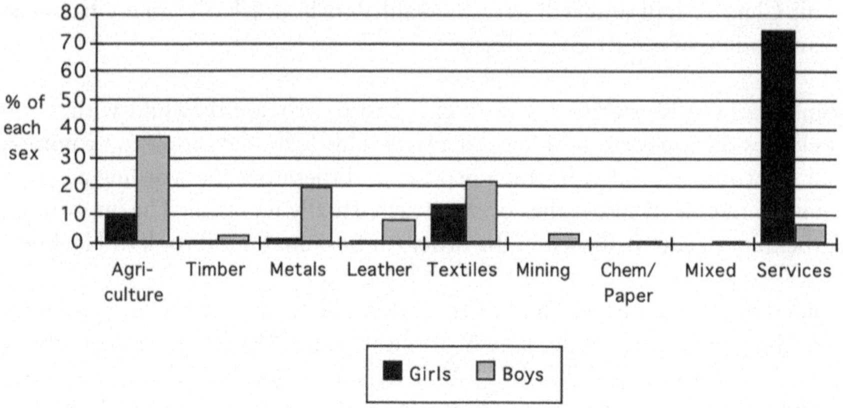

FIGURE 5.4 Distribution of Trades by Sex for Parish Apprentices, 1700–1749.

overstocked trades since many children put out by private indenture also went to unpromising trades. Instead, the patterns suggest that some trades were considered proper for 'real' apprentices and others for paupers. Yet local variations inflect this image. For example, of twelve girls apprenticed by Cannock, Staffordshire, between 1750 and 1800, twelve-year old Mary Owen went to mantuamaking for five years, but with no premium mentioned. The rest went to housewifery, to serve until twenty-one or marriage, except Mary Parker for seven years with a premium of £1.50. In Aldridge, fifteen kilometres away, girls experienced a similar pattern. None were sent with a premium and all were expected to serve until twenty-one or marriage. All twenty-seven girls went to housewifery, except Mary Gough who was sent to a bucklemaker, ten-year-old Ann Garner who went to a ropemaker, and the intriguing Elizabeth Smith who was indentured to 'anything'. Ten-year-old Martha Elleson was to become a housemaid. Since 'housewifery' could include agricultural or industrial tasks, this is more explicit than usual.[27] Chelmsford girls had a wider range of destinations, although housewifery continued to dominate. Of sixty-five girls, several went to weavers, where they probably worked as spinners since they went to the bayweaving towns of Braintree and Bocking. Rebecca Landy went to a mantuamaker, Elizabeth Reeve to a shopkeeper and husbandman. In fact, it is noticeable that six went to men in the victualing trades, three in London. The fact that they went between 1768 and 1771 suggests that someone had contacts. It was also a feature of service that those seeking servants often sought them from the countryside rather than towns because city girls were often considered unreliable. A group of nine girls went to Pendleton Lancashire, along with three boys, to cotton manufacture in 1799, the only recorded parish girls in the whole of Essex or Staffordshire to be sent to the factories in the eighteenth century. This latter is important because a common image of the parish apprentice is those who went north to the factories, and whose treatment brought concern and Parliamentary action in 1802. Figure 5.4 illustrates the trades to which parish children were sent and shows very little change over time.

This sketch is indicative of the kinds of occupational experience most parish girls would have had. Housewifery was a 'broad church' and the use of the term 'housbandry' suggests the blending of household and other work assisting in gardening and farming, or even domestic industries. For example, Dorothy Warthew was apprenticed to Thomas Jackson of Armitage, Staffordshire, to be taught 'all business proper for female apprentices in the duties of a farm'.[28] Yet, local conditions mattered, and Essex girls were far more likely to be put to housewifery while Staffordshire and Warwickshire girls, had options in a range of industries from pottery to metalwork.

Vocational training was less clear, while support of the child was paramount. Both Dorothy George and Dorothy Marshall emphasised the importance of labouring as opposed to training as a key function of parish apprenticeship.[29]

Nevertheless, parish officials functioned in a world of practicalities, and finding ways to remove girls from the rates was usually paramount in their minds. They placed children where they could. As Levene argues,

> Apprenticeship was primarily a way to ensure a child's future as a working adult, but this was related to paternalist concerns, worries about the burden on the rates for the parish and the perpetuation of idleness, and investment in human capital in a wider sense. Here, too it is likely that parish officials were still thinking in terms of settlement law and employment prospects, and applying a longstanding model of child labour and training to a changing and mixed economy.[30]

Frequently, pauper apprenticeship was criticized for providing ratepayers with cheap labour. Undoubtedly this was partly true. Parish children were more prevalent in poorer trades, such as cordwaining (shoemaking) and weaving, than in prosperous ones, which lends weight to their being cheap supplementary labour instead of receiving meaningful training. Yet, the line between training and work was clouded, since expertise was commonly acquired by association with experienced workers. In occupations requiring highly sophisticated skills, formal training was more probable in handicraft trades, especially in towns. In rural Britain many girls would be employed in agriculture where apprenticeship would provide them with useful knowledge and experience. As underlined by Marshall, in these rural communities, the work upon which they were set was preparation for the life they could expect as adults. Their position as adults would probably be little different from others in the rural community.[31] Yet, parish apprentices might find a trade this way, or the skills to take to a marriage. Girls in Harborne went to ratepayers with a wide range of occupations in metal trades, textiles trades and victualling as well as housewifery, all of which could have provided them trades in the area.

Socialisation in the values and behaviour expected by society was an important element of female apprenticeship. Thus, large numbers of parish apprentices were maintained and given social education in addition to any technical instruction they might have received. There were economic and political reasons for apprenticing pauper girls, but the female advice literature made it clear that girls' moral upbringing was of paramount concern to the middle classes. For girls lower down the scale, education in demeanour, propriety and sobriety could be derived through apprenticeship. Parish apprenticeship was thought to 'improve' children by removing them from the baneful influences of 'miserable and depraved' pauper parents into the 'good' homes of ratepayers which provided an example to emulate, as Sarah Trimmer argued. However, Cappe saw apprenticeship as working in a contrary direction, primarily because people who applied to take apprentices were not the sort who were competent or disposed to faithfully discharge their trust.

Her concern that those individuals were motivated by greed and an 'undue love of authority' indicates her belief that apprenticeship of poor children was not activated by altruistic motives or even concern for the child. She argued that apprenticeship could destroy even good people since by its very character it 'calls into practice latent vicious propensities'.[32]

Staying or leaving

For most girls, apprenticeship marked the act of leaving home, usually requiring a girl to board with her master or mistress. Occasionally she might be apprenticed to her own parents, but most left home. Some stayed quite close, in the same village or town; others travelled some distance. A variety of factors came in to play in shaping this decision, some personal and others administrative. Some apprenticeship records enable us to study the impact of apprenticeship on girls' mobility, but information is limited by weak recording practices. Parish records only partly noted destinations, and the Inland Revenue records virtually never did after 1750. Even before, it was somewhat sporadic. Thus, this section uses a small sample to suggest the kinds of journeys girls were making and how likely they were to lose connections with family and their 'home'. Nearly a hundred parish girls from Essex, Staffordshire and Warwickshire and 851 privately apprenticed girls from Bedfordshire, Essex, Staffordshire, Sussex and Warwickshire help illustrate how mobility and distance affected girls.

TABLE 5.3 Average Distance Travelled by Female Parish Apprentices, Essex, Staffordshire and Warwickshire

County	*Town*	*Average distance (km)*	*% in same place*	*Distance without those in same place (km)*	*Number*
Essex	Chelmsford	42.33	35.4%	24.25*	64
Essex	Colchester, St Botolph's	30.48	61.5%	5.77$	12
Essex	Earls Colne	38.93	0.0%	3.25	4
Essex	Witham	22.50	0.0%	22.50	8
Essex	Writtle	9.6	80.0%	48.00	10
Staffordshire	Aldridge	7.63	44.4%	13.73	27
Staffordshire	Cannock	4.65	58.3%	11.16	12
Warwickshire	Harborne	11.08	36.8%	17.54	18
Average		30.38			

Source: Per Table 5.1.

* *Excludes cotton children.*

$ *Excludes one girl sent to South Shields.*

TABLE 5.4 Average Distance Travelled by Male Parish Apprentices, Essex, Staffordshire and Warwickshire

Boys' Sample	*Average Distance (km)*	*Without Locals*	*Local*
Harborne	11.29	16.18	34.9%
Colchester	31.20	64.08	50.0%
Chelmsford	26.72	33.94*	21.3%
Witham	27.35	27.35	0.0%

Source: Per Table 5.1.

* *Excludes cotton children.*

The average distances travelled by apprentices, whether parish or privately apprenticed, shown in Tables 5.3 and 5.4, appear to show no real difference. But averages are deceiving. The data for the five counties of privately apprenticed girls show remarkable consistency, especially across southern England, with only girls in Staffordshire staying slightly closer to home. The parish figures, however, show far greater variability, and the much larger numbers of parish apprentices in Essex for whom residence and place of placement could be found skews the average significantly. Removing Chelmsford from the calculation, the average distance for parish apprentices to travel was much closer to home, 14.29 km. Another key difference between the two sets of girls is that parish girls were far more likely to stay in their own parish, or a neighbouring one. Because the poor law intended to place children to keep them off the poor registers, it was common practice to send them to local ratepayers, not necessarily willingly. Honeyman argues that 'From time to time, the reluctance of local masters to accept parish children became a real problem.'[33] There were important variations from this practice, however; sisters Mary and Mary Haward were apprenticed the same day in 1714 to two men in Saxmundham, Suffolk; their brother was apprenticed the same day, but the brief record does not say why. A feature of averages is that they can hide practices, so the other two girls from Earls Colne moved less than five miles away, and all girls stayed in Writtle except two who went to London. Frances Johnson and Mary Head were sent to London victuallers in 1715 and 1719, Ellen Cooke from Witham went to the London silk industry in 1703, and ten girls from Chelmsford went to various trades, including victualling. A common experience for girls in southern England was going to London.

Parishes were also more likely to place girls within the parish, or nearby, whereas boys were far more likely to be sent farther away. In Colchester half of boys stayed in the town, and in Chelmsford 21.3 per cent did, while in both cases far more girls stayed in the towns. At Witham, both boys and girls were sent to other parishes. At Harborne, a metalworking community, 34.9 per cent of boys and 36.8 per cent of girls stayed in the village, where there was plentiful work for children, usually hard and arduous. If we eliminate those who stayed in the homeplace, the difference between the distances girls and boys travelled becomes more apparent. Colchester boys travelled on average 30.5 km while their sisters travelled 4.4 km; Chelmsford girls went 24.3 km away from home, while their brothers went 34.0 km away. Like girls, a few boys went dramatically far; a handful of boys went to Durham and Tyneside as mariners, and three went to Pendleton with the girls to cotton manufacturing. Most parish girls, then, stayed closer to home than boys on average and in most cases were less than a day's walk away, so they could have maintained connections to their family. Nevertheless, parish apprentices were less likely to have the freedom of movement to go visiting, and many were already orphaned. The average distance for the Essex boys in the sample was farther than a day's walk, breaking the link with the place of origin more likely.

Girls whose parents arranged apprenticeships were far more likely than parish girls to leave the town or parish. Although the averages across the five counties are similar to parish girls', far fewer stayed in their home parish (Table 5.5). The southern counties were all very rural and many girls travelled distances to take up apprenticeships, often moving to county or to market towns. Since over half went to millinery or mantuamaking, a town was the best place to start a career, and the best mistresses worked in towns. Especially girls from Bedfordshire and Sussex found apprenticeships to London mistresses. Chichester and Lewes in Sussex had several firms, but Frances Heberden in Chichester was the most prominent; she drew at least one apprentice from Wiltshire and some from Kent amongst the ten she trained from 1719 to 1730. Yet, London was the magnet for aspiring girls and eight went to learn their trade in the St Martin in the Fields and St James parishes,

TABLE 5.5 Distances Travelled by Milliners' and Mantuamakers' Apprentices

County Private Apprentices	*Dates*	*Distance (km)*	*% in Same Place*	*Distance Without Those in Same Place or Outliers (km)*	*Distance Without Outliers (km)*	*Number*
Bedfordshire	1711–1720	38.56	18.75%	10.98	9.20	23
Essex	1710/11; 1750–99	30.50	25.49%	33.58	32.41	214
Staffordshire	1710/11; 1750–99	25.03	60.00%	22.71	18.58	290
Sussex	1710–52	39.25	12.63%	46.60	39.25	101
Wiltshire	1710–60	36.91	22.42%	41.78	39.42	223
Overall average		31.57				851

Source: Per Table 5.1.

making Sussex girls the farthest travellers. Half of Bedfordshire girls left for London mistresses. Girls from Essex, however, tended to stay in Essex and 73.9 per cent of Essex girls took up millinery and mantuamaking. The key town of Colchester was the place to be, and almost half of the Essex apprentices went to milliners, mantuamakers, linen drapers and mercers in Colchester. The large firm of Lucia Reeves and Co. took thirteen, Mary Gibbon took twelve, Ann and Hannah Prior had ten, as well as a myriad of smaller firms.[34] Only Katherine Franklin in Lowlayton with eight apprentices competed. The importance of reputation to families and daughters in making this decision was significant. Virtually no girls from Wiltshire went to London, but the town of Devizes was a pull for many girls while Marlborough and Salisbury drew several. No millinery firm had the clout that those in Essex did, and the premiums they charged were significantly less. Staffordshire girls were the most likely to stay in the county, probably due to good local opportunities. Obviously, it is the farthest from London, but the towns that attracted them were the cathedral and literary town of Lichfield, Newcastle-under-Lyme in the potteries, and Wolverhampton in the Black Country. Several millinery and mantuamaking firms were active in Lichfield and Newcastle, but the most prominent were Dorothy Anslow and Phoebe Moreton in Wolverhampton who took thirteen apprentices between them at the end of the century. As with the terms girls served and the premiums their families paid, the distances girls in mantuamaking or millinery travelled differed, underscoring the importance of travelling for a profession. Milliners' girls travelled nearly fifty kilometres on average (49.32) while girls looking for a place in mantuamaking stayed closer to home, 30.32 km. This also reflects the fact that milliners were more likely to be found in the county towns and centres while even small towns had local mantuamakers.

The importance of a good trade, the respectability and presence of a well-known mistress was important in deciding to whom and where to go. One of the most prestigious mistresses of the century was Mary Gibbon, and while this is not the place to detail her career, aspects of it are significant to explain why girls would travel as far as 160 kilometres to be associated with her. She was born in Suffolk in 1713 to a middling family, of whom she was the eldest girl and shared responsibility for looking after her seven siblings. Her mother was artistic and a skilled flower painter, and two of her brothers became artists, the more successful being Thomas Gainsborough. Mary trained as a milliner in Sudbury and in 1740 married a Church of England parson, Christopher Gibbon, two years her junior. They moved to Colchester about 1741. In 1753 she began registering apprentices at the Inland Revenue, although she may have taken others earlier. Her first apprentice, Tryphosa Smith, paid £25 as a premium for training, and it was agreed that she would serve three years. This set a pattern, and she continued to train girls until she left Colchester in 1761 upon her husband's death. Her fee increased to

£30, then £31 10s; the girls signed up for terms of two and three years. Significantly, her apprentices came from far and wide, mainly from Essex but a couple from London. When she moved to Bath, she shared a house with her brother, Thomas, and her millinery business continued to flourish, indeed expand. Collaboration with Thomas enhanced her standing and her millinery fees went up reaching £90 for her final apprentice, Mary Paget, in 1773. She took some girls for significantly less, and they may have been intended as mantuamakers. It has not been possible to prove, but Sarah Gainsboro may have been family. The periods of apprenticeship for these girls in Bath also increased, averaging 4.8 years. Her reputation must have been a draw since girls came from Somerset, Worcestershire, Gloucestershire and Devon; even one from Essex went to Bath. Girls from middling families or the aspiring labouring orders who could afford a private apprenticeship, then, often had to go farther away from home to train. Many stayed in the town or village, or nearby, but not as often as parish girls. Some girls seeking training that could lead to a good occupation went significant distances, especially when seeking a well-known mistress like Frances Heberden, Lucia Reeves, Phoebe Moreton or Mary Gibbon. Others had the chance to go to London, with the opportunities a good apprenticeship might offer.

Understanding girls' experiences

Sending children to other homes for learning, work and service was a long-standing practice with the underlying expectation that the child became, at some level, part of the other family, and that he or she learned manners, patterns of behaviour, servility and skills relevant to his or her station in life. In return, adults nominally acted *in loco parentis*, with responsibility for bringing them up and training them. Of, course integration into the host family varied. For the working girl, the relationship depended on the character of the placement and the nature of the home and personalities where she went. Parish apprentices could be absorbed, especially those sent to their kin. Others were virtually foisted onto ratepayers and their experience was less likely to be amicable. Girls whose families paid for their apprenticeship may have had a better hold on watching over their care, but many went significant distances. We have only glimpses into this world from the traces girls left behind. Apprenticeship, service and hiring agreements were based on the ideal that a girl would serve her full time and leave at completion, with her new clothes and armed for the world of work. For some this was probably true, or at least partly so. Girls could experience meaningful and even congenial periods in apprenticeship and service. Nevertheless, much of our information comes from poor law and court records, which inevitably concentrates on potentially dire experiences. Also, the conditions and plight of parish apprentices in factories captured the imagination of the public and has inflected our thinking about parish apprenticeship. There is no doubt that for some girls it was a horrific experience, involving physical and sexual abuse, hardship and deprivation. What is more difficult is to uncover the normative experience of girls as they traversed this part of girlhood.

Girls whose parents paid for them, especially amongst the middling sort, almost inevitably had a better experience and were more likely to have family or 'friends' to support them than poor girls, parish apprentices and orphans. Also, not all would have physically left home, while more and more stayed at home going to the shop daily. Mary and Sarah Wood from Kelvedon, or Charlotte Hossack from Hadleigh, both about 20 km from Colchester, were within a four-hour walk of home and came from families who were likely to support them. The fact that Sarah was apprenticed to Lucia Reeve in in 1760, followed by her sister in 1761, suggests all was well with the apprenticeship. Indeed, both later went into partnership with the Reeves. Charlotte Hossack was the daughter of Colin Hossack, who had been private physician to Fredrick, Prince of Wales, the father of George III. Dr Hossack left London when the prince died in 1751 to practice in Colchester and became a founding member of the Colchester medical society, then Mayor of Sudbury, Suffolk. These girls could expect the support of family, they had 'good' apprenticeships, not with 'hedge milliners' as described by Campbell, and their experience was likely good. Certainly, the Woods learned and used their craft upon completion. Many girls travelled significant distances and often to larger towns. Yet, they were also likely to be literate and able to write home, families had an investment in them, and often those who travelled farthest went to well-known mistresses, like Frances Heberden in Chichester or Mary Gibbon in Colchester and Bath, while there are hints that others went to family or friends of their parents.

Others apprenticed for less and with less reputable mistresses may not have had the same sort of experience. Their world was far cloudier, leaving few traces. Martha Pillah (or Pillow) had a successful apprenticeship, testifying that

> she was about 18 years of age, born of very honest Parents in Brewers-yard, in the Parish of St. Margaret, Westminster: That her Friends put her out Apprentice to a Taylor, and when the Time of her Service with him was expir'd, she work'd for herself, whose chief Business then was, the making and mending Men's Cloaths.[35]

Similarly, Margaret Stevenson reported that she had come to London quite young and 'was bound to a Seamstress in Chick-lane, with whom she serv'd the full time of her Apprentiship [sic], viz. 7 years; That she afterwards work'd for her self, and for a great while together liv'd an honest Life.'[36] Both later fell afoul of the authorities for small thefts of cloth. In rural areas, the community itself could act as a support network, and abuses were most likely noticed.

As population increased and poverty grew in the latter years of the century, officials adapted the long-serving policy in new contexts. One 'solution' was sending children to factories, and not always far from home; some Essex girls went to silk mills in Essex. Another was to place more girls outside the home parish, hoping to transfer her rights of settlement. Chelmsford practices are illustrative, but not necessarily typical. Over a third of girls stayed in Chelmsford, a bustling county town. Most went to housewifery, and a clutch to weavers in woollen trades, probably as spinners. However, these latter were from the first half of the century while bay and say making was thriving. From mid-century more girls went farther, seven to London, and even to the same master. While this suggests some connection between the parish and Aldgate especially, it also reflects a tendency to send girls farther away. Eleven per cent, in fact, were sent to cotton manufacture in Pendleton Lancashire, in 1799. While these girls were exceptional, their removal marked a new approach to apprenticing. However, none of the other parish apprenticeship data used here showed any shift in practices, with girls sent away or staying home depending on what was available.

In any case, distance was a factor in whether girls had any protection from various abuses. As Keith Snell argued with regard to the poor more generally, they

> had a strong *concept* of 'friends'; but away from home they lacked such people, and their predicament thus speaks to us about the historical functions of 'friends' in the make-up of communities. They had a notion of being absent from 'home'. There was little mention of 'neighbours', of the kind found in some parish vestry minutes, nor a language of fellow 'parishioners', in the places where they found themselves. Nor do the letters ever suggest solidarity among paupers or petitioners.[37]

As an unnamed servant from Essex wrote home in 1783, describing the workload and loneliness:

> I wish you would write a Littel ofenr for I have no body to speak to and I can not wright so often as i would because my place is so heavy and I have not time to wright I have nobody to do nothing for Me and I have not mended but three pairs of stockings since I have been at my place I hope these Lins will meat you alle in good health as I am at present bless God for it for I conclude with my duty to you my Love to brothers, sisters.[38]

Loneliness probably was not only the experience of parish girls, but they probably had fewer remedies and may have been less likely to return to families later—if they had one.

They were also vulnerable to abuse, sexual and physical, to poverty, even to death or a fragmented experience. Patrick Wallis suggests that younger apprentices especially may have been more vulnerable to exploitation and abuse within the household and workplace.[39] The receiving household could have been welcoming and helpful; equally it could have been fractured and unpleasant, since some ratepayers took apprentices grudgingly. Girls themselves could have been part of the problem, especially as they became older and more confident. They were 'adolescents' and their body rhythms and expectations could have made them difficult, saucy, angry or just plain difficult. For many it was a disjointed experience.

Parish officials probably did try to place girls with some sensitivity, and law specified that they were to be taught something.[40] In fact, some potential masters tried to refuse, saying they had nothing to teach them. However, this was less relevant for girls since simply helping around the house could be described as teaching her. Some parishioners took children for the small sum paid; sometimes the parish struggled because parents fought against placing out. Children had access to law, but this was difficult, often impossible without friends or family to support them. Some parishes did try to monitor the children they placed out, such as Walthamstow. In 1764 they 'order'd that Garrant do go twice a year to see after the Children that are put out apprentice . . . and to give the children sixpence to encourage them to be good'.[41] The Foundling Hospital also had their own follow-up scheme and indeed stopped sending children to the factories because of reports of their treatment. But these practices did not necessarily protect girls.

Justices could release children from abusive situations, but only when a complaint was brought. Sometimes the court only advised the master to use the child well in future and warned him. Until 1792, they could not punish the master or mistress, and then the *punishment* was to pay £10 to re-apprentice the child. In any situation, the master's powers were considerable, and a child might be sold on to another, let go to return home, driven away or abused.[42] The worst-case scenario was girls abused to death, or simply murdered. In 1758, Elizabeth Dickens murdered her apprentice by abusing and beating her, but she was acquitted.[43] In a letter to the *Monthly Magazine*, Catherine Cappe described a case in Greenwich in which Francis Jouveneaux had taken parish orphan girls as apprentices and had 'No less than seventeen miserable girls at one time in his power; that two who had at length made their escape, were dreadfully emaciated by want of food, and other cruel treatment; and that five had actually fallen victim to his brutality.' But she continued,

> It is not at all probable that Francis Jeveaux [sic], of whatever atrocities he may have been guilty, should have set out at first with the intention of

> treating these unhappy children in the manner he has done. That he must have always been an unprincipled character, we will readily admit, but it does not hence by any means follow that he was unnaturally cruel.

She argues that he had not taken them with the intention of destroying them, but that his 'motive, in all probability, was simply the desire of gain from the produce of their labour'. The court chastised the parish officers 'for never having given themselves the trouble to inquire what became of the unhappy victims' consigned to such misery and an early grave, although she notes that they probably did not expect him to treat them so badly.[44]

One of the most infamous cases was that of Elizabeth Brownrigg, a respected midwife who was appointed by St Dunstan's parish, London, as overseer of women and children. In this role she gained custody of several girls from the Foundling Hospital as servants. However, she proved completely unfitted to this responsibility. One of the first girls, Mary Jones, fled back to the Hospital after treatment that Helen Berry calls 'behaviour that today might be called psychopathic'. The Hospital was 'shocked at her injuries, obtained a discharge of her indentures' and required Brownrigg's husband, James, to keep her tendencies in check.[45] To no avail. Within two years the Brownriggs, husband, wife and son, were up for trial at the Old Bailey charged with mistreatment of two other foundling servants, Mary Mitchell and Mary Clifford who by June 1767 were suffering infected wounds which had no chance to heal. Suspicious neighbours finally called on the Hospital to investigate, and found Mitchell, but not Clifford, who was later found in a cellar. In August 1767, they were indicted

> being moved by the instigation of the devil, did wickedly, maliciously, and feloniously, [from May 1766 to 4 August 1767] make an assault on Mary Clifford, spinster; that the said Elizabeth, her the said Mary, wilfully, and of malice aforethought, did make an assault, with divers large whips, canes, sticks, and staves, and did strike, beat, and whip, over the naked head, shoulders, back, and other parts of her naked body, in a cruel and in human manner, giving to her divers large wounds, swellings, and bruises; and with divers large hempen cords, and iron chains, round . . . did bind and fasten, giving her thereby a large and violent swelling on the neck of her . . . and in a certain place, under the stairs, leading into a cellar . . . did fasten and imprison; by means of which striking, whipping, binding, fastening, confining, and imprisoning her the said Mary, she did pine and languish till the 9th of August, when the said Mary did die.[46]

Mitchell testified at the trial, as did one of James's apprentices, as well as Mary Clifford's mother, detailing the horrific treatment. She was alive when her mother found her and said 'She was in a sad condition indeed, her face was swelled as big as two, her mouth was so swelled she could not shut it, and she was cut all under her throat, as if it had been with a cane, she could not speak; all her shoulders had sores all in one, she had two bits of rags upon them.'[47] Elizabeth Brownrigg was sentenced to hang and publicly dissected; the two men were reprieved, though later sentenced to six months for their treatment of Mary Mitchell.

These two cases were the dark side of apprenticeship, certainly extreme, and not alone, as indicated by the similar case of Ann Nailor, thirteen, and her sister, Mary, who were also murdered in 1762.[48] Again, the other parish apprentice Philadelphia Downley testified, and both defendants were executed. Yet they illustrate the limits of protection and girls' vulnerability. These were both London cases, and anonymity was more probable in the large urban setting. Nevertheless, abuse and disruption crossed the urban rural divide. Peter Rushton's study of quarter session records of northeast England show that both servants and masters took to the courts to address disputes. He found that in the minority of cases brought against servants,

> masters complained that their servants were leaving without permission in nearly half of the cases [which] suggests that there was no inherent desire to rid themselves of their workforce. . . . In cases against apprentices, too, masters pursued deserters, with only a few other problems of any concern to them. More than three quarters of the cases complain of desertion, suggesting that in many instances masters were determined to keep to the original bargain.[49]

More than a fifth of the suits brought by servants (10 per cent of the whole) involved physical abuse, but more than a third concerned unpaid wages.[50]

There was also the shadow danger that girls were subjected to sexual abuse. As Sarah Toulalan argues, those accused of raping servants and apprentices were often 'older and in positions of authority over them, as a master or master's son, or men with who their master did business or was otherwise acquainted', and many were young and 'around 20 per cent of rape and sexual assault trials reported from the Old Bailey in London between 1674 and 1799 involved girls identified as between twelve and twenty.'[51] The situation of Jane Scott and Susanna Prouton, both servants, was certainly not unusual. Jane was 'pregnant of a bastard child or children, which was unlawfully begotten on her body by one George Adlam', who lived in her master's house, while Susanna was similarly pregnant by a lodger in her master's house.[52] Certainly working girls were often vulnerable, but the power relations in another's household especially left girls open to sexual abuse which is developed in Chapters 10 and 11.

Conclusion

Apprenticeship was not intended as solely industrial training for either sex. Passing on values and behaviour from one generation to the next was a significant component. Apprenticeship also may have promoted girls' mobility, because training or 'finishing' in a respectable female trade could enhance their social position, since emulation was an important feature of the initiation to adulthood. Frequently, non-pauper girls were apprenticed to trades which they probably never carried out. Girls apprenticed to farmers, mercers, drapers or even housewifery with large premiums suggest that 'finishing' or transmitting values and behaviour may have been a significant part of their education. Aspiring females, whose families could afford the premium, may have seen such apprenticeships as a means of improving their status and prospects, possibly with an eye to marriage within the trade or at least the social group. Across service, apprenticeship and the early years of work, learning remained a crucial element in girlhood, when they learned skills, behaviours and social values. These activities were themselves important aspects of the socialisation and transitions marking the years between childhood and adulthood.

Notes

1 The data in this chapter on Essex and Staffordshire comes from Simonton, *Education and Training*, chapter 5.
2 For the relationship between service and apprenticeship see Kussmaul, *Servants in Husbandry*, 4. For contractual elements of domestic service, see Hecht, *Domestic Servant*, especially 72–4. For legal definitions see Blackstone, *Commentaries*, 1, 425–7.
3 BDRO 61/7/12. See Wallis, 'Between Apprenticeship and Skill', 159, 168 and Wallis, Webb and Minns, 'Leaving Home and Entering Service', 24.
4 Gowing, *Ingenious Trade*, 1.
5 Dale, *Wiltshire Apprentices and their Masters*, xv. Simonton, *Education and Training*, 237, Rice, *Sussex Apprentices*.
6 Simonton, *Education and Training*; Snell, *Annals of the Labouring Poor*, 282.
7 In conversation, Joan Lane estimated under-registration to have been about 25 per cent in areas she knew well.
8 Crowston, *Fabricating Women*, 408–9.
9 Hecht, *The Domestic Servant*, 62.
10 Simonton, *Education and Training*, chapter 5, and Appendices.
11 See, Pullin, 'Business is Just Life'.
12 Erickson, 'Eleanor Mosley', 151.
13 Campbell, *The London Tradesman*, 208.
14 Campbell, *The London Tradesman*, 336, 208.
15 Collyer, *Parents' and Guardians' Directory*, 195.
16 *The Book of Trades*, 227.
17 *The Book of Trades*.
18 *Ipswich Journal*, 10 April 1777, 17 May 1777, and D'Cruze, *Colchester People*.
19 Campbell, *London Tradesman*, 208.

20 Campbell, *London Tradesman*, 209.
21 Campbell, *London Tradesman*, 195.
22 Campbell, *London Tradesman*, 195.
23 Phillips, *Women in Business,* 220.
24 BDRO 61/7/8.
25 'Hackney Petty Sessions Book: 1734 (No. 650)', 117–29.
26 There was no significant difference between the first and second half of the century.
27 SRO, D1054/7/20, D120/A/PO/1264-1400, D120/A/PO/1700–1750.
28 SRO, D 805/3/9.
29 Marshall, *English Poor*, 193–7; George, *London Life*, 229–34.
30 Levene, 'Parish Apprenticeship and the Old Poor Law', 917.
31 Marshall, English Poor, 194.
32 Trimmer, *Oeconomy of Charity*, 11–5; Cappe, *Observations on Charity Schools*, 19–20, 42–8.
33 Honeyman, *Child Workers in England, 1780–1820.*
34 See Simonton, 'Sister to the Tailor'; and 'Milliners and Marchandes de Modes'.
35 *OBP, Ordinary of Newgate's Account*, May 1717 (OA17170520).
36 *OBP, Ordinary of Newgate's Account*, July 1714 (OA17140716).
37 Snell, 'Belonging and Community', 22.
38 ERO D/P 245/18/6.
39 Wallis, Webb and Minns, 'Leaving Home', 23.
40 See, Honeyman, *Child Workers*, chapter 11, especially, 215.
41 Barnes, *Walthamstow in the Eighteenth Century*, 7.
42 See Pinchbeck and Hewitt, *Children in English Society*, 228–51.
43 George, *London Life*, 231.
44 Cappe, 'On Parish Apprentices', 7–8.
45 Berry, *Orphans of Empire*, 226.
46 *OBP*, September 1767, t17670909–1.
47 *OBP*, September 1767, t17670909–1.
48 *OBP*, July 1762, t17620714–30.
49 Rushton, 'The Matter in Variance', 94.
50 Rushton, 'The Matter in Variance', 95.
51 Toulalan, *Gender, Sexuality and the Body*, 127.
52 Chelsea Settlement and Bastardy Examinations, nos. 161, 162, 169, 249, 250.

6

MAKING A LIVING

Options and choices

When girls went to work, whether from home, school or apprenticeship, several factors shaped and potentially constrained their choices. For most, an income was both essential and desirable. They would also have taken it for granted that working was the next step in their journey. For some it was seen as a stepping stone to marriage and motherhood; for others it was simply what they expected to do. Parents, or officialdom, may have pressured them, but it was also 'natural' in their worlds. Even many middling girls would have accepted it as a normal part of their girlhood, regardless of their expectations of adulthood. They had choices, perhaps limited for most; but within a range of expectations they had options. Girls' work remained transitional. They were still learning and gaining know-how and their skills and abilities—and expectations—were age- and experience-dependent. Their place in the lifecycle affected the places and kinds of work they did. There are also indications that this was a period associated with anxiety and risk. Kitteridge notes 'The didactic texts written for late eighteenth-century labouring-class 15-year-olds depict young people who have similar feelings of anxiety and who struggle with the complications of making their way in the adult world for the first time.'[1] These are the issues that inform this chapter.

Poverty was a common experience amongst working people and, in agricultural districts, became acute in the last quarter of the century. Thus, there was an urgent need for all to contribute to the household, either directly by supplying labour at home or by leaving and earning elsewhere. The young made up the majority of the population, and therefore they had to earn their keep. Family strategies included juggling the labour needs of the household,

DOI: 10.4324/9781003412168-7

balancing between keeping some youthful workers at home whose labour and skills were more important to the family workload, and sending those away that they could not provide work for and whose income was an asset. Thus, girls might be kept at home as spinners and worked at preparing the yarn for weaving, whereas a surplus of boys might mean sending them away. In dairying districts, girls might leave as dairymaids while their brothers worked on the family plot. As Honeyman pointed out, 'the extent to which children were divided by gender depended on their age and availability. In much contemporary discussion of children workers, certainly before the 1830s, their sex was rarely specified . . . The textile factories established in the 1780s and 1790s were based on new ways of working, with no precedent in terms of the gender division of labour.'[2] As they moved into girlhood this became less true, and girls and youths were increasingly identified with adult roles if not with the experience or ability of adults. Other reasons than juggling the common pot also led some girls to choose to leave. For example, thirteen-year-old Mary Marsland left after being raped by her father.[3] Others saw leaving home more positively, such as offering opportunities which might open new avenues and connections, perhaps enhancing their marriage and dowry prospects, or giving them the chance of a lifelong living. Some went into service because they needed accommodation and work, often using service as a stepping stone from country to town. Many girls would marry, and they took their skills with them into marriages, so industrial, agricultural and marketing skills all offered them a wider range of choices. However, dowry accumulation could be difficult in the vulnerable world of the eighteenth century.

Learning on the job

Going to work, girls did not leave learning behind, and they continued to learn on the job. Service especially was a training ground, a space for acquiring job-related skills as well as social values and behaviours. It aimed primarily to create workers, so that girls became more experienced and skilled, and probably enhanced their chances of better positions and occupational advancement. At eight years old, Margaret Wootton of Pelsall, Staffordshire, was sent to a wheelwright who was her uncle to learn housewifery 'and to serve in the manner of a servant and apprentice' until eighteen.[4] The first three years she was a 'covenant servant' and an apprentice for the last seven years. These situations could mirror the experience of girls who learned at home, working alongside mothers and others in the family. They also had a window into how to improve their chances and recognise some of the pitfalls, and began to see how they could make choices within the worlds of service and other workplaces. Learning comprised prescriptive instruction, experience and emulation. The learning that went on depended on the nature and requisites of the household as well as a girl's position within it. Most girls were probably the only servant in the household or one of few, and thus their experiences focused on the tasks at hand, and relatively little occupational improvement was available to most. Usually moving on to another position opened the door to better chances.

They certainly absorbed what they would need as adults including the ways things were done, the behaviours and manners expected, and they gained an understanding of how workplaces and hierarchies worked. Especially in larger households, hierarchies mattered. The principal distinction was between upper servants, whose work was mainly supervisory and demanded long experience and frequently specialised training, and lower servants, whose work was directed by others and was relatively unskilled and manual in nature. A girl's upward movement in this hierarchy depended primarily on her experience and emulation of those above her. Certain positions, such as chambermaid, housemaid and lower women servants, required few skills to start, and usually built upon knowledge gained at home. Although the work of the laundry or dairymaid was more specialised, contemporaries believed that it too was easily acquired and lay within what a girl frequently would have been brought up to.[5] Experience was valued as a teaching agent, and the work practices of a household had to be acquired in addition to the mechanics of a task. Defoe acknowledged its importance when he advised on setting servants' wages: '[A] young inexperienced servant should have forty shillings per annum, til she qualifies herself for a larger sum; a servant who can do all household work . . . should have four pounds per annum; and those who have lived seven years in one service should ever after demand five pounds per annum.'[6]

Servants could also be learning skills which were not strictly occupationally relevant, like reading and writing. Perceptions of the poor girl as a servant can lead us astray. Like apprentices, servants were drawn from throughout the social hierarchy from the gentry down. It was not unusual for governesses, lady's maids and housekeepers to be the daughters of clerics, widows and unprovided-for daughters. In these instances, the disparity between servant and mistress was not very great and could encourage a relatively close relationship in which the employer might have taken an interest in improving the servant's prospects. Hester Thrale described educating Laura Carter, in 1764:

> I taught her to read myself and taught her her prayers, her Catechisms, etc. Sent her out to learn washing—ironing Lacemending, clearstarching and such like, paid a Master to instruct her in Writing & then took her into my nursery—to complete her Education.[7]

Similarly, Nancy Bere was taken from the poorhouse by the Hackmans of Lymington to weed their garden. They moved her to the kitchen, and eventually to lady's maid, after Mrs Hackman 'had her carefully instructed in all the elementary branches of education'.[8] Several servants were sent to school by their masters and mistresses whilst others were taught by their employers or other servants.[9] Although literary fiction, Samuel Richardson has Pamela say at the beginning of his novel: '[A]s my lady's goodness had put me to write and cast accounts, and made me a little expert at my needle, and otherwise qualified above my degree, it was not every family that could have found a place that your poor Pamela was fit for.'[10] It is not clear how typical the learning of letters in service was, but larger households almost certainly contained upper servants able to read and write, who could have taught others. Contemporary comment also attests to servants emulating the reading habits of employers. Jonas Hanway gave 'as proof of how servants imitate their master or mistress' that he had often 'seen on the kitchen dresser, volumes of fictitious tales'.[11] Others refer to servants borrowing books or sharing the household newspapers and periodicals. A handful of 'literary domestics', including Anne Yearsley, Elizabeth Hands, Mary Leapor and Mary Collier, illustrate the possibilities.[12]

Emulation of employers and other servants served to coach the willing girl in dress, speech, manners and expectations. Dumb waiters were adopted at the end of the century to exclude eavesdropping servants. Employers encouraged a certain level of emulation in dress, cleanliness and manners, because it reflected favourably on their household. At the same time, many recognised their responsibility for supplying moral example and regulation of the household. Defoe emphasised the central role of master and mistress in ensuring good government and moral behaviour within the family arguing that their failure led to bad servants. They had a duty to instruct and improve their servants, to see that the Lord's Day was properly observed, and that servants attended family prayers.[13] So by prescriptive instruction, emulation and the forge of experience, girls in service learned the requisite skills and values.

Farm service similarly prepared girls for adulthood although the body of knowledge was largely occupational. Agricultural tasks, from the fields to the dairy, would have been acquired early since farm servants usually came from agrarian homes, and rural parish apprentices often went to farming families in the neighbourhood. Imitation and experience would have been the means of developing more sophisticated skills and techniques, supplemented by demonstration and instruction when necessary. In a rural community farm service generally concentrated on the 15–24 age group: 'They left their parents as children and departed from service as adults,' during that time getting the skills needed to be farmers themselves. In her detailed study of farm servants, Kussmaul identified a hierarchical order like that in domestic service, in which upward mobility meant moving to a more responsible position, or to a larger or better-run farm. *The Commercial and Agricultural Magazine* underlined the importance of this learning, counselling young people to move from place to place to learn a wide variety of farming techniques in a variety of geographical settings.[14] Farm service was less likely than domestic service to provide the opportunity for girls to learn to read or write, except in the communal spirit of a household once work was finished for the day. Most evidence suggests that literacy was lowest amongst labourers so that there would have been fewer persons in this cultural milieu who could have taught them.[15] It was amongst the people of rural England that the oral tradition remained strongest, and certainly learning was at its most informal.

Contemporaries expected young workers to imitate their superiors and gain experience, and they recognised this as a useful and important instrument of learning. Where it was perceived as necessary, or possible, girls got specific training in work-related practices ranging from mechanical skills to business practices, accounts and organisation. In the pottery industry, women were found in processes carrying out fine work and as shopkeepers marketing the goods, each needing knowledge fitted to the position. Women in other industries and trades would have had similar needs, and much of their knowledge would have been gained as girls. Defoe's emphasis on learning for work speaks to what was expected of girls. He envisaged that women who married traders needed the skills to support their husbands and to take over businesses if necessary.[16] Josiah Wedgwood's pottery works provide a good example of the training which took place at work. His introduction of specialisation and division of labour meant that each worker needed to become expert in one stage or process, and as new designs and glazes were developed and techniques refined, training was essential. Wedgwood used both apprenticed and hired labour, but in both instances provided training. Children were brought into the works, trained, and as they grew up and gained experience, moved into adult processes as skilled workers. Some of his hiring agreements, such as Ann Keeling's of 1781, are very similar to apprenticeship in that Wedgwood promised to feed, clothe and house her and paid wages of £3, £4 and £5 for the three years. Thus, apprenticeships could turn into regular employment, and indeed some hiring agreements blurred the distinction, like Keeling's. On completion of her training, in 1784 she was paid 15s a week, the piece rate for journeymen painters, while the works regularly trained girls to paint.[17]

Many girls gained experience and 'training' through hirings. For example, around 1716, Rachel Herbert was born in Buckingham, but her parents seemed to have separated, and she moved to London with her father. At the age of ten she was sent to a Mrs Clare Bates in the parish of St Clement Danes to learn sewing in exchange for her labour. She was not formally apprenticed, though her situation mimicked the experience of many parish girls. She stayed with Mrs Bates for three years, but lived with her father, who provided 'washing lodging board and clothes' at his room in Essex Street, in St Clement Danes.[18] Settlement examinations from Harborne, Warwickshire, and Northfield, Worcestershire, illustrate how apprenticeship could become a series of hirings or how a hiring could turn into apprenticeship.[19] Often parish apprentices completed their terms and simply stayed with the family afterwards. For example, in 1746, Anne Piper, about thirteen, was bound by Chelsea parish to a milk woman in Westminster, Mary Perry. She stayed until her mistress died about a year later but continued with her daughters at the same house in Charles Street, Westminster.[20] Some girls had virtual apprenticeships at home. Elin Stout helped her brother at market days and fairs, learned to serve retail customers 'as a young apprentice would have done'. Another young woman was a 'dutiful assistant to her mother' and in adulthood managed a milliner's shop on her own.[21]

Characterising service

Live-in service appeared to be the largest employer of girls, although it was construed and operated differently in each setting: domestic, farming and industrial. Contemporary usage was highly variable, and the term 'service' described a range of types and forms of employment. As Carolyn Steedman argued, 'Service', in fact, described the *activity* of serving rather than the *position* as 'servant' and was understood in that way in legal terminology and practice so that it was not what you *called* your employee that counted, but rather, what he *did*.[22] Yet service was consistent in that girls were subordinate and dependent workers, often in a household, or at least in a community of workers like themselves. It was a common experience for girls, and Bridget Hill estimated one in eleven girls were waged domestic servants, as were up to one in five in London. Wall says 28.5 per cent of households between 1574 and 1821 had servants. Steedman argues that the agreement to serve in a domestic capacity and the contract between man or maid and master or mistress (the moment of hiring) constituted the most common labour agreement of the later eighteenth century.[23]

Girls at home were virtually servants to the family, assisting and providing for household needs including childcare, cleaning, preparing food and laundering. When the family was engaged in agriculture, they helped on family plots, especially cottage gardens, but also as extra labour in haying and harvest. They often had a particular responsibility helping with animals in the farmyard, milking cows, feeding fowl and pigs and generally looking after their needs. Thus, they also assisted in the slaughter when the time came. The house and farmyard were understood as explicitly female spaces and female responsibilities, and in this rural world, building this repertoire of skills and knowledge were key to knowing how to run one's own home. They also supplied the know-how should the girl leave to work on another farm as a servant. In families which had lost the mother or other female adults, girls stepped into the void.

For many girls, service was an interim stage between rural roots and adulthood. For example, in Ardleigh, Essex in 1796, 29 per cent of girls aged fifteen to twenty were servants, but only 19 per cent and 10 per cent in the two successive age groups were servants.[24] For others it became a permanent job. The prevalence of service as a route through girlhood, whether farm, domestic or industrial, was significant to many girls given its strong association with women's place and its association as a phase in girls' lives. The normative story is of a lifecycle stage used to build up the financial wherewithal to set up house. As such it was central to the way youth or girlhood was traversed, and studies of adolescent years rightly emphasise the importance of service. This representation has been inherited by historians from the work of Peter Laslett, who wrote in 1977 that 'Western servants . . . were to a very large extent, young, unmarried persons—indeed sexually mature persons waiting to be married.'[25] This was the role cast for girls, who would expect the end of service and the beginning of marriage and the formation of their own household to coincide. Kussmaul found that 42 per cent of farm servants married immediately upon leaving service, for example, but Meldrum recorded only 7 per cent leaving upon marriage—though others may have married shortly after.[26] Yet, significant numbers of women did not marry or did not give up service, making a career of it, becoming part of the family, often remembered in wills. Margaret Rogers, a single woman of about twenty-eight years old of Chelsea testified

> that about five or six years ago she lived with the late Lady Catherine Jones at Chelsea aforesaid at several times in the space of six years (but not as a hired servant). And says that about three years ago she . . . lived a hired servant by the year with the then Right Honourable Sir Robert Walpole (now Lord Orford) in the station of laundry maid, and afterwards upper house maid. Where she continued for the space of two years and received her full wages for the said time at the rate of £6 per annum when laundry maid, and £7 per annum when house maid, meat, drink, washing and lodging.[27]

Rural service

Girls who went to rural service found work through word of mouth or hiring fairs, or at hiring statutes, though in the west of England, Marshall reported that they went from door to door.[28] This was not intended to be permanent work, and hirings were normally one year—but could be less, sometimes more, sometimes undefined. In Stirlingshire, 'Some of them, contented with their lot, stayed for longer: it was not unknown for a maid to stay in one situation for the rest of her life, and even to drop her own surname and go by the name of her employer.'[29] Sometimes the hiring was formalised, but it could be verbal and casual. Kussmaul shows that they did not typically travel far from home. Figures from Hertfordshire, Lincolnshire and Suffolk show that the average distance female servants travelled was 11 km (males 12).[30] Female day-labourers were far more likely to be married women with responsibilities on their own plot and house while live-in servants were more often girls between thirteen and twenty-four, although there was some overlap between the two.

They tended to live with a family on a small farm, eating with them and often socialising with them. They were usually well-fed and looked after, especially since undernourished servants were of little use, and cared-for servants were more likely to renew contracts. The work could be hard. For example: 'The dairymaid must be up every morning by four o'clock, or she will be backward in her business. At six, the cows must be milked, and there must be milkers enough to finish by seven. The same rule must be observed in the evening.'[31] Blackstone specified that 'The servant shall serve, and the master maintain him [sic], throughout all the revolutions of the respective seasons; as well when there is work to be done, as when there is not'[32] (Image 6.1). So when weather or other circumstance meant they could not do farm work,

IMAGE 6.1 George Stubbs, 1724–1806, Hay-Makers, 1791. Stipple engraving, second state, Yale Center for British Art, Paul Mellon Collection, B1985.36.1098.

girls moved to work in the house, and not uncommonly this might be industrial work; as one job description noted, 'when she has done her worke [sic] she sits down to spin.'[33] The distinction between farm and domestic service was long a false one, and 'the maidservant, for whom the kitchen door was the most permeable of boundaries, and who was likely to clean the house, cook the dinner, plant beans in the kitchen garden and milk a cow as part of a day's work.'[34] In 1723, Judith Carpenter

> 'used to do all manner of work as a servant, as in the time of Harvest she used to go every Day with the Tith Cart into the fields, to rake after the Cart, and at other times used to do all the common business of the house, as looking after the Dairy, dressing fowls for market, and if the business of the house was done she used to spin.' she also used to help dress the children of the household and to have taken them to school, 'attending on them as a servant and carrying their victuals'.[35]

Yet Sharpe argues that in Essex, and probably in other areas of capitalist agriculture where farm sizes were large, indoor and outdoor service was largely well defined.[36] Sleeping arrangements are difficult to determine. On smaller farms, there were rarely separate rooms allocated to them. Kussmaul suggests that while sons and male servants slept together, daughters and maids did not.[37] On larger farms, servants slept in outbuildings and lofts.

Rural work could also be peripatetic, like girls from the Scottish Highlands who travelled to the lowlands in summer. There is considerable debate among historians as to how much farm work was available to girls because of a perceived decline in opportunities, especially after mid-century, when population increases made more workers available. Sharpe argues that the demand for female labour was limited anyway, as does Peter Mathias, who said 'the unusual thing is that women's role in agriculture was so limited in England'.[38] Young however showed that on farms he visited in the north of England circa 1770 servants virtually matched the number of hired labourers.[39] Kussmaul, drawing on settlement exams that mentioned service, found that 44.4 per cent had been farm servants, possibly more since several did not specify the kind of service. So, she concludes they were a strong presence in English agriculture during the century.[40]

Significantly new farming practices probably affected single girls differently from their married counterparts, servants differently from day-labourers. Using settlement exams, Snell made an influential claim that female work in predominantly arable counties in the east of England became more limited and less well paid as the century advanced. Sharpe contested his interpretation showing the availability of farm work for female *day-labourers* in farm estate accounts in Essex altered little during the century.[41] However, the need for servant girls varied by region and type of agriculture. Their labour was in demand in pastoral areas which concentrated on dairying, which required permanent skilled workers. It was considered women's work, so female live-in dairymaids were in demand in areas like southwest Scotland and Cheshire and Wiltshire in England where dairying predominated. As a skilled craft, it often involved passing on skills and 'mysteries' associated with it from mother to daughter. It was also considered the most arduous work of the farm, and some commented that general maidservants on farms did much less arable agricultural work.[42] While wives and daughters made up the bulk of the workforce on smaller farms, larger commercial farms hired specialist dairymaids: 'In Aylesbury Vale, there are great Dairies carried on, that employ considerable numbers of these useful Females, who, if rightly chosen, commonly provide more hardy, more strong, and more diligent than our Country Wenches [in Hertfordshire], that are brought up more tenderly, and more unskilful in the Business of Husbandry'.[7] In 1737, Elizabeth Purefoy wrote to William Holloway looking for

> a faithful sober understanding girl to manage my Dairy and to help some other things in ye house that I shall set her about, particularly to help wash in washing time. I keep two maids besides, and she must go to the market to make the best of my Dairy . . . pray don't let mee [sic] have any raw girl that don't well understand making butter and cheese.[8]

In other areas of the country where population was growing more slowly, notably Scotland and Northumberland, farmers needed to secure and tie workers to the farm. Thus, live-in service continued longer in the north. This was especially true on small and medium-sized farms, where girls had to be versatile. They were Scottish 'in and out girls' who were expected to do housework, work with cows and take part in fieldwork. Often farmers required a man to bring a woman with him when he went into farm service. In Northumberland, 'They each had to provide a woman to do certain work, e.g. weeding and haymaking, at fixed wages; and when corn was threshed . . . a woman must be there to see to the winnowing of the grain.'[43] So, single men might bring sisters, nieces, cousins or simply other females with them to a tenancy. Furthermore, other factors were at play, and the prevalence of alternative, often more profitable, work drew girls away from farm service. In Marton, Westmorland, David Davies commented in 1795: 'There is no kind of manufactory carried on in this neighbourhood, for which reason women and children earn little, except in hay and corn harvest.'[44] Sharpe also notes that

> 'Spring' unemployment would have been alleviated in many of the south-eastern counties by the development of London-based fashion trades and services with their production closely related to the London

> Season. [and] fashion industries created work for women in the countryside, such as lace-making and straw-plaiting, which pulled women away from service or farm work.[45]

Thus, young women increasingly turned their backs on farming for 'better' jobs in domestic service or in crafts and trades.

Nevertheless, full-time permanent work did become less viable, and fewer and fewer servants were needed as farmers turned to day labourers. Farmers had to balance the cost of feeding and housing servants against the need for permanent labour. The effect on girls was more pronounced than on boys, since males hung on to most of the permanent work. Also, service, like apprenticeship, could gain a girl a right of settlement in a parish if she stayed a year, the traditional hiring period. As the poor rates grew alongside increasing rural poverty, parish officials could pressure farmers to release girls early, or to hire them for shorter periods. The farmer who hired Ann Preece in the early part of the century let her go a few days short of her year, explaining 'she could not stay longer, for it would not be safe for the parish for her to continue there'. She was paid off with full wages and sent away.[46]

Domestic service

Echoing the values of British society that increasingly valorised domestic virtues, service was the ideal position for a girl to obtain and a central theme of her education and upbringing. Girls might find places locally, but others travelled some twenty or thirty miles, perhaps to large county towns or further afield, such as from Dublin to London. Most used well-travelled routes, building on contacts with friends and family, often moving from countryside to town from the urban hinterlands. Mistresses preferred them to city dwellers who were seen as less malleable, and urban dwellers struggled to find servants because city girls found other work. For example, 30.8 per cent of London servants were from the southeast of England.[47] Mistresses looking for servants went to coaching inns to meet young women from the country, and some large cities organised a system of licensed agents, usually women, to bring them to town. It was also common for girls to begin in a country home and move to town with their employers like Sarah Weston from Bocking (Essex) who hired herself to two spinsters with homes in Black Notley and Marylebone.[48] The demand for, as well as the supply of, household servants increased substantially in the second half of the century. This added an increasing level of choice for girls, and while some continued to do non-household tasks, domestic service became a favoured opportunity for many girls. We have seen how schools and didactic literature promoted service as appropriate for girls, while the destinations for girls leaving schools demonstrated a significant increase. Housewifery was also the single most popular apprentice trade, though as we have seen, it was something of a catch-all, representing what society expected. Thus, there was a perceived insufficiency of housemaids, and many girls aspired to gain the higher positions, for which there was more competition. Sir John Fielding explained that despite the large number of unemployed servants, 'the useful housewifery servant, commonly called maids of all work, are not sufficiently numerous to supply the wants of the families in town.'[49] Despite various servant taxes, which were readily avoided, most estimates of the number of servants remain just that, estimates; but to people of the eighteenth century, they were seen as a numerous class of worker.

Housemaids like farm servants required few skills to start, since they usually built on knowledge gained at home. Though in 1764 when Hester Thrale promised Laura Carter's father to find her a place, she found 'that she could neither read, nor write, nor work, nor wash, I found no body would be plagued with her but myself'.[50] Most servant girls were 'maids of all work', responsible for an onerous burden of cleaning, scouring irons and pewter, cooking, ironing and general housework, though for some tasks extra help was hired, such as for laundry. For example, 56 per cent of households in one London sample had only one; a further 21 per cent had two. In Aberdeen, a city of about 20,000 in 1785–86, 670 households paid 'inhabited house tax' and 618 had servants. Of these, 496 were the only female servant in the house, and the remaining (122) were one of only two. No household registered more than two.[51] In Shrewsbury, Kendal and Doncaster, Steedman found 47, 54 and 61 per cent as servants in single-servant households.[52]

Often, they worked alongside mistresses, but dirtier and heavier tasks always fell to maids, so they carried heavy loads of wood, coal and laundry, emptied and washed chamber pots, and boiled clothes, menstrual rags, diapers and sheets (Image 6.2). Servants could provide personal service to family members and look after children, and, if they had time at the end of the day, they could be expected to sew, spin or knit. The variety and blurred boundaries of the work were also apparent. Few servants serviced only a household's domestic wants; many spent much of their time in industry and husbandry. Their time was constrained and leisure time restricted since, as Susannah Whatman explained, 'A servant is not to go out without leave.'[53] She also set timetables and insisted on going to bed early because they had to be up early.

The relationship to household members varied, of course, and their experience of service depended on numerous factors, including the wealth of the household, its geographic location and the work expected. Certainly, some servants were treated well and became close to the family, like Susan O'Brien's maids Hannah Borgi and Edith Shears who were left annuities. The relationship was mutually dependent, especially with upper servants and ladies' maids, like Caroline Fox's maid Milward, who 'wrote letters for Caroline and read to her, she managed the household when her mistress was in

IMAGE 6.2 Richard Houston, ca. 1721–1775, Domestic Employment: Washing, undated. Yale Center for British Art, Paul Mellon Collection, B1977.14.11953.

Bath, and she was often left with the children when their mother was away'.[54] Nevertheless, Caroline threw a fit when Milward married (another servant) without her permission. She also mourned a servant who had been with her forty years when she died in 1797, as a 'true and faithful servant of the old sort', but she continued, 'not now to be met with'.[55] Smaller households may have been less formal and the working relationship closer if not necessarily cordial.

Most mistresses had their own clear ideas of the tasks they wanted to be done and how to do them, especially in larger establishments. They could be very detailed in their instructions, some writing handbooks for the household, and could be especially piqued when they were not followed. In the first part of the century, Scotswoman and mistress of Mellerstain House in the Scottish Borders, Grisell Baillie, directed her housekeeper to watch over the servants:

> Keep the maids closs at their spining till 9 at night when they are not washing or at other necessary work weight out to them exactly the soap, and

> often go to the wash house to see it is not wasted but made the proper use of, and that there be no linnen washt there but those of the family that are alowed to do it. Often see that they waste not fire either in the wash house or Landry and that the Landry be keept clean. [language correct][56]

Whatman instructed servants to leave a hand space between furniture since the plaster will come off if the wall were hit; she meticulously told them when the sun came into each room and how to protect the furniture, using blinds, etc. She laid out which jobs were to be done on which day—and by whom. Servants were not to dust anything with a gilt edge, and 'The books are not to be meddled with, but they may be dusted as far as a wing of a goose will go.'[57] Like Baillie, Whatman was persistently concerned that servants would cause waste. Such expectations defined girls' work and constrained their time.

In larger houses such as these, girls had a chance to improve their positions. Moving jobs was one strategy for 'getting ahead', but also learning new skills, building relationships within a household and moving up the hierarchy was a time-tested way of improving one's position. For example, the lady's maid whose work comprised personal service to the mistress held first rank among women servants followed by the housekeeper whose work was supervisory. The inferior ranks of female servants, such as the chambermaid, who cleaned rooms and prepared beds, and the other maid servants were more utilitarian. Their work centred on the actual physical maintenance of the household.

On the one hand, servants' positions were clearly inferior, dependent entirely on the families they served, subject to their vagaries and reliant on them to honour their wages. Since many employers were susceptible to downturns in trade cycles, poor harvests and other tragedies, servants were usually the first casualty of their reduced circumstances. They were also sexually vulnerable. If they complained of advances by males in the household, they were as likely to be out of a position as not, and their chances of saving for marriage were effectively thwarted. On the other, domestic service was the ideal female job, performed in private, and adhering to the feminine ideology of service and dependence.

Workers

While it is difficult to track apprentices and servants, in some ways drawing out girls as other workers is far more difficult. Largely accounts record them amongst either children or women, while the best records date from the nineteenth century and various committees and commissions on child labour. Jane Humphries's work on working-class autobiographies as well as Emma Griffin's indicate, as we would expect, that women's are much less common than men's and shed only an opaque lens on girls' industrial activities. Records like those of Wedgwood's also do not indicate what age they considered workers as girls or women. At Cromford, there is some evidence that a child worker was seen as aged seven, later ten, to fifteen. But it is rarely, if ever, defined.

Many girls stayed at home, working in family trades or protoindustries, or hired themselves out to work in the same or similar industries in which they spent their time on such tasks as hand spinning, winding bobbins for weavers, embroidering, straw plaiting and button making (Image 6.3). For example, during her girlhood while she lived at home and until she married at twenty-six, Sarah Hurst worked in her father's tailoring business, serving customers, keeping his accounts, assisting with tailoring and frequently travelling to London to restock the shop and to bank or invest the profits.[58] Textiles and the need for spinners formed a normative experience for numerous girls across Britain, preparing fibres, silk, wool or flax, spinning it into yarn for weavers, nominally male, though women and girls often took a turn. Probably, girls were most commonly spinners of thread and yarn of every sort. It was normal work in households, and girls often left home as servants

IMAGE 6.3 Spinners and Stocking Making, engraving, 1750. Wellcome Collection. Source: https://wellcomecollection.org/works/r9h5us6f.

or apprentices to spin for others. This was work that could keep them in the countryside, where a wide range of other protoindustries peppered the countryside, including lacemaking, straw plaiting, and in areas like the Black Country in the Midlands, a vast array of metalworking. But many protoindustries as well as a plethora of craft shops existed in towns and cities, whose population was swelled by young migrants of both sexes. Young described the range of work that girls could find, noting that in Knutsford in northern England, a silk mill employed children, as did a thread manufacture, and a worsted manufacturer.[59] Heywood notes

> that this early phase of development saw the 'high-water mark' of child labor during the eighteenth century in the British case. At the very least, there is plenty of evidence that child labor was 'endemic' in the early industrial economy. It is also worth emphasizing that even in a family workshop, so often romanticized by critics of the factory system, the pressure on children to produce was likely to be intense.[60]

Girls also worked on their own, in other's homes or workshops and in clusters of women who pooled their labour. Large numbers of single women worked in urban workshops, where towns created more opportunities than in the countryside. These provided ready-made food, rental accommodation and other women like themselves. Across Britain, females usually composed the majority of the urban population, many as migrants. Workshops relied on unskilled labour and especially on women and children as subcontractors and workers. Thus, significant numbers of girls operated in urban economies, often earning small incomes and a precarious living, whether working for wages or independently. Younger ones more likely became attached to households, effectively as industrial servants, whereas older ones might make their own way more successfully. In parts of Scotland, 'the income from spinning, knitting and especially the embroidering of muslins discouraged young girls from going into service, allowing them to remain at home and contribute to the family's income or to set up on their own.' *The Statistical Account* for Aberdeen, where spinning and stocking-knitting were important, noted 'while most of our [girls] remain at home, many of our young men emigrate to other places.'[61] In the second half of the eighteenth century, commercial spinning spread beyond the main weaving areas largely because better paid sources of employment for women enticed women from spinning into muslin embroidery, the bleachfields and ultimately the mills. Iain Whyte claims that relative high wages in spinning and weaving could lead to earlier independence than day labouring or service.[62] Furthermore, Berg and Sharpe were able to show that in some trades, like lacemaking, independent lives could be forged by single women.[63] However, such opportunities were probably achieved by older and more experienced workers.

On balance, income did not often provide the incentive for single women to establish separate households, but women-only households were a strategy for coping with economic necessity. In Scotland, the economic disadvantages of being single were buttressed by legal and institutional constraints. Effectively women who had never been married were not supposed to live alone or work on their own account, but in part this reflected the persistence of corporate controls so that officials attempted to restrain anyone without official privileges in Scottish society. But just as importantly, the good men wished to prevent any immorality and scandal which might arise from women living alone. Nevertheless, milliners Janet Forbes and Misses Ramsay and Mackenzie lived and worked in the same building in Aberdeen, the latter two sharing accommodation as renters from Forbes, while Janet Muschet, Cecily Murray and Ann Bucanan lived and worked together in Edinburgh (Image 6.4).[64]

Increasingly, as textile industries became mechanised and gathered in 'manufactories', girls were needed to work at spinning and later in weaving. Larger manufacturing works and early factories also hired girls, sometimes as part of family labour, other times on their own, especially older girls. Some began quite young but stayed on after marriage. They were a flexible resource,

IMAGE 6.4 The Dressmaker, *The book of trades, or, Library of the useful arts.* Part III, Vol 3, 31. Abel Dickinson, 1807.

better able to leave home to go to distant, sometime remote locations, than married women, especially ones with children. Thus, they composed most of the embryonic factory labour forces. As Berg has argued, this was a workforce that was imagined as young and female: they were also small enough to work at repairing threads, and sometimes girls found they became redundant when they got too big.[65] Although the tasks and workers in mills shifted over time, at the outset of factory development, women and children dominated the workforce. Stanley Chapman argued that 'the cotton mills of the Arkwright era typically employed about 200 to 250 people, mostly unskilled juveniles and females who proved easy to train and manage.'[66] There is little doubt that in the right localities, girls had options to choose between farm service, domestic service, and factory work. While manufactories were spread across Britain and Ireland, however, they did not always cater for the same cohort of girls. In Essex, for example, the alternative to farm service was usually domestic service since few manufactories emerged in the eighteenth century, while in areas where early factories developed, such as Cromford in Derbyshire or Penicuik at Esk Mills in Scotland, they had more options. However, at both sites it was necessary to build housing to attract and house workers, so both daughters and wives were hired to spin.

The linen industry is a useful case study because it utilised various systems of protoindustry, was among the first and most important of the mills in Scotland and provided work for large numbers of women. The development of the water-powered twist mill at Paisley in the 1720s was an important step and one advertised in 1762 claimed it was '"capable of turning not less than 2,000 spindles in a year (which when fully manufactured is worth £500)", and required "only one girl, instead of strong women, to perform two-thirds more work with an easier motion".'[67] Not surprisingly yarn spinning was female-dominated, and in Edinburgh thirty-four mistresses and forty apprentices and servants continued using the hand twist mill. In Aberdeen in 1767 no fewer than twelve thread and bleaching companies existed. Some mistresses and companies hired their own spinners to ensure the quality they needed for profitable sales.

Girls also worked in shops, small workshops and larger works like Wedgwood's. Technology may have been a factor in textile works, as Berg suggested, since the water frame relied explicitly on girls' labour. Similarly, in other industries they were taken on because of the suppleness of their fingers, and they were thought to learn more easily. Wedgwood employed girls to paint on biscuit, but 'they also paint upon the glaze and after the second dipping. They work with camel hair pencil in painting patterns upon the ware, sitting at the table.'[68] Of 220 workers in 1790 at Etruria and 450 by 1810, roughly a third were female. Of 135 'children' at least 35 were girls, (some names are unclear). A further 100 were 'women', but there is no indication of ages.[69] Berg argues persuasively that the early industrial labour force was overwhelmingly female, and not only in textiles, but also in metal trades, potteries and even coalmining:

> It is evident in Britain that women and children were simply assumed to be the key workforce to be targeted with any novelty in manufacturing methods. Machines and processes were invented with this workforce in mind. New techniques in calico printing and spinning provide classic examples of experimentation on a child and female workforce. In calico printing, processes were broken down into a series of operations performed particularly well by teenage girls who contributed manual dexterity (learned at home) with high labour intensity. The spinning jenny was first invented for use by a young girl, its horizontal wheel making it uncomfortable for an adult worker to use for any length of time. . . . Thus when we talk of industry in the eighteenth and early nineteenth centuries, we are talking of a largely female workforce.[70]

Honeyman claimed that many factory owners preferred girls as workers and 55 per cent of her parish factory apprentices were girls; eighteen of the fifty-seven firms preferred girls, sixteen preferred boys, and the remaining twenty-three were apparently indifferent. Richard Arkwright advertised for cheerful girls and his associate, Samuel Oldknow confined his search to female apprentices: 'I will thank you to inform me . . . whether it would be compatible with your engagement there to procure for me 40 or 50 females from 8–12 years old.'[71] He also noted 'a connection between firms that preferred girls, good treatment during the apprenticeship, retention at the end of the term and longevity and prosperity of business'. Newspaper advertisements echoed these preferences. For example:

> Peter Noaille, silk manufacturer and thrower at Greatness, near Sevenoaks only employed girls who 'seldom leave me unless they are bribed to leave me to go to any other manufactories or to go to service'. Flax spinners in Shrewsbury, Benyon and Co., 'took only girls, as did Newton at Cressbrook mill, Whitaker at Burley, Woolley and McQueen, Atherton and Harrison, and Cresswell at Edale.'[72]

It is notable that many firms were keen to retain girls whom they had trained. Girls also offered employers a longer working life for full-time working, and their mobility made them an ideal labour force. Girls were also perceived as cheaper labour, but employers thought they earned well. Also, employers believed girls were healthier and more robust. In the midlands, John Bott tended to retain girls when out of their time, not boys, and at his Tutbury mill girls were retained as hired workers and paid well: '[W]e had the pleasure of seeing many who had been employed in the spinning mills for several years beyond the term of their apprenticeship.'[73] A similar pattern operated in Scotland whereby girls were retained and boys went to other work. Thus, girls might leave home for service, but also for 'service' in a protoindustrial household, in silk-reeling sheds and in early factories run by waterpower, amongst others.

In a twist to this pattern of apprenticeship leading to work, Ann Maynard began work and then gained an apprenticeship. From Berkshire, she moved with her parents to Chelsea when she was only six months old. Her father then died when she was about nine and a half, so she hired herself as an annual servant to 'Mrs Hall, who kept Salters Coffee House in the said parish of Chelsea, with whom she lived four years and a half at the wages of 50s., and after, wages at £4 a year'. When she was about fourteen 'her mother gave a sum of money to Mrs Elizabeth Collins, a mantua maker in Watermans Court in the aforesaid parish of Chelsea, to teach her the art of mantua making. From thence she went to Deptford in the county of Kent, where she has followed her business as a mantua . . . maker ever since.'[74] Her story confirms the need to go to work on a father's death, and it also underlines the need to work until she was of a normative age to go to apprenticeship.

Honeyman, suggests a tension with employing girls in the face of the dominant ideology of homemaker and mother, and argues many girls were directed into domestic activity particularly during the latter period of their apprenticeship. Thus, their work identity was correspondingly weakened.

> Ellis Needham, proprietor of Litton mills, reassured St James parish, which was concerned that girls there received insufficient training in domestic skills, suggesting that girls' competence in domestic tasks was as important as the ability to earn a living wage. 'I think it exceeding proper that every woman should know something of household business.' [and] 'I assure you that many thousand women get a very good living by the same business in this country as well as in Lancashire and Cheshire . . . I however think it exceeding proper that every woman should understand the management of a family'.[75]

While most girls of the working orders needed to work, as girls and as women, the normative ideology still held purchase. They were expected to both be competent workers and have appropriate domestic skills. It was assumed that many would leave work upon marriage, and especially after childbirth, and this was often the case. While domestic service was prized as an occupation, their right to work in industry was unquestioned—as long as they also learned domestic skills for the future.

Institutional work

Institutions provided another form of work for girls from orphanages and workhouses to Magdalen homes and penitentiaries. As we have seen, schools and especially schools of industry incorporated working for girls and echoed the view that work and industry were beneficial to labouring girls. The same motive led to incorporating labour in other institutional settings. However, there were clear differences. Firstly, defraying costs was important to many of these establishments, especially when they did not have the funds for materials and tools. Secondly, girls were not working for themselves, as those who went to service and hired labour did. In some cases, training was a feature of the institutions, but in others, punishment was a more fundamental reason to put girls to work. While some attention was paid to providing work according to age and ability, it was different in character from earning for oneself.

Shifts in institutional management also played a part. In workhouses and orphan asylums, girls old enough to go to service or apprenticeship were sent out quickly. Younger children, however, could be set to work, often alongside some schooling, as in the Aberdeen Poor's Hospital where work 'included picking of oakum, beating hemp, carding and spinning coarse wool and flax, manufacturing coarse cloth and knitting stockings'. But here too, the trend was to increasingly relieve the poor in their homes. In any case, girls were a minority, thirteen girls and fifty-one boys in 1742.[76] The Birmingham Asylum for the Infant Poor was a singular experiment, which was designed specifically to house infant children over five in an 'infant manufactory', instead of the workhouse. By 1797 it housed more than 200 children, and the use of child labour saved the institution more than £500 compared to out relief or the workhouse. Children housed in the asylum were expected to work for their keep, earning their board and lodging from as young as five years of age. Links had been established with a local pin manufacturer for the employment of child workers before the institution opened: '[T]he Manufacturing Committee have agreed with Mr. Samuel Ryland for the use of twenty-three children to be employed in the Pin Manufactory at the rate of one shilling per head per week each from the 22nd Inst'.[77]

Opened at the end of the century, it also marked a shift in how institutionalisation was perceived. For example, criminal behaviour witnessed a shift in approaches, especially for women. Whereas transportation was a dominant form of punishment in the first half of the century, redemption became a higher priority than punishment, offering offenders the chance to reintegrate into society after the 'completion' of the punishment. Susan Menis argues that the understanding was that 'few or none are committed to the common gaol [jail] . . . but they come out worse than they went in. And few are committed to the House of Correction or Working House but they come out better'; indeed 'it appears that magistrates found the houses of correction to be a better alternative for dealing with petty offenders, and especially women.'[78] Robert Shoemaker also shows that in Middlesex the trend was to shift women to houses of correction.[79] Yet, work as a goal for these institutions was limited and John Howard noted in the 1770s that very few houses of correction could provide any work, because most of them had no allowance for tools or materials.[80] Yet, these trends manifested themselves in the 1778 Hard Labour Bill, which spoke to the concerns about providing work and carried with it the support of those like Jeremy Bentham who opposed transportation and valorised work and industry. Nevertheless, the final bill did not significantly change anything and only two of these new houses were constructed.[81]

Magdalene institutions, nominally for 'fallen women', also took in girls without family support. The Magdalen Hospital for the Reception of Penitent Prostitutes was founded in late 1758 in London by silk merchant Robert Dingley together with Sir John Fielding and Jonas Hanway. Bristol, Bath, Dublin and Edinburgh followed suit. Like industry schools, they put women and girls to work to help financially support the house and became especially known as laundries. Girls could earn small sums of their own in the Middlesex institution, but generally they did not, and they operated more as penitentiaries than as reformative. Thus, while these institutions might aim to provide work, many were unsuccessful, and found this work did not pay sufficiently. Despite their limitations some girls fell into these institutions, and at best may have received some useful skills to take out with them.

Relationships

Most live-in girls were probably well-treated, since hungry or ill servants were of little use. On smaller farms and households, they often shared with a family, and the relationship could be relatively close. In many cases, girls were from the same community and had family locally who could provide support. Orphans, of course, could not count on this, but notably, some parishes were careful about monitoring children. In larger farms and households, however, the relationships were more likely to be distant, perhaps except for girls who worked intimately with the family like nursemaids or ladies' maids. Nevertheless, they remained dependents and were entirely dependent on their employers. They might stay briefly, they could be fired at any time, and any perceived indiscretion could lead to being sacked, often without pay. If a girl became pregnant, no matter who the father was, she was usually sent away, though in many parishes the employer was required to keep her until her term was up and a month thereafter before releasing her. Servants were also usually paid at the end of their term and thus had little money to spend while in service. The failure of a farm or business could lead to being sent away without pay. Yet appeals to courts were rare and usually related to money, not treatment. For example, in Newark in 1755, Mary Rawlins was hired for a year 'in the business of husbandry' by John Lighthouse of North Collingham, at an annual wage of 37s. When he discharged her without paying the whole of her wages she appealed to Justices and Nottingham. Lightfoot was found guilty and ordered to pay 40s to the Court and half was to be paid to her.[82]

In contrast, Mary Farrant told the Chelsea officials that she had been a hired servant in several places, the last being with Mr Duffell, but she left because she was sick.

> She being very ill told her said master that she was not able to do his work, and desired of him to let her go to her father and mother's house, and he answered her and said that she might stay there if she pleased or go, and accordingly she . . . went home . . . 21 days before her year's service was expired. And in two or three days after she was gone her said master sent her £2 11s., which money with £4 2s. 6d., which she was paid before, made £6 13s. 6d., being the money paid to her for the wages for the eleven months and ten days. And he also further made her a present of 12s and also a further sum of 21s. for her Christmas box or vales.[83]

Thus, he was prepared to keep her, and when she decided to go, paid her wages in full and added a present of 12s as well as a sum for her 'Christmas box'. This marks a genial and honourable relationship. Yet contracts and situations were often unclear, and servants and potential employers could end in court disputing them.

Baillie and Whatman's accounts also illustrate the tensions of mistress and servant. Baillie insisted that her housekeeper keep a careful watch on the keys—a comment on her fear of theft, real or imagined—and distrusted servants. Whatman similarly insisted:

> As it is very wrong to lay temptation unnecessarily in the way of anyone, the large joints are not to be left open to the inferior servants . . . This duty of keeping away temptation is very necessary, as it would be difficult to detect depredations on a large joint, and a dishonest servant might contract a habit of doing injustice.[84]

She was particularly concerned that maids were trained properly, and watched until they got it right. 'Every new servant must be very particularly attended to in doing her business till she is got in the way of the family. It is easier to *prevent* a bad method of doing the work than to alter it afterwards.' Her reasoning was that 'If the underservants could be depended on for doing all their business *according to the instructions that could be given them*, a Housekeeper would not be necessary to keep everything going in its proper way. But this is never to be expected.'[85]

Baillie reminds us that many servants were expected to undertake other chores on the estate from spinning to haying. She also set her own timetable to the servant tasks.

> One week the body linnin is washt, the second week table and bed linnin and always bouckt when the weather will alow of it, the third week the

> landry maids must be keept closs at spining and at all times when they have not other necessary business, such as Hay and Harvest and the Barn which the dairy maid goes to when she has a moments time for it, and always to the miln with any melder. The dairy maid, house maid and kitchin maid always to spine when they are not otherways necessarly imployd which they will often pretend to be if they are not diligently lookt after and keep to it.[86]

These tensions speak to reality but also to class difference and expectations, and as Amanda Vickey wrote, 'The mistress-servant relationship was nothing if not complex and paradoxical. Relations with some servants were characterized by fondness and intimacy, with others by distance and antagonism.'[87]

Reading between the lines, these accounts suggest that the mistress-servant tensions lay especially with younger servants, precisely the girls this book is about—who were often described as careless, obstinate, disobedient and wont to leave with great frequency. Whatman employed six maids in 1778, but only two remained in 1779. Indeed, she complained, damage 'is one of the inconveniences of changing housemaids often, because it is sometime before one can make them understand these kinds of things.'[88] Steedman argues that the root of the tensions, and endemic complaints about servants, were the result of the complicated relationship between master/mistress and servant. While mutually dependent, friction arose about who was *responsible*. As Blackstone explained, this relationship was 'founded in convenience, whereby a man is directed to call in the assistance of others where his own skill and labour will not be sufficient to answer the cares incumbent upon him'.[89] Indeed, argued James Barry Bird, 'in strictness every body ought to transact his own affairs', and only 'by the favour and indulgences of the law . . . can [he] delegate the power of acting for him to another'. That was why 'the acts of servants are in many instances deemed the acts of the masters'.[90] Law reinforced this by levying tax on servants, crystalising the act of hiring and the mistress's acquisition of the servant's labour. While authors like Smith saw the skills of the servant belonging to the master, not the servant, tax law flipped that so that capabilities belonged to the servant—the servant becoming not an object, but what she does.[91] Mistresses might act as if they owned the servant, while the servant was prepared to assert her own identity and self as a person.

Complaints were persistent, but a shift in tone emerged near the end of the century with advice books promoting a desire 'to see things from the servant's point of view, to attempt to understand why they did all the things that irritated you so profoundly 'shutting the door; doing everything with maddening slowness; always making three journeys upstairs when one would do'.[92] As an anonymous author commented,

> We are dinned on every side with the history of bad servants, let us not be deaf to the oppressed voice of our inferiors, who may whisper, though

> scarcely loud enough to be heard, that there may exist also bad masters and mistresses . . . I can recollect but few bad servants. [They were] in the powers of superiors [with] an infinity of means to aid . . . a helpless female.[93]

Indeed, Bird believed that the placement should not be a prison but an asylum. Thomas Gisborne argued that Biblical texts 'strongly inculcat[ed in] servants the duties of conscientious fidelity, respect and obedience'. Mistresses were also to understand these duties, ensuring 'just and humane treatment on [her] part'. They should allow servants to visit their families; teach them to read; perhaps make them a loan when they married, or set up in business. Indeed, a very

> strict oeconomy and accountableness should be required from every servant . . . and should be enforced by a uniform adherence to settled rules and systematic plans [but not] by the master's acting the part of suspicious spy . . . and thus incurring the hatred and contempt of his domestics and whetting their ingenuity to impose upon him the more.[94]

The tension between their expectations and what mistresses saw servants doing is clear in the guidebooks written by Baillie and Whatman.

Hired girls had more independence, but were still highly reliant on their employer, and were especially vulnerable to trades cycles and the character of the workshop or factory. Paternalist employers might have been more protective, and where accommodation and food were provided, girls were probably less at risk. Yet, sexual vulnerability always lurked in the shadows and is dealt with more fully later.

Birds of passage

Clearly service and hired labour did not necessarily end with marriage, and marriage was rarely the end of a working life. But beyond the idea that girls were passing through this lifecycle stage, they were also frequently passing through a range of jobs and positions. They were highly mobile, migrating to take up positions and moving jobs frequently. Contracts were rarely renewed, their placements were seen as temporary, moving for better wages or conditions was common and servants played an important part in this. Their reasons for changing positions were many and varied. Some moved to leave a hard master or mistress, or because they did not like the work. Some simply wanted a change of scene and new people. In a world where finding a marriage partner was important, moving places was one strategy to meet potential mates. Once a girl had found a potential spouse, she might choose to move nearer the chosen man while they both saved for marriage. Girls also moved nearer home—or away from it—depending on loneliness or dysfunctional relationships with family. Some migration was semi-annual, others' was annual; they could stay shorter or longer periods, depending on contracts and preferences, as well as the wishes of the employer. By the time of the OSA in the 1790s, temporary migration of youth seeking employment in the south was a feature in northern parishes. At Canisbay, Caithness, it was reported in 1791 that 'there are annual emigrations from the parish, both of males and females in the menial line, who leave the place of their nativity in quest of superior wages in the south of Scotland'.[95]

Servants often stayed relatively short periods of time in one position and were willing and able to move frequently. Also, many girls left rural jobs to move to cities and towns that provided particularly rich opportunities to establish extensive and fruitful contacts, allowing them to decide how to move in the labour market. Many saw service as a first step, changing to other work once they became more secure; others alternated between service and other work. In London over half stayed less than a year. Mary Weaver, 1757, about nineteen years old, came from Whittington Shropshire. When she was about thirteen or fourteen, she had gone to service in Whittingham, and the last place that she lived in as a hired servant was with John Reaves in Whittington, 'with whom she lived about 16 or 17 months at the wages of 40s. per annum and a shift'. She left and went to London where she 'worked about in the fields and gardens in the parish of Kensington and Chelsea, laying about in barns and out houses and under the hedges'.[96] Mary Welbeck served in Essex and in her home county of Kent before taking up places in London. Eleanor Ashwood described interchanges between farm and domestic service, explaining that in addition to various places in London, 'she has lodged at several places in the country within the said time upon haymaking and harvest work.'[97] Farm servants moved regularly and several hirings during girlhood were normal.

Girls on average, stayed in their first place about eight months and in their second about ten. Sixty-eight per cent of farm servants hired at Tetney, Lincolnshire, between 1780 and 1830, stayed only one year. They were usually hired annually, starting at Michaelmas, Martinmas or May Day, when 'the roads were crowded with farm servants leaving their places and hying to the fair.'[98] Many also broke their career in service and returned home. There were various reasons for this but Kussmaul suggests that death of a family member or family acquisition of a larger holding requiring more labour were the most likely reasons.[99] The demand for servants fostered mobility, although at any one time, many were out of place, looking for a new position.

Settlement examinations illustrate the variety of motives and routes girls took as they moved through this period of their lives. These examinations usually speak to the bad fortune that befell them, but their testimonies also show how mobile they were. Importantly in terms of settlement, each hiring cancelled out the first, meaning the last one was the one that counted.

In 1745, Jane Scott applied to Chelsea and explained that while she was born in Stortford, Hertfordshire, she became a hired servant at age sixteen to a Captain Hogan at Chelsea, who she served for two years and 'received her full wages for the said time at the rate of 50s. for the first year, and £3 for the last year'. After she left, she was hired to one Joseph Batts of Chelsea where she also stayed about two years and 'received her full wages of her said master for the said time, at the rate of £3, meat, drink, washing and lodging'.[100] In 1756 Lydia Bridgemen similarly testified that her father was a parishioner in East Barnet, and said she had been a hired servant in several places in London and Chelsea.[101] Both, in fact, were pregnant when applying for settlement. Mobility marked out the period of girlhood as girls made their way from one place to another, from one position to another. Sometimes they were scooped up by the systems, especially the poor law, but they also used the poor law together with networks of family kin and acquaintances to seek out opportunities for work. While many would have been out of place frequently, the demand for servants and workers operated in their favour, and barring disaster like pregnancy, many made their way successfully through this part of their girlhood.

Notes

1 Kittredge, 'For the Benefit of Young Women Going into Service', 108.
2 Honeyman, *Child Workers*, 153.
3 *OBP*, January 1739, (t17390117–25).
4 SRO, D120/A/PO/1264–1400.
5 See Hecht, *Domestic Servant*, 35, 60–9.
6 Defoe, *Everybody's Business*, 13.
7 Thrale, *Thraliana*.
8 Quoted in Hecht, *Domestic Servant*, 183–4.
9 Hecht, *Domestic Servant*, 35–6.
10 Richardson, *Pamela*, vol. 1, 1.
11 Hanway, *Virtue in Humble Life*, vol. 1, 407.
12 See Lonsdale, *The New Oxford Book of Eighteenth-Century Verse*, nos. 173, 218, 269–71 and 479.
13 Defoe, *Great Law of Subordination*, 261, 291–4; and *Everybody's Business*, 19–21.
14 Kussmaul, *Servants in Husbandry*, 55–6, 70.
15 Altick, *English Common Reader*, 35, 39.
16 Defoe, *English Tradesman*, vol. 1, 35.
17 Wedgwood Archives, nos. 133–26816; 133–26818 and Josiah Wedgwood, 'Letters', xi, 130, 146.
18 LL, 'Rachel Herbert, bc 1716'.
19 BDRO 61/7/12; BDRO 14.
20 Chelsea Settlement and Bastardy Examinations, No. 242.
21 Ben-Amos, *Adolescence and Youth*, 242.
22 Steedman, 'The Servant's Labour', 27.
23 Steedman, *Master and Servant*, 66; Hecht, *Domestic Servant*, 33–4; Hill, *Servants*, 15–6; Wall, 'Mean Family Size', 151–3.

24 Kussmaul, *Servants in Husbandry*, 71.
25 Laslett, *Family Life and Illicit Love*, 34.
26 Kussmaul, *Servants in Husbandry*, 84; Meldrum, *Domestic Service and Gender*, 121.
27 *Chelsea Settlement and Bastardy Examinations*, No. 133.
28 Marshall, *Rural Economy of the West of England*, vol. 1, 109.
29 Barty, 'Kilbryde in the Olden Days', 76.
30 Kussmaul, 'Ambiguous Mobility of Farm Servants', 225, 228–9.
31 Young, *The Farmer's Kalendar*, 164.
32 Blackstone, *Commentaries*, i, 425.
33 *Purefoy Letters*, 147.
34 Steedman, 'Servants Labour', 11.
35 Quoted Hill, *Women's Work*, 82.
36 Sharpe, 'Female Labour Market', 175.
37 Kussmaul, *Servants in Husbandry*, 41.
38 Sharpe, 'Female Labour Market'; Mathias, 'Labour and the Process of Industrialisation', 41–2.
39 Young, *A Six Months' Tour Through the North of England.*
40 Kussmaul, *Servants in Husbandry*, 19.
41 Snell, 'Agricultural Seasonal Unemployment'; Sharpe, *Adapting to Capitalism*, 73–80.
42 Ben-Amos, *Adolescence and Youth*, 76.
43 Bailey and Culley, *General View of the Agriculture*, 53.
44 Davies, *Case of Labourers in Husbandry*, 185.
45 Sharpe, 'Female Labour Market', 175.
46 Quoted, Hill, *Women's Work and Sexual Politics*, 80–1.
47 Meldrum, *Domestic Service and Gender*, 19.
48 ERO, D/P 264/13/4, 1792.
49 *London Chronicle*, 1758, III, 327c.
50 Thrale, *Thraliana.*
51 NRS, Inhabited House Tax; Female Servant Tax Rolls.
52 Steedman, *Labours Lost*, 40.
53 Whatman, *Housekeeping Book*, 53.
54 Martin, *Wives and Daughters*, 137, 138. Both are members of the Fox family.
55 Martin, *Wives and Daughters*, 145.
56 Baillie, *The Household Book*, 278.
57 Whatman, *Housekeeping Book*, 37–42, quote 39.
58 Hurst, *Diaries*, 80, 88, 106, 111, 113, 128, 201, 206.
59 Young, *Six Months Tour Through the North of England*, 300.
60 Heywood, 'Children's Work', 130.
61 OSA, Aberdeen, 293.
62 Whyte, 'Proto-industrialization in Scotland', 240, 247.
63 Berg, 'What Difference Did Women's Work Make?', 32; Sharpe, 'Literally Spinsters'.
64 *Aberdeen Journal*, 22 June 1767; Stirling County Archives. Murray family of Polmaise and Touchadam papers.
65 Berg, 'What Difference Did Women's Work Make?'.
66 Chapman, *The Early Factory Masters*, viii.
67 Durie, *The Scottish Linen Industry*, 113.
68 Quoted, Berg, 'What Difference Did Women's Work Make?', 35.
69 Wedgwood Archives 46–29123.
70 Berg, 'What Difference Did Women's Work Make?', 27–9, 34.
71 Honeyman, *Child Workers*, 156.

72 Honeyman, *Child Workers*, 157.
73 Honeyman, *Child Workers*, 159.
74 Chelsea Settlement and Bastardy Examinations, No. 367.
75 Quoted Honeyman, *Child Workers*, 159.
76 OSA, Aberdeen and Aberdeenshire, XV, 305; Dennison et al., *Aberdeen before 1800*, 68.
77 Nejedly, 'Earning their Keep', 206–17.
78 See Menis, *A History of Women's Prisons in England*, 40, 48.
79 Shoemaker, *Prosecution and Punishment*, 161.
80 Howard, *The State of the Prisons in England and Wales*, 8.
81 Menis, *A History of Women's Prisons in England*, 52.
82 Hill, *Women's Work*, 81.
83 Chelsea Settlement and Bastardy Examinations, No. 372.
84 Whatman, *Housekeeping Book*, 43–5, quote, 45.
85 Whatman, *Housekeeping Book*, 51, 52.
86 Baillie, *Household Book*, 279–80.
87 Vickery, *Gentleman's Daughter*, 143.
88 Whatman, *Housekeeping Book*, 4, 56.
89 Blackstone, *Commentaries*, i, 422.
90 Anon., *A Present for Servants*, 14–5.
91 Steedman, *Master, and Servants*, 84–5.
92 Steedman, *Master, and Servants*, 138.
93 Anon., *Hints to Masters and Mistresses*, 5.
94 Gisborne, *An Inquiry into the Duties of Men*, 455. See Steedman, *Master and Servant*, 138–9.
95 OSA, Canisbay, VIII: 156.
96 Chelsea Settlement and Bastardy Examinations, No. 351.
97 Meldrum, *Domestic Service and Gender*, 20–1.
98 Marshall, *Rural Economy of the Southern Counties*, 233.
99 Kussmaul, *Servants in Husbandry*, 73.
100 Chelsea Settlement and Bastardy Examinations, No. 161.
101 Chelsea Settlement and Bastardy Examinations, No. 306.

7
MONEY

Introduction

Whereas the previous chapter focused on girls' work, this one concentrates on the money they earned, comparing different areas of work, and what they were able to do with it, from subsistence to saving to operating in a credit economy. The growth of a waged female labour force throughout the eighteenth century is indisputable, and consistent with an increase in wage dependency throughout the economy. How much they earned and what form it took varied significantly. Importantly, age was a factor in how much they worked and earned, and whether they worked at home, in the home of another, or independently. Some girls worked for room and board, sometimes clothes, like many servants. They might receive wages as well, but sometimes not. Some girls received a fixed sum at the end of a contract, day wages or piece rates depending on their rate of productivity. Some received perks, and in the case of servants, gifts, tips and other benefits could be substantial. These factors influenced what they could then do with what they earned. Often, making ends meet was difficult if not impossible; sometimes mothers or fathers expected any monetary income to be handed over, either fully or partially. Where a girl was more successful, she might be able to live tolerably well and even spend on trinkets or other personal items. Some managed to save up for their own home, pooling with a mate perhaps, and setting up in business or a trade. Girls also engaged in the credit economy, lending small sums and sometimes borrowing them. This chapter therefore examines girls' interactions with money and how they engaged with earning, living, spending, saving and lending.

DOI: 10.4324/9781003412168-8

Wages

These are not straightforward issues. Gender, place, control, age, supervision and structural factors played a part. As Jane Humphreys and Keith Snell argued, the 'wage' was

> a complex cultural product that was also linked to different forms of social relationships. In some cases it had particular meanings in relation to girls or young women, and could be paid in distinct ways. Thus the gendered nature of the wage extended beyond the obviously different levels of pay or types of payment in kind afforded to men and women, to manifest itself in the partial dependency relationships of female service, female apprenticeship, agricultural bondaging, live-in millinery or sempstressing, indentured 'house-wifery', or governessing. . . . There could be payments to parents rather than to the employee, and for longer durations than was usually true for boys.[1]

Seeking an average wage is beset with hazards, not least because some wages tended to rise, but also because they varied significantly by age and occupation, whether they were paid daily or annually, and whether 'in kind' income is counted or not.

Eighteenth-century wage data is scattered, often in records of a single farm, factory or workshop. Longer data runs come from surveys and studies usually associated with nineteenth-century Parliamentary inquiries and the like. Less is known about the eighteenth century. Significantly, girls were not always recorded separately from women, and single and married women were frequently lumped together. Detailed studies by Humphries, Joyce Burnette and colleagues make the best attempts to arrive at an understanding of wages, and are careful to note the range of variables and assumptions that go into arriving at notional 'averages', but to fully understand them, it is essential to turn to their original research.[2] Their data is used here as indicators of the level of women's wages and not as absolutes (Table 7.1). Also, they mostly describe women's wages, and girls usually did not earn at the same level. To impose some sort of order on these multifarious variables, this section looks at four broad groups of girls: those in agricultural labour, domestic servants, those in workshops, and factory girls.

The process is complicated by the simple fact people could be paid singly or as members of a group or team, but they were also paid 'in kind' or with perquisites composing all or some of their income. These issues especially affected women and children, often included in group payments, such as in cloth production when the final product was remunerated, not the work of individuals. Similarly, those on annual or long-term contracts often

TABLE 7.1 Mean Wages in Pence per Day of Unskilled Women by Decade

	Women Casual	*Women Annual*
1710–10	5.50	6.12
1710–20	6.53	7.33
1720–30	6.07	7.29
1730–40	5.59	8.48
1740–50	7.09	8.19
1750–60	6.31	8.04
1760–70	6.54	8.51
1770–80	6.19	9.18
1780–90	6.37	9.37
1790–1800	7.53	10.62

Source: Humphries and Weisdorf, *Wages of Women*, Appendix, Table A1.

benefitted from payment in kind, like room and board. For example, 15.5 per cent of eighteenth-century children received board, 12 per cent had lodging and 2 per cent received clothing.[3] Some independent workers were paid by the piece, notably spinners, and outworkers like seamstresses. Furthermore, girls' wages or piece rates were likely to be less than adults' because of lack of experience and expertise. Ann Keeling was paid incrementally more as she gained experience, and female pottery painters at Wedgwood's earned significantly more than she did. Young said that female gilders earned 7s 6d per week in 1771 (nearly £20 per year), for example, while painters (many of whom were men) earned 10s to 12s compared to Ann's £3, £4 and £5 per year.[4] Girls might start with only room and board, much like apprentices, and move to a wage after a trial period. For example, Elizabeth Pope worked for a cheesemonger for six months for room and board and for the next half year was paid at the rate of £1 15s per month.[5] In the 1790s, 'women' could average between £7 10s and £10 10s a year, and children's wages hovered around 5 pence per day or around £8 per year.[6] Girls in annual service almost always earned less than those who worked for daily or weekly wages, usually at piece rates. Farm servants might earn between £3 and £5 a year, but also have room, board and sometimes clothing, but frequently did not see any or all of their wages in cash.

Farm and household servants

Farm servants usually worked on annual contracts, especially dairymaids. Most lived in and benefitted from food and accommodation in addition to wages paid at the end of their service. Also, the requirement for many men to provide a female worker for no wages as part of an arrangement complicates the picture. The nominal annual farm servant's wage could be deceptive, not only because she often lived in, but also because she did not always get the cash that the contract suggested. For example, at Nantwich in 1769, Thomas Furber hired Martha for a year on his large dairy farm with a hiring fee of a shilling, at a wage of £2 7s 6d. During the year he advanced her small sums totalling £1 10s. The remainder of her wage he spent on 'shoes, "cloth for a shift", a handkerchief, a coat and a pair of stockings'. He also recorded 6d for a bottle of tincture of myrrh. At the end of the year, therefore, she was overspent on her wages by 2s 1d. It appears he 'forgave' it.[7] It is unclear whether she asked him to make these purchases or not. Kussmaul shows that for the sixteenth through the eighteenth century, female servants' wages averaged less than males' in the ratio of 0.60 to 1, and in the last half-century, in Spalding, Lincolnshire, male wages averaged £6.5.0 whilst women's were £2.15.0 (a ratio of 1 to 0.44). Similarly, for the period 1751–1836, Snell shows women's wages to have been two thirds to one half of men's throughout southeast England. Kussmaul also found that very young servants might receive no wages, only being kept by the farmer. They received only adult wages in their late teens or twenties, and she found that the median age at which a girl could expect an adult wage was eighteen. Yet all women's wages were low, with little real increase with age. However, in southwestern pastoral counties, where dairying was prominent, women's wages were often higher than men's, as contemporaries noted (Table 7.2).[8]

In Cumberland where men could earn between £9 9s and £12 12s per year, Eden commented, women 'who here do a larger portion of the work of the farm with difficulty get half as much'. He continued, 'It is not easy to account for so striking an inequality; and still less easy to justify it.'[9]

An important contribution to our understanding of Scottish wages is the work of T.C. Smout and A.J.S. Gibson, who derived detailed assessments of wages and prices, and importantly, included female workers, sometimes segregating single women and daughters. They argued that 'by far and away and most useful account of contemporary opinions, however, were those collected by Sir John Sinclair from all the parishes in Scotland in the *Statistical*

TABLE 7.2 Maids' Wages in Selected Parts of England

	Young, North	*Young, East*	*Marshall, Devon*	*Granger, Durham*
Maids	50s—£5	£4	£3 10s—£3 2s	£4—£6
Dairymaids	£3—£6	£5		
'undermaids'		£2s 10—£3		

Sources: Young, *Tour of the North*, and *Tour of the South*; Marshall, *Rural Economy west of England* v. 1, 109; Granger, *Agriculture of the County of Durham*, 44.

TABLE 7.3 Men's and Women's Wages at Marykirk, Aberdeenshire

	Men	*Women*
1740	£1 10s	
1750	£3 0s	£1 4s
1760		£1 10s
1771	£4—£10s	£2—£2 10s
1795	£10—£12	£2—£2 5s

OSA, XV, 205.

Account of the 1790s [OSA].' Reports having been made mainly by clergy, they tended to be supportive of agricultural improvement and critical of the past, but 'Nevertheless, there is a consistency and pattern in their reports which itself should encourage the historian to consider them seriously.'[10] The rates in northeast Scotland, reported in the OSA, showed considerable variation with maids in Inverbervie, south of Aberdeen, earning between £5 and £6 a year, but most earning between £2 and £4. A feature of Scottish hiring, however, was a tendency to hire for the summer half-year. Also, wages were much higher at the end of the century when the data was collected than it had been forty years earlier (Table 7.3).

Smout and Gibson noted two areas in southeast Scotland

> where the common people seemed to be quite clearly better off by the 1790s. One was in rural areas which were close enough to urban labour markets for the people to feel the strong upward tug on wage rates and regularity of employment, and also for them to be involved in selling a surplus of grain or animals either to the towns or over the Border to England. The other type of favoured locality were centres of manufacture, in town and country alike.[11]

Thus, wages at Inverbervie, Marykirk and Inverurie reflected their proximity to Aberdeen, and regularly correspondents bemoaned the increase in flax and thread spinning in Aberdeenshire complemented by an increasing number of manufactories in Aberdeen which drew girls away from farm work. One complained that male and female servants are 'repairing to Aberdeen where they readily find employment in the extensive manufactories lately established in Aberdeen, and get high wages' so that servants' wages were pushed up to at least double of what they were a few years ago, and it was 'very difficult to get them at any rate'.[12] At Alford, Aberdeenshire, the minister reported that day rates were so high that many preferred not to sign annual contracts and frequently 'desert' their service.[13]

During the century, war and harvest failures also affected wage rates, but as Humphries and Weisdorf argued, young women who could accept annual contracts were better placed by the end of the eighteenth century, since their wages stayed in touch with unskilled men's wages and were in line with the daily rates of female factory workers in cotton and wool.[14] In part, this was driven by competition with other work, like putting out protoindustries and small manufactories of Aberdeen, like the linen and cloth factory at Grandholm Mills. At the same time, more farmers increasingly employed more day labour rather than full-time live-in servants, contributing to pushing girls out. The hiring of girls for only a half-year in Scotland reflected the ways farmers tried to cut their costs but keep workers.

Simultaneously, wages in domestic service rose as demand for servants increased and more and more girls left farming. It was seen as a cut above, while agriculture was thought dirty, arduous and unpleasant. Both protoindustries and household service challenged farm service, wages rising significantly after mid-century. As farmers in Aberdeenshire reported, 'when these works bring tolerable prices, it is difficult for those that need them to get female servants.'[15] Competition therefore for working girls was dynamic. Importantly, however, not only the perceived character of domestic service was a draw, but so were the potential rewards. Compared to farm service, a girl was far more likely to earn relatively well. As Hecht stated, 'Numerous as were those who thus in one way or another entered service in order to gain shelter and maintenance, many more were led to embrace it as an occupation by its promise of economic and social advancement . . . the prospect of a comfortable life operated far less powerfully than the hope of profit and increased prestige.'[16]

Data on wages drawn from contemporary sources, without adjusting for the elusive perks, is shaped by location, age, gender and type of work girls did. As Sharpe noted, 'Domestic servants wages were subject to a wide degree of variation to a point which almost defies analysis.' Jacob Field drew together several existing data runs and compared them to his own dataset (Table 7.4). Given the variation, different locations and sometimes small numbers involved and sources used, none of these are completely convincing. For example, Essex and London data are based in part on settlement exams, Field's on elite homes and Hecht's on advertisements and household records which also prioritise the wealthier household. They are, however, suggestive, with a range for maids between £3.60 and £7.50. This gave domestic servants a consistent advantage over many farm servants. Snell and Field argued that wages were essentially dormant, not rising significantly, and that increasing population growth increased competition for the places available. Yet Hecht demonstrates that wages rose consistently for the maids-of-all-work and laundry maids after 1743.

Smout and Gibson did not include domestic servants in their wage data, and the servant tax rolls for 1785–92 did not give wages either. However, a snapshot of female servants' wages can be gleaned from records of some

TABLE 7.4 Listings of English Domestic Servants' Annual Cash Nominal Wage Compared to the Dataset of Jacob Field (in £ decimalised)

Place	*Type of Servant*	*Dates*	*Mean £*	*Number*	*Field, Mean £*	*Field, Number*
Bath[1]	Female	1730–1837	7.5	34	6.5	549
Essex[2]	Female	1741–1825	3.6	143	6.4	531
London[3]	Female	1700–59	4.0	53	3.6	136
St Martins in the Field[4]	Female	1750–60	4.7	712	3.7	43
England[5]	All maids	1702–95	7.5	175	4.7	414
England[5]	Cooks	1703–98	10.3	94	8.1	46
England[5]	Housekeepers	1719–95	13.5	21	18.8	21

Sources: [1]Neale, *Writing Marxist History*, 121.

[2] *Sharpe, Adapting to Capitalism, 115.*

[3] *Meldrum, Domestic Service and Gender, 188.*

[4] *Kent, 'Ubiquitous But Invisible', 118.*

[5] *Hecht, Domestic Servant, 142–49.*

Table extracted from Field, 'Domestic Service, Gender, and Wages', 254.

TABLE 7.5 Comparative Wages for Sample Households in Eighteenth-Century Scotland

	Baillie 1692–18 (£ Scots)	*Baillie 1740 (£ Scots)*	*Beattie 1783 (£ Sterling)*	*Lamont ca. 1800 (£ Sterling)*
Housekeeper	£4 to £5	£5 0s 0d	£5 0s 0d	£18 0s 0d
Cook	£1 13s 4d to £3 0s 0d	£8 0s 0d		£15 0s 0d
Chamber/ladies' maid	£1 13s 4d to £2 10s 0d			
Housemaid		£2 0s 0d	£3 3s 0d to £6 6s 0d	£10 0s 0d to £12 0s 0d
Kitchen maid	£1 3s 4d to £2 10s 0d	£2 0s 0d		£6 0s 0d

Source: Household Book of Lady Grisell Baillie Beattie's Day Book, Georgian House.

urban and country houses (Table 7.5). These include the landed estate of the Baillies at Mellerstain in the Scottish Borders, Professor James Beattie of Marischal College, Aberdeen, who lived with his sons and housed his incurably insane wife elsewhere, and the Lamonts, the first residents of 7

Charlotte Square in Edinburgh's New Town. They are not strictly comparable since they represent families of different status and size of establishment. For example, in 1740, Lady Grissell Baillie had seventeen servants at Mellerstain House and seven in London, while forty years later, James Beattie had two or three at Schoolhill, Aberdeen.

These snapshots tend to confirm that Scottish wages were lower than English ones, but comparable to or better than girls in farm service. For comparison, Smout and Gibson consider the Scottish £ to be one twelfth of the £ sterling.[17] Notably, the wages of the Lamonts servants reflect a general rise in wages by the end of the century, demand for servants and the prosperity and cachet of Edinburgh's Georgian society. The rates do suggest that a girl with the ability and presence to get a housemaid's position would have been better placed than those who could not.

Money wages were a significant draw but as Meldrum argues, 'the importance of a mixture of earnings in a customary context—a moral economy of service—persisted for this large and important sector of the London labour force.'[18] Living-in remained a key component of non-monetary emoluments for farm and domestic servants. They received room, board and washing, which Snell estimated to amount to 80 per cent of their 'wages', while Meldrum valued bed and board as adding some £14 6s for fifty-two weeks, at the beginning of the century.[19] Tips and vails as well as 'gifts' from employers and visitors, especially the elite, effectively increased servants' incomes. For example, Parson Woodforde's maid Betty was given a silk bonnet by Mrs Davie after she had stayed at the parsonage in 1781, and Mr de Quesne gave each maid a muslin apron after a visit in 1789.[20]

Wage disputes were frequent and one of the most common reasons for servants to end up in court, often at their own initiative. On 10 September 1708, Elizabeth Hawkes petitioned the Middlesex Sessions:

> That There being due to your Petitioner for a years Wages from Thomas Barkham Gt Acton in This County Gentleman the Sum of fifty Shillings which he refuseing to Pay though often demanded yor Petr [petitioner] thereupon made her Complaint to ye Worshippfull Justice Cullum who Granted his Warrt [warrant] for the sd Mr Barkham to Appeare before him who did Appeare accordingly. But . . . yor. Petr. being a Poore Servant wanting her said Wages which is still unpaid.
>
> Your Petr. therefore most humbly prays yor. Worshipps to be pleased to Grant that she may be paid . . . her said Wages as unto your Worshipps shall Seeme Meete
>
> And yor. Petr. shall ever pray
> Eliz [signed X mark] Hawks[21]

On the other hand, Margaret Rogers, who worked for Robert Walpole, 'received her full wages for the said time at the rate of £6 per annum when laundry maid, and £7 per annum when house maid, meat, drink, washing and lodging'.[22]

Making and selling

Girls could be tempted by the wages in handicrafts and protoindustries, and especially new manufactories that emerged later in the century. There were three main ways for women to earn wages in the clothing trades: working in shops, especially in millinery; working at home for the shops and paid as piece-work; and via intermediaries who employed women as outworkers or in small workshops for the bespoke trade.[23] A key factor for girls was that this sort of work frequently meant that they could stay at home, contributing to the family pot, and benefitting from the support of the family around them. Ian Whyte argued that in Scotland, 'the income from spinning, knitting and especially the embroidering of muslins discouraged young girls from going into service, allowing them to remain at home and contribute to the family's income or to set up on their own.'[24] Furthermore he claims that relatively high wages in spinning and weaving could lead to earlier independence than day labouring or service.

It is impossible to be precise about protoindustrial earnings, since rates depended on several variables, including the kind and quality of work, the type of product and the amount of time put in, as well as local and regional economic factors. Experienced workers earned more than beginners because they worked more quickly and with greater skill, and full-time workers also earned more. These were usually those who were single and dependent for their sole income on spinning as opposed to those who spun or knitted as a sideline. Not only were weekly wages not comparable but girls' needs were different. In 1795, Davies reported a family of seven in which two girls spun; the eldest aged seven

> can earn 2d per day, spinning near 1 lb. of such flax and suffusing her also to lose two days in the week in going of errands, tending the infant, etc, her earnings will be [8d per week]; the *little girl* age five can also spin adroitly; she goes to the wheel when her sister is otherwise employed, but is not kept closely to it, as that might hurt her health.[25]

Often domestic industries developed where there was little other paid work for girls, except at harvest time. For example, in the Scottish Highlands and Orkney, small-scale subsistence agriculture rather than 'agricultural improvement' led to women and girls taking up commercial spinning. Typical were the practices of the British Linen Company which expanded linen production across Scotland, often targeting women where there was less work for them. As Smout and Gibson argue,

> It could well be that in the areas of specialised textile production in the central belt children were less readily sent into farm or domestic service in another household, but kept at home to contribute to family income until they left on early marriage to set up their own households. . . . Two daughters in their late teens in the 1790s, living at home and working constantly at a wage of 12s. a day could each earn £180 Scots a year, and thus easily bring the household income to three times the sum that the adult male alone was able to earn.[26]

Daughters working at home were unlikely to receive wages so that their skill and knowledge had to serve as a dowry. Urban girls might, of course, take employment in town, returning home at night. In this way, they might be less exposed to risk than country girls who migrated to town without family protection. Girls with craft skills but without family resources probably hired themselves to out where they operated as assistants carrying out minor tasks, like sewing on buttons in a tailor's shop. A sample from eighteenth-century contemporary sources shows that obviously full-time work was more remunerative than part-time so that even with less experience girls could earn tolerably well, and their income could increase over time (Figure 7.1). Lacemaking stands out partly because it was the one industry that was virtually controlled by women throughout the process.

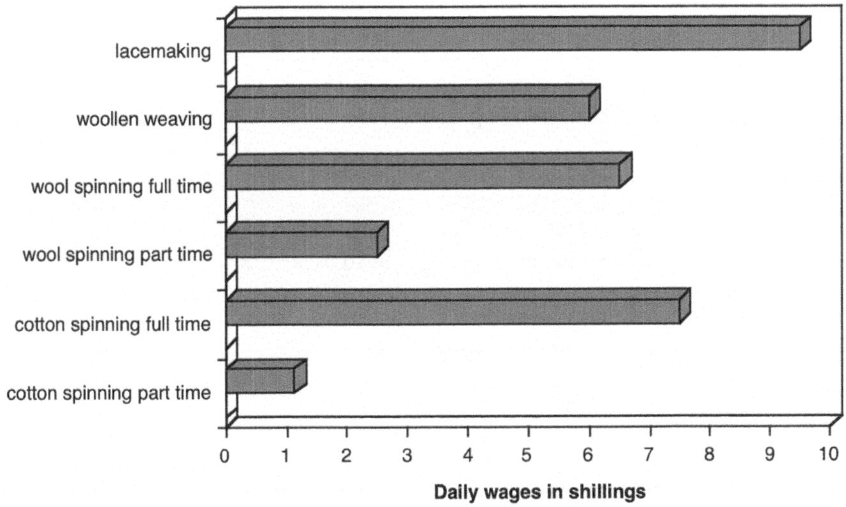

FIGURE 7.1 Wages of Women in English Protoindustries

Like England, data is dispersed in Scotland, but Durie said that in Kintyre in 1744 a good linen spinner might have earned 7s.–8s. a week, but 'it is perhaps safest to say merely that earnings varied widely'. Wages also had to account for the cost of materials so that in 1755 a flax spinner might earn 16s a week at Brechin in Angus, but only 12s at Banff and even less at Huntly in Aberdeenshire. In 1775, Smith thought that in most parts of Scotland 'she is a good spinner who can earn twentypence a week' or 20s. Scots. He further argued that any woman who tried to earn her living solely by spinning would 'earn but a scanty subsistence'.[27] Yet, in those areas where rural textile work became most important, a girl's contribution to family income, and potentially to her own independence, could be substantial. There is no doubt that these earning opportunities were extremely important for families and for girls themselves, and despite the range of income, in contrast to Smith, James Steuart thought women could subsist with ease by spinning (Table 7.6). In 1769 he quoted earnings of 20s. to 24s. Scots a week in Lanarkshire, saying that 'with this they are clothed and nourished'.[28] Smout and Gibson thought £15 a year was feasible for daughters in their late teens in the 1790s working constantly while Arthur Young thought women in potteries earned about £27 a year. These figures, then, suggest that girls could earn enough to save for the future or have the money to spend on 'little things' for themselves. There are caveats of course in that sometimes costs were taken from this sum, like clothes, or materials like flax or cotton for spinning, or like Rebecca Cakebread who earned

TABLE 7.6 Wages in Scottish Protoindustries from the OSA

		Scots, per day	
Dumbarton	Flowering muslin	12s	And upwards
Kirriemuir, Aberdeenshire	Flax spinning	15s	More than male farm servants
Galashiels, Borders	Spinning wool	6s to 8s	Slightly more than female farm servants
Old Monkland, Lanarkshire	Spinning wool	6s to 8s	'eight-year-old girls'
Auchtertool, Fife	Flax spinning	6s to 8s	
Keithall and Kirkell, Aberdeenshire	Stocking knitting	3s to 6s	Poorly paid trade
Lethnot, Angus	'work'	18s	Fourteen- and fifteen-year-old girls, same as mothers

Source: Smout and Gibson, *Prices, Food and Wages*, 354.

about 8s 7d each week. Out of this sum she paid for light and heat, the wages of the second loom operator and depreciation on two looms. She was probably a full-time worker. Girls may also have felt an obligation to contribute to family, perhaps even as 'gifts', and many could have been paid as a part of a family wage, so what she might have for herself was dependent on family circumstances and attitudes.

Not all girls had a household to fall back on; some deliberately set out to manage on their own. Often, they went to town, but not always. A common strategy was forming partnerships, or households of single women which could allow production to be divided, and they could gain some control over markets and income by working directly for a merchant. The existence of numerous merchants in an area competing for women's labour was to their advantage compared to areas where a few or a single merchant controlled raw materials. Sharpe showed how, in a community like Colyton, Devon, the protoindustries of lacemaking and wool spinning worked to their advantage because women did not need to operate within a family economy and were not dependent on or subsidiary to men's work.[29] Furthermore the poor law system at Colyton was sufficiently supportive to enable such households. Her study focused on adult singletons, but she reveals girls like Ann Rick who went to live with a poor woman when her apprenticeship ended, or Ann Snell, who became ill, left service and lived with Alice Long who nursed her, then at eighteen, with Sarah Newbury, who 'seems to have maintained her own household in Colyton from the age of 20'.[30] She argues that these girls could have made at least a self-supporting livelihood. Spinning wages were not high enough to encourage women to establish an independent household but were high enough to permit it. Sanderson listed ninety-one 'partnerships' of women, usually kin, and often sisters, in Edinburgh, in commerce perhaps combined with manufacture. Janet Muschet, a milliner, took two cousins into partnership, Cicely Murray and Ann Buchanan. However, Buchanan's later letters home suggest she thought she was being undervalued, and both partnerships ended in acrimony. No income was mentioned but the size of the stock suggests they could have been doing quite well.[31] Millinery especially provided girls opportunities, and female collectives were common. It could also be lucrative for girls, and trade guides indicated that a journeywoman in a milliner's shop could earn between £13 and £30 a year, which exceeded the wages of most girls. However, though they could earn 6s a week, they still had to find board and lodging.[32] The picture of independent households is, therefore, somewhat mixed. On balance, income did not necessarily provide the incentive for women to establish separate households, but women-only households were a strategy for coping and perhaps living relatively well. If wages were too low for a single woman to gain an independent existence, then in combination with others she could ensure her room and board.

Manufactories

There was overlap between the protoindustrial workforce and manufactories since sewing, for example, could be carried out in workshops or put out to households. Humphries and Weisdorf's calculations show a rapid and stark increase in female wages, especially in the last quarter, and clergymen in Scotland attributed competition especially from the manufactories to forcing up servant wages. The foray into cotton complemented the vast investment in linen spinning, concentrated in the Highlands, where there were 252 mills by 1772, working in association with the number of domestic workers and promoted by the British Company, and some 10,000 women, including girls, across the northern counties spun linen thread.[33] Thomas Griggs, a worsted clothier, hired female spinners on piece rates in their own homes, all within a fifteen-mile radius of his base at Sudbury, Suffolk. He similarly hired weavers, usually based on his premises, some of whom were women on lighter fabrics. These rates were highly variable and linked to market conditions. Mary Hayward, who had a single loom, earned an average of 2s 9d per week over seventeen weeks. A worker weaving the more expensive and difficult says could earn 7s 6d to 8s a week, possibly 10s a week for a quick skilful worker.[34] All wage rates were flexible and relied on market conditions; therefore they could fall and rise. For example, Young reported in 1767 that a girl of fifteen or sixteen in Sudbury was not able to earn more than 6d a day; he later reported, in 1784, a lower figure of 3d a day.[35] A snapshot from his northern tour illustrates the variation encountered by location but also by the type of work (Table 7.7). Girls could have been included as either women or children, depending on their age, and worsted spinners were probably all females.

Honeyman elaborated on the sorts of wages that girls finishing apprenticeships in mills at the end of the century could expect to earn if they stayed on:

> At the Holywell Twist Company, for example, 'when out of their time . . . girls may then earn from 5 to 7s per week, boys from 10 to 15s or more according to their ability'. Confirmation that this was within the usual range of pay for girls is provided in the case of the Nantwich firm of John Bott where 'girls when grown up may earn from 4/6 to 6/- per week if attentive to business'. . . . At Backbarrow, once apprenticeship was completed, 'the girls get from 6s to 7s per week. The men from 12s to 14s and upwards they can board in the neighbourhood men for 6s women 5s per week'.[36]

Throughout England, Honeyman noted that boys always were paid more than girls, and their apprenticeships taught them to expect differentials: Apprentices were given 'pocket money' for working 'over hours', to which

TABLE 7.7 Industrial Wages in the North of England, ca. 1770

Place	*Work*	*Women*	*Children*	*Men*
Knutsford, Cheshire	General	4s to 6s, pw	8d to 2s, pw	
	Threadmill		1s to 2s	
	Worsted	2s 6d	2s	
Kendal, Westmoreland	Spinners in stockings	3s	2s 6d	
	Cotton weavers	4s 6d		
	Cotton spinners	3s 3d		
Warrington, Lancashire	Sailcloth, spinning	2d		
	Ditto winding	2d		
	Ditto weaving	5s		Men 9s
	Ditto, sacking, spinning	6d		
	Winding	2s	4d a day	
Warrington pins			1s to 2s	
Staffordshire	Potteries	5s to 8s		Men 7s to 12s, 'but few girls.'

Source: Young, *Tour of the North*, 171–72.

boys had greater access. 'Henry Churchill . . . has 2/- a week allowed him for pocket money and is nearly out of his time . . . Martha Kelly almost out of her time has long had 1/- a week for pocket money.'[37] However, she thought there was some leeway in the amount of pocket money earned: Margaret Chamberlain 'could earn sufficient pocket money when she pleased'. Thus, in England it was more usual for girls to earn around half the male wage, although they could in certain circumstances match boys' wages.

In Scotland, however, mill girls commonly earned higher wages than boys, who were likely to seek other work anyway. The OSA did not distinguish between women and girls but reported that at the three key linen thread mills in Aberdeen, many earned 5s to 6s a week, but those who worked at home earned less because they were not full-time.[38] Bleaching too was strongly female, and provided much competition to farmers since the bleaching season was precisely when farmers needed labour. At Salton virtually the same numbers of men and women were hired between 1768 and 1772, and the men earned between 7d and 9d and the women between 4d and 6d per day, earning more with more experience.[39] Thus their wages, while potentially good and better than servants' wages, still did not match men's.

Female wages were depressed partly because of the belief that women did not need the same income as men—that they supplemented men's income—and partly because plenty of women were available for hire. If the rate did not suit them, merchants simply replaced them. To even begin to deal with the persistent wage gap between men and women, we have to remember that wages were highly variable, often not paid in money anyway, and work varied by age and sex, meaning most girls did not necessarily do what women did, and vice versa, nor did they do what men and boys did. Similarly, their work hours and allocation of time varied. Thus, the fact that women simply did not do as much as men because they had to juggle with more domestic responsibilities than men is important. As Burnette said, 'The existence of the wage gap between men and women is well known and not disputed; what is disputed is the interpretation of this gap.' She therefore argued that 'the wage gap in agriculture reflected differences in productivity, because of their household duties. [And] because of differences in strength women tended to be given lighter tasks, and when they did the same tasks as men, they had a lower output per hour.'[40] The gender wage gap has been a thorny question for historians. For some the blame falls on capitalist structures, for others on endemic patriarchal attitudes amongst both men and masters. It can also be argued that women's work was seen as casual, and as subsidiary to men's, as supplementary labour and therefore not 'real' work. Also, strength is often used as an excuse rather than the reality of what women could do.[41] Humphries and Weisdorf point out that the widening gap began about 1760 which coincided with changes in spinning.[42] Other things changed about that time and coincided with an increase in tracts depicting women's work as primarily domestic. Single women, and thus girls, were judged by the notion of 'women's work' and by *married* women's household responsibilities, especially childcaring. Research is ongoing and should be, since the data is difficult to find and analyse, and inevitably a complex of factors contributed. However, an important point for this chapter is precisely that girls were not adult women, and there are very few sources which help disentangle this. Some of the snapshots in this chapter suggest that girls, 'young women' if you will, may well have had competitive incomes. What is more useful here is the comparative earning opportunities girls had and how these moved across the century. What a girl's options were depended on household circumstances, where she lived, what she was capable of, how old she was, and even what she wanted to do. Birth order in the family was often a feature as well. Education and apprenticeship probably aided some girls in making this decision, as did a stable family background. Whether they made enough to support themselves was also a question, and beyond that, what they spent their money on.

Balancing the budget

The cost of living has long concerned historians as well as late eighteenth-century commentators like Eden, Davies and Malthus, whose main interest was to assess the risk of falling into poverty and becoming chargeable for poor relief. However, rarely, if ever, did anyone ask about the income and expenses of girls, who were not chargeable to poor relief usually—unless they had an illegitimate child. In fact, the child was the recipient of relief. The 1801 list of the poor in Terling confirms that girls and youths were effectively not eligible for relief and were usually sent to apprenticeship rather than supported. The common view is that girls might earn enough to support themselves in some occupations and circumstances, even earning enough to save a little toward their futures. Kussmaul estimated that two servants marrying who had been in service from six to ten years could save between £27 and £60 together, depending on their combined length of service and whether they were able to save one half or two thirds of their wages.[43] Muldrew argued that the period of demographic stability from 1650 to 1760 allowed labourers, as well as English society in general, to build up savings for consumption and capital for investment, which otherwise would have been spent on feeding more young people.[44] Thus we need to recognise that the ability to save was not constant across the century, nor was it the same for all girls whose income and demands on it varied. Significantly large numbers continued as singlewomen workers, for whom savings could prove useful, perhaps crucial.

We do not have budgets for girls, but we can make a few estimates. In 1795, Davies included a budget for an unmarried man, age unknown, which suggests what a singleton household might spend (Table 7.8). Eden noted that an elderly female singleton, who spun for a living, balanced earnings and expenses of £4 1s 7½d. She rented her deceased father's small farm and used the interest on £10 profit after selling his animals and possessions for her rent payment: 'This woman's earnings are small; but she makes her expences [sic] correspond. She seems perfectly happy, content and cheerful; and always takes care to avoid debt.'[45] However, after rent she spent mainly on food,

TABLE 7.8 Sample Single Man's Budget, 1795

EXPENCES	*£ s d*
Two bolls one firlot of oat-meal	1 11 6
Potatoes bought	0 10 0
Shoes, 2 pair	0 3 4
Clothes of different kinds	1 0 0
Pays for washing, 1 s for soap for shaving, razor, etc. 6d	0 1 6
Buys a little milk when it can be got	0 2 0
At particular times to make merry with his friends	0 5 0
Saves annually, which enables him to take up house	3 5 1
Total per annum	£6 18s 5d

Source: Davies, *Labourers in Husbandry*, 60.

very little on clothes and virtually on nothing else; for example, a pair of clogs every two years and a pair of shoes every seven and no more than 12s on shifts, etc. This snapshot of working singletons' living costs suggests that £5 a year was probably a minimum to live alone. Yet, if earnings were greater, or young women lived in shared households, these budgets indicate that disposable income was feasible.

Saving depended on the simple balance between living and earning. Managing this was often less simple. As the elderly singleton earlier showed, making ends meet could be challenging but was possible. A variety of strategies like living and working together helped with light, fuel and rent; girls however found this strategy difficult. Social mores tended to assume and require them to work in a household, whether a master's as apprentice or servant, in domestic or farm service, or at home or in the home of kin. While this provided basic subsistence, what was less likely was independence, and this could mean an independent income to save or spend as they liked. In best-case scenarios, girls' earnings could be accumulated, especially if paid properly at the end of a hiring and if they could move to another without depleting their resources. Meldrum argued that saving was difficult for London servants, but not impossible, and an eighth of female servants stated in church court depositions their worth was over 170, £10.[46] Thus, when things went well, girls certainly had the possibility of saving for the future. They could also buy things they needed or wanted. They could also use it for other purposes, such as lending, maybe even investing. While the prospects were better for the middling working girl, possibilities did exist.

Spending

The expression 'to cut your cloth to fit your purse' is apt, because working girls earning the best wages would have been far more likely to spend on personal items, fripperies and luxuries than their poorer sisters. Girls are often depicted as striving for fashion, desiring to be attractive, perhaps even trying to 'catch a husband'. Indeed, many of the criticisms of spending during the period targeted girls, especially house servants and milliners' and their apprentices. Commentators were often critical of the expenditure patterns of working people, while spending rather than poor wages was often perceived as a cause of poverty. Eden and Davies thought they could spend more wisely and frugally.

On the one hand, servants' employers encouraged a certain level of imitation in dress, cleanliness and manners, because it reflected favourably on their household, and they frequently passed on garments, and they often promised 'cast cloths' at hiring, as a regular perquisite. Woodforde habitually made 'presents' of dresses to his two servants, 'sensibly' buying

> the same material each time he made a gift to both maids: peagreen stuff in 1783, and early in 1801 a pink and white cotton gown for each of them at

> 2s 6d a yard, a price which suggests a Sunday gown rather than a working one. They had a 'cotton gown apiece' from London in 1789 and a gown each of cotton at 2s 3d a yard in 1795 at the same time as Nancy had cotton for a gown at 2s 6d.[47]

Such gifts could become a virtual uniform, as in a house at Norfolk, in 1756, where all maids dressed for church in green stuff gowns, though in fact it was inadvertent since 'a green camblet used for many years to be an annual present of her mother's to those servants who behaved well . . . and that now indeed as they all behaved well and had lived there so much longer than the limited term this was constantly their old master's New Year gift.'[48] Vickery argues that a servant's right to clothing was hotly disputed. While employers might see such gifts as patronage, many servants regarded them as a right. For example, in 1707, Mary Hill's mistress refused to give back clothes, so she returned four days later with a friend, and the dispute was overheard by a neighbour who said 'Fie, fie, give the poor servant her clothes, what do you keep them for?'[49]

Such 'involuntary consumption' assisted servants who were saving or who desired other things, but it does not tell us much about personal choice or aspirations.[50] Ann Buck pointed out that castings of morning gowns of printed cotton passed from mistress to upper servants were intended for Sunday or best wear. However, finer clothing was often included, sometimes a whole wardrobe in a bequest. The practice gave servants the freedom to sell on to other servants, or to pawn to have money for other things. In some cases, such gifts were a recognised perk, but in others, they may have been genuine presents, rewards, even bribes.[51] The lack of uniforms gave license to female servants to follow fashions according to their own taste and means, and Buck argues the readiness of women to pass on their own clothes to their servants shows there was no sharp division of dress, nor even a social convention against servants occasionally buying the same garment as the mistress. Woodforde recorded: 'Nancy bought of Bagshaw this morning . . . a very genteel Shawl at 10 shillings. Both my Maids bought 2 Shawls the same as Nancy.'[52]

At the same time, contemporaries commented negatively about the practice of cast clothes, claiming servant girls copied their employers (Image 7.1). They argued, somewhat absurdly, that these practices blurred visual marks of class distinction and confused observers about the status of the wearer. Defoe, for example, claimed 'it is now become frequent in middling Families, that the Chambermaids have better Laces, and finer Silks than the Mistresses, and it is not easie to know the Servants from the Daughters of a Family.'[53] Hester Thrale described 'Wenches with umbrellas and Workmen with muffs' in Paris.[54] Defoe further grumbled,

> our servant-wenches are so puffed up with pride nowadays, that they never think they go fine enough: it is a hard matter to know the mistress from

IMAGE 7.1 John Raphael Smith, 1752–1812, Like Mistress, Like Maid, 1781. Mezzotint on medium, slightly textured, cream laid paper, Yale Center for British Art, Paul Mellon Fund, B1970.3.813.

> the maid by their dress; nay, very often the maid shall be much the finer of the two . . . in short, plain country Joan is now turned into a fine London madam, can drink, take snuff, and carry herself as high as the best.[55]

While Defoe's critique was situated in a defence of domestic manufactures, he directed it at female servants, whose ubiquity and visibility were seen as tending to destabilise relations between master and mastered.[56] As the tea table became an icon of polite society, contemporaries criticised working people for wasting time and money on tea and coffee drinking. Tea also became a guarded perk among servants, so that Hecht noted that when a grocer stopped 'gifts' to servants to attract their custom, they announced they would stop drinking tea.[57]

The consumer revolution of the eighteenth century fostered a wider array of goods, and for many an increased ability to spend, and reshaped the world of the consumer, so that '"luxuries" came to be seen as mere "decencies", and "decencies", came to be seen as "necessities". Even "necessities" underwent a dramatic metamorphosis in style, variety and availability.'[58] Smith argued necessities are 'not only commodities which are indispensably necessary for the support of life, but whatever the custom of the country renders it indecent for creditable people, even of the lowest order, to be without.'[59] As John Styles, Cissie Fairchilds, Daniel Roche and others have argued, these practices included the plebeian classes. Fairchilds points out that a salient feature of the consumer revolution 'was the penchant of the lower classes for . . ."Populuxe" goods, that is cheap copies of aristocratic luxury items'.[60] George argued that labourers and artisans frequently possessed silver watches as investments that could be pawned when needed, a feature applicable to many small luxury items like silver spoons.[61] McKendrick contentiously claimed that women had a 'pent up desire' to compete with their betters and lay new consumer demand at the door of the 'the mill girl who wanted to dress like a duchess'.[62] Thus the proliferation of consumer commodities made the specific connection between female appetite and the world of goods; with the birth of consumer culture, women were assumed to be hungry for things.

While the elite and middling orders were the primary drivers of the expansion of goods, in this 'new culture of appearances' there is no doubt that these practices included working people.[63] Clothing and personal accessories served to mark out personal and social identities so that what people owned and what they wore was an expression of meaning, embedded in concerns about age, gender, sexuality and position. Fashion was central to the culture of appearances, and it was inextricably linked to females. Young women were knowledgeable, and wished to project themselves the best they could, and they learned about fashion from shops and as they traversed the streets. Despite the concern of the elite, this was not necessarily emulation. A key difference was not necessarily in style but in quality:

> There were many variations of cloaks and hoods . . . Although in the country cloth cloaks might be fashionably worn in winter, silk was the usual fabric of fashionable cloaks made warm by being lined with fur or thickly wadded. . . . Madame du Bocage visited the cottages of shepherds and farmers Oxfordshire in 1750: 'People of this class have their houses well furnished, are well-dressed and eat well; the poorest country girls drink tea, have bodices of chintz, straw hats on their heads and scarlet cloaks upon their shoulders'.[64]

The dress of northern women was originally homemade but became more frequently shop-bought because it was cheaper. A woman's dress consisted of

> A black stuff hat, of the price of 1s 8d.; a linen bed-gown (stamped with blue) mostly of home manufacture—this usually costs in the shops 5s 6d; a cotton or linen neckcloth, price about 1s 6d; two petticoats of flannel, the upper one dyed blue, value of the two about 11s 6d; coarse woollen stockings, home manufacture, value about 1s 8d, linen shift, home manufacture, 2½ yards at 1s 3d a yard. Women usually wear stays, or rather

> bodices of various prices. Their gowns are sometimes made of woollen stuff at 1s 6d the yard. The women, however, generally wear black silk hats and cotton gowns on Sundays and holidays.[65]

Missing girl Martha Thedham of about fifteen was described as wearing 'a plain Muslin Cap and an old black hood, a yellow Stuff Gown and Petticoat, with red stripes, pretty old, her under Petticoat of old Silk of Gold colour and black, and old pair of Stays on, white sticht with red, the Stomacher with some Gold in it.'[66] A late eighteenth-century Scottish commentator compared the clothing of 'ordinary' people in 1798 with 1778:

> Then, there was not one black cap; now, all the women wear them. Then, the gowns of the women were camblet [wool/silk] and their aprons woollen; now, the gowns are of printed linen, and the aprons of white muslin. . . . Then, in short, the whole articles of the dress of the people were home-made, excepting their bonnets, and a few shoes; now, they are all bought from the merchants of Dunkeld.[67]

Stubbs painted women in the fields in black caps, and historians have argued about how realistic this was, but this evidence from Scotland suggests it could well have been (see Image 6.1). Styles makes this point forcefully showing how plebeian clothing was marked by substantial improvement across the century. Shop-bought rather than homemade became decidedly more fashionable and cotton became the common fabric for working girls' dresses. He argued that when English plebeian girls bought cheap silks and muslins aping the fashions of the wealthy, it was not to wear at the balls and assemblies frequented by the genteel, but at the fairs and hirings, the parish feasts and harvest homes, that featured so prominently in the customary festive calendar.[68]

One April afternoon in 1780, Elizabeth Hicks, a London streetseller, left her belongings in her rented room in a lodging house, to return and find them gone. She 'lost two cotton gowns, a silk crape gown, a woollen cloth cloak, a silk handkerchief and a muslin handkerchief'; these included 'many of the costlier items owned by other kinds of labouring people.' Another, Esther Hudson, owned a scarlet cloth coat and two printed calico muslin gowns. Notably, Paul Sandby's drawing of a London milkmaid shows that despite the fact that many street sellers were amongst the most ragged of dressers, she is shown with 'a short red cloak, a large white apron and a straw hat over a red-spotted handkerchief. None of them is ragged'[69] (Image 7.2). Paintings of labouring people were notably romanticised, but they could, as the previous quotes suggest, also reflect a reality.

Eden and Davies's budgets show that families spent only a small proportion of earnings on clothes, perhaps 10 per cent, and Davies believed that children's clothing was 'usually partly made of up of the parent's old clothes, partly bought

IMAGE 7.2 Paul Sandby, 1731–1809, London Cries: A Milkmaid, ca. 1759. Watercolour, pen and brown ink with graphite on medium, slightly textured, cream wove paper, Yale Center for British Art, Paul Mellon Collection, B1975.3.209.

at second hand' and amounted to around £1 a year.[70] Eden compared the costs of a man's and woman's clothing and found the total per year to be almost the same, £1 16s for a man and £1 16s 11d for a woman in 1796, although higher than Davies did.[71] He thought that a woman would buy, in a year:

A common stuff gown	£0 6 6
Petticoat	£0 4 6
Two shifts, 3s 8d each, 1 made at home, will cost	£0 6 0
Two pair of shoes, at 3s 9d	£0 7 6
Coarse apron 1s, Check ditto, 2s	£0 3 2
A pair of stockings, 3s if knit at home	£0 2 6
Hat, once in two years, 1s 8d	£0 0 10
Pair of stays, once in 6 years, 6s	£0 1 0
Coloured neckerchief	£0 1 0
Two common caps	£0 1 8
Cheapest cloak, 2 years, 4s. 6d	£0 2 3
	£1 16 11

TABLE 7.9 Clothing Lost by Working Females in a Fire at Brandon Suffolk, 1789

Clothes lost	*No. Items*	*Value*	*Value per Item*	*Gowns*	*Shifts*	*Stockings*	*Hand-kerchiefs*
Sarah Homes, servant	69	£10 4s 6d	3s 0d	4	5	7	8
Mary Cooper, servant	37	£4 18s 8d	2s 9d	4	4	3	10
Elizabeth Cooper, mantuamaker	22	£2 13s 0d	2s 5d	3	1	3	1

Source: Styles, *Dress of the People*, 335–38.

The working girls who lost clothes in a fire in Brandon Suffolk in May of 1789, listed by styles (excluding what they were wearing), gives texture to the previous accounts (Table 7.9). Several handkerchiefs were lost, but only Mary Cooper had a silk one, valued at 2s. The main difference between these items and those of the wealthier inhabitants was in quality rather than in kind. All three lost gowns of either cotton/linen or stuff, typical of standard daily wear for girls of their station: a linen shift worn with stays over it, a petticoat and a gown on top. They added shoes with removable buckles, stockings, an apron, a linen cap, a hat and neckwear, either a handkerchief or shawl.[72] Sarah Holmes's workday stuff gown was valued at 4s 6d, much more than Eden estimated. However, this clothing could have been handed down or gifted. Then too, they could have made their shifts and knitted their stockings to make savings or purchased items second-hand (see Image 7.3, for example).

There was a vigorous second-hand market in eighteenth-century Britain. As Beverly Lemire says, 'For the second-hand trade to thrive . . . there had to be at least the small occasions of surplus, as well as the desire for extra, the means to enhance comfort and reflect some material complexities in their lives and on their persons.'[73] Fashion was an important feature of the trade, which enabled servants and other working girls to access the markets for items beyond the bare necessities, those that had become at least decencies to them, the extras that made working worthwhile. The wages paid at the end of service or redeeming the piece of linen a girl had been weaving could operate exactly as these moments of surplus.

Fashion was not always expensive, and early in the century, commentators criticised servants for buying calico, instead of wool and linen, and calico merchants, recognising the purchasing power of working women, targeted them in their marketing.[74] In defending maidservants' consumption, an anonymous author linked servant dress to sartorial self-assertion:

> And why may it not be as reasonable with Respect to Servants Dresses; that Those, who are Honest, Careful, and Pains-taking should lay out the

IMAGE 7.3 Paul Sandby, 1731–1809, A Girl with a Watering Can facing left: Sarah Hough, Mrs. T.P. Sandby's Nursery Maid, ca. 1805. Grey wash, pen and grey ink and graphite on moderately thick, slightly textured, cream laid paper, Yale Center for British Art, Paul Mellon Collection, B1981.25.2694.

> Wages they work for, in such Cloathing, as well for Ornaments as Use, to their Satisfaction; since they are as much their own [as his—Defoe's].[75]

By the end of the century, plebeian women's gowns were almost exclusively made of cotton compared to approximately a third at mid-century, with a similar trend for other bits of clothing, like stockings, and far more was purchased rather than homemade. The elements of clothing remained largely the same, and also similar to the clothing of the elite, but the fabrics and styles showed they were not resistant to fashion.

While we know relatively little about girls' consumption of clothes, we know less about their acquisition of trinkets and accessories. While they tended to own a change of clothes, they often owned only one set of buckles. The two servants (see earlier) lost decorative and protective items in the Brandon fire: removable shirt sleeves, ruffles to attach to gowns and caps and

IMAGE 7.4 Thomas Rowlandson, 1756–1827, A Young Woman in a Blue Striped Dress, undated. Watercolour and graphite on medium, slightly textured, cream laid paper, Yale Center for British Art, Paul Mellon Collection, B1975.3.2.

pattens to keep shoes dry in the wet. One lost a bedgown, a garment coming into wider use. Accessories that plebeian women frequently purchased included handkerchiefs and neckcloths in multiple colours since 'they were relatively inexpensive, but highly conspicuous'[76] (Image 7.4).

Robert Heaton (1726–1794), a worsted manufacturer and small landowner, kept records of servants' purchases showing how spending might have worked in practice. Servants bought items and charged them to his account, and the character of their purchases suggests that he did not determine them. He also advanced money to spend at fairs and allowed them to 'overdraw' their accounts, sometimes over several years, though it seems most were repaid. Heaton's twenty-eight female servants spent 86 per cent of outlay on clothing, clothing materials and upkeep of clothing, mainly workday clothing, but also on the most fashionable linen and cotton gowns. Accessories were their second most plentiful of purchases, which allowed them to alternate and show off, especially the omnipresent neckcloth, as well as hats and caps. They bought different fabrics and patterns, from common ones to checked or printed and in muslin or even silk and ribbons, which could be changed frequently, to decorate hats. Buckles to adorn shoes also enabled making a statement. Styles concludes that most of these servants fell between two extremes—careful and profligate—although the majority did buy at least two expensive showy items of clothing each year of service. They were not relying on hand-me-downs and or second-hand purchases.[77]

Credit relations

The historiography of borrowing and lending largely focuses on businesswomen, middling and elite women with money to spare; working women are more likely to be depicted engaging in pawning and the second-hand trade, especially clothing.[78] Nevertheless, servants and working girls shared in credit networks, although drawing them out of the literature is challenging. Most obvious is that, once again, materials lump women together, and if they are segregated, the divide is based on lifecycle rather than age. Also, many records used to find women are probate materials, dominated by older women, not the young. However, there are three points at which girls may be seen in the shadows: as borrowing against expectations; as lenders of small amounts, often to friends and family; and as young businesswomen, especially petty retailers. While they may have intended surpluses to go for a future, they also could use them within credit markets.

Eighteenth-century Britain existed on credit. Money supply had increased over the previous centuries, but there was still a lack of hard currency, and many financial relationships were built on credit and trust. Small shops commonly offered credit so local knowledge and confidence were key features in these transactions. Wages were not always reliable or sufficient, and girls regularly relied on stratagems, like borrowing, sharing and pawning, to make ends meet. Pawning was a time-honoured way to manage 'cash-flow' issues, and although fees charged by pawnbrokers made this an uneconomic route, for some it was the only option—pawning Sunday clothes or small objects, like watches, and hoping to redeem them before they were needed.

Wages paid in arrears operated as savings which could be used for acquiring a small stock in trade, or for setting up a girl when she left service—or to tide her over until she found another place. The accumulation of wages in the hands of masters and mistresses represented an indebtedness on their part, or a credit to be drawn on by servants. These could act like little 'banks' and were used for clothes and other necessities. Also, the elite borrowed from their employees, creating a subtle web of pledge and promise that was more than pecuniary obligation. Margaret Hunt has argued that 'the main method of accumulating investment capital in the eighteenth century was through personal connections, relatives, or close friends, rather than through relatively impersonal institutions like modern day banks or investment companies.'[79] The sums involved were occasionally staggering suggesting that monies owed to servants were allowed to accumulate. Muldrew listed numerous debts owed to servants from probate accounts like the widow Ann Inglefield, who owed '£1183 9s . . . (comprising 92 per cent of the value of her movables worth £1285 6s), including many debts to servants for wages as much as three years in arrears.'[80] He also cites a small number of servant's inventories from Cheshire and Kent, and almost all were owed considerable sums often on bond ranging from £20 to £41.[81] Girls might also borrow against their wages or expectations. Communities were small and it was likely that people knew each other, so that reliability and personal credit was a factor even in small-scale loans and debts. Servants also received 'arles' or a hiring fee, which could put a small sum in their hands that they could spend, lend or invest, while tips and vails increased their pocketbook. Working girls in industry and retail trades could also earn well, potentially building up small sums. As we have seen, while balancing the budget could be challenging, girls could also acquire little nest eggs which gave them disposable income.

Little surpluses could allow them to lend small amounts, usually to family and friends, as they evolved strategies to survive, or to take a small loan to build up their own position, maybe buying tools or marrying. Girls operated within a credit nexus that allowed them space within the urban economy, and they developed extensive networks and connections in a larger commercial marketplace in which financial transactions and pawning of goods could become a virtual and very lucrative occupation. Issues of credit are usually thought of in monetary terms, but many debts were on merchandise, to be repaid later. Alexandra Shepard demonstrates the importance of 'worth', linking material possessions as well as virtue, showing how women were embedded in commercial transactions that were far more than lending and borrowing among friends and families, and upon which networks of credit were built.[82]

Girls had access to larger credit markets, and the growth of lotteries and investment opportunities provided them the chance to share in these new opportunities. Amy Froide notes that workingwomen, especially servants, often lent money and could invest with the new public institutions. Even if lottery tickets were relatively expensive for them, they could pool their money to buy a ticket. For example, Dorothie Hawes of Cheapside wrote on her ticket, 'We put in one lott, poor mayden we be ten: We pray God send us a good lott, that we may all say Amen.' As Froide notes, another ticket was divided into shares including a servant, though the sex of the shareholder is unknown, while another went to a cook maid. Furthermore, women invested in the Bank of England as stockholders, one of whom was a servant: Elizabeth Green, who worked in Covent Garden, and who invested £25 together with another servant.[83] Thus investing was not only the privilege of the middling and elite orders; girls with a little spare cash could also do so.

Older girls setting up in businesses also relied on credit. Small capital was necessary to set up even a small retail trade, like John Mitchell's daughter who sold confectionery in Aberdeen, to rent premises and buy in stock or materials. Young milliners were in the same position and Buchanan relied on family support to allow her to buy into a going concern with Muschet. Ann's father wrote to his brother seeking further family support of his daughter's business venture in 1756 explaining that the first ninety pounds was not sufficient:

> She is obliged to give long credit to many customers who are so kind to buy of her & to keep a necessary Stock of Goods always ready for her Shop for them to look at to please their fancy without which She can expect little or no Business . . . I now hope you will in your great and goodness assist me & Daug^{r} in our present wants & also to enable her to prosecute Business effectually hereafter by making the whole Sum that is to be lent Three Hundred Pounds the consequence of which Friendship will in all respects prove of the utmost service & greatest benefit & make her capable in proper time to repay you all back with most hearty thanks.[84]

She also acknowledged family support when she joined Muschet in 1757:

> I had a letter from Buntine Last week where she tells me that Mama and Grandpapa is very well pleased with the proposal and is willing to give as much credit as is needed; so I hope there is no fear of my getting Employment as I have so many relations; for there's all the Kier folk, Lady Helen Colquhoun; Lady Grace Campbell; Mrs Smalet and many my Dr than is needed to name.[85]

Personal credit and respectability underpinned her requests, but family was a key source of support. The practice of young women taking up little shops was so common that the Merchant company of Edinburgh tried to stop it in 1736, specifically citing servants: 'A great many women servants and others, who turning wearie of their services, have, out of a principle of avarice and habit of laziness taken up little shops, albeit they have no title to the privilege of trade in this city.'[86] This concern about numbers of servants suggests that girls in particular saw shopkeeping as an employment option through which they could operate to maintain themselves. Nevertheless, they still needed to find credit.

Conclusion

Girls' wages varied widely: farm servants were at the bottom of the scale, while domestic servants, especially with room and board, and perks and vails, did better. Girls in manufactories could earn well, and Honeyman showed that apprentices kept on in factories could be earning £27 a year. Income in protoindustries was particularly variable, since it depended on demand, family situation and the kind of industry. It also depended on whether she was full-time or not, since full-timers were better placed to earn well, possibly a third more than adult males in their families. Girls could spend on their 'expectations' since employers held their wages, and thus could buy things for them, clearing the debt when wages came due. Saving was therefore possible for some, to allow gathering a dowry; similarly in the world of increasing consumption opportunities, girls could certainly have been players. They were not the drivers of the consumer revolution, but they could buy small items, often to vary a daily outfit, or buy fashionable goods of a lesser quality from the purchases of the middling orders. They also operated in the credit worlds on a small scale, benefitting from enforced savings since many wages were paid in arrears, or using hiring monies to give them a little nest egg to lend or spend. Commercial credit networks were also open to them, especially if they gathered a group of friends to buy a lottery ticket, for example. They also usually had some money to spend on sociability and pleasures, as described in Chapter 8.

Notes

1 Lane et al., *Women, Work and Wages*, 6.
2 Humphries and Weisdorf, *Wages of Women.*
3 Horrell and Humphries, 'Exploitation of Little Children', Table A1.
4 Young, *Tour of the North*, vol. 3, 254–5.
5 Hembry, *Calendar of Bradford-on-Avon Settlement Examinations.*
6 Horrell and Humphries, *Women and Children*, and Humphries and Weisdorf, *Women's Wages.*
7 Davies, *The Agricultural History of Cheshire*, 80.
8 Kussmaul, *Servants in Husbandry*, 37–8; Snell, 'Agricultural Seasonal Unemployment', 414, and *Annals of the Labouring Poor*, 29–47.
9 Eden, *State of the Poor*, v. 2, 47.
10 Smout and Gibson, *Prices, Food and Wages*, 337–8.
11 Smout and Gibson, *Prices, Food and Wages*, 339.
12 OSA, XV, 520.
13 OSA, XV, 396.
14 Humphries and Weisdorf, 'Women and Children', 429–30.
15 OSA, XV, 721.
16 Hecht, *Domestic Servant*, 22–3.
17 Smout and Gibson, *Prices, Food and Wages*, v.
18 Meldrum, *Domestic Service and Gender*, 186.
19 Snell, *Annals of Labouring Poor*, 86; Meldrum, *Domestic Service and Gender*, 198.
20 Buck, *Dress in Eighteenth-Century England*, 114–5.
21 *LL* Middlesex Sessions Papers—Justices' Working Documents.
22 Chelsea Settlement and Bastardy Examinations, No. 133.
23 Earle, *City Full of People*, 142.
24 Whyte, 'Proto-industrialisation in Scotland', 240.

25 Davies, *Labourers in Husbandry*, 85.
26 Smout and Gibson, *Prices, Food and Wages*, 355. Data from the OSA are in £ sterling.
27 Smout and Gibson, *Prices, Food and Wages*, 355; Durie, *The Scottish Linen Industry*, 43, 76–7; Smith, *The Wealth of Nations*, vol. I, 106.
28 Steuart, *Considerations on*, 16.
29 Sharpe, 'Literally Spinsters', 55.
30 Sharpe, 'Literally Spinsters', 60.
31 Stirling County Archives, PD189.
32 *A General Description*, 149–50; Campbell, *London Tradesman*, 208.
33 Wilson, *The Annals of Penicuik*.
34 Burley, 'An Essex Clothier', 295.
35 Young, *Tour of the South*, 70; Young, *General View of the Agriculture of Suffolk*, 233.
36 Honeyman, *Child Workers*, 161.
37 Quoted Honeyman, *Child Workers*, 163.
38 OSA, XIV, 319.
39 Durie, *Scottish Linen Industry*, 369–71.
40 Burnette, 'Women's Wages in Agriculture', and Burnette, 'Testing for Occupational Crowding'.
41 Simonton, *History of European Women's Work*, 82.
42 Humphries and Weisdorf, 'The Wages of Women in England', 429.
43 Kussmaul, *Servants in Husbandry*, 81–3.
44 Muldrew, 'From Credit to Savings', 409.
45 Eden, *State of the Poor*, vol. 2, 74.
46 Meldrum, *Domestic Service*, 204.
47 Buck, *Dress in Eighteenth-Century England*, 112.
48 Buck, *Dress in Eighteenth-Century England*, 112.
49 Meldrum, *Domestic Servant*, 199.
50 Styles, *Dress of the People*, chapter 15.
51 Buck, *Dress in Eighteenth-Century England*, 113, 115.
52 Buck, *Dress in Eighteenth-Century England*, 119.
53 Defoe, *Great Law of Subordination*, 6.
54 Tyson and Guppy, *The French Journals of Mrs Thrale and Dr Johnson*, 148.
55 Defoe, *Great Law of Subordination Consider'd*, 6.
56 Maza, *Servants and Masters*, 133.
57 Hecht, *Domestic Servant*, 173.
58 McKendrick, *Birth of a Consumer Society*, 1.
59 Smith, *Wealth of Nations*, 869.
60 Fairchilds, 'Production and Marketing of Populuxe Goods', 228.
61 George, *London Life*, 173.
62 McKendrick, 'Home Demand and Economic Growth', 200, 209.
63 Roche, *People of Paris*, 227.
64 Buck, *Dress in Eighteenth-Century England*, 130.
65 Eden, *State of the Poor*, v. 1, 556–7.
66 Quoted Gowing, 'Marked Bodies and Social Meanings', 133.
67 Quoted Nenadic, 'Necessities: Food and Clothing', 150.
68 Styles, 'Custom or Consumption?', 103–15.
69 Quotes Styles, *Dress of the People*, 68, 69.
70 Davies, *Labourers in Husbandry*, 137.
71 Eden, *State of the Poor*, Appendix, cccxliii.
72 Eden, *State of the Poor*, 31–6.
73 Lemire, *Business of Everyday Life*, 88–9.

74 See Smith, 'Callico Madams', especially 40–2.
75 Quoted Smith, 'Callico Madams', 44.
76 Styles, *Dress of the People*, 285.
77 Styles, *Dress of the People*, 285–8, tables on 357–8.
78 The introduction to Spence, *Women, Credit, and Debt* is a useful overview.
79 Hunt, 'Time-management, Writing, and Accounting', 150.
80 Muldrew, *Economy of Obligation*, 107–9.
81 Muldrew, 'From Credit to Savings?', 407.
82 Shepard, 'Crediting Women'.
83 Froide, *Silent Partners*, 8, 31, 64.
84 Mungo Murray to William Murray of Polmaise Esq. 4 March 1756, SCA, Murray of Polmaise Collection PD189/2/334.
85 Ann Buchanan to Janet Muschet, 22 March 1757, SCA, Murray of Polmaise Collection, PD189/2/337.
86 Sanderson, *Women and Work*, 39.

8

SOCIAL LIFE, SOCIABILITY AND ASSOCIATIONS

Introduction

Girlhood was not all work and no play. They had times and spaces for leisure and sociable activities. As Chapter 2 argued, the Enlightenment agenda saw play and amusement as part of learning and growing up which became more widely acknowledged as the century progressed. We know less what this meant for girlhood since girls sat between the worlds of children in which play might be both allowed and encouraged and the worlds of adults in which work and industriousness were seen as priorities. To the wealthier classes, leisure for the plebeians was often problematic and commonly described as laziness. This debate ran through the century and indeed became more fraught as the century passed, and by the nineteenth century, leisure for the plebs was supposed to be 'rational exercise', not frivolity. So, while popular culture and girls' worlds gave them opportunities for leisure, pleasure and sociability, critics often condemned it for its potential lewdness and bad behaviour as well as simply laziness. This chapter examines the issues of time and opportunity for girlhood leisure and sociability against this context, recognising the clash between popular and elite concepts of time and sociability. Girls' activities were embedded in plebeian culture and much of it took place at home or in the community. Sociability included times when friends could enjoy socialising while working, but also included the fairs, harvest celebrations, weddings and other similar events, often including sports and games. Their associations also embraced work solidarities and collective action, while the use of friendly societies provided not only sociability but also insurance and protection when sickness, accidents or death hit them.

DOI: 10.4324/9781003412168-9

Time, gender and leisure

Much of our concept of time is tied up with modern ideas of a division between work time and leisure time. The world of the eighteenth century was more fluid. Certainly, there were concepts of time, but demarcating it was not managed in the same ways or with the same cultural considerations as today. Work time was not 'time-disciplined' in the same way, though by the later parts of the century, 'factory' time would come to define 'work' and 'not work' hours. Cunningham argues that as leisure became a more studied topic from the 1970s, historians increasingly segregated work and leisure as oppositional concepts. The emphasis on and valorising of leisure tended to devalue work itself as a negative other, as something to be done to permit leisure.[1] In many respects, such conceptualisations of time, and of work and leisure relies on a notion of time as male and modern. Arguably, time for many in the eighteenth century was shaped by other considerations. It was about tasks and inflected by traditions and customs as well as by environmental factors. Time was marked by seasons and the religious calendar. The year was broken into quarters, and the quarter days, such as Michaelmas or Martinmas, were key dates in the rural calendar as traditional dates for hirings to begin. These were recorded in the almanacs that permeated eighteenth-century society from humble homes to the elite. How people understood time also depended on whether they lived in town or country and what their social position was.

Society recognised a notion of a 'working day' with regulations and legislation dating back to 1495, and they continued to be imposed and amended into the eighteenth century, sometimes specified for single trades, like tailors. Control of hours was often based on an anxiety that workers would idle away their time, but as Cunningham noted, 'Statute law represented an ideal, reality was often different. This was not so much because workers or employers did not accept the assumptions of the law but because circumstances made it impossible to uphold them.'[2] Other factors came into play such as weather conditions, supply and demand of materials, products and workers. Nevertheless, there was an idea of what constituted the working day, Campbell suggesting twelve or fourteen hours for London trades, beginning primarily around 6 a.m. Hans Joachim Voth, using Old Bailey testimonies for 1749 to 1763, found that on average people got up just before 6 a.m. and were at work from shortly before 7 a.m. until about 7 p.m., or two hours less. They were in bed by 11 p.m. This pattern was virtually unchanged at the end of the century, though working hours increased by about half an hour.[3] Timing suggests the significance of light and dark, and before the onset of street lighting, people of necessity tended to operate around hours of daylight. Girls experienced this as schools shifted attendance hours by seasons. Town lighting began at the end of the seventeenth century and spread relatively slowly across Britain. While this is pertinent for work time, people also walked and associated for pleasure, and shops benefitted from extended passing trade. People traversed the town using the moon, lanterns and ambient light where streetlamps did not exist. Making the city secure and safe to navigate was a priority. Disorder and crime were constant concerns, physical and sexual safety assuredly so. While working in daylight was pragmatic it also reflected an endemic fear of the dark. Nights were a particularly alarming time, and 'gave cover to the disorderly and immoral, and made the public spaces of the city stages for violence, theft and latent evil'.[4] As Pamela Phillips argued, '[D]ay and light, providers of order, knowledge, and safety, are enhanced by their opposition to the nighttime hours that harbor danger, mystery, ignorance, and transgression. This dichotomy lies at the foundation of human culture by organizing a code of "correct" human behavior and "proper" spaces.'[5]

The meaning of time had specific salience for women and girls. The authors of *Women's Leisure, What Leisure?* suggested that 'the artificial separation of areas of life entitled "work" and "leisure" into different subsections of the discipline both marginalized the experiences of women and obscured the significant "overlaps" that happen in real life'.[6] Women's work and leisure were in tension with one another, since no clear delineation existed between the two. They had long supported others' leisure, feeding and looking after households, but also preparing and organising outings so men's time might be seen as more clearly work and not work while women's time merged one into another. Thompson argued that women had 'an imperfect sense of time' imbedded in a pre-modern world in which '"task-orientation" in relation to the "natural work-rhythms" operated instead of time-discipline'.[7] Such a sense of time undervalues women's strategies and undermines ideas about what leisure meant to women. Firstly, they operated to many of the same regimes as men did. They endured the time-discipline imposed on domestic industries by market dates, raw material deliveries and putting-out networks, a discipline greatly amplified by the intensification of labour driving down piece rates. Shifting international markets brought spells of highly intensive labour followed by periods of unemployment. As servants, workers and apprentices, girls operated within these occupational structures. Yet, because much of their work was task-oriented, working around seasons, deadlines and household needs, their work time and not work time tended to merge.

Women's leisure time was not seen as time for relaxation, as Ingram commented: 'While the men were engaged in cultivating the earth, and other occupations abroad the females employed their leisure time, in the intervals of their ordinary domestic avocations, in the manufacture of woollen and linen for the use of the family.'[8] Thus, distinguishing between work and leisure was more problematic for women than for men. Girls were expected to fill their hours with work around the house, purchasing, preparing, and clearing away meals, cleaning, washing, and minding small children. Virtually all girls were supposed to knit, spin or sew in their 'time off'. Ingram advised: '[A]ccording to the circumstances of the district, they may most profitably employ their leisure intervals, or gain a livelihood, when destitute of other work, or, again, supply themselves and families with some articles of primary necessity.'[9] Servant's time was constrained, and leisure time restricted since 'A servant is not to go out without leave'.[10] Work and leisure were not compartmentalised, and many women found themselves regularly moving between them, as part of their life flow. As a time-disciplined workforce developed especially after mid-century, girls became increasingly tied to forms of work that structured their use of time, rather than fitting between other tasks of domestic life. They also marched to the same cultural norms of time: hiring conventions, seasons and the annual calendar of feasts and holidays, secular and religious. Cunningham reckoned adding 'all the Sundays, the Mondays and Tuesdays at Easter and Whitsun, and the saints' days, it amounted to seventy-nine days in the year rest days for prayer and worship. These complemented other church events, as well as local traditional feasts, celebrations, May Day and the annual village feasts or wakes, often associated with Whitsun or harvests.'[11] But women and girls did enjoy leisure and moments of repose, as Tammy Proctor said: 'Despite the demands of childrearing, family care, work in fields and factories, religious instruction and devotion, women have always found opportunities in their days for private joys or civic revelling.'[12]

Popular culture

The elision between work, leisure and recreation was important throughout popular culture. Community activities from market days to fairs involved exchanging gossip, pleasure and sociability. Proctor argued that

> leisure in the modern capitalist world meant establishing an identity apart from work and family and escaping from the predictability and lack of autonomy . . . Whether in rural areas or cities, amusement meant socialization, and leisured time was usually spent with others. Such popular culture cemented social ties, provided a chance for reaffirming local mores and rules, and reflected the importance of communal life in pre-industrial and industrializing societies.[13]

Thus, interwoven with working and busyness were occasions that gave people respite and pleasure, perhaps helping to while away the time.

Popular culture was not static and transformations in this 'traditional' culture began appearing by the end of the century as economic and social changes had an impact. Increased literacy and innovative ideas and laissez-faire attitudes to business and trade fed the growth of capitalism. Corporate entities, like guilds, confraternities and communalism were declining, while high rates of mobility, both geographic and social, fostered openness and made interpersonal relationships harder to sustain. Migration was also a factor in shifting the parameters of popular culture. Town and country had an umbilical connection, but their cultures were framed by important differences, which made towns seem more open and fluid than rural communities. There is little doubt that cities of all sizes offered opportunities and constraints to individuals. People left smaller towns for larger ones, dormant towns for vibrant ones, the countryside for urban opportunities. Towns acted as a magnet for the young, the ambitious, the underemployed, even the elderly. Commonly women looking for subsistence, married or single, formed the bulk of migrants creating a steadily rising female-to-male sex ratio in many European cities with an expanding range of jobs open to women. Some migratory patterns retained links with the place of origin, but in many cases, those links broke, and local customs and identities were gradually absorbed into a new cultural nexus. Forms of community leisure also shifted. For example, local rural fêtes continued more regularly than in towns, while large fairs like London's Southwark Fair gradually declined. Yet, despite an image of towns as spaces where strangers and rootless congregated, free from the constrictions of the rural world, cities could generate new forms of community, belonging and identity.[14]

The informality and regular rambunctiousness of many plebian leisure activities were also part of their death knell. Historians regularly point out attempts for a more organised, controlled and rational approach to leisure by the end of the century, and as Howard Newby says, 'This meant that the traditional round of festivals, ceremonies and celebrations was in decline and it had not yet been supplanted by modern forms of mass, commercialized leisure.'[15] Similarly Golbie and Purdue argue

> the general movement was one towards more orderly and organised celebrations, in which there was a greater role for women and children, and a compromise between the concepts of community and recreation held by the dominant sections of society and those which were developing within the lower classes. Even in the countryside, festivals and sports became more organised and limited to specific arenas—the rectory garden or squire's park loaned for the occasion or the cricket field, and later the football field, donated by a benefactor.[16]

Home and community

Girls were involved in communal activities on their doorstep much as others were. They ran errands for workplace and home, taking them into the streets and markets. As Malcolmson noted, 'A trip to the market combined business with social pleasures; exchanging news and courtesies with a craftsman or dealer introduced sociability into an economic or service transaction.'[17]

Street trading blended conversation with market activities and were typical gathering places for the labouring orders and a significant location of intercourse and casual sociability. Religion was also a focal point for leisure and provided 'a supportive communal and cultural life', and 'formed relatively enduring structures for social intercourse', especially for those engaged in Methodism or cottage religions.[18] Girls shared in activities and events which elaborated social values and morals in the community as well as shaping local culture and expectations. These were activities which welded communities together—though, of course, disruptions and rancour also ran through these worlds. In addition to conviviality, pleasure and relaxation, such activities were part of courtship, which is addressed explicitly in Chapter 9.

Much of what has been written about Georgian sociability reflects elite and middling activities. Balls, theatres and music venues are perceived as settings for a certain level of society to relax and enjoy themselves, and to see and be seen. While largely true it also erases the way working people, male and female, related to such ventures. Price alone could exclude many girls. In Aberdeen, for example, an evening's concert cost 2s or 2s 6d in September 1751, and several were held as part of a seasonal subscription series.[19] Although 'free' plays formed part of the entertainment, you had to get in first, and charges excluded the plebeians. Indeed, they were frequently advertised as 'concerts for the ladies'. Theatre attendance was cheaper, and gallery seats could be had for 1s. in 1788.[20] Theatre catered to wide audiences including artisans and servants, and lower middling girls would also have access. Spatial distinctions were important. Multiple descriptions refer to the maids among the crowd in the gallery, and Rebecca Wright pointed also to the 'the fruit women, selling refreshments, copies of plays and books of songs, and the prostitutes who worked in the auditorium', and John Brewer to 'servants and the hoi polloi looked down from the upper gallery, price one shilling, while the whores cruised the upper boxes and orange-sellers offered fruit at exorbitant prices'.[21] While detailed evidence is slim, then, girls might also have shared in this form of formalised leisure, and the liminal character of many plays, especially farces, suggests they were not exclusive and intended only for the better off.

While urban pleasure gardens discouraged working people and charged a fee, about 1s, which was beyond most working girls, gardens and open spaces offered places to meet friends. Many formal parks and garden derive from the nineteenth century, but towns and the countryside provided options for many. Peter Borsay argued that rural pleasures and a growth in the rural nature of health grew significantly in the eighteenth century, and it is likely that some of these ideas also became of more importance to workers, especially those in towns. Artists depicted working girls in London parks, such as Rowlandson's *Milkmaids and Gentlemen in St. James's Park* and Benjamin West's *Milkmaids in St. James's Park, Westminster Abbey Beyond* (see Chapter 10, Image 10.2). Thompson also commented that when Princess Amelia tried to close access to Richmond New Park in the 1750s, 'she was opposed by a vigorous horizontal consciousness.'[22] Logically the countryside was a workplace for agricultural workers, but it was also where they might take their leisure. Certainly, many competitions and feasts, like May Day, took place in rural spaces.

The inn or pub was popular gathering space for socialising, sharing with others, enjoying company. Yet girls' access is hard to trace. Inns were perceived as male spaces, but this does not reflect the ways girls and women interacted with them. As Daniel Maudlin says,

> this picture does not take account of the women also attending meetings, dances, performances and exhibitions, dining in mixed groups in the public rooms downstairs or the relatively large number of elite female travellers who would have been a constant presence in parlour, lobby and coach yard and on the stairs and corridors that led to bedchambers. That is, while male drinking clubs were a common and colourful feature of inn-life they were but one of the many activities hosted by an inn, most of which involved women.[23]

Others also confirm that plebeian women were active participants in pub life although probably at more modest inns (Image 8.1). Brewer argues that these'were places of pleasure and business, catering to customers from all walks of life, centres of rumour, news and information. In these snug centres of conversation and conviviality, groups of men (and, less usually, women) gathered to drink, gossip, trade, debate and intrigue'.[24] Clark further claims that 'Women's culture extended beyond the home into the streets. The acceptability of female drinking in plebeian society gave women access to public space and the intimacy intoxication could render. Women drank together as well as in the company of men.'[25] Also, female Friendly Societies met up in pubs. Women and girls might accompany a father or husband for a meal and drink, or groups of women might visit a tavern to celebrate a special event or occasion, such as the birth of a child or a carnival celebration, or even stay as guests at inns, especially travellers.[26] In Birmingham, the Robin Hood Free Debating Society met at the Red Lion tavern while the Amicable Debating Society met at a coffee-house, and women were encouraged to attend, though placed behind a barrier in the balcony. In 1773, Samuel Riley reported that in Saddleworth Wales, 'He went into an alehouse that was crowded with men and women rolling about drunk and singing indecent songs.'[27] Drinking was seen as not respectable for women, though plebeian culture did not share this prohibition. Beer was commonly supplied for farm workers, and as Davies said, 'Time was when small beer was reckoned one of the necessaries of life, even in poor families: and it seems to have been designed by Providence for

IMAGE 8.1 Thomas Rowlandson, 1756–1827, Two Girls Tippling, undated. Watercolour with pen and grey ink over graphite on medium, slightly textured, cream laid paper, Yale Center for British Art, Paul Mellon Collection, B1977.14.347.

the common drink of the people of this country.'[28] Drunkenness was criticised by the middling orders, but girls are seldom mentioned in this context.

Clearly, working girls were present in inns as servants and workers, serving beer and food. Also, many innkeepers were women, often as partners or widows, like Mrs McGhie in Aberdeen's New Inn. Women were associated with the hospitality trade across the social scale in the eighteenth century. But this was work. Inns were, however, conflicted spaces, 'neutral in terms of use, they were not at all neutral in terms of user'.[29] It was a liminal space wherein female respectability was often suspect, and girls and women were vulnerable to abuse and sexual advances in these arenas. The elision with prostitution of the girls, and even innkeepers, had grounds in truth, although many were, in fact, respectable places, but dependent on the class of clientele and landlady. They also were potential spots for prostitutes to solicit, which created dilemmas for servant maids. The inns on Aberdeen's Castlegate were seen as quality places for businessmen to meet, while at the same time, the street was often cited in complaints against prostitutes. Yet, in no complaints do the servants or landladies appear.[30]

Plebeian women operated in worlds which were not always separate, with public spaces overlapping with private or domestic ones. The context of plebeian culture was significant here because it did not operate in the ways that middling folk expected and as Clark says, 'Plebeian women often shocked middle-class observers by their enjoyment of the pleasures of public life . . . Still, they could not indulge in libertinism as easily as artisan men could, for their respectability was much more fragile, based on sexual reputation rather than skill.'[31]

Work and leisure

Girls joined in collective activities which combined work and leisure, sharing in such a way that encompassed tasks but also sociability. Patterns of socialising while working had a long history. In Germanic countries, the *spinnstuben* (spinning rooms) were a feature, and in France the *veillée* played the same role. In America they took the form of spinning bees or quilting bees. In England, they were simply gatherings while in Scotland and Ireland the ceilidh, or céilí, performed the same function, the word meaning simply 'gathering'. It has also given us the concept of a traditional music-and-dance evening in modern Celtic communities, but its origin lies in the evening gatherings at which people congregated to work, often with reading, music, singing and sometimes dancing as part of the evening activities. They were conceived initially as a way for people to share light and warmth while continuing work after dark, spinning, knitting, mending fish nets, etc. in a collective setting. As Malcolmson explained, 'story-telling might accompany the work of spinners, harvesters, or servants. Weavers sang at their looms, haymakers in the fields. Women gossiped over their sewing. Among some groups of workers one of their members was appointed to read aloud as the others worked.'[32] Some communities had a dedicated space where people gathered, in Scotland the eponymously named 'ceilidh house'; in others they met in homes, barns or wherever there was space. These gatherings often focused on girls who brought 'their spinning wheels, knitting needles as well as their news, love stories, anecdotes about dances and other matters. There will be knitting, spinning, laughing, teaching and telling stories, all waiting longingly for the appearance of the courtiers, and then the game will begin all over again.'[33] Although they played a role in courtship, men and boys were often excluded, and offered girls and women a chance of same-sex sociability. What Rosemary Sweet says for polite urban socialisation could be paraphrased to describe the working girl's use of these spaces: sociability marked these leisure spaces as women intermingled, producing and reproducing their own identities through their sociability.[34]

As basic literacy improved, solitary leisure also meant reading for pleasure (Image 8.2). Chapbooks, available throughout Europe, provided access to romances, pious tales like Hannah More's *Cheap Repository Tracts*, folk tales and 'true crime'. Popular books like Defoe's *Robinson Crusoe* and *Moll Flanders* were abridged and widely available, as were multiple versions of the exploits of popular heroes like Robin Hood. They included almanacs, children's literature, folklore, nursery rhymes and poetry. Printers produced them cheaply, using woodcuts, cheap paper and flimsy binding and sold them for pennies. Short simple texts were available to a wide range of people, and girls would have spent spare pennies on these. Improving literature used similar formulas, and while probably not such popular reading as tales of excitement and romance, many were intended for girls, like Trimmer's *The Servant's Friend* written specifically for girls going into service as was Eliza Haywood's

IMAGE 8.2 Philip Dawe, ca. 1750–ca. 1790, Reading by a Paper-Bell Shade, 1768. Mezzotint and etching on medium, moderately textured, cream laid paper, Yale Center for British Art, Paul Mellon Fund, B1970.3.856.

Present for a Servant Maid (1743) or Jonas Hanway's *Advice from Farmer Trueman, to His Daughter Mary, Upon Her Going to Service*. There is debate over whether moralistic tracts had a real readership or whether they were produced by well-meaning persons because they were 'good' for the poor. Reading for many members of the working classes, women included, was not easy nor habitual, so that some material would have been beyond their ability. However, Richard Altick claims that by 1789 the Wesleyans represented the largest group of lower-class readers, numbering some 56,000.[35]

This was a society in transition from an oral tradition to a reading public, and chapbooks were part of that shift. Even more so were ballads, which were increasingly written down and published as single-page broadsides. They served a similar function of providing cheap and accessible reading, and as Barclay shows they often provided reading for girls and youths with frequent references to courting, love and intimacy.[36] That many were written down from women who sang them in communal settings speaks to their importance in female culture. Thus, ballads, the stories which found their way into chapbooks, as well as information about work and community practice were part of transmitting culture and were another route into leisure for girls. While we think of reading as a solitary activity, it too took on a communal character in a society in which those who were literate read aloud to others. This could take place in a workshop wherein one read to the others, in the evening gatherings and in inns and other communal spaces. Girls shared in this culture, perhaps even becoming the designated 'reader'.

Fairs, festivals and frivolity

For all members of society, amusements were found locally in the variety of entertainments that came from festivals, fairs and other community pursuits. Girls were frequent, numerous and sometimes noisy participants at the fairs, dances and festivals of local communities. Maria Spilsbury's *Greenwich Fair* clearly shows the mix of age, sex and sociability they offered (Image 8.3). Rowdy and exuberant, maids and other working girls, usually identifiable by their caps, contributed to the large crowds, enjoying the entertainments, eating and drinking, and sharing company with their peers. Fairs had sprung up around the country, often linked to markets and annual agricultural sales, serving practical needs as well as sociable spaces for all classes of society like the Pitlessie fair:

> Pitlessie Fair, held twice a year in May and October in what was a tiny community of 300 inhabitants, was just one example of hundreds of such events that took place each year in half the towns of Scotland. They were great occasions these—a combination of commercial enterprise and social junketing that to my understanding has no comparison today. The fairs

IMAGE 8.3 Maria Spilsbury, 1777–1820, Greenwich Fair, ca. 1800. Oil on canvas, Yale Center for British Art, Gift of Gilbert W. Chapman, transfer from the Yale University Art Gallery, B2022.6.

provided the biggest shopping opportunities of the year, and in fact originated in medieval times specifically to encourage and facilitate trade.[37]

The Hallows Fair on Edinburgh's Grassmarket was usually held on 1 November, and memorialised by Scots poet Robert Fergusson in 1772: it was clearly a chance for boys and girls to have some fun:

HALLOW-FAIR
At Hallowmas, whan nights grow lang,
And starnies shine fu' clear,
Whan fock, the nippin cauld to bang,
Their winter hapwarms wear;
Near Edinburgh a fair there hads,
I wat there's nane whase name is,
For strappin dames and sturdy lads,
And cap and stoup, mair famous,
Than it that day.
Upo' the tap o' ilka lum,

The sun began to keek,
And bad the trig-made maidens come,
A sightly jo to seek,
At Hallow-fair, whare browsters rare,
Keep gude ale on the gantries,
An dinna scrimp ye o' a skair,
O' kebbucks frae thair pantries,
Fu' saut that day.
Her country John in bannet blue,
An' eke his Sunday's claes on,
Rins efter Meg wi rokelay new,
An' sappy kisses lays on;
She'll tauntin say, Ye silly coof?
Be o'yer gab mair sparin;
He'll tak the hint, and criesh her loof,
Wi' what will buy her farin,
To chow that day.
Here chapman billies tak thair stand, . . .

Local fêtes were sprinkled across the landscape, and the flourishing local traditions involved both men and women. The young were singularly active, even if they did not dominate, but some events like May Day mornings were specifically for them. In 1715, Nicholas Blundell reported that at Little Crosby, 'the Little Boyes and Girles of this Town diverted themselves with Rearing a May-pole in the West-Lane, they had Morrys dancing and a great many came to it both old and young.'[38] Girls were ever-present even if accounts tend to mention youths more frequently. They decorated rush carts, maypoles, food stalls and other paraphernalia of the fête. Weddings also were a focus for communal leisure involving especially young people, and girls certainly took an active part. Eden noted that 'a custom of a general feasting at weddings and christenings is still continued in many villages, in Scotland, in Wales and in Cumberland . . . indeed it is not singular that, marriages, births, christenings, house-warmings, etc., should be occasions in which people of all classes and all descriptions think it right to rejoice and make merry.'[39] These were often sizeable communal affairs to which everyone contributed something. In 1712, Blundell described the preparations for a celebration rewarding his workers for their work marling the fields.

July 4. Some of the young Foulks of this Town met those of the Morehouses and of Great Crosby to consider about the Flowering of my Marl-pit . . .
July 8. I was very busy in the after Noone making Kaps etc: for my Marlers and Dansers, severall of Great Crosby Lasses helped me. The Young Women of this Town, Morehouses and Great Crosby dressed the Garlands

in my Barne for Flowering of my Marl pit. I tought my 8 Sword Dancers their Dance, they had Musick and Danced it in my Barn.

July 9. . . . The six Garlands etc: were carried by Young Women in Prosestion, the 8 Sword Dancers etc: went along with them to the Marl-pit where they Dansed, the Musick was Gerard Holsold and his Son and Richard Tatlock, at Night they Danced in the Barne.[40]

More dancing, eating and drinking followed as the marling continued over nearly two weeks (Image 8.4). Regular events, like haymaking, were also communal events which embodied a combination of work and festivity. Imagery like that of Stubbs (*Reapers* and other haymaking paintings, like Image 6.1) shows girls and youth 'wearing their Sunday best clothing, according to the conventions that associated haymaking no less than Harvest-Home as an occasion of festivity and courtship when best clothing was worn, perhaps to be gleefully discarded as rustic youths and ruddy maids labored and sweated together.'[41]

Many fairs and markets were chaotic and rumbustious affairs; paintings show girls as ever present, sharing the fun, and probably at risk of some of the semi-violence of sexual harassment that was part and parcel of many events. As Malcolmson explained,

> Fairs were probably the recreational events which were most commonly employed for sexual licence. An apt illustration of this feature is the October fair at Charlton in Kent which was vigorously condemned, but also perceptively observed, by Daniel Defoe. 'The village, he said, is . . . infamous for the yearly collected rabble of mad-people, at Horn-Fair . . . The mob indeed at that time take all kinds of liberties, and the women are especially impudent for that day; as if it was a day that justify'd the giving themselves a loose to all manner of indecency and immodesty, without any reproach, or without suffering.'[42]

IMAGE 8.4 David Allan, A Highland Dance, about 1792. Dipper Historic / Alamy Stock Photo.

Hiring fairs, common in a wide range of communities, were specifically attended by girls and youths looking for work and remained the means of finding new employment. An annual statute fair for hiring servants in husbandry was advertised at Alfreton in Derbyshire in October 1784 which promised suitable encouragement and some entertainment for young people. Like many markets, they were not only a pragmatic way to deal with a regular necessity for employers and girls to connect but also migrated into a range of sociable opportunities from taking drink before returning home to becoming a virtual 'fun' fair with music and dancing. For many girls these were annual occasions on which they could participate in the hubbub and stimulation of the wider world.[43]

Fun and games

Fairs and festivals were also the occasion for contests, sports and games, sometimes informal, sometimes organised. For example, they hosted smock races in which women and girls ran a set course in little more than their shift. This was a crowd-pleasing event, but also a chance for young women to demonstrate their physical prowess. These races fit within a larger tradition of foot races, involving men and women, and had evolved from when masters might promote races between male servants. But as Peter Radford showed, in the eighteenth century, women and girls were even more likely to compete with one another than boys and men were. 'In an analysis of 50 such events, less than one-third had running events for men or boys, but nearly 80 per cent had running events for women or girls. Viewed as a folk-event, running races seem, therefore, to have been largely a woman's affair.'[44] Contrary to some versions of these races, they did not only compete for a smock or dress, but for a wide range of prizes, including a leg of mutton, and for younger girls, perhaps an apron. They might take place in association with fêtes, weddings, horse races, church festivals and other fairs and festivals. In 1790, the *English Chronicle* reported, for example, 'The wedding was attended with the usual divertissements, a horse and a foot race, a bull baiting, wrestling &c . . . The whole concluded with dancing.'[45] In 1749, the *Aberdeen Journal* reported

> We hear, that at the new Market at Fettercairn; which began the 26th called Lambas Fair, belonging to George Middleton, of Seaton, esq. There was a great Number of Sheep, black cattle quantint of linen and woollen cloth etc. . . . besides several Prizes to be run for by Men, Women and Horse, and the Market custom-free, all which he continues next Year.[46]

Woodforde described watching a smock race in May 1784 at the Heart Inn in Norfolk for Whitsun festivities, to which he 'let all my people go except

Lizzy', his maidservant who had been ill.[47] They were especially prevalent in the last decade of the century, and although the light attire of the women and girls was often criticised, they remained popular and common events, and were 'part of the traditional life in England and Scotland'.[48] They were meant for fun, and participants knew they would be laughed at—it was the spirit of the thing.

Other types of competitions for women were popular spectator sports. Some like boxing were more common in urban areas, and Proctor notes,

> often the combatants were poor women, and many of the matches were set up to represent larger issues, such as the Englishwoman versus an Irishwoman. One eyewitness described a Drury Lane fight between two women thus: '[They were] engaged in a scratching and boxing match, their faces entirely covered with blood, bosoms bare, and the clothes nearly torn from their bodies.'[49]

Betty Rizzo argued that working women had to be strong, wore clothing that enabled physical exertion, and could shout or exhibit themselves in public.

> It was, therefore, perfectly acceptable and amusing that plebeian women such as Christian Davies, daughter of an Irish maltster, had 'too much mercury' in her for a sedentary life, loved ploughing, raking, and exercise as a girl, rode bareback . . . 'My inclinations, while a girl, were always masculine'.[50]

Girls played cricket and other competitive games especially in rural areas, sometimes becoming well-organised affairs such as the first recorded organised women's cricket match held in 1745 in Surrey, between Bramley and Hambleton maids. They were dressed all in white, and 'The Bramley maids had blue ribbons and the Hambl [sic] maids red ribbons on their heads. The Bramley girls got 119 notches and the Hambleton girls 127 . . . the girls bowled, batted, ran and catched as well as most men could do in that game.'[51] Many sports that emerged during the century were for men, but this belies the extent to which girls took part as participants and observers. Normally they also had more freedom from responsibilities than married women and mothers. Certainly, many sports required investment and mainly involved elite and middling women, but the communal character of local entertainment and activities meant that girls were present, and because of their youth and agility, were more likely to attend and take part.

Solidarities

A feature of girls' lives is that they rarely spent their lives in isolation. They worked with others, often other girls; they were usually one of a couple apprentices or more, and workshops also had women working in them. Maids of all work may have been the only servant in a household, but they would gather and chat with others and associated with sellers and shopkeepers in the course of their duties. Prostitutes too were known for working together, and many of those in Aberdeen charged with streetwalking or disorderly behaviour were charged in pairs. Girls had multiple ways of socialising and people to relate to inside and outside the home and workplace. They could create powerful informal social lives embedded in friendships, kin networks and neighbourhood and community. They shared experiences and provided support in a female network of solidarities. This is not to suggest they were always convivial, because disputes and altercations surely could break out. 'Traditional' forms of community action were resilient, including charivari, carnival, ritual and inversion tactics, which included women and girls. Girls also had access to other groups and associations through which they could become embedded in different concerns and activities, such as mutual benefit organisations, labour movements and political societies. Many of these were in their infancy, and girls were less likely to be prominent, but they nevertheless were a fundamental part of collaboration, communication and socialisation.

In many forms of collective action, girls were invisible. Some like labour disputes and political actions tended to be dominated by and led by men. This does not mean women and girls were not there, but that often we cannot see them. In part this is due to historical reporting which for generations has been gender-blind and accepted a notion of public/private that suggested women did not take public action or were unimportant to it. Bob Bushaway, for example, argues that women and children were not normally regarded as powerful elements in the structure of the community, implying they were rarely involved, and says when they were involved, it was symbolic of community strength and played on the rubric of role reversal.[52] This diminishes the role we see women playing. Furthermore, contemporary comment, including male protestors and local officials, tended to ignore or obscure women's participation. To some extent this may have been partly true, but examples from Europe suggest such activity was not so unequivocal or absolute.[53] Women, however, are often described as dominating, organising and promoting food and bread riots, reflecting a notion that women were responsible for feeding families. However, historians have increasingly shown that women were virtually ever present. Across eighteenth-century Europe women participated in sundry protests; they did not 'think only with their stomachs'.[54] They may well have had a better knowledge of bread and grain prices, positioning them to instigate protests, but this regularly repeated argument has led to a perception that food riots were a specific province of women, belittling their contribution to other forms of civic protest. Although Thompson saw them as 'those most involved in face-to-face marketing, most sensitive to price significancies, most experienced in detecting short-weight or inferior quality', he argues there is no 'myth of the feminine food riot', and no historian has shown that they were the monopoly of women.[55] Other historians also are sceptical of women's special prominence, since many male workers were also evident, and like Wendy Thwaites, for eighteenth-century Oxfordshire, they note 'food riots concerned men, as much [as] or more than women.' The same is true in Scotland where Jane Rendall suggests that 'women's leadership in food riots seemed conspicuous because it contrasted with the rarity of their appearances in other forms of political action.'[56] Women's marketplace activities and food provisioning certainly contributed to provoking women to act.

They were less likely to be involved in artisanal disputes. In England, women were more prominent in resisting early textile machinery, explicitly spinning technologies, but less so against the flying shuttle for which they were secondary workers or in cloth dressing from which they were excluded. This reflected their workplace position and their point of contact with civic power.[57] Rendall also suggests that women did not appear in political movements until after 1815, although they were present in the Wilkite, Gordon and anti-Jewish naturalisation riots in London and the Porteous riots in Edinburgh.[58] In part it is simply hard to 'see' women in protests, but one example comes from riots about the anti-Militia Act riot in Tranent, Scotland, in August 1797 which enacted a compulsory levy of men for the army. Several women, beating drums, led the crowd, against which soldiers opened fire, killing twelve people, including Joan ('Jackie') Crookston[e] (1768–97), who has been memorialised with a statue, and Isabel Roger.[59] As Karen Hunt argued, women were primarily involved in the relatively rare economic and religious disturbances with political overtones. For example, women participated in riots in the 1720s prompted by rumours of the extension of indirect taxation, though not to the same extent as men. But she echoes the fact that recording women's presence was sporadic. They could also act with other women or with men, or provide the incitement to revolt and then leave more violent action to the men.[60] Thus, women were no doubt present as members of crowds, sometimes leading as with Crookstone and Roger, but plebeian women adopted a more overt political presence in the next century. How gender operated in popular disturbances is highly debated but knowledge of their communities shaped how they acted during moments of unrest and collective action. Women characteristically networked, shared information and guided actions. They exploited their knowledge of how society worked, monitoring events through local contacts, neighbourhood intelligence and information networks.

In all reports however, 'girls' were decidedly invisible, which does not mean they were not there. Some accounts referred only to women, and some to women and children, and thus once again girls were shrouded by their age and social position. The 'housewife' nomenclature serves to promote that cloak. Girls' position as largely subordinate to masters as servants or apprentices could have made them wary participants. On the other hand, and especially in largely female company, they could well have joined in. Although the age of the 'sister' referred to hereafter is not clear, her role and position could well have suggested she was a girl. At Leicester,

> A certain manufacturer of worsted threatened a sister of ours, whom he employed, that he would send all his jersey to be spun at the mill; and further insulted her with the pretended superiority of that work. She having more spirit than discretion, stirred up the sisterhood and they stirred up all the men they could influence (not a few) to go and destroy the mills erected in and near Leicester, and this is the origin of the late riots there.[61]

The sense that girls had 'spirit' comes into play regularly, and they were prepared to find ways to resist what they saw as injustice. Thus, on 13 September 1755, the *Norwich Mercury* repeated a report from the *Newcastle Journal*:

> Newcastle, Sept 6. We are advised from Penrith, that lately a young girl in Kendal being with child and near her time, sent for a physician in town to do her the office of a midwife, which he refused, and giving her hard names, left her: She in return for this usage, and willing to do good for evil, dignified the man by declaring him the father of the child.

Collective action could take many forms. On 10 October 1716, two men and three women amongst a larger crowd of some thirty were indicted for a 'Riot, in assembling themselves with diverse other Persons in a Riotous Manner under a Pretence of celebrating in a publick and insulting Manner the Death of Thomas Bean, a Malefactor convicted last Sessions for Felony'. Hester Tibbs was a servant and Anne Lane possibly also, and all of them claimed that they had been invited to the funeral and only went to celebrate his memory; nevertheless they were fined.[62] As expected, few women turn up charged for riot at the Old Bailey, and when they were, they were part of a larger crowd, but were especially visible and in one case probably the leader of the mob. They also appeared as witnesses, and in a case against Thomas Downs in 1780, Elizabeth Frazer, a servant girl of fifteen, was the first witness to a mob housebreaking where she lived with her mother. Notably, her testimony was vigorously challenged, and she was virtually bullied by the counsel, far less than her mother who testified after her.[63] In Aberdeen on 4 January 1755, Janet Pirie was 'complained on for inciting a mob at the Church previous Thursday; held to behave herself decently and discreetly and not be guilty of such practices in time coming, 200 merks.'[64] Her age is indeterminate, but she may have been one of the mantuamakers described in the next section. This handful of examples shows that girls were part of these collective actions, sometimes the instigators.

Friendly societies

In Britain there were no specifically female guilds, unlike in France, and they relied on men to protect their interests. However, guilds were also one of their biggest challenges. In Aberdeen in 1726, the bakers prohibited 'female pastry bakers' from using members' ovens for firing cakes, biscuits and other pastry. Similarly, the tailors had a long-running dispute with mantuamakers dating from the early years of the century in which they first tried to prohibit women from encroaching on their male privilege of making women's clothes, then granted 'tollerations' [sic] to permit individual women to do so, and finally made them pay a fee to the guild as well as a fine for doing so, in 1717 recording Rachel Baxter, who signed her agreement and in 1728, Janet Pirie, daughter of a shipmaster.[65]

A phenomenon of the century was the 'friendly society', which could create a distinctly female space. The majority were male, some admitting women, and 'friendly societies offered working people an element of security through providing mutual insurance against sickness, while also offering opportunities for regular, sometimes ritual-based, sociability.'[66] In *Essay upon Projects* (1697), Defoe shows friendly societies already were widespread by the beginning of the century, and he saw them as a kind of contributory insurance scheme in 'which in short, a Number of People enter into a Mutual compact to Help one another, in case of any Disaster fall upon them'.[67] The numbers continued to grow so that over 5,000 with over 700,000 members were registered after the passage of *Rose's Act* (1793) to prevent financial abuses, although this is an underestimate since many smaller ones did not register.[68] They were not the only forms of 'brotherly society' forming during the century, which saw an increase in Masonic Lodges. As Rendall argues, these organisations 'were linked to and intertwined with existing masculine patterns of work, sociability and ritual.'[69] While some women may have benefitted from association with a male member, largely they were not members.

Female friendly societies grew most rapidly toward the end of the century, with the Howden Women's Friendly Society, East Yorkshire, founded in 1763.[70] Eden reported several in 1797: for example, one in Carlisle for women, five in Lancaster and six in Wolverhampton with 351 members. The earliest in Scotland was founded at Dundee in 1789, and Rendall identified sixty-six female societies in Scotland before 1830. Like Lancashire, Scottish societies tended to be in industrial cotton districts, especially Ayrshire, but were not necessarily trade-related. Women involved in the philanthropic movement founded many of them, following a pattern set in women's connections with and management of charity schools discussed in Chapter 3.[71] Broadly they were rooted in ideas of 'fraternity, benevolence and social union' using terms like 'Humane', 'Benevolent', 'Beneficent', 'Agreeable' and 'Amicable'.[72] As Cappe argued,

> In a state of Society, like that of this Country, it will always happen, that many Ladies, especially in the middle ranks of life, will be free from the cares of a family. Of what importance would it be to the happiness of such persons, voluntarily to take upon themselves the patronage and protection of forlorn and friendless young Women?[73]

Philanthropic motives underpinned many female friendly societies, such as the 'Original Female Friendly Society' in Lichfield in 1794, or in York.[74] Cappe's description of the York society shows the relationship between philanthropic founders and girls who were intended to benefit:

> This institution, in common with many others, consists of Honorary and General Members, who contribute equally toward the Fund; but with this peculiarity that we have also a second Fund, formed by the contributions of the Honorary Members solely . . . the object of which is the relief of Members in any particular exigence, to which the relief of the first Fund cannot extend. . . .
>
> At our first meeting, twenty Ladies presented themselves as Honorary Members: and eight young Girls from the Grey Coat [charity] School, and seven from the Spinning School were admitted General Members, paying 2s. 6d. each for their entrance. . . . General Members, . . . whose wages amounted to 3£ per annum, were to contribute 2s. 6d. per quarter, and those whose wages fell short of it, 1s. per quarter, till their wages should reach that sum. The benefits were, a weekly allowance of four shillings to every Member confined to her bed by sickness, two shillings for slighter indisposition, and one shilling per week, if admitted into any Hospital, with the limitation, however, in respect of all three payments to the term of six months at one time. These rules also provided a reward of five shillings for every Girl who had continued a Member, and behaved well, for the space of three years; and the sum of twenty shillings, on the same terms, at the expiration of seven years.[75]

Honorary members also had the right to introduce a girl to the society who had not attended the specified schools. Clearly a philanthropic endeavour, and one with behavioural conditions attached, this initiative nevertheless not only created material support for working girls but also provided potential connections with other girls, as well as with the 'ladies' in charge, who could and would be useful contacts and references for work. This kind of society was a further step in promoting the well-being of what Trimmer called the 'better glass' of working girl.

The York Society, founded in 1788, like the Lichfield one in 1794, were essentially straightforward sick clubs, with added rewards for good behaviour and constancy.[76] Importantly, friendly societies did not spring up in isolation. The York Society was copied and Eliza Fletcher, who claimed to be a founder of the Dumfries Female Society in 1789, had come from near York and would have known of the York Society. She with other middling women, founded the Edinburgh New Town Female Friendly Society, intended mainly for domestic servants, with both honorary middling women and working-women as members. However, objections to women running such a public institution led to a long battle with the magistrates.[77] It was a common pattern that benefactors founded and managed the societies but admitted regular and working members. In the midlands, women who belonged to the Ashbourne Society (founded 1806) were usually unmarried when they joined and aged under twenty years.[78] From 1805, in Scotland, the Irvine and Halfway Female Friendly Society restricted membership to girls between sixteen and twenty-five, limiting the number to 150. Evidence suggests that most societies had significant numbers of girls.

Some societies struggled with assisting married women, because of the risk of pregnancy, and so in some cases, single women were able to pay less to receive benefits. For example, the Female Benefit Benevolent Society of Lancaster refused payments for pregnancy, and if a single woman gave birth twice, she was excluded. Similarly, the Carlisle society stated, 'If any single or unmarried woman, having had a child before she entered this Society, shall commit the same crime . . . she shall be excluded.' Most societies like the Lancaster Benefit Benevolent society did not pay anything for drink-related illness and the Drury Lane Society did not pay out if an injury was caused by fighting or quarrelling, unless in self-defence, or by being in a riot. They were also fined for bad behaviour, swearing or calling another member by a nickname along with other exclusions.[79]

Rates of subscription and benefits varied, but notably those recorded by Eden charged smaller entrance and box-money fees than in York: Carlisle at 1s 9d entrance fee and 7d box money, and the Benefit Benevolent Society, 9d box money and they spent 1d in drink at the meetings, while those in London tended to charge more than 2s entry fee.[80] Drink money was important because many held meetings in pubs, so the publican wanted a return on his benevolence. The Irvine and Halfway Female charged an entry fee of 1s and only 1d in weekly payments, somewhat less than the English societies, reflecting the relatively poorer wages in Scotland. While these rates were within the range that girls could afford for membership, and sickness benefit also corresponded to wage levels, they also demanded a certain level of 'prosperity and respectability making distinctions that suggest nascent class divisions within plebeian society'.[81]

While they provided benefits, usually sickness support, they were spaces for collectively meeting, discussing and socialising. Most had at least an annual meeting, and some had monthly or more frequent meetings often with weekly fees. At meetings, members paid in their fees, and often drink was available and sometimes meals, though in Lancaster, some clubs paid for it and others did not. They met in a variety of places, some in taverns, like the Drury Lane Friendly Society of Women, as well as the Cripplegate and Hoxton societies. Scottish societies, however, appear to have met elsewhere, using schools or a local assembly room. Describing women clubs in London, *The new art and mystery of gossiping* satirised London women's societies:

> The Weaver's Wives Club in Spittlefields
> The Milliners Club by the Royal Exchange
> The Butcher's Wives' Club by Cow Cross
> The Fish Women's Club at Billingsgate
> The Quilters Club in Long-Acre
> The Mantua Maker's Club in St. Martin's-Lane
> The Basket Women's Club in St Giles
> The Bunter's Club in Tyburn-Road
> The Shoemakers' Wives Club in Cranburn-Alley
> The Taylor's Wives Club in Monmouth-Street
> Mrs. Pug the Penny Barbers Wives' Club in Rag-Fair
> The Whores and Bawds Club in Drury-Lane

While we cannot be sure these were real, nevertheless they intimate that girls could have been members of some if not all. The author's intention was to ridicule the associative nature of these clubs especially ascribing to them the sin of gossip. He described a ribald series of episodes and suggested one of his issues was wives out of control. However, the text indicates that girls were present, drinking and meal sharing, and a comment shows one of the gossips trying to protect her reputation: 'O don't, says Ruth, I'd not for the world have my name brought into question.'[82] As Clark noted,

> The pamphlet presents a mouthwatering, if comic, picture of the tailors' wives' club annual feast, where they consumed nine geese, six legs of mutton, and french beans, rolling out into Monmouth Street after having smoked 'pipes and tobacco' and drunk 'royal gin'. One can only imagine why the Fore Street Society added the rule that 'no member shall commit any indecent act with the victuals' at the annual feast.[83]

Nevertheless, despite the ribaldry of the pamphlet, reading between the lines, it depicted the socialising character of the clubs and reflected the 'relaxed' associative character of plebeian life.

Rituals and communal activities marked these female societies and in York they decided

> In order to attach the young Women more generally to the institution, it was thought expedient in the year 1797, to institute a Procession, which should take place on the 15th of May, once in two years, when the whole Society, Honorary as well as General Members, should attend Divine Service at the Cathedral in this City, distinguished by a green Ribband placed in their hats, and afterwards be regaled with Tea and Cake, in a room engaged for the purpose; the whole expence to be paid by the honorary Members, from their private Fund. The Children belonging the two Schools, and their Mistresses, also attend upon this occasion, and follow in procession.[84]

They sometimes combined with men's societies, and 'The Ruthwell Female Friendly Society accompanied the male friendly society in a procession to church, with music and flags flying, every year before their annual meeting; once a year the female society also drank tea together.'[85] They also orchestrated their own sociable activities and on 5 August 1814, a carefully stage-managed procession took place when

> the Montrose Female Friendly Society availed themselves of the annual procession of St John's Lodge of Free Gardeners, to accompany them through the principal streets of that burgh. The females, to the amount of nearly 200, neatly and uniformly attired in white muslin dresses; their caps ornamented with blue ribbon, corresponding with their neckerchiefs, proceeding from the Town-hall in which they assembled, headed by their office-bearers uncovered, and preceded by their patroness, Mrs Carnegie of Charleton, supported by the two lady key-keepers.[86]

Thus, sociability and communal activity played an important role, whose purpose was to 'attach the young Women' to the society and to the principles of the society. But such events and practices also served the girls. Not only was their membership an opportunity for preferential treatment when they sought work and the fact that they had support at vulnerable points in their lives, but also and importantly, these could be bonding occasions for working girls. They also operated as sociability and pleasure and gave them respite from work. Lord argues that such societies were not founded because women were excluded from male ones, but because women wanted 'all female societies that reflected the single sex social groupings of the working class, and on a practical level left the husband free to look after the family on club nights and feast days.'[87] The founding 'ladies' could be seen to be using their 'privileged position to create and organise their own societies', and many did so out of genuine commitment to benevolence often fostered by evangelical religion, but girls who joined by choice may have actively sought female support. It is difficult to say how many societies may have been formed by groups of working women, but the Cripplegate London society described itself as 'a Society of Women, to prevent as much as in us lies the fatal effects which these calamities [sickness, lameness, and other disorders] must avoidably bring with them, have formed ourselves into a society for the mutual support and relief of each other.'[88] Also, the evidence is unclear but Rendall argues that it was possible that around half in Scotland were run by working women or women of fairly modest incomes though supported by patronage.[89]

Conclusion

Girls who worked also played, socialised and took part in community solidarities, whether in town or country. They sought out spaces of conviviality with their peers, as well as specifically female spaces. Popular culture, while shifting across the century, nevertheless, created opportunities from working together to sharing in the fairs, festivals and fêtes that characterised eighteenth-century society. Communal activities spread to protests and popular expressions of discontent as well, and girls would have been present in these, although almost virtually invisible, probably disguised as children or women. Friendly societies, especially from the end of the century, marked another opportunity to collectively share experiences with others while gaining the benefit of some form of insurance. Girls clearly participated in these, and some societies specifically focused on girls. Often created by benefactors, the evidence shows that girls took part, used them for sociability and may have been involved in forming them. These sociable activities clearly enabled respite from work, female sociability and fun. Many communal activities also functioned as meeting places for courting and seeking out life partners, which we turn to in Chapter 9.

Notes

1 Cunningham, see his critique of new histories of leisure of the late twentieth century, *Time, Work and Leisure*, 2.
2 Cunningham, *Time, Work and Leisure*, 32–3.
3 Campbell, *London Tradesman*; Voth, *Time and Work*, 31–6.
4 Muurling and Pluskota, 'Gendered Geography of Violence', 158; Simonton, *Gender in the European Town*, 94–6.
5 Phillips, *Enlightened Nightscapes*, 1.

6 Green, Hebron and Woodward, *Women's Leisure, What Leisure?*, 1.
7 Thompson, 'Time, Work Discipline, and Industrial Capitalism', 79.
8 Ingram, *Importance of Schools of Industry*, 3.
9 Ingram, *Importance of Schools of Industry*, 10.
10 Whatman, *Housekeeping Book*, 53.
11 Cunningham, *Time, Work and Leisure*, 12.
12 Proctor, 'Home and Away', 299.
13 Proctor, 'Home and Away', 299, 305.
14 On belonging, see Simonton, *Gender in the European Town*, 9–23.
15 Newby, *Country Life*, 92.
16 Golby and Purdue, *Civilisation of the Crowd*, 101.
17 Malcolmson, *Popular Recreations*, 15.
18 Parratt, 'More Than Mere Amusement', 52.
19 *AJ*, 3 September 1751.
20 *AJ*, 13 October 1788.
21 Wright, *Georgian Theatre Audience*, 35; Brewer, *Pleasures of the Imagination*, 261.
22 Thompson, *Customs in common*, 63.
23 Maudlin, 'The Urban Inn', 623; see also Mackay, 'Women at Work', 155–76.
24 Brewer, *Pleasures of the Imagination*, 34.
25 Clark, *Struggle for the Breeches*, 39.
26 MacKay, 'Women at Work', 172. See also Tlusty, *Bacchus and Civic Order*, 133–46.
27 In Walvin, *Child's World*, 78.
28 Davies, *Labourers in Husbandry*, 38.
29 Maudlin, 'The Urban Inn', 2.
30 Simonton, 'Inscribing the Town on Women's Bodies'.
31 Clark, *Struggle for the Breeches*, 35.
32 Malcolmson, *Popular Recreations*, 15.
33 Medick, 'Village Spinning Bees', 335.
34 Sweet, *Urban Histories*, 203–14.
35 See Neuberg, *Popular Education*, 127–38; Webb, *Working Class Reader*, 27–8. Altick suggests that Methodist tracts for which a small charge was made were regarded more respectfully than free ones, *English Common Reader*, 35–6.
36 See Barclay, 'Love and Courtship'.
37 Skinner, 'Scots Fairs and Markets'.
38 Quoted, Malcolmson, *Popular Recreations*, 55.
39 Eden, *State of the Poor*, vol. 1, 598.
40 Quoted, Malcolmson, *Popular Recreations*, 62–3.
41 Hindle, 'Rural Society', 633.
42 Malcolmson, *Popular Recreations*, 77–8.
43 Golby and Purdue, *The Civilisation of the Crowd*, 101.
44 Radford, 'Women's Foot Races', 56.
45 *English Chronicle or Universal Evening Post* (London), 28 August 1790–31, August 1790.
46 *AJ*, 8 August 1749.
47 Woodforde, *Diary of a Country Parson*, 153.
48 Radford, 'Women's Foot Races', 50.
49 Proctor, 'Home and Away', 305.
50 Rizzo, 'Equivocations of Gender and Rank', 71–3.
51 Guttmann, *Women's Sports*, 77.
52 Bushaway, *By Rite*, 200.
53 See Simonton, *Gender in the European Town*, 72–9.

54 Farge, 'Protesters Plain to See', 491.
55 Thompson, 'The Moral Economy', 115–6, and *Customs in Common*, 306.
56 Thomis and Grimmett, *Women in Protest*, 32–4. Thwaites, 'Women in the Market Place', 36. For Scotland see Logue, *Popular Disturbances*, 199–203 and Rendall, *Origins of Modern Feminism*, 201.
57 Randall, *Riotous Assemblies*, 313.
58 Rendall, *Origins of Modern Feminism*, 70–2, 235.
59 *Narrative of the Proceedings at Tranent.*
60 Hunt, 'Women as Citizens', 223.
61 'Humble Petition of the Poor Spinners', Leicester, 1788.
62 *OBP*, October 1716. Trial of James Beaver, William Eldridge, Hester Stibbs, Eleanor Hornsby, Anne Lane (t17161010–2).
63 *OBP*, June 1780. Trial of Thomas Downs (t17800628–103).
64 ACA, Enactment Books.
65 ACA, Enactment Books, 228, 256–9; See also Simonton, 'Sister to the Tailor'.
66 Rendall, 'The Principle of Mutual Support', 18.
67 Defoe, *Essay Upon Projects*, IV, 118.
68 Lord, 'Weighed in the Balance', 103.
69 Lord, 'Weighed in the Balance', 24.
70 Neave, *Friendly Societies in the Rural East Riding*, 548.
71 See also Simonton, *Education and Training*; for Scotland, see Rendall, 'Women's Associations'.
72 Rendall, 'The Principle of Mutual Support', 19, 21, 22.
73 Cappe, *Observations on Charity Schools*, 64–6.
74 Cappe, *Account of Two Charity Schools* and *Observations on Charity Schools.*
75 Cappe, *Observations on Charity Schools*, 64–6.
76 *Rules, Orders and Regulations for the Original Female Friendly Society.*
77 Rendall, 'The Principle of Mutual Support', 26–7.
78 Lord, 'Weighed in the Balance', 108.
79 Eden, *State of the Poor*, v. 1, 59: v. 2, 322–4; Drury Lane Society, *Rules.*
80 Eden, *State of the Poor*, v.2, 322–4.
81 Clark, *Struggle for the Breeches*, 37.
82 Anon., *New Art and Mystery of Gossiping*, 3.
83 Clark, *Struggle for the Breeches*, 38.
84 Cappe, *Observations on Charity Schools*, 71–2.
85 Rendall, 'The Principle of Mutual Support', 32–3.
86 Caledonian Mercury.
87 Lord, 'Weighed in the Balance', 101.
88 Cripplegate Society. *Rules.*
89 Rendall, 'The Principle of Mutual Support', 28.

9

LOVE, COURTSHIP AND INTIMACY

The problem of knowing

Knowing what working girls thought or felt about love, sex and intimacy is more opaque than many topics in this book. Historians are interested in the sexual behaviour of young couples, especially marriage and marriage patterns, in failures of courtships and in bastardy and abandonment. Most studies concern themselves with propertied and middling classes, but love is shrouded in lacunae and lapses. Even with the growth of attention in emotions and feeling in the past, studies of what couples and girls especially thought are rare. As Griffin remarks, 'sex is one of the topics about which many autobiographers could simply not bring themselves to talk about at all.'[1] Some male autobiographies give us glimpses—from the bloke's point of view. Advice books described normative behaviour and standards, and treatises depicted what society considered appropriate behaviour. But very few tell us what girls wanted, how they felt, their motivations or even their reactions to unwanted advances. There are very few surviving accounts from working girls, anyway. This chapter relies on the work of historical demographers and research on sexual behaviour to assess how girls traversed this aspect of their lives. It also uses the testimonies of a very few autobiographies from working people and must rely to some extent on men's given the scarcity of women's. The other sources of testimony are bastardy and settlement exams and court cases which, though mediated, give some voice to working girls. While this book defines girlhood in a *longue durée*, clearly matters of sex and intimacy are more significant from about the age of menarche. Younger girls were victims of sexual abuse and rape (Chapter 10), and young prostitutes could also be found, but this chapter is concerned with consensual relations, the progress of intimacy and courtship,

DOI: 10.4324/9781003412168-10

and the probable drive to marriage. Obviously, sexual urges were not only about marriage, and we find girls who moved from one partner to another, just because the fancy or circumstances took them, to girls who looked for, found and married their own chosen partner.

This chapter discusses how girls navigated their relations to men; acknowledging the importance of custom, control and culture is the background and context to this process. It could involve failed courtships, or it could be whirlwind, but family, relations and community could slow it down—or not. The route was not necessarily rational and while economic reasons were never far away, many married with little consideration of rational factors. Despite a historiography that suggests that people married when they had the wherewithal to do so, issues of chance and irrationality played a significant role in courtship and marriage considerations.

Marriage as a goal

As girlhood prepared the girl to become the woman, distinctive changes in her social and sexual persona marked the passage to adulthood. For most, marriage was a goal, and literary and customary values promoted it throughout society. However, to repeat, working girls covered a wide span from middling girls who turned to work either temporarily or permanently to help families and sometimes support themselves to labouring daughters and poor girls for whom working was a given necessity. Across this span, attitudes, money, status and parents were variables in how girls moved toward sexual encounters, intimacy and marriage. Advice literature articulated the social expectations of marriage and motherhood, and while most aimed at the middling girl, as we have seen, a number were directed at working girls. During the century, women's duty shifted subtly from marriage and duty to husbands to a much more overt focus on their role as mothers. Cappe and Trimmer like most of their contemporaries saw motherhood as the natural destination of girls, and marriage was an expected pre-condition. Their underlying assumption was that girls desired and wished for the married state. Trimmer emphasised the importance of a domestic world for women and decried 'contamination' from rough men.[2] Her comment reflects another shift in attitudes with a focus on providing girls with the moral tincture to avoid seduction, seeing a transfer of culpability from women to men.

Literature promoted the ideal of working to save for a dowry and a nest egg so that she could marry and set up a marital home, and regardless of how difficult it might be, it was an underlying trope for most girls. Similarly, their upbringing, schooling and work experience were largely aimed first at work, but secondly to provide the skills to run a household and be a helpmeet in a family enterprise. This is overt in the apprenticing of poor girls to housewifery. Although not always expressed, it was so embedded in the social psyche as to not be questioned. In practice, it was also difficult for singletons to make their way as independent adults, so marriage was a practical way to establish a working and potentially successful economic partnership. Young women also learned that most women gained strength, position and status through marriage; she became a real person who was an authority figure to servants and children. Religious dogma had long supported woman's role as helpmeet, which meant that in marriage she would achieve her highest status. The newer views of Nature supported and further sublimated that view. Women prepared trousseaus even before grooms appeared: towels, linens, quilts, clothing and personal belongings, so new husbands did not have to spend money dressing their wives. Family gifts and small items handed down from one generation to another supplemented these.

Marriage was relatively late, often dependent on the couple having the wherewithal to set up their own home. The relatively high proportion of single servants in their mid- and late twenties attested to this pattern. As Chapter 1 showed, few married before they were twenty, about half by the time they were thirty and most had done so by the time they were forty. Significantly also, many never married, some by choice and some by circumstances. Yet, during the century, women started marrying more frequently, rising from a low of about 25 per cent so that by the mid-eighteenth century only between 4 and 7 per cent never married. Location and community could be factors in when girls moved toward becoming married women. Different economic situations created differences between town and country. Also, different cultural regimes and customs mattered, and the north of England and the south could well have differed. Certainly, looking at the broader picture, Scotland illustrated these variables with age of marriage remaining higher than English figures commonly cited.[3]

Sexual knowledge

During girlhood, girls learned what it meant to be female and the values to which society expected them to adhere. However, plebeian cultural norms and those of the middling orders diverged, having an impact on how sex, sexuality and intimate behaviour was understood and practised. Girls also came to understand physical aspects of their being. Girls developed their charms to attract men, and even if the basis of marriage was economic or social standing, love and sexual attraction clearly played a part. Meeting partners, discovering intimacy and their sexuality operated as the bridge to the anticipated marriage. Girls learned about sexual behaviour in several ways. Seldom was it explicitly taught, and so most gained their knowledge from their surroundings and the proximity in which people lived. Plebeian culture was lived out in overcrowded and communal spaces, and children often shared rooms with their parents. People shared beds in inns, and private space was not yet an intrinsic part of home life. Rural girls and many town girls would have been familiar with animal procreation, and babies were common additions in any household.[4] Fanny Burney wrote about the pregnancies that surrounded her, and when she was twenty-two, her sister Hetty was unwell during her pregnancy, and she recorded that 'Susy & I sleep at her House alternately every other night, for though we cannot boast of being very useful, her affection & our Anxiety, make our being with her a mutual comfort.'[5] In practice however, it was less likely that girls would have attended childbirths, and a certain level of modesty could restrict women of all ages from talking publicly about sexual knowledge.

Boarding schools, and perhaps workhouse and industry schools where girls lived in, provided venues for exploring sexual matters. Gossip shared knowledge while experimentation offered a route to self-exploration. Prohibitions against bed-sharing and mixed-sex play were prevalent in didactic literature, as were admonitions to look into the mirror only when truly necessary. Nudity was to be avoided and certainly hidden from males. Yet, lessons designed to promote chastity and modesty must have piqued their curiosity, so that nubile young women looked for explanations for their nameless longings and desires. You cannot protect sexual virtue, unless you have an idea of what you are protecting. If taboos and psychological distance prevented intimacy, they fostered sexual awareness. Girls were discouraged from openly discussing sex, and diaries seldom mentioned it, but undoubtedly young women were not completely innocent. They gained knowledge of their bodies, sexuality, conjugal expectations and physical aspects of childbirth through word of mouth. Inevitably, women around them, usually mothers, passed on information, almost certainly about menstruation and sexual practicalities. Apprentices and servants shared information and learned trades and sexuality from mistresses.

Even modest literacy enabled young women to read literature that discussed sexual activities, including same-sex relations. As Chapter 3 argued, most records only measure one kind of literacy—the ability to write one's name—suggesting an abiding literacy, but there are recognised flaws in this measure. More women may have had a functional literacy, and were a 'potential reading public'.[6] The greatest growth in access to reading material blossomed after mid-century, 'in the wake of Richardson and Fielding', fostered by the growth in the popularity of the novel and promoted by the birth of the circulating from mid-century.[7] 'A circulating library in a town is as an evergreen tree of diabolical knowledge! It blossoms through the year!—and depend on it, Mrs. Malaprop, that they who are so fond of handling the leaves, will long for the fruit at last.'[8] Popular literature, chapbooks and newspapers became ever more widely accessible, and girls certainly could have shared in this expansion. Altick noted:

> Though these fees were by no means low considering the purchasing power of the shilling during the period, at least the renting of books was

> less expensive than outright purchase. Thus the libraries made books available to a much wider audience. From how far down in the social scale they drew their customers, it is difficult to say. If we are to believe the constant burden of contemporary satire, domestic servants attended in great numbers on their own account, not merely to exchange books for their mistresses.[9]

Widely read novels, like Samuel Richardson's *Pamela* and *Clarissa*, included allusions to desire, rape and same-sex relationships. Dublin librarian Mrs Lord assured parents that she underlined offensive passages so that girls would know what to skip.[10] As literacy expanded and popular literature burgeoned in the second half of the century, more and more material both serious and bawdy became available to girls.

While trying to inculcate morals and virtue, even conduct books could provide insights to the other side of chastity. In his *Letter of Genteel and Moral Advice to a Young Lady*, Wetenhall Wilkes understood chastity as 'a suppression of all irregular desires, voluntary pollutions, sinful concupiscence and of an immoderate use of all sensual and carnal pleasure'.[11] Hannah More attacked novels, especially Rousseau, for their proclivity to undermine virtue:

> Novels, which used chiefly to be dangerous in one respect, are now become mischievous in a thousand. . . . Rousseau was the first popular dispenser of this complicated drug . . . He does not paint an innocent woman, ruined, repenting, and restored; but with a far more mischievous refinement, he annihilates the value of chastity, and with pernicious subtlety attempts to make his heroine appear almost more amiable without it. . . . With a metaphysical sophistry the most plausible, he debauches the heart of woman, by cherishing her vanity in the erection of a system of male virtues . . . powerfully insinuating, that to this splendid system chastity does not necessarily belong: thus corrupting the judgment and bewildering the understanding, as the most effectual way to inflame the imagination and deprave the heart.[12]

While she addressed the elite, she made much the same point in 'The Sunday School' chastising a woman for distributing ribald songs and warned girls 'consisting of the farmer's two young daughters, and a couple of rosy dairymaids', on the evil character of the tracts and has the minister say 'I do again repeat, the souls of these innocent girls will be poisoned, and may be eternally ruined, by this vile trash which you carry about.' Furthermore, it would be better to teach girls nothing 'unless you keep such trash as this out of their way, and provide them with what is good, or at least what is harmless'.[13] Banning books, however, could simply entice a reader to seek them out, and girls were not protected from gossip, story-telling and ribald songs.

For example, the ballad *A Remedy for the Greensickness* joked about sex as a cure for this common female ailment:

> A Handsom buxom Lass lay panting in her bed
> She lookt as green as grass and mournfully she said
> Except I have some lusty lad to ease me of my pain
> I cannot live
> I sigh and grieve
> My life I now disdain.[14]

Women like midwife Jane Sharp and almanack writers like Sarah Jinner and Mary Holden also contributed sexual information when they wrote about women's bodies.[15] Thus the burgeoning print culture of books, pamphlets, ballads, stories, collections of jests, ballads and advertisements promoted the wide circulation of tantalising information.

Custom and control: law, family and community

Courtship and intimacy were governed primarily by custom and control. Family, communities and social status were significant for monitoring the progress of courtship and practices of intimacy. Couples also self-policed what they were prepared to do and what they actually did, and their motives could be complex, reflecting self-interest, desire and respect for family, community and legal structures. Emotion and feelings inevitably played a part. There were a multitude of ways that girls could learn what they *should* do, perhaps what they *could* do, but ultimately what they *would* do was partly their decision. A girl also operated in a gendered context and had to work out how to understand and manage what potential suitors and sexual partners might do. If literature and community norms told her what she was expected to do and how to behave, girls had the potential to make their own decisions and weigh the factors involved. Of course, they could get 'carried away', literally.

Marriage law was not homogenous across the British Isles, and in the *Act of Union* of 1707, Scotland retained control over marriage law, both black-letter and case law. Ireland, while still ruled by England, similarly retained older marriage practices and legal authority. Church law and custom retained a role across the British Isles. While Anglicanism dominated in England, Presbyterianism predominated in Scotland and Northern Ireland (not yet separated from Ireland), while Catholicism was the rule for the rest of Ireland. This is somewhat complicated in the case of Scotland however, because there were important pockets of Episcopalianism and Catholicism, alongside the Church of Scotland, itself subject to disputes and splits.

The *Clandestine Marriages Act*, 1753, commonly known as *Hardwicke's Marriage Act* (26 Geo. 2. c33, or *The Act for Better Preventing Clandestine*

Marriage), was the first legislation to insist on a formal church wedding following the publication of banns or obtaining a marriage license.[16] However, it applied only to England and Wales, and exempted Jews and Quakers. Since Scots law remained under the jurisdiction of Scotland, it was not operable there, nor did it operate in Ireland or abroad. Its key aim was to prevent irregular, or clandestine, marriages 'and the unruly culture that surrounded them' which had begun 'to threaten power and property'.[17] Children under twenty-one required parental approval to marry under license, banns should otherwise be posted and only if parents objected was the wedding stopped. Couples also had to marry in a parish where one of the parties lived. It was intended to stop weddings not properly conducted by the church. Prior to the *Clandestine Marriages Act*, simple consent was often seen as sufficient. In part, the act was intended to prevent propertied heiresses from being married off to unscrupulous men, but the concern was broader than this.

Marriage law had largely operated under the principles of mutual consent across Britain, and this remained significant in Scotland and Ireland, although a 'regular' marriage requiring marriage banns to be read in church in the weeks preceding the nuptials was the usual practice. But 'irregular' marriages could be recognised, and cases of contested marriage illustrate how complicated and variable these might be. In Scotland, three patterns comprised most of these. A couple were legally married if they declared themselves to be so in front of witnesses, whether or not the declaration was followed by intercourse. It could also be legal if undertaken without witnesses but was much harder to prove without substantiating evidence such as correspondence to confirm it. A promise of marriage followed by a sexual relationship could also be recognised, but usually proof could be required, like a written promise of marriage, or an oath sworn before witnesses. Marriage by 'habit and repute' in which a couple presented themselves in public as wife and husband, even with no formal declaration of marriage, was legal in Scotland until 2006.[18] Irregular marriages were frowned on by law and the churches, and couples who admitted to them were fined, but they had the same inheritance rights as regularly married couples, and their children were legitimate. However, the Church of Scotland tolerated them because it feared that if the law did not recognise such relationships, the couple would end up 'living in sin', and as Barclay argues, the Kirk was less concerned about morality than about an orderly society. Such marriages could be contracted without banns being posted, residence requirements or parental consent. Thus, they also acted as a route to marriage for English couples unable or unwilling to meet the conditions of English law, so that border communities, notably Gretna Green, but also others like Coldstream and Berwick-on-Tweed, were common destinations for couples seeking this loophole.[19] As Barclay says, 'As the legal will of the child carried over into marriage law, regardless of parental desire, that youth was a moment of nascent independence informed how such decisions were argued and explored by the court.'[20]

Family interests, together with community values within and outside legal systems, influenced girls' understanding of what was permitted and what was acceptable in their exploration of love, intimacy and courtship. As this book argues, girlhood was a time of learning to be an adult, and it involved negotiating family and individual interest while they relied on families for help and support in managing love, sex and courtship. Courtship involved family at various important points. Men continued to ask parents' permission to marry their daughter, and so, Quaker John Grubb wrote to Hannah Lynes for permission to marry Sarah Lynes, who had been nanny to his sister Sarah.[21] Failure to get parental consent 'not only undermined a relationship's validity, but also highlighted youthful folly'.[22] The families then usually came together to agree upon the terms of the marriage, and the wedding was celebrated by family and community, often entire villages coming together to eat, drink, dance and be merry. In towns, commonly members of the trade also turned out to share in festivities.

Whether a girl was still at home or had travelled for work or apprenticeship partly determined the level of observation, supervision or control she experienced. Servants and other young people working away from home had the most freedom to socialise without being supervised by parents or family. While parental approval and encouragement probably mattered to many girls, those living at home, or where there was family land or prestige involved, even amongst plebeians, were more likely to consult families in making a decision. Remember that the working girl came from a broad span of social orders, including the lower middle classes, shopkeeper and artisanal families and smaller farmers, as well those from labouring households and even the poor. Many families had their position to retain and valued their property and respectability which factored into the choices a girl made and the permission her parents were prepared to give.

Parents owed their children care and attention, while increasingly, as adolescents, the children might challenge parental authority. They also relied on their support and throughout the records of marriages we see children trusting parents for guidance, collaboration and protection. For example, 'fourteen-year-old Elizabeth Duncan's father, a vintner, protested her abduction and marriage in 1753, noting that Lieutenant Malby Brabson carried her off "without the Knowledge, Advice, or Consent of the said James Duncan her Father or any other of her Friends".'[23] When Jedediah Strutt proposed to servant Elizabeth Woollatt, she hesitated and finally showed his letter to her master, before accepting him.[24] Family relationships therefore mattered when girls began to explore their sexuality, as they experienced romantic love and sexual desires. Families could be a barometer for them in making decisions regarding emotional and sexual behaviour.

Residence contributed to whom she met and whether the youths she encountered would have been acceptable to her parents. Even employers could take on the role of *in loco parentis* providing the back-up a girl needed as well as spaces to meet and 'court'. Such protection was implicit, and sometimes explicit, in apprenticeship contracts and hiring agreements. Girls were aware of the values of their community, and these expectations added to the boundaries within which they might operate. While the age of marriage could be as young as twelve, communities and law regarded this as far too young. Thus 'Agnes Young, the daughter of a writer (solicitor), who married her schoolteacher, William Allen, the day after her twelfth birthday, was widely agreed to be too young to have made this decision; her stepfather—rescuing her after the ceremony—refused to let the couple go to bed even "for half an hour", "reasoning upon the absurdity of going to bed with a Child".'[25] Concern with an 'orderly society' figured in community approaches to young people's marriages, and challenged those unions perceived to be dangerous to such orderliness.[26] Gillis argues that marriage had particular resonance in plebeian cultures:

> [P]lebeian marriage was a public act and a highly ritualized event. Even among the lower classes, where the big peasant wedding symbolic of the establishment of a household had fallen away, there persisted a set of very public rites that confirmed the status of the newlyweds in the community. The very publicity of plebeian courtship and marriage was the source of its meaning and the essence of its utility to a population denied other sources of social recognition and respect. . . . And they relied on their friends, kin and neighbors to provide them with an appreciative audience for this social drama, a fact that had a determinative effect on how and when they wed.[27]

'Courtship took place within a matrix of relationships, and courting couples themselves operated according to a set of internalised expectations.'[28] Although Diane O'Hara wrote this in relation to the sixteenth century, it remained a truism for eighteenth-century girls. Kinship, friendship and neighbourhood networks could be a pivotal influence, speaking to reputation, prospects and appropriateness of the marriage partner, as Gillis noted: 'One might even say that among this strata of society it took a community to make a marriage.'[29] In eighteenth-century society, the process and route to marriage had become far more nuanced and complicated.[30] As Steven King argued, 'In crude terms people often did not behave as macro-theories say they should. . . . David Levine . . . concluded that there was little system in the marriage decision, which took place "for their own reasons". . . . Whether long or short, the process of "getting married" was littered with pitfalls and the end result was never certain.'[31]

Being able to afford marriage often hampered the process to courtship, and men regularly repeated this as a restraint. Girls frequently saw saving for a dowry as a prerequisite, and being 'without means' figures in many accounts. Although as the opportunities for waged work increased, a couple did not necessarily have to save large sums to get married. In 1740, Jedediah Strutt, a young apprentice wheelwright, became intimately acquainted with Elizabeth Wollatt, a servant, and daughter of the family he lodged with. However, as a dependent he was not free to marry, and even when he moved to Leicester to continue his trade, he felt unable to marry. Only when he was left a farm by his uncle in 1755 did he feel he could do so, and he immediately wrote:

> Feby 3rd 1755
> DEAR. BETTY,
>
> Since our first acquaintance, which is now many years ago, I have often wrote to you but never in a strain like this; nor did I think I ever should for though we were then more intimately acquainted than since and though then I thought you had some degree of kindness for me, yet as my conduct and behaviour to you has been such as could neither raise nor continue your regard, together with the years that have passed since then . . . therefore it is upon this foundation I promise to tell you that from a wandering inconstant and roving swain I am become entirely yours! I am ready to become all that you could wish me to be if you loved me and which is all I wish your husband.[32]

Their acquaintance had continued over seven years, though he was uncertain that her regard for him persisted. She responded carefully and expressed her concern that her own lack of 'fortune' was an impediment:

> As to myself was I possessed of any desirable qualification, and had I enjoyed the greatest affluence, I should not then hesitate a moment, but comply with whatever you will desire; but my consciousness of my own inferiority in points of fortune as well as anything else, makes me extremely fearful that you should find cause to repent, when it is too late.[33]

Suffice it to say, she was persuaded in following letters, and they married. Romantic love and deep affection mattered, but popular literature and communities still believed that a girl should take practical considerations into account. She should expect a good provider, with a good trade, a reliable man whom she could respect. Impulsive mates were not uncommon, but girls usually consulted kin, employers and neighbours about the potential of a match.

Getting to know you

Meeting and socialising took various routes, often beginning as friendships and flirtations (see Image 9.1). Not all were intended as courtship since young people enjoyed their youth and sociability. King described courtship as a process that began 'with the decision to enter the courtship market in the first place, continued through an individual finding the ceiling and floor

IMAGE 9.1 Love at First Sight. George Shepheard, after Henry William Bunbury: January 10th, 1796. The Elisha Whittelsey Collection, The Elisha Whittelsey Fund and Harris Brisbane Dick Fund, by Exchange, 1970. The Metropolitan Museum of Art, 1970.541.170. https://www.metmuseum.org/.

to their marriage expectations imposed by social and economic status, identifying potential partners, entering into successful courtship, and only then ending with marriage.'[34] But girlhood was often filled with several flirtations, especially when they were still dependent, too young and essentially enjoying the discoveries of love and intimacy. Gillis notes that it was a peculiarity of Britain and northern Europe that 'young people experienced love as a form of polygamous play, only gradually narrowing the field of choice as they approached marriageable age'.[35]

'Neutral', coded language often veiled sexual knowledge and female passion. Sarah Hurst formed an attachment with Henry 'Harry' Smith in 1752 when she was only sixteen, but over the next ten years, often while he was away with the navy, she had many flirtations. In her diaries she described 'romping' and other flirtatious behaviour, including kissing and kissing games with men she did not marry. On 19 September 1760, 'Jack Ellis calls to see me two or three times, flatters me sufficiently & kisses me enough.'[36] Then on 11 December, she wrote, 'Romp with Captain Miller, he washes my face with a knife cloth.' On the twelfth she romped with him again but adds that 'he pinches my arms black and blue, which puts me in violent pain.'[37] Throughout this period, she was involved in an extensive correspondence with Smith with whom she eventually eloped.

Similarly, on 26 January 1758, Hertfordshire gentlewoman Elizabeth Raper recorded in her cypher diary,

> Word was brought me Mr. Houblon and Mr. Lipeat were come. . . . went to them, chatted very agreeably, a little after 12 Uncle came in, found the fire smoking, so invited them into the study. Mr. L. desired to see the great room whither I attended him but found it was more for his sense of feeling than his sense of sight, kissing being his chief business there. That over, we adjourned to the study, drank chocolate, then the gentlemen went into the Observatory . . . In due time they came down again, L. came hopping before to get a kiss or two 'though the devil was in him'.[38]

And on 26 August, she 'dined, talked, worked, walked, romped, supped, upstairs a great deal of kissing from my young he-cousin, romped and to bed'. From 1 to 9 September wrote that she spent her days 'reading, working, eating, sleeping, walking, romping and kissing.' In May 1760, she wrote, 'up before 7, dressed and to Stortford before 8 to Bkft. with Mrs. Dimsdale. . . . Bkft. over we all walked in the garden, the lover very pensive, kept close to me, sighed, squeezed and sighed again; his mother looked very arch but said not a word.'[39] None of these men became her husband; she married Dr William Grant of Inverness-shire after a very swift courtship and moved to Scotland. As King concluded, frequently little planning went into courtship. Serendipity, proximity and simple physical attraction played a part.

While not distinct from adult and community values, youth culture was an important aspect of negotiating love, passion and getting to know one another. Young people utilised available spaces, often in group settings where the rituals and peer pressure of youth groups encouraged association, but which operated to restrain premature 'pairing off'. Joan Scott and Louise Tilly argued,

> Adolescent boys particularly policed the behavior of courting couples. . . . A wide discrepancy in the ages of the couple, for example, or promiscuity or adultery, could attract the ridicule of local youths. They would engage in elaborate rituals, following the couple, mocking them, singing profane songs under the woman's window. A bad-smelling bush planted before a girl's door indicated her low moral standing. A group of young men might fight or fine strangers.[40]

Gillis too noted that youths would chase away strangers, protecting their 'rights' to local girls, so at Pudsey, 'he is looked upon as an interloper . . . and a poacher on their preserves.' He also suggests girls joined in the preservation of their 'turf', with coarse rhymes and name-calling. Men they fancied were rewarded with kisses and hugs.[41] In the countryside it was common for young people to engage in such 'policing' activities and charivaris, setting boundaries and evoking values that might or might not coincide with those of their elders.

As Chapter 8 showed, numerous community activities provided group spaces for girls and boys to meet, like ceilidhs, harvesting festivals and community dances, fêtes and weddings (Image 9.2). While these were not solely youth events, 'that descriptions of such events featured more prominently in the testimonies of young people in legal records is suggestive of their important function for that group.'[42] The Donnybrook fair was notorious in Dublin for 'riot and dissipation', with girls competing in their underwear, and kissing games, though Jonah Barrington explained that it was not until the evening that 'sweethearts made up their matches'.[43] Even these could be fleeting encounters. While leisure spaces increased, girls of the middling and labouring orders had their spaces and places to socialise and meet those of the opposite sex, even if less formally.[44] Minister's daughter Dorothea Herbert described the social world of the young members of the Protestant community in and around Carrick-on-Suir in the 1780s: 'we had always dancing in the Evening on the green Turf and regular Assemblies once a Week in Carrick'.[45] Elizabeth Ham recounted an array of social activities in Weymouth, then a regular place for royal visits, and she described fêtes, plays and walks on the esplanade as social activities taken with friends.[46] Ann Taylor says that as children she and Jane spent a lot of time in the parlours because their mother did not like leaving them with servants, and they frequently experienced the social life of parties and visits.[47]

IMAGE 9.2 John Eginton, active 1763–1800, Setting out for the Fair, 1792. Stipple engraving, Yale Center for British Art, Paul Mellon Collection, B1977.14.14534.

Many couples would have known each other from childhood, growing up in the same community, going to the same church, meeting at markets and other local sites. They shared connections of family and friends and met at social gatherings in the community. As Luddy and O'Dowd discovered, analysis of marriage licenses primarily from the Protestant community of the diocese of Ossory, 1739–1804, indicated that over 60 per cent of people married someone who lived in the same county as themselves while over 50 per cent of people chose a partner from within their own parish and some from within their own township. In Catholic Ireland, numerous couples sought dispensation to marry kin, and in some protoindustrial townships, it is likely that not only did they know their partners but were related to them.[48] Many Quaker diarists met through their religion, and their letters do not reveal much about the courtship. Reserved and respectful, Margaret Lucas commented briefly, 'A little past the twenty-fourth year of my age, I was married, with the approbation of my friends, to Samuel Lucas: he was a worthy man and well respected.'[49] Similarly Deborah Bell, also twenty-four, returned home from ministerial duties and commented, 'The spring following, my friend John Bell and I came to a conclusion to accomplish our intended marriage, and it was with great awfulness and reverence, having a due regard to the peace and freedom of my own mind, that I consented to enter into a married life.'[50] Hannah Gibbons commented simply, 'Sometime after my return from the journey above-mentioned, I was solicited in marriage by William Gibbons, son of Abraham and Lydia Gibbons, of an adjoining county. The subject to me felt very weighty, and I trust we both were desirous of seeking for Divine direction in the proposed important step. But after endeavoring solidly to weigh it, momentous as indeed it was, and the way appearing open to proceed, we were accordingly married.'[51] Ruth Follows noted, 'As I was thus made willing to obey the Lord, he was pleased to bless my undertakings; and about the twenty-third year of my age I was married to a young man far more worthy than myself; and I can truly say, it was because he was well inclined that I had so much love for him as to have him for my husband.'[52]

Those who were isolated from community and family structures, often having moved away for work, were most liable to make their own choices. But it remained a largely communal society, and few were without friends or kin. Settlement exams reveal how such girls might make their own matches. Sarah Stubbington was born in Croydon but her parents died when she was three years old, so she moved to her grandmother's in Chelsea where she lived twelve years until her grandmother too died, and Sarah went into service. When she was about nineteen, she married Jonathan Cook, a soldier, at the Fleet and had a daughter. Unfortunately, she then heard he was already married, though he denied it.[53] The Fleet Prison was a common venue for clandestine weddings, presided over by a minister without either banns or a marriage license and commonly away from either partner's parish. Interviewed in 1759, Ann Williamson from Leicestershire became a servant when she was fifteen or sixteen to Lord George Bentick at Soho Square where she stayed nearly two years 'in which time aforesaid she came acquainted with Martin Williamson, to whom she soon after married at Chesterfield in the county of Derby, by whom she hath one child alive, 4 years old, named William, and is now with her uncle Ward in the parish of Rippon, a farmer.' Her husband was pressed into the army and sent to Germany so she returned to service.[54] She appears to have made her own marriage but was in contact with family and not totally isolated. In contrast a Cheshire girl, Elizabeth

Ashbridge, was in a loving family with a devoted mother, and her father, a sailor who gave up sailing when she was twelve, and thus she had a settled life. Yet she eloped at fourteen. She remorsefully wrote,

> I believe I was as innocent as most children, about which time my sorrows began . . . by giving away to a foolish passion in setting my affections on a young man who courted me without my parents' consent till I consented . . . I suffered myself to be carried off in the night, and before my parents found me I was married.[55]

While she loved her husband, she 'was soon smote with remorse for thus leaving my parents, whose right it was to have disposed of me to their consent, or at least to have been consulted in the affair.'[56] Left a widow after five months, her father refused to speak to her.

The process of getting to know one another and considering or proceeding to marriage involved more than collective events. It was also an individual and necessarily private affair, and couples sought out privacy to carry on their business. William Drennan asked his sister to help find out when Margaret Jones would travel to Dublin, because he did not want to meet her in Belfast where he suspected her father might not approve of him. When he later wished to court Sarah Swanick, he sought to have her invited to Dublin, 'as he considered his going to England to visit her in her parents' house, "imprudent"'.[57] Churches provided opportunities for observing, meeting and perhaps strolling home. Gradual pairing off provided the chance to speak privately, to gauge the other's affections and to consider the potential of the relationship. Often it came to nothing, but it could lead to further intimacy, parental consultation and perhaps marriage. Courtship followed a familiar pattern in that public association then private concourse could lead to closer affection, greater intimacy, gift-giving and ultimately parental and/or public acknowledgement. Gift-giving was an important part of courtship, and often marked the promise to marry, and the giving of rings during the ceremony, a pledge to the partners. In a largely oral culture, the 'exchange of objects served as an apparently speechless dialogue between courting couples' and 'as an aspect of intimate behaviour in the making of marriage'.[58] When and how gifts and tokens were given denoted 'a socially identified structure which progresses from a stage of early courtship, to one of pre-betrothal communications of love and marriage, through to a stage of more formal betrothal, and finally to a post-contractual period.' They operated within courtship to publicly 'conduct the parties through these vulnerable times'.[59] Love letters (Image 9.3) and loving correspondence featured widely as tokens and functioned to maintain connections when a courtship was carried on at a distance or was lengthy, as with Wollatt and Strutt. Betty Leeming's courtier, Benjamin Shaw, in fact learned to write when she left to go to Preston to

IMAGE 9.3 Thomas Rowlandson, 1756–1827, The Love Letter, ca. 1790. Watercolour, pen and grey ink, and graphite on thick, slightly textured, beige wove paper, Yale Center for British Art, Paul Mellon Collection, B1975.3.104.

work in a mill. He explained: 'She sent me letters by the waggon from dolphinholme, & I frequently wrote to hir—this was the begining of my writing, for I never went to any school to write in my life—and wanting to send to her I was ashamed to let anybody know my secrets, I set about writing love letters &c'.[60] Sally Holloway points out that: 'The period from *c.*1714 to 1830 saw a momentous increase in the volume of love letters written and exchanged by couples,' while Clark maintains that increasing evidence indicated 'that husbands and wives wrote more affectionately and romantically to each other in the eighteenth century'.[61]

Love, passion and sex

In 1762, Sarah Hurst commented: 'How much perplexity attends love affairs of all kinds whether the Heart is engag'd or not, it takes away all the pleasure of that part of Life most capable of happiness, when health glows on the cheek and the spirits move in a brisk circulation.'[62] Courtships and dalliances involved romantic love, passion and a range of sexual behaviours which marked couples' intimate practices. The progress of romances and courtship could move from 'getting acquainted' to various levels of intimacy, kissing, a little fondling, to more intense petting and physical exploration of each other. It also might also involve 'night-visiting' or 'bundling', and ultimately penetrative sex. For some girls romance and ideas about romantic love were important, and for others a deep attachment marked their feelings. Hurst referred to a meeting with her beloved: 'Sat up till three with my dearest Harry, he is all modesty, love & tenderness.' When he left he took 'a tender leave of me.'[63] Such veiled language was common in women's reminiscences, but speaks to loving, romantic, intimate associations.

As studies of emotions have surged, authors have pointed to romantic love as an increasingly important aspect of courting during the century. Certainly, it has a longer history, but it became more acknowledged and referenced in making matches and a more pervasive ideal for marriage. Romantic love was a feature of ballads while broadsides were replete with tales of romantic courtship. Novelists too explored romantic love not only as an overwhelming passion but also as an emotion reflecting sensibility, while ideology shifted to expect marriages to be based on love and not property. It was also tied to the idea of self-validation and identity. Ruth Bloch made the point that romantic love came to be valued in part because of the evangelical revival in the latter part of the century, which stressed intense personal conversion experiences.[64] While the musings of philosophers may have held little interest for working girls, they operated in a setting in which the mood and ideals of love had shifted, especially during the last half of the century. At the same time, 'love, romance, sex before marriage, and the appropriate emotions within courtship and marriage were discussed at length in popular culture . . . affecting how people felt about each other and expressed such feelings.'[65] Adolescence was long seen as a time for romantic love but during the century it gained special resonance.

There is no doubt that romance, love and physical passion were tied up in girls' minds. Love was complicated—it could be provoked by physical attraction while sexual behaviour could foster love, but passion and intimacy did not always lead to love. Association and less personal factors could also promote it, and Barclay emphasises the importance of time in creating intimacy and 'as the popular term "wooing" suggests, love was often envisioned as something to be created over time, a feeling produced through appropriate behaviour towards a beloved.'[66] Love was individual, and we have little knowledge of their real feelings; we can only observe behaviours and occasionally hear their comments.

Quaker Sarah Lynes gave a reserved insight to her feelings. A nanny from age fourteen, in 1787, she maintained a 'long attachment' of some sixteen years to John Grubb, brother to her mistress. He wrote her mother in

May 1803, intimating that 'the precious friendship and unity of spirit that has long subsisted between thy beloved daughter Sarah and myself, may not be much of a surprise to thee, viz., to avow my near and tender attachment for her, and the desire of my heart to obtain her as a companion in the closest and most endearing connection in this life.' Sarah wrote him several letters over the next few months and from them we get glimpses of her attachment and hesitations because she was to move to Clonmel, Ireland, from London, upon marriage.

> I think that some of those seasons we have lately enjoyed in each other's society, when we felt the sweet influence of our heavenly Father, like a sanction to our attachment, may, from time to time, be recurred to for our mutual and united strengthening. . . . [My hesitation was] the prospect of separating from my near relations and friends in my native land is trying . . . [I wish] that if I do go, our habitation may be like his where the ark was, which, it is said, was blessed. I well know that this is thy desire also . . . Ah! my endeared friend, our attachment is not indeed 'the sudden impulse of a moment,' but (as thou says) hath its foundation in the deeps, and hath been proved by many storms. Oh! may He who hath already blessed it in measure to thee and me, continue to bless it as a thing of His own (dare I say) preparing. . . . Alas! what would, what could a union like that which we now hope for, be to either of us without such a possession?[67]

Her comments reflect Quaker reserve and her religion, but they invoke a depth of feeling and slide over the period of courtship which began as friendship. Farmer's daughter Margaret Ferguson's courtship in the 1770s was somewhat more passionate. David McKie, a twenty-two-year-old teacher, wanted her 'to make a quick decision to marry as he had an economic opportunity to take up elsewhere if she refused him'. When she averred, he complained that

> 'he had been constant in his Love to the defender but that she had not given him the return he expected and that he did not chuse to linger any longer in a Vain Courtship'. On this, the tears 'rushed' into Ferguson's eyes and she declared 'her love was as strong to him as ever And that she loved him better than any other Man in the World' . . . before she 'put her arms about his Neck pulled him down a little and kissed him'.[68]

Only Ferguson used the term love, but there is little doubt that love informed Lynes's attachment.

Intimate behaviours short of penetrative sex were common amongst adolescent couples. It was a gradual move from kissing and light touching to more physical intimacy, even for girls who saw it as a mere flirtation. Hurst and Raper alluded to kissing, hugging and 'romping', and with Harry, Hurst talks about tenderness. Irish Quaker Mary Shackelton Leadbeater 'watched with fascination the courtship of her sister, Margaret, by Samuel Grubb. It involved a great deal of physical touching, with Margaret sitting on Samuel's knee and being pulled by him into the second parlour in the house where the young couple spent a "long time" in the evenings alone together.' And yet there was no evidence that either she or her sister Mary had sexual intercourse before marriage.[69] A wide repertoire of sexual play, echoed in first-hand accounts, suggests strategies to pursue a relationship while avoiding pregnancy, shame and sin. Couples acknowledged that sexual attraction was normal, while at the same time they often struggled to avoid intercourse. John Cannon's first serious relationship, or 'love intrigue', with his uncle's servant, Mary Rose, quickly moved from 'jesting complements' [sic] to more physical fun and games. They shared 'amorous talks & quaint glances, kissing and toying when together in private . . . [which] brought on by degrees a more close familiarity even to a plain discovery of such matters & concerns which modesty teaches me to omitt'. As Griffin points out, 'John insisted that their adventures fell short of sexual intercourse—we "never carnally nor criminally knew each other", he wrote. Once, he admitted, he had had the "lust to debauch her", but the "thoughts of the crime . . . soon quelled that flame".'[70] As Hitchcock suggests, we need to 'think of sex not as a single set of unchanging behaviors with a consistent relationship to making babies but, instead, as a physical culture possessed of rapidly moving boundaries.'[71]

Relationships frequently moved on to intimate physical behaviour, not always marriage, of course, though couples seen to be committed to marriage were often given far more latitude. Night-visiting was one aspect of community and family consent that gave girls and their 'chosen' a chance to know each other better. Often supervised, girls had a certain level of protection. Gillis described a common practice in Wales whereby farmers' sons and servants went courting together—the son to see the daughter of the house and the servant to see the maidservant. This allowed a couple flexibility in deciding whether to continue the relationship and also helped to overcome any inhibitions they may have felt.[72] Parents or employers might go off to bed leaving the couple to themselves. In the Carnmoney Presbyterian session book, one woman described in 1804 how she and her husband permitted young men to visit their female servant at night and she acknowledged that she did not know when or if they had left to go home.[73] Gillis reported a farmer who would not allow his daughter to walk in the woods with a man, but would allow her to be courted under his own roof. It also gave space to terminate a relationship before it bloomed and became public, thus protecting the couple and parents' interests. Nights could be a valuable time for courting, especially in rural areas where distance and workloads were restrictive. In Wales it was called 'nights of watching', in Cheshire, 'sitting up', and a term more common in Ireland, bundling was practised across Britain.[74] In

Kilfinnan, Scotland, Isobel Middy and Duncan McCurrie were called before the Kirk session, where he stated 'That he lay in Naked bed with Isobel Midy . . . at the shearing in harvest last, that it was the Custom of the place for Neighbours and Country Bairns to ly together, and that there were many others who lay together as they did: he absolutely denied any Carnal dealings with her.'[75] Notwithstanding official disapprobation, night-visiting could be explicitly or quietly condoned by girls' friends and family. Griffin argued that sexual purity was not prized nor expected, and it was taken for granted that their courting would lead to sexual exploration.[76]

In contrast to punishment, shame and official interference in premarital sex, rural communities displayed a relative lack of concern attached to illegitimacy. It was not taboo; frequently the pair was an acknowledged couple who expected to marry eventually. Scottish couples usually acknowledged Kirk discipline and accepted punishment, but people seemed not particularly anxious about illegitimacy. Penance re-established a girl's character, and in the Highlands, 'if a young woman lost her virtue and character, then she was obliged to wear a cap [as married women did], and never afterwards to appear with her hair uncovered'.[77] This was hardly a stigma if it simply linked her with married women. The role of sex and sexual relations in courtship or as a part of adolescence demonstrates contradictory pressures. Inevitably it happened, but the extent to which it was regarded as normal and customary is debatable; it was also often culture-specific with important geographic variations.

Hitchcock argued that sexual behaviour became increasingly phallocentric, moving away from fondling and touching, shifting from a 'ragged and uncertain boundary' around ideas of sex, to an 'increasingly phallocentric definition of sex that excluded nonpenetrative activities from what was considered normal sex and placed greater emphasis on putting a penis in a vagina as the only acceptable definition of sexual behavior—with all other forms of sex becoming literally foreplay.'[78] We have little direct evidence of such a shift, but demographic data tend to support it. Clearly, premarital intercourse figured in courtship, and figures of rising illegitimacy suggest a change in its frequency by the last half of the century, with the dramatic rise in the number of births inside and outside marriage as population grew rapidly, and a higher proportion of the population got married, with a third of brides already pregnant on their wedding day.

Churches clearly disapproved, but people do not always do as they are told, and alternative moralities played a part. Not necessarily subscribing to middling values, for most plebeians, illegitimacy and irregular marriage derived from an alternative morality. Relatively free from the domination of the church or the upper classes, many viewed premarital sex after a promise of marriage as completely acceptable. Thompson made the case for a distinct plebeian culture while Gillis constructed these views in terms of familial affection.[79] They contended that the lower orders did not have an identity of interest with the middling orders and that the operation and system of values of the former owed relatively little to the latter. In plebeian culture, a double standard was much less marked and the resulting injunctions about female image, role and chastity were also far less significant.[80] In commenting on the 'companionate marriage' identified by Lawrence Stone as a feature of bourgeois family life, Gillis argued that Stone negated the values of the poor because his central point of reference, affective individualism, did not begin to comprehend the way that plebeians felt and acted. Their personal and social relations did not easily fit the sharply defined moral and emotional categories he employed.[81] 'Among the eighteenth century plebs . . . the compatibility of individual affection and collective solidarity was an ideal worth struggling for.'[82] Creative common law practices suggest a collusion between partners against parents and, from 1753, against 'the triumph of property, patriarchy, and male dominance' embodied in *Hardwicke's Marriage Act*.[83] In particular, he argues that since the family constituted a productive unit, marriage could be regarded as forming a partnership which involved individual rather than parental choice. In the face of greater need to control the labour of children, parental control appeared to be lessening. 'Sex and age relations had become simultaneously more equal and more problematic.'[84] Betrothal had become the private concern of the young couple. But cultural patterns came into play. Contemporaries Jonas Hanway and John Smeaton noted the plebeian practice of 'trial marriage' implying a variant mode of behaviour from that found in middle-class culture.[85] Yet, Rosalind Mitchison and Leah Leneman dismiss the contention that 'bride testing' was a feature of courtship in Scotland, arguing that the level of antenuptial pregnancy was too low to justify such a belief.[86] Although sex before marriage was the norm, plebs seemed to happily engage in intercourse with little expectation that marriage would follow, and even in bastardy cases, a promise of marriage was seldom used as a defence. Yet incidences of irregular marriage increased everywhere in Scotland over the century, with significant regional variation.[87] Like Protestant Scotland, Presbyterian communities in Ireland tolerated premarital sex, as long as couples then married. 'In Carnmoney between 1767 and 1819, the sessions considered thirty-eight cases of fornication and seventy-nine of pre-marital fornication (i.e. where the couple had married subsequently). By contrast there were only twenty cases concerned with the paternity and maintenance of children born outside marriage.'[88] In Wales, Angela Joy Muir argued that it is likely that many unmarried men and women engaged in consensual sexual activity with no intention of marrying at all, while the illegitimacy level rose from just below 3 per cent to over 8 per cent between 1680 and 1830. Furthermore, she points out that in many parts of England, unmarried fathers were identifiable in fewer than 50 per cent of cases and in some areas in as few as 7 per cent, but some Welsh parishes identified unmarried fathers in over 80 per cent of cases.[89] Premarital sex certainly was common but varied significantly by location. Some 20 per cent or more of English brides were pregnant, while probably 7.5 to 11.4 per cent in Ireland were pregnant, and despite wide regional variation, Scotland averaged 3.6 per cent in the 1760s.[90] Illegitimacy is dealt with in more depth in Chapter 10, but it illustrates that premarital sex was a part of adolescent life—and while courtship might begin in girlhood, many were not girls by the time they became brides.

Sexual desire was a normal feature of courtship, and 'songs, ballads and chap-books explored sexual intimacy as part of ordinary courtship practices and even a necessary part of a successful romantic relationship'[91] (Image 9.4). Furthermore love could be a metaphor for sexual desire, so *A New Song of Mallinger* described 'when we had Drunken / two Bottles of wine, / I found my Dear Mistriss / both Loving and Kind', in which 'loving and kind' meant sexually available. The proximity of young people together working

IMAGE 9.4 A Girl Singing Ballads by a Paper Lanthorn. James Watson (Irish, Dublin ca. 1740–1790), 1767–81, after Henry Robert Morland. Harris Brisbane Dick Fund, 1953. The Metropolitan Museum of Art, 53.600.1892. https://www.metmuseum.org/.

as servants and farm hands and in workshops provided the ideal proving ground. Thrown together frequently, often away from home, possibly lonely, and operating within a shared youth culture provided adequate opportunity. Alexander Chrystal, a farm servant, described the conviviality and jocularity that groups of young people working together shared. The female servants slept in the kitchen, and he described frequent 'daffing' (merry-making) beside the bed and to get them up in the mornings he pulled off the covers, and 'he has seen dancing going on and all kissing one another'. He emphasised that he was never in the bed and never took 'a stolen kiss from her privately'.[92]

Broadly speaking, girls seem to have been prominent in setting the boundaries of the relationship and in policing sexual activity. For example, while John Cannon and Mary Rose abstained while he was out of work, when he got a good job as an Officer of the Excise, she became more eager to explore more physical intimacy, and attempted to persuade John 'to consummate' their private agreement to marry by proposing a time and place where they might meet and have intercourse. John, however, cooled because he now saw himself as having the potential for a better match. He also had shifted his interests to Joanna Stephens, an attractive young woman living across from his lodgings. Shortly his frequent visits had developed into a relationship

> spiced with a fair amount of physical intimacy. One evening, emboldened by the liquor running through his veins, John went to pay her a visit, and after 'some lovetoyes & amorous expressions', swiftly proceeded to attempting 'a great piece of indecency . . . Joanna responded by laying out her conditions for access to the terrain under her petticoat. She offered John 'absolute command' over her body, short of 'deflowering or debauching'; in return, John must 'be constant to me above all others & in due time to make me your lawful wife'.[93]

In fact, the ploy did not work, but it was common for girls to try to obtain a promise of marriage by getting pregnant. Joanna pressed John and shifted the territory, wishing she were pregnant, but like Rose, he averred. As Griffin explained,

> John, Mary and Joanna all negotiated the ground between sexual fulfilment and social acceptability in a fundamentally similar way . . . as their relationships progressed, all three believed that marriage would be unavoidable should a pregnancy occur. The power of family, employers and neighbours to coerce young couples into wedlock was very real in the minds of John, Mary and Joanna. It was this knowledge that prompted Mary and Joanna to urge John to consummate their affairs . . . And, of course, it was the very same knowledge that caused John to resist their overtures.

Being too 'forward' could hamper their chances though. Andrew Russell admitted an illicit converse with seventeen-year-old servant Elizabeth Beatson, but argued that it 'was mainly brought about by the imprudent forwardness of the pursuer who was in the habit of inviting the Defender into her Master's kitchen where opportunities of course occurred too frequently for indulging in familiarities'. Similarly, Brabson accused of absconding with fourteen-year-old Elizabeth Duncan, admitted to a flirtation, but claimed she provoked him and 'he thought her very forward & Impudent' and certainly not suitable as a wife.[94] Benjamin Shaw resisted carnal knowledge too, but when pressed, and fearful of losing Betty's affections, 'at last I went we spent the day together, & things were ajusted . . . I stayed all night with her, and went home the next morning &c.'[95] From this time she dated her pregnancy. We don't know her motives or whether it was natural affection and lust that came into play. It is harder to describe Leeming and Shaw as being 'in love', though the editor of his autobiography thought so. Shaw certainly was strongly attracted and attached to her, despite their rocky courtship.

Conclusion

These examples illustrate the range of directions that flirtations and courtship could take. Raper and Hurst came from supportive families as did Elizabeth Ashbridge. All three engaged in flirtations and two eloped. Hurst's courtship was not only secret but also lengthy, and when she married it was by private license and remained secret for some time. She admitted his parents were one of the issues. Ashbridge like Hurst eloped, but with quite a different outcome. Raper's courtship was quite swift, and her family supported her choice and helped the young couple financially. Sarah Stubbington's parents and grandmother had died, and she was employed as a servant when she had a clandestine marriage that turned out to be problematic. Also, servant Ann Williamson had quite a good place when she 'became acquainted with' her future husband. Notably, she married him in the midlands, nearer family, and her child went to live with her uncle when her husband was pressed into the army, and she returned to London for work. Another servant, Elizabeth Wollatt, experienced another lengthy courtship, often at a distance, and money and the ability to support themselves was a dominant theme in Strutt's delay and her response. Betty Leeming's courtship speaks to the kinds of tribulations that couples could experience, and Hurst too expressed concern about her fiancée's commitment. Despite her flirting, she was dedicated to him, and constantly worried about his well-being, wanting to see him while also fretting about the relationship. Leeming was prepared to leave home to go to work in another mill, leaving Benjamin behind. Although they had quarrelled, they had 'made up', but clearly this was a tempestuous relationship. And, although he wrote that 'on the whole we could not part', she appeared to have her own flings. They ultimately married, though he recognised 'she as unfit for a wife, as I was for a husband'.[96] These courtships were marked by regard, love, passion and intimacies; they were acted out with families, friends and employers in the background, but they were also private and individual and mattered to the girls involved.

Notes

1 Griffin, 'Sex, Illegitimacy', 143–4. Important contra-examples are Barclay, *Caritas, and Love, Intimacy and Power*, and 'Love and Courtship in Eighteenth-century Scotland'.
2 Trimmer, *Oeconomy of Charity*, 66.
3 Wrigley and Schofield, *Population History of England, 1541–1871*, 122, 534, and Wrigley et al., *English Population History from Family Reconstitution*, 131; Houston, 'Age at Marriage of Scottish Women', 65 and 'The Demographic Regime', 19–20. Flinn, *Scottish Population History*, 276–8.
4 Bailey, 'The Vexed History of Children and Sex', 192.
5 Burney, *Early Journals*, vol. II, 54, see also 52, 63, 200.
6 Cowan, *Growth of Public Literacy*, 105; Webb, *British Working Class Reader*.
7 Altick, *English Common Reader*, 63.
8 Sheridan, *The Rivals: A Comedy*, 1775.
9 Altick, *English Common Reader*, 62.
10 Kaufman, *Librarians and Their Users*. 172.
11 Wilkes, *A Letter of Genteel and Moral Advice*, 77.
12 More, *Strictures*, 32–3.
13 More, *Cheap Repository Tracts*, 41–2.
14 Quoted Crawford, *Parents of Poor Children*, 66.
15 Crawford, *Parents of Poor Children*, 96–7.
16 26 Geo. 2.c33.
17 O'Connell, *Origins of the English Marriage Plot*. See also Probert, 'Control over Marriage'.
18 Not to be confused with 'common law' marriage which effectively did not exist in Britain.
19 See Barclay, 'Marriage, Sex, and the Church of Scotland'.
20 Barclay, *Caritas*, 75.
21 Grubb, *Life and Letters*, 87. She was thirty years old with a career as a minister, though from respect, he still wrote to her family.
22 Barclay, *Caritas*, 76.
23 Barclay, *Caritas*, 75.
24 Strutt, *Jedediah Strutt*, 371–84.
25 Barclay, *Caritas*, 76.
26 Strutt, *Jedediah Strutt*.
27 Gillis, 'Triumph of Hope over Experience', 50–1.
28 O'Hara, *Courtship and Constraint*, 237.
29 Gillis, 'Triumph of Hope Over Experience', 49.
30 Levine, 'For their Own Reasons', 255–64. See also Gillis, *For Better, for Worse* and *Adair, Courtship, Illegitimacy and Marriage*.
31 King, 'Chance Encounters?', 26.
32 Strutt to Woollat, in Strutt, *Jedediah Strutt*, 371–84.
33 Woollat to Strutt, 15 February 1755, in Strutt, *Jedediah Strutt*.
34 King, 'Chance Encounters?', 26.

35 Gillis, *For Better, for Worse*, 37.
36 Hurst, *Diaries*, 163.
37 Hurst, *Diaries*, 123.
38 Raper, *Receipt Book*, 15–6.
39 Raper, *Receipt Book*, 17, 21.
40 Scott and Tilly, *Women, Work and Family*, 39.
41 Gillis, *For Better, for Worse*, 28.
42 Barclay, *Caritas*, 72.
43 Barrington, *Personal Sketches*, ii, 331.
44 See Luddy and O'Dowd, *Marriage in Ireland*, 106.
45 Herbert, *Retrospections*, 81.
46 Ham, *By Herself*, 44–9.
47 Gilbert, *Autobiography*, 102.
48 Luddy and O'Dowd, *Marriage in Ireland*, 101–3.
49 Lucas, 'Life of Margaret Lucas', 29.
50 'A Short Journal of Deborah Bell', 16.
51 'Journal of Hannah Gibbons', 4.
52 'Journal of Ruth Follows', 2.
53 *Chelsea Settlement and Bastardy Examinations*, No. 366.
54 *Chelsea Settlement and Bastardy Examinations*, No. 373.
55 Ashbridge, *Life*, 4.
56 Ashbridge, *Life*.
57 Luddy and O'Dowd, *Marriage in Ireland*, 141.
58 O'Hara, *Courtship and Constraint*, 61.
59 O'Hara, *Courtship and Constraint*, 75.
60 Shaw, *Family Records*, 28.
61 Holloway, *Game of Love*, 'Introduction'; Clark, 'Heterosexuality', 16.
62 Hurst, *Diaries*, 22, 43, 62.
63 Hurst, *Diaries*, 120–5.
64 Bloch, 'Changing Conceptions of Sexuality', 38–40.
65 Barclay, 'Love and Courtship', 38.
66 Barclay, 'Love and Courtship', 45.
67 Both quotes, Grubb, *Life and Letters*, 86–9.
68 Barclay, *Caritas*, 37.
69 Luddy and O'Dowd, *Marriage in Ireland*, 146.
70 Quoted Griffin, 'Sex, Illegitimacy', 143–5.
71 Hitchcock, 'Reformulation of Sexual Knowledge', 826.
72 Gillis, *For Better, for Worse*, 30.
73 See Luddy and O'Dowd, *Marriage in Ireland*, 110.
74 Gillis, *For Better, for Worse*, 31.
75 Quoted in Leneman and Mitchison, *Sexuality and Social Control*, 181.
76 Griffin, 'Sex, Illegitimacy', 145.
77 Stewart, *Sketches of the Highlanders*, 1, 94.
78 Hitchcock, 'Reformulation of Sexual Knowledge', 826.
79 Thompson, 'Patrician Society, Plebeian Culture', 382–405; Gillis, 'Affective Individualism', 121–8.
80 Gillis, *For Better, for Worse*, 114–6, 126–8.
81 Gillis, 'Affective Individualism', 126. See Stone, *The Family, Sex and Marriage*, 374.
82 Gillis, 'Affective Individualism', 127.
83 Gillis, 'Resort to Common Law Marriage', 12.
84 Gillis, 'Resort to Common Law Marriage', 10.

85 Quoted in Malcolmson, *Life and Labour*, 104–5. See also Macfarlane, *Marriage and Love*, 303–7.
86 Leneman and Mitchison, *Sexuality and Social Control*, 183.
87 Leneman and Mitchison, *Sexuality and Social Control*, 107–8, 176, 181, 182.
88 Luddy and O'Dowd, *Marriage in Ireland*, 147.
89 Muir, 'Courtship, Sex and Poverty', 61, 64.
90 Muir, 'Courtship, Sex and Poverty', 148, Leneman and Mitchison, *Sexuality and Social Control*, 156.
91 Barclay, 'Marriage, Sex, Lower Orders', 171.
92 Barclay, *Caritas*, 72. See also Ben-Amos, *Adolescence and Youth*, 178–80.
93 Quoted, Griffin, 'Sex, Illegitimacy', 144–5.
94 Barclay, *Caritas*, 80.
95 Shaw, *Family Records*, 29.
96 Shaw, *Family Records*, 26.

10

WHEN THINGS GO WRONG

Introduction

Most working girls moved through girlhood and arrived at adulthood having successfully travelled a well-worn path of home, school or apprenticeship and work. This is not to suggest their paths were always easy, and many would have encountered bumps along the road because they were potentially vulnerable to a range of vicissitudes. This chapter, then, looks at what happened 'when things went wrong', from poverty and ill health to broken promises and failed courtships, to illegitimacy and sexual violence. The records do not always state the age of the girl, so some may have been 'adults', but they were single and often servants or young workers. Girls could and did recover from misfortune, but for many, their troubles shaped the rest of their lives.

The story of Elizabeth Hewit, alias Giles, describes the ranges of misfortunes that could beset a girl. She was

> born at Rochester of mean Parents, who gave her no Education. Being unkindly treated by a Mother-in-Law, she left her Father, who took little care of her when young, and serv'd in any mean Station, till about a Year ago she came to London, and serv'd in a Victualling-house in the Strand. There she got acquainted with one Giles, who upon promise of Marriage, unlawfully convers'd with her. And she being reduced to a distrest and desperate Condition, and finding an opportunity, when her MASTER Mr. Kirk, and her Mistress were both out, she broke open a Trunk in a Closet, and took thereout fourteen Guineas and a half, 3 l. 13 s. in Silver, and two gold Rings, value 10 s. the 14th of July, 1733, and then went out of Town in a Coach, but was soon pursued and taken at Badgers-hill in Kent,

DOI: 10.4324/9781003412168-11

> in a day or two after the Robbery; . . . Being thus taken, she was sent to Maidstone Goal [sic], and when Health permitted, brought to Newgate, by a Habeas Corpus in order to be tried at the Old Bailey. This Robbery she own'd, but deny'd that she was a Thief before, but acknowledged her being addicted to and frequenting vicious Company; she was in a miserable and poor condition, and some Weeks before she died, she was wholly deaf and could hear nothing. She was very ignorant of Christian Principles, but declar'd herself Penitent, in Peace with every body, and own'd the Justice of her Sentence. Her Sickness and troubles increasing, upon Saturday the 15th, of June, between five and six o'Clock in the Morning, she died of a violent Fit of the Convulsions.[1]

She had dysfunctional parenting from both a stepmother and her father, took up whatever jobs she could find, was seduced by a man who left her after promising marriage. She was probably pregnant, since she was recorded as lying in at Maidstone jail, and becoming desperate she turned to theft, was arrested, found guilty and sentenced to death. She clearly was in poor health because she died of convulsions before the sentence could be carried out. In this one account several of the misfortunes that girls encountered are recorded; certainly, she was not typical, but poverty, ill health, pregnancy and lack of decent work contributed to pushing her to crime. This chapter and the next examine these issues, beginning with when things went wrong.

Poverty

Probably the most common calamity for a girl was to encounter poverty, either with her family or on her own. As Laurence Fontaine argues,

> To be poor meant having to rely solely on one's work to survive, which meant that at the first misfortune, the slightest illness, there was no state-provided safety net: you lost your job, your income, and 'fell' into poverty. To be poor wasn't to be unable to meet one's needs, but to constantly be at risk of being unable to do so.[2]

This concept of poverty as risk rather than a state of being is useful as we trace the girls' trajectories. They were not always nor necessarily poor, and they used an array of strategies to keep afloat, but the circumstances of their lives frequently left them at risk of falling into poverty. Living close to the edge, many girls found that once anything went wrong, a cascade of things could go wrong. Poverty was one of the main reasons why girls left home to work to send money home as well as to relieve the burden on the family, or to be apprenticed, often through the poor law. It was common practice for Overseers of the Poor to require families to give up children for apprenticeship before allowing the remaining members relief, as in Terling in 1801, when only four girls over fourteen remained at home, including the thirty-six-year-old 'idiot', because the rest had been apprenticed, or at least sent to live with kin or others.[3] Sarah Gale's family slid into pauperism in the 1770s, and in 1777 aged eleven, she was admitted to the parish workhouse of St Clement Danes. Shortly thereafter she was apprenticed to Joseph Walker, a tailor of some means. But he fell on hard times, possibly due to age since he was sixty-eight, and went into the workhouse; she followed shortly after, pregnant by his son.[4]

The most likely cause of poverty was simply lack of work, lack of well-paid work, or inability to work due to poor health. There is a sense from settlement exams and other testimonies that girls were peripatetic, moving from one place to another looking for work, and often 'making shift'. Mary Ann Ashford depicted a life of movement as a servant over seventeen years. Born in 1787, as an infant she was put out to a nurse, who clearly neglected her. When she was twelve her parents died, and despite relatives offering to apprentice her to a milliner, she went into service. What followed was a catalogue 'of wage theft, false accusations, deceitful fellow servants, and unhealthy and flooded sleeping quarters'. Her first employer refused to pay her wages; her next position paid a paltry wage of £2 10s annually, and there she was forced to drain a basement that regularly filled with water, 'till I have been nearly exhausted with pumping, and almost poisoned with the smell'. Her next position paid only £5, and she left since this 'would never find me in apparel' and was turned out into the rain immediately.[5]

Rachel Herbert's story is typical of many. Born in 1716 in Great Marlow, Buckinghamshire, she moved with her father to London, probably before 1726, her parents having apparently separated. She was sent at age ten to a Mrs Bates in St Clement Danes to learn plainwork. Because this was neither an apprenticeship nor a secure form of service, she did not gain a legal settlement. She lived with her father in St Clement Danes and stayed with her teacher for three years. At twenty-four she was picked up as a homeless vagrant, reporting that she was 'poor [and] not able to maintain herself'. Though her claim to settlement was vague, she was not removed and seems to have worked from time to time and to have been lifted again as a vagrant nine years later. She then disappeared from view.[6]

Mary Saxby's memoir described her life as a vagrant, having run away from home on more than one occasion, often just about managing. She confessed to being culpable in creating her situation by her bad behaviour, and

> nights that I staid in town, I was forced to creep under hulks, or any where, to hide myself from the watchmen; and as soon as day broke, I went into the markets, to pick up rotten apples, or cabbage-stalks; as I had nothing

> else to support nature. [She continued] How I lived, I cannot now remember; but . . . there fell a very deep snow, and I had nearly perished with cold and hunger. I can recollect sitting in a black-smith's shop, and holding my feet in my hands, to get some warmth into them.[7]

These snapshots indicate the risks girls faced. Within this risk culture they benefitted from help from friends, relatives, acquaintances and a solidarity of the working orders. But these resources often fell short, leading some to the poor law officials, others to crime and prostitution, some to death. Some, of course, may have found solutions. Herbert disappeared from the records, and she 'may have married and taken another name, making it difficult to trace her. . . . It is possible that she was able to survive without parish assistance'.[8] Mary Saxby married and despite some tribulations, was secure on her husband's military pension.

When sex goes wrong

A common risk for working girls was the result of sexual intimacies, because of broken promises of marriage, 'misunderstandings' between partners or even 'carelessness'. Sexual intimacy and penetrative sex amongst the unmarried were on the increase and inevitably unmarried girls became pregnant. However, it is worth noting that the number and proportions were relatively tiny, and therefore the exception, not the norm, with 3 to 8 per cent in Wales, 2 to 6 per cent in England and 4 to 6 per cent in Scotland, though with significant regional variations across the period.[9] Recording of birth and marriages was relatively haphazard, and some clergy did not note legitimacy consistently anyway. Others used oblique language like the Hertfordshire clergyman who entered a child as begotten by 'her master', another in Gloucestershire as 'supposed daughter', and 'Sarah the reputed daughter of William Pope (shearman) & Sarah Clark *als* Hobbs his supposed wife'.[10] Churches, families and communities might ensure a marriage, for better or worse, but equally, men might abscond, or refuse or be unable to take responsibility—especially if they could sow doubt as to paternity. Girls might not know who the father was, or they could have been in a position such that to 'name and shame' was to lose their livelihood, especially if a master or his son was the sexual partner. Their own shame restrained some from acknowledging a child, and families may have assisted in a subterfuge. Girls could decide to hide the pregnancy and pass the child off to another, family or friend, to preserve their place in work. Authorities carefully monitored illegitimate births, Kirk sessions in Scotland and poor law authorities in England, particularly if mothers and children were likely to become a financial burden to the community. A fundamental purpose was to identify fathers, whom they required to support children. Concealment of pregnancy was criminal, ostensibly so that the mother would not endanger the child by 'neglecting' her pregnancy. A common example before poor law officials was the settlement exam of twenty-two-year-old Elizabeth Bridgen, who worked as a servant to a tailor and then for the matron of the Foundling Hospital. When she became pregnant, her partner absconded, and she appeared before the Justices, destitute. Her case was complicated by disputes over where she had a right to a settlement and she was moved at least four times, before she disappeared from the records.[11]

Sarah Gale, introduced earlier, went to the workhouse pregnant by her master's son. He apparently went abroad, and his father died in the workhouse, leaving her with no recourse. Two years later she became pregnant again, naming William Underwood, a glass polisher's employee, and gave birth to a second daughter. Three years later she was pregnant again, giving birth in the workhouse, naming a journeyman dyer as the father, 'he having had Carnal knowledge of this Examinants Body sometime in the Month of February last and at several times since'. She is not noted in these records as having any work, and there is no indication of financial support, though one suspects she lived a precarious existence with the men who fathered her daughters. It is possible that she then married in 1792, still only age twenty-four.[12] While she might have become a 'repeater', Laslett argued that single-cause explanations for the number and timing of bastards were dubious. He suggested that bastardy 'in England may well be partially understood on the hypothesis that something like a sub-society of the illegitimacy-prone may have existed over time [and] that it is possible that the shadowy society of the bastard-bearers itself grew larger'.[13] Certainly bastardy cases figure large in poor law accounts, mainly because the authorities wished to keep supplicants off their poor register if they could pass them to another or at least get support for the child. The single woman might not gain support from local officials, but the officials were less likely to neglect a child. One result was that they acknowledged the child's place of birth as the place of settlement, although the mother's might be elsewhere. For example, in 1743 Southampton All Saints ordered relief to Argentine Long's two-year-old bastard, but not to her.[14]

Girls may have willingly engaged in sexual intercourse, feeling secure that they would be married to their chosen mate. To reiterate, communities did not necessarily see intercourse as wrong, though churches might. Scottish Kirk sessions became increasingly lax in requiring and enforcing penalties for irregular marriages but continued to call girls, and men when they could be found, to account for 'unclean behaviour'. In 1712 in Dumfries, Marion Irving and Edward Maxwell were required to stand on the Sabbath and be rebuked for their irregular marriage. By the 1790s, the same Kirk did not formally admonish couples, although they were expected to demonstrate remorse. John Monteith and Janet Nanning were irregularly married without proclamation of banns in 1795, 'for which neglect they profess their sorrow & promise faithful adherence to one another'. The Session Clerk noted only that the couple gave seven shillings for the use of the poor.[15] Aberdeen Kirk session recorded fewer cases of unmarried mothers by the end of the century.[16] In England, church courts ceased to prosecute fornication, though civil authorities still ensured child maintenance, and couples often married before children were born. However, Sarah Hurst was born several months before her parents married, a common enough story.[17] In Presbyterian Ireland, premarital sex was tolerated, but couples were expected to marry—in Carnmoney between 1767 and 1819, in seventy-nine cases of premarital fornication all couples married subsequently. Similarly Catholic Ossory tolerated premarital sex, but not when the man refused to support the child or marry the woman.[18]

'Interrupted or frustrated courtship' accounted for a significant number of cases and King 'reminds us of just how precarious and highly contingent upon circumstances "getting married" actually was'.[19] As we saw, John Cannon's relations with three girls illustrate this well. While he and Mary Rose secretly agreed to marry, they resisted 'carnal knowledge' because they knew they were in no position to marry as servants. When John's situation improved, he lost interest and turned to Joanna Stephens who laid out conditions for access to her body, short of intercourse. Both she and Mary pressed him to marry and saw pregnancy as a route to that end. Yet again, he turned away. His third relationship with Ann Heister took a different course; a servant where he lodged, she made no conditions. When John found himself alone with her in the house late one evening he decided to try his luck, slipping his hand 'under her coat to her knee'. Encountering no resistance, he then 'boldly ventured higher'. Within a matter of weeks, he had had 'Carnal knowledge of her', and the pair continued at the 'same sport frequently'. All the while she had been telling John that she would use 'all ways & means with me till she was with child in hopes to force me to marry her. In short, in her eyes, pregnancy took her directly to the place where Mary and Joanna had ended up wishing themselves to be.'[20] She, however, lacked the promises and expectations they had, and he only agreed to help support their illegitimate son. In contrast when Betty Leeming finally allowed Benjamin Shaw to consummate their relationship, she was quick to press for marriage when she discovered she was pregnant, even though they were still in a poor situation. For girls with poor prospects in the marriage market, sex may have been the price for gaining a marriage promise from their lovers. Such bargaining, however, was full of risks.

In Scotland, Leneman and Mitchison argue that women rarely used pregnancy to force a marriage. If girls who bore illegitimate children did so because they expected their partners to marry them, then one would have expected this to have been a common defence under interrogation, particularly if the girl had been abandoned or repudiated. In fact, this is not so, and the phrase 'under promise of marriage' virtually disappeared from Scottish records during the eighteenth century.[21] Tanya Evans also points out that amongst petitions to the London Foundling Hospital, 'only 18 per cent of unmarried mothers mentioned that a promise of marriage had passed between the father and mother before sexual relations commenced,' despite the need to have 'a sharp eye on the presentation of their moral status'.[22] On the other hand, women and men did seek legal redress to deal with broken promises, the numbers rising across the century, especially in cases involving an alleged irregular or clandestine marriage. Thus, Jean Low, a tenant farmer's daughter claimed that Francis McFarlane had 'frequently made love to the Complainer and upon the faith and belief that the defender was sincere in his Courtship for Marriage and upon his actually promiseing and Engageing to Marry the Complainer, she was induced and prevailed upon to admitt of his Embraces'. Unfortunately, there was no decision lodged in the file.[23] Importantly for the working girl however, the simple issue of cost would have kept many out of court, while isolated or friendless girls would have lacked the support and probably knowledge to do so. If she did try, she needed proof, and 'sweet nothings' in the bedroom would not hold up in court. Letters or public declarations might.[24]

Eliza Haywood's *A Present for a Servant Maid* took great care to warn girls of the dangers of flirtations, especially with those for whom hope of marriage was non-existent:

> Every Street affords you Instances of poor unhappy Creatures, who once were innocent, till seduced by the deceitful Promises of their Undoers; and then ungratefully thrown off, they become incapable of getting their Bread in any honest Way, and so by Degrees are abandoned to the lowest Degree of Infamy. . . .
>
> But there is yet a greater Trial of your Virtue . . . and that is when your young Master happens to take a Fancy to you, flatters your Vanity with Praises of your Beauty; your Avarice with Presents; perhaps, if his Circumstances countenance such a Proposal, the Offer of a Settlement for Life, and, it may be, even a Promise of marrying you as soon as he shall be at his own Disposal. . . . such Matches have sometimes happened, [but] Examples of this kind are very rare, and as seldom happy.[25]

Ballad and broadside stories of broken courtships, tragic endings or other fatalistic outcomes reminded the public of the poignant dangers of sinful choices. These were stories and songs that portrayed desire as a natural and human behaviour, but one that required an exercise of a stoic and Christian self-control, that was largely construed positively as both moral and ethical in its protection of women.[26]

Clearly some girls were seduced by men who had no intention of marrying them, but also circumstances could turn a genuine promise of marriage into a courtship failure. Mary Rose was the victim of her suitor improving himself and deciding she was no longer an appropriate wife. Migration for work and economic uncertainty could undercut a couple's plans, while the difficulties of gaining mastership and a position at the end of apprenticeship could thwart plans. Couples might find their economic situation never improved or that families succeeded in keeping them apart. Men could be pressed into military service, leave to seek fortunes in the colonies or move to get work and drift away, sometimes not knowing a sweetheart was pregnant. In 1733, 'sixteen-year-old Sarah Norton, deceased, gave birth to a daughter at Avery Farm . . . and that William Norton, a soldier in the Scotch Guards, was the reputed father of the said girl', though probably unmarried despite taking his name.[27] Mary Corrick was pregnant by a fellow servant, George Newman, who upon hearing she was pregnant 'went a soldier and I have never heard of him since'. She did everything she could to look after the child but found herself totally unable to support the child.[28] These stories echo a refrain that runs through the records.

Britain was a mobile community with both men and women leaving rural areas for work. Illegitimacy statistics suggest that girls in urban areas were more vulnerable than rural ones, with fewer family and friends around them and lacking the supporting community which ensured that the man married them. Urban migrants were not necessarily so well supported, and rural girls may have taken their faith in the durability of a promise to town with them and been disappointed. However, urban statistics undoubtedly reflected pregnant girls forced from their village, or who chose to leave to avoid shame and punishment. Susannah Harman from Bath, 'wishing to keep my Character good entreated a friend to lend me some money to Come to London to lie in'.[29] Yet, poor law officials monitored incomers liable to become reliant on them for support and, whenever they could, sent girls back to their places of 'settlement' to have their babies.

If premarital sex was accepted by many couples, then they could and would engage for the pleasure of it, because of the juxtaposition servants and workers. Asking why did they do it: 'Sheer proximity and opportunity form one obvious answer. A young man and young woman working in the same household would be thrown together frequently, and the large proportion of cases involving fellow servants—echoing a trend found in England—shows that this temptation was indeed difficult to resist.'[30] We know nothing about the emotional relationship between Sarah Gale and her master's son, father of her bastard child, but it speaks to the proximity and opportunity available to young people working in the same household. Putting it somewhat flippantly, girls will be girls and boys will be boys. The settlement exams are full of stories of girls who slept with a partner, and instead of being a one-off encounter, it was repeated. Girls rarely said anything in their testimonies to suggest their consent but neither do they complain of being forced. Thus in 1757, nineteen-year-old Ann Bingham, a servant at the Kings Arms in Compton Street, Westminster, testified that

> she is now great with child or children, which is or are likely to be born a bastard or bastards. And that Michael Como, an upholster lodging at Mr Jarrett's aforesaid, had carnal knowledge of her body in the month of February last, upon a bed in the room up three pair of stairs forwards in the house of Mr Jarrett aforesaid, and several times afterwards at the same place. . . . And that he, the said Michael Como, is the true and only father thereof and no man else.[31]

In 1757, nineteen-year-old Margaret Bingham, an unemployed lodger, told the Chelsea examiner an almost identical story, claiming ploughman Thomas Yerby was the true father.[32] This is a refrain in many of the accounts indicating repeated sexual intercourse, apparently with little plan or promise. While a few acknowledged seduction or rape, commonly they accepted a level of responsibility or at least acquiescence. The bastardy examination of Ann Bingham is typical in wording and content. She does not mention seduction, she noted that they had relations several times and that they worked in the same house, and she named the father.

Other girls became victims of a cynical ploy for a man to get sex with no intention of marriage. Elizabeth Hewit, who opened this chapter, served at an inn in the Strand, where 'she got acquainted with one Giles, who upon promise of Marriage, unlawfully convers'd with her' and abandoned her.[33] Such casual encounters surely led many girls to be deserted and alone. Certainly they felt betrayed like Mary Seymour, who 'trusting too much to the Deceits of a Man whom she really loved, and by whom she believingly thought herself reciprocally regarded until the Fruits of her unlawful Connection undeceived her'.[34] With little control over their fertility, girls engaged in sex and took the risk, but they also could be led astray by broken promises or the assumption that relations would lead to marriage.

Understanding sexual behaviour from girls' point of view is often obscured by tropes about female sexual passivity and male aggression. As Evans argued, 'This aggressor/victim dichotomy, founded on the double standard (and closer to a language of sexual politics that emerged in the late-twentieth century) masks the ambiguities of the power relations involved in sexual attraction, courtship and the formation of marriage.'[35] Embedded in a concept of seduction, allowing women little agency, does not reflect the kaleidoscope of these girls' stories and experiences nor the characteristics of plebeian behaviour. Depicting them as victims without thoughts and motivations of their own further obscures the already relatively opaque realities of girl's

IMAGE 10.1 The Coffee House by Thomas Rowlandson, ca. 1790. Purchased in 1954 with income from the Webster Bequest. City of Aberdeen Art Gallery and Museums Collections, ABDAG003913.

behaviour and emotions. Notably in most of the texts cited so far, little blame is placed on the men with whom the girls had sex: although it was not always consensual, men would divert blame to forward and flirty girls (Image 10.1).

Sexual violence

Courts struggled with determining sexual assault, violence and rape. Given the ideological perception of men as dominant and virile and women as submissive, sexual behaviour from harassment to rape in modern eyes could be seen as another sexual practice. When a girl seemed to know her assailant, or had spent any time with him, or had acted in a friendly way toward him, courts often acquitted. The shift in ideology away from the seventeenth-century lusty woman created a prototype of the ideal feminine woman who was supposed to protest or be submissive in the sexual act, while men were expected to be the aggressor.[36] Still the image of the vulnerable female must be balanced against an ability to protest vigorously. On 29 June 1767, the *Aberdeen Journal* reported:

> A young gentleman riding into town, accosted a girl who was leading a cow on the road, and would fain have persuaded her to retire with him

> behind the dyke. . . . The lass, who was more tenacious of her virtue than he expected, gave him so smart a reception, that after throwing him upon the ground, she administered the ordinary school-discipline with a very heavy hand. At length on the appearance of some persons on the road, he was suffered to go: which he did with so much precipitation, that he forgot to take his hat and whip . . . the heroine picked up and carried home with her the trophies, which have never yet been called for.

Gillis noted that in Wales a bridegroom and his mates 'fetched' the bride, and it was common for the young woman to show reluctance, demonstrating that she was sufficiently modest and not overly lustful: 'The Girl makes great moans & lamentations, and if she can counterfeit tears & Tearing of hair it is reckoned a merit.'[37] Such activities were symbolic challenges to the groom to demonstrate his ability to 'master' his wife and protect her from other males. The language used by men in their diaries 'to discuss sex suggests control and dominance: they write of "the use of her body", of having their "will and pleasure" of a woman, or of satisfying an "itch".'[38] Thus, rape and seduction tended to be confused by the culture of the time. As Wiliam Garrow said in the case of Anne Barret, 9 December 1789,

> Gentlemen, these are cases in which Courts and Juries find considerable difficulties in the consideration; because from the nature of the offence, it is almost always attended with a secresy which makes it necessary for Courts and Juries to find their way as they can, and to judge from the probability and improbability of the story told by the person who complains of the injury.[39]

Courts did not have clear definitions of indecent assault until the nineteenth century, and rape was only distinguished from assault if penetration took place, while courts frequently required proof that seminal emission had occurred.[40] In fact, prosecutions of rapes of adult women were rare at the Old Bailey, while cases of rape of young girls were significantly more prevalent. Working girls, like the rest of their social milieu, had access to courts using petty sessions and magistrates as a first step. Serious crime, like rape, was then sent before professional judges. In Ireland, testimonies were mediated, in that the courts structured the stories they wanted girls to tell, by their questioning and views of law, 'and the newspapers that reported those cases were an extension of the courts, broadening the court audience'.[41]

A girl's age had an impact on how accusations of rape were treated. While the legal age of marriage was twelve across Britain, in rape cases in which the victim was aged under ten the defendant could not claim the girl had consented to intercourse because she was deemed too young. This created a grey area between age of marriage and age of consent. A murky area, intercourse with girls under twelve was often punished as a misdemeanour.[42] Of 232 cases at Old Bailey Online, nearly a quarter recorded girls under ten (23.3 per cent); 37.1 per cent were recorded as under twelve (including those under ten). The remainder for whom ages were given (fourteen to twenty-one) accounted for another 20.3 per cent, so that 57.1 per cent were under twenty-one, which perhaps not coincidently was the permitted age for female apprentices to marry. No age was documented for another 28.4 per cent, although trial texts showed that they were spinsters, servants and a few apprentices. While some may have been older, up to 85.8 per cent could have been girls. The remainder constituted widows and wives. The large proportion of those under twelve, and since society did not really believe girls under fourteen should be married, suggests that protection of young girls was of serious concern. The importance of age is explicit in the case of Mary Sherwin who was raped in the workhouse. The vestry clerk testified that he had been told that she had been 'ill-used', but because he thought it was 'a grown person', not a child, he 'therefore did not take much notice of it till the next morning . . . She appeared to be a child of ten years of age'.[43]

Conviction still could be difficult because some believed a girl's anatomy made it impossible for them to have intercourse, and courts found that young girls could not necessarily understand the charge and testify. In 1715, eleven-year-old Elizabeth Robinson, her mother and a midwife testified, saying, 'he threw her upon the Bed, and put something into her; but she not understanding the meaning of an Oath, what she said was not taken as Evidence', and David Bonnely, a weaver she worked with, was acquitted.[44] William Nichols of St Ann Aldersgate, who raped Dorcas Reeves, the five-year-old daughter of a neighbour, was also acquitted of the rape, but convicted of an assault. This was despite her 'being in a very bad condition', and a doctor and surgeon testifying that

> she had been very much injured, that the Parts were much inflamed and excoriated, and that there had been a manifest Perforation. . . . Mr. Fern the Surgeon, who was of this Opinion, and that the Child had been very much damaged; and that the child did say it had been done to her by the Prisoner. [But] The Child being too young to swear to the Fact, the Jury acquitted him of the Rape.[45]

Proof of penetration, and corroboration that the accused actually did it, were required. Otherwise, the court acquitted, often in the face of otherwise overwhelming evidence as with Dorcas Reeves. For example, Joseph Eason was indicted for raping Catharine Pitman, 'a Virgin, within the Age of 10 Years'. The court accepted that it had been 'clearly prov'd that the Girl had been abus'd by a Man' but determined that the evidence did not prove it to be a 'Consummate Rape', and the jury acquitted.[46] The level of questioning and the detail of the trial records confirm that the court was determined to find definitive evidence. Thus, they probed girls' testimonies in depth and asked questions repeatedly in different constructions. While it looks as though they were trying to trip them up, it was also because the penalty was death, so a firm grasp of evidence was required. This meant that in several cases in which a girl gave detailed evidence, and was old enough to swear, men could be acquitted. In the case of Jane Harris, a girl of twelve, despite her evidence and that of her mother and a midwife, the court determined, 'either their over-much modesty, or for some other reason, it was so favourable, that no positive Proof being thereof, he was Acquitted.'[47] Similarly, William Cash, who was indicted of raping a twelve-year-old girl, 'in his Defence had a Witness who swore, the Girl said he try'd, but could not enter her; and two Surgeons, who depos'd there had been no Penetration.'[48] Again, he was acquitted. In 1768, Elizabeth Hall, age eight, said the labourer who worked for her father 'had had to do with her' and she produced a venereal discharge, sworn to by the doctor. While he was convinced the rape had taken place, the justice asked, 'Do you think it possible for a man to lie with a child of eight years old, without an extension or laceration of the part?' Doctor Barrel responded, 'No, it is not possible', so William Allam was acquitted.[49] However, Thomas Padget was found guilty of rape of five-year-old Catherine Burchet. The doctor found her lacerated, bruised and inflamed and that 'the Parts had received an infection; that the Child had not suffer'd penetration, but an injection had been made on the Orifice'. Given that he had beaten her and wounded her, the jury 'considering the barbarity of the Crime, brought him in guilty.' He was, however, fined and not hanged.[50] That young girls made up such a substantial portion of the cases indicates that this was seen as a more heinous crime than those performed against older girls, and in the cases of older girls the prosecution often tried to besmirch their characters. When Charles Earle was charged with raping Mary Matthews (the younger), the court asked 'Do you know the nature of an oath. Now if you was to sware that which is not true, what do you think would become of you? Matthews. I should go to hell.' Her evidence was compelling and confirmed by her mother and several doctors so he was sentenced to death.[51]

We have to accept that some girls did make up their story, sometimes under the influence of others, or because they were ashamed, were ill with the pox or pregnant, and wanted to obscure their actions. Elizabeth Broadbent, fourteen, testified that she and a friend Rachel Hannet followed Sarah Clifton, a servant, into an alley, where Broadbent was given strong beer and gin. They then went to a public house where Clifton took her upstairs and sent her for more beer. When she returned she found a man there. Clifton locked the door and undressed her since she refused to do it. She claimed they put a handkerchief in her mouth and pulled her onto the bed, where Baynham fondled and ultimately raped her, while Clifton held her legs. Examination of the girls, accused and witnesses was lengthy and detailed, with the prosecution attempting to unpick their stories. While the girls corroborated each other, other testimony confused the issue, and witnesses gave the prisoners a good character. Both were acquitted. The next day the girls denied their whole testimony and said it was their master who debauched them, and he was remanded to Newgate.[52] Frances Adams, eighteen, deposed that while her mistress and the other servants were at the market, she was asked to put a child to bed, in January 1716. Returning downstairs, her master, William Atterbury, a butcher, 'spread a Great Coat on the Ground and swore he'd cut her to pieces it she refus'd to let him lie with her, stop'd her Mouth, and forc'd her after she had spent herself an Hour and a half wite'd, struggling'. She was afraid to tell her mistress in case Atterbury killed her but told her brother about a fortnight later. However, Atterbury denied it, witnesses said he was out playing at cards with them, and her mistress said only the servant was up when she came home. He was acquitted. The truth of this story is unclear, and she could have invented it—or not.[53]

Girls were vulnerable to men who shared the same house, neighbours, casual acquaintances and indeed total strangers. In 1721, Sarah Pearse, twelve, was a servant to Mrs Loo, a lodger in Christopher Graff's house. Her version was that he enticed her upstairs, pulled her into his room and raped her so violently that she bled. He then tried to pay her off, telling her not to report it and offered to marry her if his wife died. She did not tell for a week but a surgeon then reported that 'he found the Vagina extended, torn and bruis'd with a forcible entry, that she had been penetrated even to the inner Matrix, and that he was forc'd to use the utmost Art, both by external and internal Medicines, to prevent a Mortification, and that the Child told him the Prisoner had forced her, but she was ashamed to speak of it.' Graff claimed that she seemed willing and found witnesses to testify that she had lain with him several times before—but he was found guilty and sentenced to death.[54] Another servant, Ann Cooling, was prostituted by her mistress, Lucy Roberts. She had been at the house only a week when Roberts dressed her up on Christmas Day and 'sent her to drink when the ladies had any company'. Roberts then fed her more drink and pushed her upstairs where a 'gentleman' was waiting. He raped her with Roberts holding her legs open. A week later, the same scenario unfolded but Cooling refused and was turned out. She found lodging and her parents were sent for. She said 'I was very bad, and my mother examined my body. I had a very bad distemper after this affair, and have it still very much'. Unfortunately for her, her parents showed no sympathy, saying she had run away and knew it was a bad house—he was acquitted.[55] Likewise, John Sheridan, journeyman baker, was indicted for committing a rape on the body of Mary Brickinshaw, not quite twenty, a servant to an innkeeper, whom she had served six months. He was a neighbour, and as she returned from delivering beer, he dragged her into lane and raped her, twice. She waited to tell her mistress after the inn was empty and at the trial, she was quizzed about why she did not report it immediately. He was given a good character by witnesses, while one claimed that Mary said she 'did not want to hurt a hair on his head'; she was also offered money to change her accusation, and she swore on her oath that these stories were false. He was sentenced to death.[56]

A recurrent theme is attempts to make a girl change her story or accept money to withdraw her accusation. Because the penalty was death, girls were under pressure, and Mary Hix said she would rather marry John Harris than hang him.[57] When Elizabeth Banks was raped by a casual acquaintance as she travelled to Salisbury, despite horrific injuries the doctor persuaded her to say she made it up. She only brought a prosecution when she heard he had come to London, apparently believing he was a threat to her there. When accused he offered to pay for a cure for her health, but the wagon carrier who had travelled with them persuaded the jury that the weather could have caused her illness.[58] Being alone and undefended, like Elizabeth Banks, was always a risk for girls as Jane Bell discovered (Image 10.2). A milkmaid, she pastured her mistress's cows in Green Park, and on one July evening as she was doing so, a stranger grabbed her, dragged her away and raped her twice. Although the park was usually busy, it was not at this time, and she was only rescued

IMAGE 10.2 Benjamin West, 1738–1820, Milkmaids in St. James's Park, Westminster Abbey Beyond, ca. 1801. Oil on panel, Yale Center for British Art, Paul Mellon Fund, B2014.2.

by John Smith and Sarah Scott using the park as a route home who heard her cries. Again, a very detailed account in which she was quizzed on the layout of the gardens, the gates, etc., with suggestions that she might have invented the story, and a series of questions of which pubs she went to—none, she said. One of the odder questions was why she was out at 9 p.m.—she pointed out that it was July and still light. Witnesses however claimed that she had drunk with him, at least three times, suggesting she had also lain with him, and others said she was offered money to not testify. Throughout however, she was consistent in her version, and ultimately, he was convicted and sentenced to death.[59] Attempts to question and damage the character of a victim were frequent.

Characteristic of the testimonies is the detail of the occasion and especially of the physical assault and resulting injuries to the girls. The questioning was intensively probing and oftentimes seems to throw shadow on the girls' character. It is natural that defendants sought to proclaim their innocence, and their witnesses frequently provided the most potentially damning evidence. The court had to ensure guilt and juries probably tended to err on the side of caution, but there is no doubt that these cases demonstrated violent rapes on girls. The relatively small number of guilty verdicts speak to a concern with sentencing a man wrongly rather than belief in innocence, since death was the usual punishment. The prosecution pointed this out regularly, as well as ensuring girls knew the implications of lying. A few men were fined, and some were found guilty of assault instead. Another feature of these cases is that the men and girls virtually all came from the same class of working people; the middling sorts and wealthy did not appear.

A few cases spoke to a different set of patterns, and becoming friendly and offering to marry a girl was one device. For example, Barton Dorrington, 1788, claimed he was in love with Eleanor Masters, a servant, and followed her and visited her several times. Then on 16 May he went to her house when everyone else was out and raped her. It appears she left with him and was away several days and 'it was with difficulty she was taken from him when she was found'. William Garrow prosecuting said that she had given him a note, promising to marry him or forfeit £20. So, 'though a bad case of seduction, it is not a case of a rape, the man will be intitled to an acquittal.' But further he commented that

> on apprehending him there was found in his pocket-book . . . a list of young women whom he had seduced, and . . . the note signed by the young woman, Eleanor Masters, is pinned to several other notes, signed by those unfortunate young women whose names are in the list found in his pocket-book; the notes all of them are in these words, the same as this given by the prosecutrix.[60]

Garrow warned him of preying on women again, while the court confirmed:

> The seduction of these young women, under pretence of marrying, is not a crime of much less criminality than that which you have been tried for; and you will some time or another get your neck into the halter, if you do not leave off these practices. . . . Oh, he is a very bad man, certainly; but we cannot convict without evidence.[61]

A rare case of incest rape came to court in 1768. Mary Sherwin, mentioned previously, was asked, 'has anybody played any tricks with you?' She responded 'Only my daddy, my daddy, put his hand up my coats. Did he do any thing more?—Yes; he put his cock up into my body. Did he give you a great deal of pain?—Yes.' She said they were alone at her father's lodging, and he said if she told anybody he would not come and see her anymore. Jane White from the workhouse confirmed the injury and Mary's story, but a neighbour claimed

> He came to my house with his daughter about two o'clock . . . and took my little boy and his own girl into the fair; he brought him back about four o'clock. When he came back, he left his girl with me till about seven o'clock in the evening; then he came and took her home to the work-house. Did she say she had been used ill?—No; nor did I see any thing the matter with her.[62]

He was acquitted on her evidence.

Several of the girls described were raped more than once; others suffered gang rapes. In 1735, Margaret Macculough was not only gang raped, but publicly beaten and humiliated. Martha Mulzer, a midwife, deposed that 'She found her bruised on her Arms, Legs, Thighs, Back, and all over, like the Bark of a Tree; and fore, swell'd, and in such a shameful Condition, that she never saw any thing like it, and believed she would never be her own Woman again.'[63] She was accosted as she left home between three and four in the morning to go and sell mackerel. She was attacked by three men, and then 'a great many more followed'. After Togwell had abused her, Arn, Pug and Harding, and 'three more of the Company lay with her in the like manner; and then they left her and were followed by some of the Neighbours into Drury Lane, where they met another Woman, and pulled up her Coats and whipt her in the Street'. Testimony confirmed the details of the attack, and that Pug was well known. His defence simply was that he didn't do it. The others obfuscated and witnesses had some difficulty distinguishing the perpetrators, but these three were sentenced to death.[64] The rest appear to have not been charged. In a similar incident in Aberdeen, three men were 'placed at the bar, charged with committing a rape on Mary Munro, a girl of seventeen years of age'. Although the jury found that William Turnbull was guilty of the rape, being assisted by Edgar and Potts, they were simply allowed to go away and join the army.[65]

Many rapes, or attempted rapes, probably did not make it to court, as we know from contemporary experience. Reputation of the girl and her family as well as shame were discouraging factors. So were the pressures and publicity of the trials, the intense questioning, and potentially the cost of mounting a prosecution, a factor mentioned by Mrs Mary Matthews. Isolation and the lack of friends, especially girls away from families, possibly in larger towns where they might not get support, were also disincentives. The victims, either young girls or servants, were left with the damage caused. As the trial transcripts showed, many were severely injured, and would certainly have carried mental as well as physical scars. The trials showed a tendency to question a girl's testimony, obviously to ascertain guilt, but also to challenge her version of events. Neighbours and even family might be wary of the truth and might have wanted to disassociate with them. It could have been possible for a girl to seek lodging or work elsewhere, though references might have been difficult to obtain. Certainly, some midwives, doctors and witnesses showed sympathy for the girls and supported them. Mary Matthews had full support of her mother who brought the case. Other times, parents were unhelpful like Ann Cooling's parents who virtually condemned her. The nature of the evidence leaves us only to speculate what was in store for these girls.

Conclusion

While many girls travelled through girlhood encountering only the normal vagaries of obtaining a livelihood, a significant minority experienced the pitfalls of the eighteenth-century world, in which poverty, poor health and sexual snares tripped them up. Certainly, some recovered and moved on, usually disappearing from the records. Many ultimately did marry or achieved a successful singlehood. The support systems of family, neighbours and community as well as the intervention of poor law, churches or courts helped some reassert themselves. But inevitably some did not. While economic disaster and ill health may have affected more, the problematic character of sexual relations and sexual violence undoubtedly left some, especially young rape victims, damaged and vulnerable. When things went wrong, besides recruiting the support of family and community, girls deployed several strategies, some successful, or even more desperate as recounted in Chapter 11.

Notes

1 *OBP, Ordinary of Newgate's Account* July 1734 (OA17340709); *OBP*, April 1734 (t17340424–55).
2 Fontaine, 'In the 18th Century, Poverty Was More a Risk Than a State'; see also her *Vivre pauvre*.
3 Terling List, ERO, D/P 299/12/3.

4 'Sarah Gale, b. 1769', *LL*, compiled Sharon Howard.
5 Boos, 'Mary Ann Ashford', 173–6.
6 'Rachel Herbert, bc.1716', *LL*, compiled Charlotte Clapham.
7 Saxby, *Memoirs of a Female Vagrant*, 6–7.
8 'Rachel Herbert', *LL*.
9 See Leneman and Mitchison, *Sexuality and Social Control*, especially chapter 5 and Muir, 'Courtship, Sex and Poverty'.
10 Quoted Crawford, *Parents of Poor Children*, 32.
11 'Sarah Bridgen, fl. 1750–1773', *LL*, compiled Victoria Philpott.
12 'Sarah Gale', *LL*.
13 Laslett, *Family Life and Illicit Love* 107, 177, 147, 150; Laslett, 'The Bastardy Prone Sub-Society', 217–46.
14 Froide, *Never Married*, 41.
15 Barclay, 'Marriage, Sex, and the Church of Scotland', 175.
16 Diack, 'Motherhood and Poverty in Aberdeen', 175.
17 Hurst exhibition, Horley Museum.
18 Luddy and O'Dowd, *Marriage in Ireland*, 146, 149.
19 King, 'Chance Encounters?', 23–46.
20 Griffin, 'Sex, Illegitimacy', 143–5.
21 Leneman and Mitchison, *Sexuality and Social Control*, 181.
22 Evans, 'Unfortunate Objects', 142.
23 NRS, CC8/6/15/77 Jean Low a. Francis McFarlane, 1757 in Barclay, 'Love and Courtship', 46.
24 Leneman, *Promises, Promises*, 8.
25 Haywood, *Present for a Servant Maid*, 44, 49.
26 Barclay, 'Love and Courtship'.
27 *Chelsea Settlement and Bastardy Examinations*, No. 4.
28 Evans, *Unfortunate Objects*, 121.
29 Evans, *Unfortunate Objects*, 114.
30 Leneman and Mitchison, *Sexuality and Social Control*, 183.
31 *Chelsea Settlement and Bastardy Examinations*, No. 349.
32 *Chelsea Settlement and Bastardy Examinations*, No. 369.
33 *Ordinary of Newgate's Account*, July 1734, OA17340709.
34 Quoted Evans, *Unfortunate Objects*, 144.
35 Evans, 'Unfortunate Objects', 128.
36 Harvey, *Reading Sex*, 192–3.
37 Gillis, *World of Their Own Making*, 139.
38 Shoemaker, *Gender in English Society*, 68.
39 *OBP*, 9 December 1789, t17891209–91.
40 Shoemaker, *Patterns of Crime and Prosecution*, *OBP*.
41 Luddy and O'Dowd, *Marriage in Ireland*, 14.
42 Toulalan, '"Unripe Bodies"'; Simpson, *Age of Consent*, 181–205.
43 *OBP*, January 1779, t17790113–36.
44 *LL*, 13 July 1715, t17150713–35.
45 *OBP*, 26 February 1724, t17240226.
46 *OBP*, September 1707, t17070903–25.
47 *LL*, 12 December 1683, t16831212–24.
48 *OBP*, July 1715, t17150713–54.
49 *OBP*, September 1768, t17680907–40.
50 *OBP*, February 1727, t17270222–72.
51 *OBP*, December 1770, t17701205–39.
52 *OBP*, December 1755, t17551204–29.
53 *OBP*, April 1716, t17160411–34.

54 *OBP*, December 1721, t17211206–67.
55 *OBP*, January 1758, t17580113–34.
56 *OBP*, April 1768, t17680413–30.
57 *OBP*, May 1723, t17230530–26.
58 *OBP*, September 1717, t17170911–41.
59 *OBP*, September 1797, t17970920–12.
60 *OBP*, September 1788, t17880910–46.
61 *OBP*, September 1788, t17880910–46.
62 *OBP*, January 1779, t17790113–36. See also July 1726, t17260711–69.
63 *OBP*, September 1735, t17350911–55.
64 *OBP*, September 1735, t17350911–56, t17350911–55.
65 Black Kalendar, 233.

11

DEALING WITH MISFORTUNE

Introduction

Misfortune is the term many girls used to describe their predicaments when things went wrong. To deal with them they deployed whatever strategies they could see and under stress these were not always the logical or even obvious ones. As Chapter 10 showed, poverty, ill health, casual sex or even sex with promises as well as sexual and physical abuse could leave a girl with few choices. If she was in a supportive situation, family and friends could come to her aid, which is one reason most of the working girls that turn up in unfortunate circumstances are more likely to be amongst the poor or those at risk, rather than middling girls, those still with a family or a community around them. This chapter picks up the stories of girls 'in trouble' looking at routes they took to resolve their problems—with varying degrees of success.

Encountering misfortune

Bearing an illegitimate child without subsequent marriage often led to poverty. Unless she had family, friends or employers upon whom she could rely, pregnant girls had few choices, and for many, there seemed no choice at all. As we have seen, many applied for poor relief, and the records are replete with these girls. Some may have returned to their families, but as with Cheshire girl Elizabeth Ashbridge who eloped, families were not always willing to receive them home. For those who could successfully hide the birth, sending the child away was sometimes an option, and family or friends could be invaluable leaving them to continue working, or attempt abortion which was not illegal before 1803 if the child had not quickened. These girls made

DOI: 10.4324/9781003412168-12

decisions in a climate that was often hostile; poor law officials were not necessarily sympathetic, and an Aberdeen girl who abandoned her child in a doorway was described by the newspaper as 'unnatural'.[1] They might flee, especially if they could move to another part of the British Isles—border crossings offered an alternative.

For others, child abandonment or infanticide seemed the only alternatives. Mary Anslay's plea to the governors of the Foundling Hospital is indicative of their predicaments. She was a single servant deserted by the father, and wrote: '[I am] in a Miserable and almost Starving Condition having parted with Every Thing But what is on my Back for its [the child's] support and have no way of Giting my Bread but by Servitude Which has Reduced Me to the loest Pitch of Misery and Distress and am no longer able to Suport my Tender Infant.'[2] Single mothers were the most vulnerable, needing to work, often as servants where a child was unwelcome or not allowed. They faced dismissal and potential isolation and in small communities often were no longer welcome. In 1771, Grace Scott lost her place 'of a common servant' because of her pregnancy.[3] Migration was not necessarily a solution since she would have to find work and become even more isolated, distant from previous networks of support, lacking the belonging which would give her an entitlement to parish assistance, and likely to be punished as a vagrant.[4] They were also the most exposed women, often giving birth alone, potentially in poor health, making stillbirth or early infant death common. Although there were safe places for lying in, the poorest girls probably had little access to them either because of cost or lack of information.[5] The perils were strong deterrents, and they were motivated to set boundaries in 'sexual relations by far more than the loss of reputation. Considerably more serious than a tarnished reputation was the reality of trying to raise a child without a male breadwinner for support.'[6] Recognising the difficulty of surviving with a child certainly restrained some women. Some single mothers, at wit's end and fearing the ostracism and shame that could come their way, escaped through suicide.

Abandonment

Abandonment was one alternative. Children were left at church doors, hospitals or any likely venue for the child to be found (Image 11.1). The *Aberdeen Journal* regularly reported children left on doorsteps, 'exposed' or worse, but commonly mothers probably wanted them to be found; it was 'a last gasp of maternal love rather than neglect.'[7] They only abandoned a child if they could see no alternative and probably hoped that it might give the child a chance of a better life, though this was often a fruitless expectation. Most single mothers were young, usually migrants who had come to town to find

IMAGE 11.1 A baby has been left outside the town-house of an old bachelor, and a young woman watches from the corner of the street. Engraving, 1794. Wellcome Collection. Source: https://wellcomecollection.org/works/gh82j6gj.

work. Their partners had similar origins and were men they met at work, in the household and the neighbourhood; many were servants or apprentices. With the fluidity of urban society, men had opportunities to abscond in a myriad of ways—but in a large city like London, they could simply move to another part of town. Sometimes, of course, they were simply too poor to take on a child, while some died leaving a girl literally 'holding the baby'.

Abandonment did not necessarily mean a lack of love as historians like Tanya Evans, Samantha Williams and Patricia Crawford showed. In contrast, others took a sharper view. Keith Wrightson suggested that those who gave their babies to vagrants or otherwise unsuitable nurses were virtually infanticidal. Hitchcock saw 'abandoning' mothers as doing so to move on to lead new lives, though he acknowledged their distress: 'It would be condescending and simply wrong to suggest that the mothers of the thousands of abandoned children who passed through the institutions of London did not feel their loss to a devastating extreme. But, it is likewise apparent that having abandoned their children, these women went on to essentially new lives.'[8] For the girl

IMAGE 11.2 Charles Grignion, 1717–1810, A Perspective View of the Foundling Hospital with Emblematic Figures, 1749. Engraving, Yale Center for British Art, Paul Mellon Collection, B1977.14.17125.

'in trouble', abandonment could make it easier to move on with her life, and evidence suggests that some lived in hope. They hoped for a better life for the child, and hoped that without a child, they could improve their own circumstances. For example, Mary Jackson was 'anxious to conceal her misfortune from the Knowledge of an ancient parent and the world, has reduced herself to very great distress, is unable to support herself and child, which could it be received under your charitable care might be saved from ruin'.[9] Servants almost certainly would not been able to keep a child and return to service.

When leaving a child at a hospital girls couched their situation as 'misfortune' (Image 11.2). As Evans argues, these women saw themselves as 'unfortunate objects' but not as

> hopeless not without desire . . . The language of the petitions challenges the representation of unmarried mothers as passive, seduced victims and tells us instead of the myriad fortunes and misfortunes of infanticide. . . . Economic need rather than shame was the all-important criterion in the admission of a child into the hospital.[10]

They knew how to frame their stories so that hospital authorities would accept the child, and those who sought help from the poor law authorities also knew how to portray themselves to gain support if they did not abandon it. Most stories did not claim seduction or shame but recounted tales of misfortune including unemployment and poverty, illness, deaths of those who could help support them, and betrayals. Evans reports that 'Out of a total of 1,138 accepted petitions for admission [at the London Foundling Hospital], 867 referred to children who were illegitimate; of these 391 included accounts of seduction but 476 did not.'[11] Yet, they also learned to buy into the preconceived notions of governors who were largely unsympathetic. So, some created stories as victims of seduction, often obliquely. The insecurities of a working girl's life were ever present. Sarah Hall had suffered a catalogue of misfortunes since the age of five:

> I am sorry to be thus unfortunate an particular as it is intirely out of my power to suport it as the father is absent . . . to had [sic] to my misfortune I have been deprived of parents ever since I have been five years old and have not a friend to apply to and no not in wat manner to support the enfant an I have thus been so unfortunate an only been a servent sence I was fourteen.[12]

Some girls did have support, of course, and family, friends, co-servants and employers might help with writing petitions to the foundling hospital. Families also stepped up and took children. Employers were not always unsympathetic and some helped, so Mrs Scott in Holborn helped Hannah Holden, her unmarried domestic servant, supporting the child along with the father. Similarly, Mrs Etchers of Goodge Street, London, supported her servant's application to the Foundling Hospital, saying that 'her Misfortune (has not) been . . . so as to be injurious to her future Character' and promised to keep her place open.[13]

Infanticide

Abandonment was linked to infanticide since many children were left outside, on doorsteps or in fields, leading to death. Other cases appeared far more deliberate. Infanticide was viewed with severity and authorities were relentless in their search for culprits. In 1771, dealing with a complicated case of child abuse and abandonment, the editor of the *Aberdeen Journal* expressed the desire that: 'It is apprehended that detecting and discouraging such Practices very much concerns the good order and Police of the Country; and it is therefore hoped, that civil Magistrates will lend their aid, as well as Ministers of the Kirk-Sessions, and others, endeavour to obtain . . . all the Information in their power.' Later, when a newborn boy was discovered, a notice in the *Journal* stated that 'Any Person who will make a Discovery to the Kirk Session, who is the Mother of the Child, shall upon her being apprehended receive a Reward of Five Pounds Sterling.[14] Anne Marie Kilday argues that abandonment was a far more likely alternative than infanticide, and strenuous efforts to find the mother of an exposed child tended to be made only if the child died.[15] Few indictments for exposure appear in records: Leneman and Mitchison recorded only 78 cases of infant abandonment amongst the 8,429 instances in seventeenth- and eighteenth-century Scotland, only a handful appeared in the *Aberdeen Journal*, and Nick Woodward uncovered just two cases of infant abandonment in Wales between 1730 and 1830.[16]

Official concern about infanticide and immorality worked together to create a dangerous atmosphere. The fact that physicians could not distinguish between a stillborn child, a newborn who had died of natural causes or murder made the situation more perilous. A midwife was obliged, and usually inclined, to alert authorities, and may have insisted other women present backed her up. Any unmarried woman whose baby died before baptism after a concealed pregnancy was deemed guilty of infanticide regardless of mitigating evidence. Certainly, in desperation, some girls took what they saw as the only alternative of killing their baby. Across Britain, girls were charged with concealing their pregnancy, giving birth in secret and killing the infant almost immediately after delivery. It was a distinctly female crime with few men charged. Of 131 cases recorded between 1700 and 1799 at the Old Bailey, 97 per cent charged women. Three men were prosecuted as accessories, and only James Field was charged alone, since the mother died after labour; he was acquitted. It is a matter of historical debate about how widespread it was, and Kilday and others talk about the 'dark figure' of infanticide. She argues that there were sharp disjunctures between official practices and popular perceptions and customs. Also given the very nature of infant murder and the necessity of concealment, it is difficult to find and investigate infanticide effectively.[17] However, despite moral abhorrence, there is also clear evidence of a growing degree of leniency around the offence after the mid-eighteenth century. Old Bailey records show that only 20 per cent of the cases before the court resulted in a guilty verdict, and towards the end of the century, fewer cases came before it, while in the last two decades of the century, there was not a single guilty verdict.[18] It was a hidden crime of necessity, and many were unreported, others recorded as stillbirth.

Girls' principal interest lay in self-preservation, and their testimonies in infanticide cases depicted a variety of strategies: that they had not known they were pregnant, that the child was stillborn, that someone else did away with it, or even that she was confused, out of her mind and did not know what she was doing. While infanticide was a violent crime, most girls tended to smother the child rather than use bloodshed. It was simpler and less horrific. Suffocation did not leave visible marks, and girls commonly claimed that the child had been stillborn, an easy option since many gave birth alone, often after hiding the pregnancy. Girls also commonly tried to show that they had prepared for the birth, implying that they had not planned to kill the child. Certainly, babies born too soon, often undernourished, did die naturally, and poor mothers were most vulnerable to stillbirth and early deaths. But such defence was not always convincing since linen could be placed afterwards, or even 'beforehand by a cold-blooded women intent on killing her child and avoiding punishment'.[19] Hiding the pregnancy, while a self-preservation measure, could also be held against them. Legislation presumed that if she had hidden the birth or not sought help during labour, then she had intended to kill the child.

The key difference between English and Scottish legislation was that the Scottish judiciary placed much more emphasis on there being a direct link between concealment and intent to commit murder than English law. So, in Scotland, 'concealment of pregnancy and failure to engage help at parturition (*as well as* concealment of the actual death of the infant itself) were sufficient grounds for an indictment. This was true where deliberate killing was not clearly evident and even when murder was suspected but a corpse had not actually been found.'[20] Thus, when Janet Whiggham of Haddington, near Edinburgh, was convicted of hiding the birth and making no provision for the child, she was not condemned for the child's murder or burial. They found that the child had been murdered and buried but could not say whether she or her partner had done so, and decided that he had 'influence' over her, so accepted her plea to be banished while the charge against Thompson was vacated.[21] Similarly in 1798, Janet Yarrow of Selkirkshire was found guilty of concealing her pregnancy, but the plurality of the jury found she was not guilty of the actual murder of the child. The judge, finding this a tricky situation, sought further information for a later date and she went back to prison in the meantime.[22] The court clearly struggled with these cases, and in 1798 the High Court of Justiciary reversed a decision of the Circuit Court of Jedburgh against a guilty verdict on Janet Ramsay of Eccles in Berwickshire. She was initially found 'guilty on her own confession', but the record showed she had pled 'not guilty'. Thus, they decided no punishment could follow on this verdict, so the case was dismissed.[23] In contrast, in England these circumstances were only grounds for *suspicion* of murder.[24] Yet Ann Price 'was got with Child by a Man that was her fellow Servant; and carried it so cunningly, that no Person in the house did in the least suspect her till after she was delivered, which was without help, when wrapping the Child in an Apron. She locked it up in her Box; and rising betimes in the Morning, made a Fire and went to Bed again'. Her mistress however called a midwife who declared that she had given birth. Price argued that the child was stillborn, and the pains had come on her suddenly, and claimed she knocked for help. But concealment of the child was a material point of evidence against her, and she was found 'guilty of Murther'.[25] Thus, asking for help, not concealing a pregnancy and preparing for a child's birth were mitigating circumstances. Also, medical knowledge was less precise than today, and cessation of menses could be attributed to several factors, including poor nutrition. Lynn Abrams noted that doctors could mistake a stomach complaint for pregnancy.[26]

In July 1752, Elizabeth Dunkin's story of murdering her newborn daughter combines several familiar elements. She denied being married or pregnant the day before she was delivered, but on 22 July her daughter was found in a box, in her room dead, but with no marks of violence on her. In her defence, she said

> it was her first child, was taken in labour sooner than expected, and being surprized, had not proper assistance as is necessary. She called the person who was ordered to search her room, who produced a quantity of child-bed linen; and called Mr. Clark, who lives in the Temple, who depos'd, she came to him about two months ago and told him her case; and that he would assist her in speaking to a surgeon to help her; and that a Jamaica gentleman, one Mr. Roberts, was the father. James Mophat deposed, that one Mr. Roberts, who is now gone to Jamaica, had applied to him to assist a young woman with proper conveniences, who he expected would be delivered of a child about Christmas, but did not mention the prisoner's name.[27]

She was acquitted. She demonstrated her inexperience, thought the birth was too soon, did not dispose of the child, had prepared bedlinen for her child and sought help two months prior to the event. The father had left the country, but he too had sought help for her. Midwives' testimonies were crucial in infanticide cases and when Ann Wood of Cripplegate was tried for murder, the midwife declared it 'was an Abortive Birth, and she wanted so much of her time, that the Infant was altogether imperfect, and consequently not alive; the Jury Acquitted her'.[28] In Aberdeenshire a young girl was found in July 1754 in a park with two female infants in her lap, 'newly brought forth'. She was examined by the Justice of the Peace with a minister in attendance, and she claimed they had been born dead. 'She never discovered her being with child, to any body, nor had any Person suspected her.' She said she had set out that day to ask her uncle for help when she felt the pains unexpectedly, since she reckoned that she was ten weeks short. The doctors and midwife summoned concurred that the twins had probably been born in the seventh month and found no signs of violence on them. However, 'the unhappy Woman in the meantime is secured till she be in Condition to be imprisoned', presumably because she was guilty of hiding the pregnancy.[29]

Others, however, hid the birth, sometimes throwing the child in the 'necessary' (the toilet), covertly smothering it, or at times violently killing the child in cold blood. Janet Trigg was closely questioned, and it appears that she went into the toilet with what she called bad bowel pains, gave birth and left the child there. Several witnesses confirmed seeing the child there, even removing and cleaning the child. But the justices probed whether she could have given birth and not known it, and although the surgeon was thoroughly convinced this could not have happened, she was acquitted.[30] These cases endorse Emsley's view that 'when the coroner did register a verdict of murder, the assize jury was generally reluctant to return a verdict indicating culpability on a mother's part'.[31] Other bastards certainly had a violent death. Mary Forest, of Stepney, strangled her child with her hands, presented no defence and was sentenced to death. Mary Radford's child was found in a chamber pot with a broken jaw and a torn cheek which continued bleeding; she too was sentenced to death. Mary Morton's child was found buried in a garden with two stab wounds in 1724, while Mercy Hornby, of Stoke-Newington, was found guilty of casting a child 'alive into a Privy' with a 'mortal Bruise on the left side of the Head,' of which it instantly died, and Elizabeth Ambrook, 'was indicted for the murder of her male Bastard Infant, by throwing it, as soon as born, out of a Window 2 Stories high'.[32] The *Aberdeen Journal* carried accounts of babies left on hillsides, and in January 1758 reported, 'Last week a new born child had been thrown into the water in the parish of Kildrummy. . . . [The child] was found half-eaten by dogs . . . [and] the perpetrators of the crime were being looked for.' Insanity was often considered and courts and the public saw infanticide as unnatural and aberrant.

Girls behaving badly

Crime itself is the result of constantly shifting definitions of acceptable behaviour and sometimes criminal behaviour was determined by what was socially acceptable rather than what was against the law. Thus, a shady area of behaviour which was unacceptable or 'harmful' to society rather than illegal often caught girls who were struggling to manage their lives. Proportionately, they appear more often in the court records for 'keeping disorderly company' or for 'being persons of bad fame and character' than for any other offence. For example, in 1758 alone, eighteen out of the twenty-nine women recorded in the Aberdeen enactment books were convicted of misdemeanours (no ages given). Vagrancy was a persistent concern, because inhabitants recognised that often miscreants were transient, or incomers, often with no obvious means of earning. The English 1744 *Vagrant Act* frequently referred to persons 'wandering abroad'.[33] Legislation often victimised paupers, but certainly prostitutes, seasonal workers, street pedlars and aggressive beggars were prosecuted for vagrancy, 'including all the ill-defined "crimes" of "wandering and begging", and of being "loose, idle and disorderly"'.[34] Aberdeen banished women perceived as disorderly or suspicious 'incomers' as vagrants of 'bad fame and character and no visible means of support', like Helen Anderson, Christian Fotheringham and Elizabeth Smith, banished on 7 December 1758.[35]

Most girls would do all they could to avoid poverty by developing self-help strategies such as small-scale saving, trading, selling homemade goods or, ultimately, even resorting to crimes like prostitution and theft to earn an extra bit of money, because it was a matter of survival. Poverty and unreliable work left many of them turning to selling sex, sometimes for a loaf of bread, a room or something similar. For others it could become a way of life, and a way to cope with the uncertainties of working girls' lives, especially those alone and in towns. It was a source of income, and a means of getting by when times were hard. So, servants, needleworkers and others in casual or seasonal trades were vulnerable since they were subject to periods of slack employment and low wages and often turned to prostitution from time to time, and as Campbell warned, mantuamakers' pay was frequently so low as to make prostitution the alternative.[36]

Many were migrants who used urban support networks and access to information from friends, pedlars or people who had migrated earlier—part of the 'floating mass' of urban inhabitants. Most were born into the ranks of the unskilled working classes with little opportunity to learn a skill, and often the death of one parent was the catalyst.[37] Although part of an economy of makeshift, frequently prostitution was a choice since earning power, labour relations and independence were usually better than they would have found in service, industry or seasonal textile work. The trope of the servant falling into prostitution is belied by the lack of servants charged, and provision of room and board meant servants were not desperate.

Despite no law against prostitution itself, there was a consensus of authorities and the public on the definition of behaviour that is 'harmful' or 'unacceptable' in society. The records of London Bridewell are replete with a string of women and girls bound over as loose, idle and disorderly persons; in 1797 alone, 188 women were bound over.[38] England's *Disorderly Houses Act*, 1751, required that no place be kept for public entertainment within the City of London and Westminster and twenty miles around without a license granted by the local authority.[39] Most towns, like Aberdeen, lacked effective policing, so magistrates relied on vague but useful euphemisms 'disturbing the peace', or 'disorderly behaviour', 'lewd and disorderly', and similar phrases. Constables were instructed to 'to apprehend offenders against the peace, vagrants, frequenters of disorderly houses, and such as can give no account of themselves, and carry them to the next justice; to suppress riots, with the assistance of the neighbourhood, and apprehend the rioters'.[40] It was the lusty, sinful behaviour of workingwomen whose behaviour was regarded as lewd who were singled out in attempts to protect the town. Misdemeanours and other behavioural crimes were likewise met with disciplinary punishment. These were minor offenses, such as keeping bad company or roaming the streets at nighttime, and they were typically met with punishments designed largely to shame the offender, like public whipping or exposure in the stocks.

Girls who behaved indecently or annoyed passers-by could be targeted, and coded language referred regularly to houses where prostitution was conducted as 'disorderly houses'. Those deemed to be sexually promiscuous figured large in Aberdeen Council's efforts to create a virtuous civic society. 'Flexibility, compromise and absence of system were almost the defined characteristics of the policing of street prostitution. . . . The process of policing itself constituted a relationship between police and policed, the nature of which was determined by the needs and activities of both sides.'[41] Frequently prostitutes were dealt with summarily, often released before seeing a magistrate after a few hours incarceration; others saw only a few days of imprisonment; first offenses were increasingly dealt with outside the courts and repeat and blatant offenders received the strictest treatment. Two examples illustrate how Aberdeen Council dealt with persistent prostitutes.

In June 1759, William Lamb, a Sheriff's officer, bound himself not to harbour his daughter Janet without notifying the magistrates under penalty of himself being banished. In August, they found 'that she is a person of notorious bad character and that she has been banished several times from the Burgh and ordain her to be conveyed out of town by the executioner & tuck of drum.'[42] Yet in 1767 she was before them again, under the certification that 'if she returned she would be corporally punished and publicly disgraced, and having returned from banishment' they would banish her again from the burgh, never to return. She was to remain in prison and then 'publickly whipt threw [sic] the streets of this Burgh by the executioner with the tuck of drum and then banished'.[43]

In November 1785, Margaret Adam and two others were found by the guard walking the streets about one or two in the morning. She claimed she was a stockingknitter and came to the well to find out the time and collect thread. Because she could not confirm her supplier, she agreed to leave the town since she was an incomer. It came out in testimony from her former employer that she had lost her job in service because of her 'irregular behaviour and haunting loose and disorderly company. [He] Declares that for some time past the said Margaret Adam has been a common streetwalker and Prostitute.'[44] On 1 December she asked the magistrates for money to leave but commented that she had been in the infirmary with a sore throat. She was asked if she had venereal disease, then admitted she was a streetwalker.[45] She was again found on the street between eleven and twelve, with two men in her company, but they ran off. She was finally banished, but on 1 October 1786, she was back in town and the sheriff's officers were ordered to carry her off to the Tolbooth, with others. They were to be detained until

Friday 13 January at 12 noon, when they were to be taken 'from the Prison and brought to the head of the stair at the Railing with Labels on their breasts and ordained them to stand there with the Hangman attending for one full hour thereafter'.[46]

Both obviously had made a virtual career out of prostitution, and Margaret Adam was in a volatile and poorly paying trade. We don't know when or exactly why they had turned to selling sex, but their stories mirror many girls who would have taken this route to survive—indeed it often paid better than knitting, spinning or sewing. Hogarth drew on the vulnerability of the young girl who came to town unprotected in *A Harlot's Progress* (Image 11.3). She was greeted at the staging post by a woman who complimented her beauty then groomed her as a prostitute. She later found herself in Bridewell with other prostitutes and ultimately died at age twenty-three of venereal disease.

IMAGE 11.3 Moll Hackabout, dressed in fine clothes, is beating hemp, used for making rope, with a mallet, in a prison with other inmates who are mostly prostitutes. Engraving by William Hogarth, A Harlot's Progress, Plate 4, before April 1732. Harris Brisbane Dick Fund, 1932. The Metropolitan Museum of Art, 32.35(5). https://www.metmuseum.org/.

A moral tale, it underlined how exposed girls could be without family and friends.

Criminal behaviour

Throughout the eighteenth century, significant numbers of females were accused in only a few offences, like pick-pocketing, shoplifting and receiving stolen goods, and behavioural crimes such as defamation, keeping bad company and fornication. On the other hand, relatively few women were accused of deception, violent assault and robbery, and even fewer of murder. Women do not often appear as the perpetrators of more physical crimes and were mostly seen as the victims of violence and murder, partly because some crimes are gender-specific: women were more likely to be accused of prostitution, infanticide, concealing a birth and unlawful abortion. Crimes also reflected social attitudes in that men were seen as prone to violence, obstinacy and selfishness while women were allegedly driven by their bodies and emotions.[47] 'Aggression was certainly not one of the celebrated traits of the "fairer sex", yet its existence suggests ideals of femininity could be—and were—challenged, particularly by women of the lower orders.'[48] This raises a tension in understanding crimes of women and girls. Kilday argues that 'Women could be just as shocking and brutal in their criminal behaviour as men.'[49] In eighteenth-century Aberdeen few women were charged for violent crimes, but 'the figures for non-lethal violence amongst women may be an underestimate, as many male victims of minor female aggression might have been reluctant to risk public humiliation by prosecuting such attacks'.[50] But as we shall see, both women and girls did commit violent acts. They also joined highway robbery gangs. In 1753 Elisabeth Brown and her daughter (age unknown) were on trial for 'belonging to Gun's crew', a famous Scottish robber, John Gun, and banished from Aberdeen.[51]

Identifying girls involved in criminal activity is difficult because testimony usually described women, ages were only occasionally mentioned and the designation of 'girl' was subject to various interpretations. Jane Gibbs, depicting herself the victim of theft, argued that she was an honest **girl** robbed by a strange man; however, witnesses described her as a **woman** of suspicious manner overly tall and masculine-looking.[52] Very few cases of girls as perpetrators turned up in courts or even the press. They were charged occasionally with fraud and deception, a handful for theft, arson and sometimes murder other than infanticide. But more often they were the victims of mistresses, masters, other servants and acquaintances. Girls were vulnerable as rape cases illustrate, but they could also be proactive and disputes with other servants, members of the household, masters and mistresses could lead to criminal behaviour, but so could poverty, desire for money or goods and the availability of things in a household provided opportunity. Social conditions created a situation in which women's occupations were overstocked, ill-paid and irregular, and therefore it is not surprising that 'women's instinct to protect themselves, their interests or their families were the main reason why they committed criminal acts'.[53] Malcolm Feeley and Deborah Little have argued that the female offender vanished from violent crimes by the end of the century, and from mid-century women were less frequently charged, while insult and defamation constituted the main crimes charged to women. Kilday argues that 'authorities tended to regard [females] with pity rather than disdain', while Laura Gowing maintains that girls would have been entitled to some assumption of innocence and protection, and Peter King suggested that women's 'Pleas of poverty, unemployment and economic vulnerability . . . may have received a more sympathetic hearing in the courts because women were marginalised in the employment market in this period, forced into lower-paid and less secure types of work.'[54] There was a shift toward benevolence, and a movement away from physical and public punishments across the century.

Poverty undoubtedly provoked crime, as did the low and uncertain wages most girls earned. When theft was successful the offender usually sold on the stolen goods to make a bit of money, or in some cases have someone else sell them on. It was probably the most frequent crime girls were changed with, and servants especially had opportunity to steal. For example, in Aberdeen in 1762, Elizabeth Sinclair from Caithness, a former servant, was childminding when she was charged for having 'no attestation as to her character . . . opening a trunk belonging to [her master] and of having left his child with some strangers'. Apparently, she did not steal anything—but she might have. Doubting her character, the magistrates banished her.[55] Girls might obtain goods claiming they were for their mistress. In November 1796, Ann Lemon, nineteen, said she was sent by her mistress, a regular customer of haberdasher Lucy Todd, for a pair of worsted stockings and a muslin handkerchief. Mrs Richardson explained that Lemon had been her servant but had left in July, and she had not seen her since. Lemon was found guilty and transported for seven years.[56] When Alice Pendergrass, Margaret Gill, sen. and Margaret Gill, jnr. were convicted of stealing a great amount of money, Margaret Gill, jnr., 'being a girl was young, acquitted' while the other two were branded.[57] In February 1762, Sarah Morring was indicted for stealing three silver spoons, valued at 16s and three pairs of laced ruffles, valued at 10s and accused of setting fire, but witnesses could not prove that she had done either, and with a spotless character confirmed by witnesses she was acquitted.[58] In October 1703, 'Margaret Richards, a little Girl of the Parish of St. Pauls Covent-Garden, was indicted for privately Stealing 6 Yards and a half of Ribbon out of the Shop of William Smith, on the 23rd of July last. The Jury considering the Tenderness of her Years, and that she was not sensible of her Fault, acquitted her.'[59] Testimony, age of the girl and probably the value of the property often worked in the girl's favour. In contrast, Mary Speerman, described as a girl, was sentenced to death for stealing 7 Guineas and 25s. from a man sleeping in the same room as her. Despite claiming she found it on the ground beside the bed, the jury did not believe her and concurred that she had taken it from his pocket.[60] The value of the money and the fact that she was believed to have taken it from his person weighed against her. Ten-year-old Hannah Starky was a regular offender being charged for the theft of a watch, a smock, tablecloth and other things. She had been taken in by the prosecutor, in charity, but within a few days she ran off with the goods and pawned the watch for liquor. On the same day she was named as Hannah Norman for stealing a bodice and a petticoat, which she also pawned. Charged with grand larceny and stealing from a place, she was transported.[61] Multiple other girls appeared before the Old Bailey for theft, and it appeared a common occurrence. They stole from houses they lived in and others in the neighbourhood, and they shoplifted, usually goods of relatively small value, like Jane Finch who was accused of stealing 'Childbed-Linnen, a Silver worked Stomacher, a Child's Frock and Petticoat, and other Things, to a Woman that crys old Iron.' In an interesting twist, however, she claimed it was the master's own daughter, aged eleven, that had broken open the trunks and sold them and that she had been stealing from her father for years, 'young as she was'.[62]

Girls could be induced to collude as well. Susanna Moor of St. Martin in the Fields was indicted for stealing certain Tea, Chocolate, &c. from Samuel Hawkins, and seducing 'a Girl he kept', to rob him of his Goods &c and receiving the same. Hawkins, said he had taken a poor girl 'from the Country to keep and bring up out of Charity; he received a Letter' that his Girl us'd to give away his Tea, Chocolate, &c. to the Prisoner [Moor], who had a great many Companions she us'd to treat therewith. The Girl deposed, that she gave the Prisoner Tea twice at her desire . . . who carryed it out of the House: That she also induced her to take half a Crown out of her Master's Drawer . . . and that she saw the Prisoner take her self a Candle, starch, and Pounds of Chocolate at a time. The girl was never named, but Moor was transported.[63]

Certainly, girls were charged with violent crimes on property and person. Nineteen-year-old servant Elizabeth Sedgwick was indicted for 'wilfully, maliciously, and feloniously' setting fire to two barns and a stable and then to the out-house belonging to her master John Taylor of Feltham Hill, Middlesex, on 10 and 17 December 1786. It was clearly a difficult case since she claimed to be not guilty and was calm at the time of the events and well regarded. But physical evidence tended to point to her, and after trying to blame others, she confessed fully. However, she said it was to prevent others from being indicted, and claimed an unverified altercation with a neighbour. She was sentenced to death.[64] And though murder was not a common accusation against girls, they did accost and kill others. In 1744, servant

Elizabeth Sevill was 'indicted for feloniously, wilfully, and of her malice aforethought', assaulting Mary Cartwright, a co-servant, with a smoothing iron. During the trial it was disclosed that the two of them fought regularly, and Sevill saw herself the victim of Cartwright. Despite the gravity of Cartwright's injuries, after much questioning the doctor admitted he could not be sure her death had been caused by the assault with the smoothing iron, and Sevill was acquitted.[65]

The infamous yet complicated case of case of twenty-two-year-old servant Sarah Malcolm shows the potential for girls to steal and kill. Born in Durham, she was raised in Ireland and by 1733 was on trial in London for killing three women. Her infamy was such that she was sketched by Hogarth, figured in broadsides and took up several pages in the *Newgate Calendar*, a popular book of heinous crimes, and her execution drew an enormous crowd (Image 11.4). At her trial, the evidence was compelling, and her manner was

IMAGE 11.4 After William Hogarth (British, London 1697–1764), Sarah Malcolm, after 1733. Harris Brisbane Dick Fund, 1932. The Metropolitan Museum of Art, 2.35(184). https://www.metmuseum.org/.

bold and sharp, questioning the prosecution and offering differing interpretations of events and the physical evidence. Although her co-conspirators were arrested, there was no direct evidence against them, and indeed the court assumed that she had named them only to exonerate herself and paid them a *per diem* while in jail. The murders of an elderly respected widow, her elderly maid and a young maid were horrific, and it is likely that the court and public wanted to convict someone. Hogarth said that 'she is capable of any wickedness' though his image of her shows none of this.[66] Twenty years later Henry Fielding included her in his bizarre list of 'heroines', or impassioned and criminal women, in *Amelia*.[67] It took the jury fifteen minutes to convict her, but even up to the moment she was hanged, she denied her part in the murders, only accepting that she was present on the stairwell as a lookout, and took her share of the spoils.[68]

Conclusion

Encountering misfortune on their route through girlhood, girls adopted different strategies to deal with them. From poverty and ill health to failed courtships, and sexual abuse, they often had options, but the way out was equally obscured and difficult. Those with backup and support did best while those isolated and alone or simply vulnerable by circumstance used the tools at their disposal. This chapter has concentrated on two main groups of decisions: those related to sexual misfortune and those skirting the boundaries of crime. Abandonment was useful especially if a girl believed that it could bring hope to her child and perhaps enable herself to recover her bearings. Some took the expedience of leaving a child where he or she might be found—churches were popular. Many who used foundling charities might have hoped they would recover their child, but the reality was rather different. Sometimes abandonment was tantamount to infanticide, when live infants were left in obscure places, perhaps the countryside. Child murder was not easily distinguishable from stillbirth but social concern about immoral behaviour coupled with suspicion of murder made this a dangerous situation for girls. There is no doubt that they did kill their babies, but also it could have been accidental, or they could have been alone and distraught and lacking knowledge. It is noticeable that attitudes shifted in that it became less likely that a girl would be criminally charged by the end of the century, a feature also apparent in other crimes committed by women and girls. Crime was to some extent a moveable feast in that definitions shifted, especially with respect to sexual misdemeanours, but also with petty crimes. Many petty crimes were provoked by poverty, and as the examples in the chapter showed, girls in particular may have been treated sympathetically. Nevertheless, especially crimes of violence gained little sympathy.

Notes

1 *AJ*, March 1759.
2 Quoted Evans, '"... Overwhelmed with Shame and Destitute of Friends"'.
3 In Crawford, *Parents of Poor Children*, 40.
4 Crawford, *Parents of Poor Children*, 41–2; Gowing, 'Giving Birth at the Magistrate's Gate', 137–50.
5 Gowing, *Common Bodies*, 156–7.
6 Griffin, 'Sex, Illegitimacy', 148.
7 Bailey, 'Family Relationships', 21.
8 Wrightson, 'Infanticide in Earlier Seventeenth-Century England', 16; Hitchcock, 'Unlawfully Begotten on Her Body'.
9 Evans, *Unfortunate Objects*, 113.
10 Evans, 'Unfortunate Objects', 130–1.
11 Evans, 'Unfortunate Objects', 133.
12 Evans, 'Unfortunate Objects', 134–5.
13 Evans, 'Unfortunate Objects', 104, 113.
14 *AJ*, 18 March 1771; 16 February 1778.
15 Kilday, *Infanticide in Britain*, 84–5.
16 Leneman and Mitchison, 'Scottish Illegitimacy'; Woodward, 'Infanticide in Wales'.
17 Kilday, *A History of Infanticide* and 'Maternal Monsters'; Sharpe, *Crime in Early Modern England*; Beattie, *Crime and the Courts*.
18 Thanks to Rita Lima Fernandes for data calculation.
19 Kilday, 'Maternal Monsters', 160.
20 Acts of the Parliaments of Scotland, 195, Kilday, *History of Infanticide*, 18.
21 *AJ*, 22 July 1801.
22 *AJ*, 10 July1798.
23 *AJ*, 10 July 1798.
24 21 Jac. 1 c. 27.
25 *OBP*, 13 April 1681, t16810413-1.
26 Abrams, 'From Demon to Victim', 187.
27 *OBP*, 14 September 1752, t17520914–66.
28 *OBP*, 12 May 1687, t16870512-1.
29 *AJ*, 30 July 1754.
30 *OBP*, 12 September 1750, t17500912–76.
31 Emsley, *Crime and Society*, 41.
32 *OBP*, 6 September 1710, t17100906–10; 16 January 1723, t17230116–38; 26 February 1724, t17240226–72; 24 April 1734, t17340424–21; 16 January 1735, t17350116–11.
33 17 George II c. 5.
34 Simonton, 'Inscribing the Town'; authors' calculations; Hitchcock and Shoemaker, *London Lives*, 305.
35 ACA, *Enactment Books*, 19 November, 1 and 2 December 1785.
36 Campbell, *London Tradesman*, 227.
37 Norberg, 'Prostitutes', 470; Pluskota, *Prostitution*, 5; Henderson, *Disorderly Women*, 14.
38 *LL*, 'Bridewell Prison and Hospital'.
39 *Statutes*, 25 Geo. II.
40 Erskine, *Institute of the Law of Scotland*, 86.
41 Henderson, *Disorderly Women*, 140.
42 ACA, Enactment Books, 5 June and 21 August 1759.
43 ACA, Enactment Books, 4 April 1767.
44 ACA, *Enactment Books*, 19 November, 1 and 2 December 1785.

45 ACA, *Enactment Books*.
46 ACA, *Enactment Books*, 2 December 1785; 10 January 1786.
47 Emsley, 'Gender in the Proceedings of the Old Bailey'. *OBP*.
48 Kilday, 'Women and Crime', 175.
49 Kilday, 'Women and Crime'.
50 Durston, *Victims and Viragos*, 61.
51 Black Kalendar, 89.
52 Gowing, 'Marked Bodies and Social Meanings'; *OBP*, September 1799, t17990911–18.
53 Kilday, 'Women and Crime', 175.
54 Feeley and Little, 'The Vanishing Female', 719; Kilday, 'Women and Crime', 176; Gowing, 'Marked Bodies and Social Meanings', and King, 'Gender, Crime and Justice', 64–5.
55 Black Kalendar, 239.
56 *OBP*, February 1796, t17960217–72.
57 *OBP*, February 1712, t17120227–33.
58 *OBP*, February 1762, t17620224-11.
59 *LL*, 13 October 1703, t17031013–6.
60 *OBP*, June 1720, t17200602–17.
61 *OBP*, July 1722, t17220704–59.
62 *OBP*, October 1725, t17251013-10.
63 *OBP*, February 1719, t17190225–29.
64 *OBP*, February 1787, t17870221–11.
65 *OBP*, December 1744, t17441205–33.
66 Hogarth, *Anecdotes of William Hogarth*, 178.
67 Fielding, *Amelia*, 35–6.
68 *OBP*, February 1733, t17330221–52. Knapp and Baldwin, *The Newgate Calendar* 336–43; Magrath, '(Mis)Reading the Bloody Body', 223–36.

FINAL THOUGHTS

The end of girlhood

As girlhood prepared the girl to become the woman, distinctive changes in her social and sexual persona marked the passage to adulthood. Girls expected to acquire their adult status primarily through marriage, a feature marked in apprenticeship indentures which could end 'age twenty-one or marriage'. They developed their own distinct identity, learned skills and behaviours and gained a knowledge of what society expected of them. They also matured sexually, explored sexual relationships and tested the romantic waters. Theoretically they gained the tools to be an adult woman. Clearly what they achieved during their girlhood depended on family, community, their place in the social order and often on geography. Scottish, English, Welsh and Irish girls drew on different communities, values and expectations. Not all girls needed the same skills as adults, nor did they acquire them. They also often ended girlhood in a very different location from where they began.

For most girls, marriage marked the end of girlhood, and the skills, knowledge, customs and dowries they had acquired were necessary to set them up as married adult women. They learned as a wife, most women gained a credible adult status and position; she gained power and more independence than girls had in relation to the household and servants, though under her husband's authority. The understanding of eighteenth-century coverture, described by Blackstone, that 'the husband and wife are one person in law: that is, the very being or legal existence of the woman is suspended during the marriage' has definitely been challenged and nuanced over the last two decades. The hegemony of coverture was partial and contested rather than monolithic; the law was variously interpreted and resulted in a more

DOI: 10.4324/9781003412168-13

complex, and often less oppressive, set of social relations.[1] Thus the newly minted adult woman and wife did move into a new realm of responsibilities and power.

Undoubtedly for many girls this was true and shaped how they experienced their years of girlhood and the ways they used this period in their life—as a recognised period of transition. However, several variables meant that the timing of both entering and leaving girlhood, as well as its duration, were flexible. Both beginnings and ends could be influenced by economic and political trends, biological and familial factors and customs, as well as simple personal choice. Many servants were, in fact, older than the youthful idea of a maidservant, often at least in their twenties and thirties. This was partly a function of a high level of permanent celibacy across society and of a general trend to delay marriage. However, ages of marriage varied, so burgess daughters in Aberdeen tended to marry younger than the average, because family connections and wealth made it feasible, and their role as members of a commercial network meant they played an important role in creating alliances. In addition, fishing communities often saw earlier marriages since fishermen were more likely to have money and the opportunity to marry sooner than their farming cousins. Protoindustrial families also had the potential for daughters to marry younger than servants and those who had to find their own work. In conditions of a rising population, not all young people could be absorbed into the rural community; they had to wait their chance, and for many it never came.

Custom and control based on social class and local cultures within which young women operated circumscribed courtship and marriage partners. Women were often bargaining tools between families to secure alliances, property and inheritance, and daughters played an important role in building up trade and farming networks. Even amongst working families, dowries sealed contracts, and those with no dowry could find marriage difficult. Marriages varied from pure love matches to unfeeling unions of sheer dynastic policy or money. Girls were not oblivious to family predilections but recognised that their own interests played a part. Even a decision to agree to a clandestine marriage could represent a girl's wish to retain a separate legal position, a right to her name, property and children, and could protect her access to trade. Thus, a woman gained public validation of her private life without loss of her legal identity.

The wedding marked a rite of passage, which had more meaning for young women than men, as they transferred from fathers' houses to husbands'. Older customs of large community weddings shaped by local traditions persisted, and weddings could be boisterous community affairs or simple private affairs. True, most brides had achieved maturity, and perhaps their activities remained unchanged, but marriage represented a change of status and role. Wives became persons in their own right. Culture marked the passage from maiden to wife by overt and recognisable symbols. Shifts in the traditional clothing of girls, single maids, married women and widows denoted changes in status. Commonly girls started to put their hair up, instead of flowing locks or plaits. Walking to their weddings, brides' hair remained unbound as a last sign of maidenhood. They also adopted the 'cap of a married woman' after marriage.

While ideology shaped the context and law set the rules, couples negotiated practice behind closed doors. Historians have argued that we see far more of romantic love in the eighteenth century than in earlier eras, and that affection formed a more substantial element in marital relationships. Nevertheless, several forces, including a period of relative peace and stability, emergent Enlightenment notions of the companionate rational marriage and growing prosperity for large sections of the European population may have fostered a respect for affection, even among the labouring orders. So, shifts probably did take place in the balance between affection and obligation in marital relationships.

Marriage discharged families from responsibility for daughters' support, and a couple's self-sufficiency marked success. They wished for a 'good' marriage, and women valued marriage to a man of substance, in a trade or with the skills to work. Characteristic patterns of sociability played a key role, since young women usually associated with their own social strata and encountered young men broadly acceptable to their parents. They married men who were close in proximity, from mutual trade or work backgrounds or the same community and who shared many of the same cultural expectations.

Importantly, society often saw girlhood ending upon marriage—regardless of when it took place—and marriage and service were frequently seen as mutually exclusive, and indeed many contemporaries and regulations enforced single servanthood.[2] However, older and married servants worked in both domestic and farm service. Also, married service was not necessarily non-resident. Sometimes couples married within a household and retained their positions, perhaps as cook and butler. Frequently, when a female domestic servant married, she retained some of her duties as a 'daily' servant, or switched to take in laundry. In 1739, Mary Collier's poem, *A Woman's Labour*, described the activities of a married woman working in both farm and domestic service. She was drawn into the haying and harvest, but also went 'a charring', doing laundry as well as cleaning pots and pans: 'For my own Part, I many a Summer's Day / Have spent in throwing, turning, making Hay; . . . Hard Labour we most chearfully pursue, / And our, abroad, a Charing often go.'[3] Residence was a factor in whether or not servants married, since particularly for domestic servants, families tended to be reluctant to have married workers as residents. Particularly in the case of women, this related to aspects of control, since tensions could arise if a woman was seen to serve two masters. Magistrates engaged in adjudicating on English servant taxes frequently dealt with hiring agreements that involved domestic servants living outside the employer's household. Between 1715 and 1752, Meldrum found that 8.5 per cent of London female servants were married and another 9.2 per cent widowed, while Earle found 5.5 per cent of occupied married women worked as domestic servants between 1605 and 1725. Furthermore, Earle noted forty-three wives (16.8 per cent of employed married women) and sixteen widows charring or doing laundry. Laundry could have been done on the premises or taken into the home; some may have been specialist ironers.[4] Dame Hilder came in to do the two-day wash at New Place Farm at Guestling in Sussex, while Frances Hamilton recorded at great length the various tasks her 'daily' Betty Huckleborough undertook in 1798 and 1799.[5] Thus, service and marriage could be intertwined, and service was not the sole property of singletons.

While the cultural norm was courtship, marriage and motherhood, large numbers of women remained single for long periods, or never married at all, some by choice and some by dint of circumstances. Some expected to marry but never did, remaining self-supporting or dependent throughout their lives. Significant numbers of women did not marry or give up service, making a career of it—or married when they were much older.[6] Poor women with few skills and no dowry could find it difficult to marry, disadvantaged by an excess of women over men in towns. Girls who had lost their honour were damaged goods in the marriage stakes, since the stigma of sexual taint and loss of reputation was clearly disadvantageous.

Remaining single was a lifestyle alternative, and of course, cohabitation was common, and it is unlikely that all singletons remained celibate. Convents still provided a route to single life in Ireland, and religious conviction or a desire for the contemplative life led some to this decision. Not all women in convents chose it, though, since some families sent daughters because they were unlikely to marry. But others saw the potential for a single independent life, perhaps embracing a degree of power and influence. Girls might choose not to conform if they had sufficient resources, control over income and strength of character. They used female business partnerships, ranging from well-capitalised concerns to petty trading and spinning to maintain a single existence. Many thrived. Mutual dependence, combined business activities and halving the overheads could make these successful, or at least attractive options. Poorer women might also choose to live without men, but maintaining themselves was extremely challenging. Some turned to the economy of expedients, and clustered with other women to make shift and survive. Remaining single could provide other sorts of opportunities, if a woman had the courage to pull it off. Some posed as men, and certainly not all were lesbian. Others entered into same-sex unions, even marrying. At issue was not only their need for support, or even their perceived failure as a woman, but the fact that 'unmastered' women were seen as disorderly and dangerous. Gender boundaries were bent and challenged across society.

Female agency

Girls took part in the decisions which shaped their lives, staying at school when the opportunity allowed, using service and apprenticeship to set themselves up, changing jobs and moving from place to place (Image 12.1). While parents shaped many of these decisions, a combination of high mortality and the commonsense view that coercion probably played a minor role indicates the positive force girls may have exerted on their journey through girlhood. Girls used school, service and apprenticeship as well as work, at home and away, to gain knowledge and experience they could usefully deploy as an adult. Throughout the literature and listening to girls' voices we have tangential evidence of the choices girls had and the ways they manoeuvred themselves through girlhood.

A question that this study cannot answer is the extent to which girls had choices, and the level of agency they could exercise as they moved toward adulthood. The question of agency underpins much of the research on

IMAGE 12.1 Joseph Highmore, 1692–1780, Sketch of a Young Girl, ca. 1735. Oil on canvas, Yale Center for British Art, Paul Mellon Collection, B1981.25.341.

contemporary girlhood, and it is useful to gain some understanding of how it could have operated in the early modern world. Agency was more than just having choices:

> If agency clearly refers to a capacity for action in the world and is therefore closely linked to the notion of choice, it is also embedded, as Giddens and Bourdieu have argued, in a set of deeply internalised dispositions (*habitus*) or in institutional and structural constraints (structuration theory). These constraints—or opportunities—are explicitly generative of agency, an agency that is always embodied in power relations and has to be contextualized within them.[7]

These girls had to negotiate multiple levels of power constraints: parents, siblings, officials, benefactors, masters/mistresses, courts and community and normative expectations. Although this volume argues for the significance of girlhood as preparation for adulthood, as a stage of learning to be adult and to gain knowledge, skills and practices they would need, it is also true that often this simply did not happen. Many slipped through the cracks, moving in and out of the poor law system, or turning up in court. Many of the few testimonies we have of working girls' experience come from settlement examinations and court testimony. Whilst opaque, they provide glimpses of the roles girls played in their own attempts to traverse girlhood.

The period to fourteen was most likely to be spent near or within the family home, working or attending school. In Chapter 4 we saw evidence of girls having a hand in making choices about schooling and apprenticeship. This period varied considerably in terms of length and location, and the extent to which they were able to play a role in the decisions and strategies adopted by them and their families. Leaving home often loosened parental control and fostered the shift into adulthood, and there was a long tradition of leaving home to find work elsewhere. Girls took advantage of schooling, staying on, frequently for longer than many historians have indicated. They sought out informal avenues of learning. Even after going to work, many girls continued their education through Sunday schools, and even attending lectures when they were available.[8]

Poor girls, however, could find themselves apprenticed as young as seven, especially if they were orphaned or parents needed to claim poor relief. While most parish and private apprentices stayed relatively close to home, certainly, some went considerable distances away, necessitating cutting ties to family, friends and familiar surroundings. Parish girls were more likely to stay nearer home, and far more likely to be apprenticed nearby. For girls apprenticed by their parents, however, as evidence from milliners' apprentices indicates, where there was the pull of a good trade and the opportunity to do so, on average, they travelled the farthest of all girls in this study. It would be surprising if a daughter had had no input in the decision to go to a milliner at a distance, even several counties away.

The story of Elizabeth Palmer, with whom this book opened, is indicative. She went apprentice at age ten, served two months, then went to her father for three years, then back to Solihull but was sent onward to Lapworth, then taken to Northfield because her master was there on poor relief, then put to another farmer for a year.[9] Travelling over 130 km, she does not speak to us; we don't know what she thought or what choices she had or made. Nineteen-year-old Mary Weaver's testimony suggests she made some of the decisions on her movements, going to service at thirteen in her home community, but then she left to go to London where she did day-labour in Kensington and Chelsea.[10]

A commonly repeated phrase is that 'I hired myself out.' Thus, in Northfield, Warwickshire, in 1760, Mary Bowers explained that she had hired herself about thirteen or fourteen to a yeoman for a year. This was followed by several hirings.[11] So did Catherine Smith, who applied for a settlement in Sheldon, near Birmingham in 1770.[12] Similarly, Sarah Weston from Bocking, Essex, hired herself to two spinsters.[13] Indeed servants were especially mobile, acknowledged by historians and as examples here have shown. Once in service, girls moved regularly, usually for what they saw as a better position, one with better pay or for advancement. Mary Bowers moved several times, as did Mary Welbeck who served in Essex, nearer her home in Kent and then took up places in London.[14] Eleanor Ashwood moved between country and town, while Jane McDaniel left Ireland after serving Dublin. She was born in New Towne, County Down, Ireland:

> About eight years since I left the said town and came to Dublin and there lived as a servant . . . to Mr Nicholas Southerden, an upholder in Cable Street, Dublin, and thence removed and was a servant to Mr Charles Cao at Indian Queen on Essex Bridge in Dublin and then removed and was a servant to Mr Dugan, a taylor in Michaels Lane in Dublin, and there marrying, I came for London.[15]

Indeed, mobility was more than distance, and servants commonly moved around since their hirings were often a year. Susanna Whatman employed six maids in 1778, but only two at most remained in 1779.[16] Eleanor Ashwood explained that in addition to various places in London, 'she has lodged at several places in the country within the said time upon haymaking and harvest work'. With opportunity, many moved far more frequently, staying in one place on average eight months.[17]

Girls also had a hand in their courtships and sexual behaviour, and while they may have been circumscribed by community values and parental wishes, and to some extent simply by who they met, usually of their own social status, they often moved forward as they wished. Sarah Hurst, the other opening example, certainly had a hand in deciding on her marriage partner, keeping it secret and ultimately eloping when she was twenty-six. She also went on business trips on her own, suggesting a degree of independence, and potentially agency. However, family was one reason she was private about the liaison, especially his parents who did not approve of the match. The girls John Connon met and fancied all had their own ways of moving toward sex and marriage—even if unsuccessfully. As Gillis noted, couples in the plebeian orders were far more likely, certainly later in the century, to make their own marriage with less interference from parents, and marriage was one area girls had a larger say in. Girls in trouble, certainly, often took matters into their own hands, although it is hard to couch their actions in terms of agency. They were actions and decisions, some made with some thought and others as spur of the moment. Their situations spoke more of desperation isolation and a simple lack of support of other options.

Girls operated in a system that had multiple purposes. In principle, parents and girls wanted to find a living for daughters and used schools, apprenticeship and forms of service to do so. Girls staying at school for lengthy periods suggest that between them there was agreement that this would give them a step up for the future. Good apprenticeships could do the same and suggest the investment in fees and time offered potential. Poor children, who were more overtly subject to the systems, had less control over their lives. However, when it worked and girls gained an apprenticeship or service, locally perhaps, they remained in their community, may have married and worked to maintain a home and family, or to seek a living that could sustain them. Girlhood was understood by eighteenth-century society, and it embraced several routes toward adulthood, some related to work and gaining a living as well as learning the practices and skills they would need. Girls themselves had a hand in making decisions about how they traversed these years. So, while girlhood had significance within the social constructions of eighteenth-century Europe, it also had meaning for girls themselves.

Notes

1 See Simonton, 'Coverture and Capability'.
2 See Sarti, 'All Masters Discourage the Marrying', 417–49.
3 Collier, *The Woman's Labour*.
4 Steedman, 'The Servant's Labour', 11; Meldrum, *Domestic Service and Gender*, 18; Earle, 'Female Labour Market', 339. See also Erickson, 'Married Women's Occupations', 271–7.
5 Steedman, 'The Servant's Labour', 14.
6 Simonton, 'Birds of Passage'.
7 Simonton and Montenach, *Female Agency*, 4.
8 Simonton, *Education and Training*, chapter 6.
9 BDRO 14.

10 *Chelsea Settlement and Bastardy Examinations*, no. 351.
11 BDRO 14.
12 ERO D/P 264/13/4; BDRO, 42.
13 Earle, *City Full of People*, 139.
14 Meldrum, *Domestic Service and Gender*, 20–1, 43.
15 Earle, *City Full of People*, 192.
16 Whatman, *Housekeeping Book*, 56.
17 Meldrum, *Domestic Service and Gender*, 21, 43.

BIBLIOGRAPHY

Abbreviations

ACA Aberdeen City Archives
ERO Essex Record Office
FL Friends Library
LL *London Lives, 1690–1800*. www.londonlives.org
NAS National Archives of Scotland
OBP Old Bailey Proceedings Online. www.oldbaileyonline.org
PP Parliamentary Papers
PRO Public Record Office. Board of Inland Revenue. Apprenticeship Registers, 1710–1808
SRO Staffordshire Record Office

Archives

Aberdeen City Archives, Council, Baillie and Guild Registers

Barnes, Stephen J., ed. *Walthamstow in the Eighteenth Century Being Extracts from the Vestry Minutes, Churchwardens and Overseers' Accounts*. Walthamstow Antiquarian Society, 1925–1927

BDRO. 14, Saint Lawrence, Northfield, Examinations Re: Settlement, 1699–1802. Overseers of the Poor, Bundle II

BDRO. 42, Poor Law No. 7, Box 2, St Giles, Sheldon

BDRO. 61/7/8. Harborne Parish Apprenticeship Indentures

BDRO. 61/7/12, Saint Peter Harborne, Settlement Examinations, 1752–1807

Dale, Christabel. *Wiltshire Apprentices and Their Masters, 1710–1760*. Wiltshire Archaeological and Natural History Society, 1961

ERO. D/AEM 2/4, Archdiaconal Returns to the Bishop of London, 1807/8

ERO. D/DRa E16, Documents Relating to Terling Place Estate, List of Labouring Persons, 1778

ERO. D/NC 9/1, Coggeshall, Minutes of the Congregational Sunday School, and Accounts, 1788–1800

ERO. D/NC 9/1, Proceedings of the Committee of a Congregational Union for Promoting the Knowledge of the Gospel in the County of Essex and its Vicinity, 1798–1807
ERO. D/P 18/2/2, Ashdon, Draft Returns to the Bishop of London, 1810, 1814
ERO. D/P 18/3/75, Ashdon, Mr. Saltier's Account Book, 1745–1776
ERO. D/P 18/3/75B, Ashdon, Account Book of Rectory, 1799–1809
ERO. D/P 18/11/3, Ashdon, Overseers' Rate Book Including School Children, 1793–1794
ERO. D/P 18/12/3–4, Ashdon, Overseers' Accounts, 1770–1789
ERO. D/P 18/14, Ashdon Parish Apprenticeship Indentures
ERO. D/P 30/14, Witham Parish Apprenticeship Indentures
ERO. D/P 94/14, Chelmsford Parish Apprenticeship Indentures
ERO. D/P 203/14, Colchester, St Botolph Apprenticeship Indentures
ERO. D/P 245/18/6, Colchester, St Leonard, Overseers' Correspondence, 1745–1831
ERO. D/P 264/13/4, Braintree, Overseers, Settlement Examinations, 1703–1827
ERO. D/P 275/28/2, Great Yeldham, Girls' Industry School Minute Book, 1789–1798
ERO. D/Q 8/1, Chelmsford Charity School Minute Book, 1787–1808
ERO. D/Q 8/3, Chelmsford Charity School Accounts and Lists, 1773–c. 1830
ERO. D/Q 24/1A and D/Q 24/2, Romford Charity School Account and Minute Book of Trustees, 1710–1803
ERO. D/P 299/12/3, Return of the Poor Inhabitants of the Parish of Terling, 1801
ERO. T/A 461, Chelmsford Charity School Minutes, 1716–1763
ERO. T/A 613, Colchester Charity School Cash Book and Ledger, 1710–70
GLRO. Greater London Record Office, Kingston upon Thames, Apprenticeship Indentures, Camberwell, St Giles, P73/G13/122
Hembry, Phyllis. *Calendar of Bradford-on-Avon Settlement Examinations and Removal Orders, 1725–98*. Wiltshire Record Society, 1990
Jenkinson, C.H. *Surrey Apprenticeships, 1711–31*. Surrey Record Society, vol. 10, 1929
Jenkinson, Mrs. Hilary. *A List of Bedfordshire Apprentices, 1711–1720*. The Records of the Bedfordshire Historical Record Society, IX, 147–76. Boydell and Brewer, 2023
NAS. RH2/4/81/82. Narrative of the Proceedings at Tranent, on Tuesday the 29th of August
Rice, R. Garraway. *Sussex Apprentices and Their Masters, 1710–52*. Sussex Record Society, 1924
SRO. D120/A/PO/1264–1400; D120/A/PO/1700–1750, Aldridge Parish Apprenticeship Indentures
SRO. D204/1, Tamworth, Rawlett's Trust Charity Book, 1759–1862
SRO. D805/3/9, Armitage Parish Apprenticeship Indentures
SRO. D1054/7/20, Cannock Parish Apprenticeship Indentures, D120/A/PO/1264–1400
SRO. D1157/1/5/1, Wolverhampton Charity School Minute Book, 1716–97
SRO. D3720/4, Tamworth, Rawlett's Trust, Apprenticeship Indentures
Stirling County Archives. Murray Family of Polmaise and Touchadam Papers, 1450–1926, PD189, Ann Buchanan Letters
Surrey County Record Office. Apprenticeship Indentures, Mitcham, LA 5/6
Wedgwood Archives, V&A Wedgwood Collection

Newspapers

Aberdeen Journal
Birmingham Gazette
Chelmsford Chronicle

English Chronicle or Universal Evening Post (London)
Ipswich Journal
London Chronicle

Web Resources

Ancestry.com

Chelsea Settlement and Bastardy Examinations, 1733–1766. Edited by Tim Hitchcock and John Black (London, 1999). British History Online, http://www.british-history.ac.uk/london-record-soc/vol33/

FL. Friend's Library, https://www.friendslibrary.com/

OBP. 'Hackney Petty Sessions Book', 117–29. In *Justice in Eighteenth-Century Hackney: The Justicing Notebook of Henry Norris and the Hackney Petty Sessions Book*. edited by Ruth Paley (London Record Society, 1991). British History Online, http://www.british-history.ac.uk/london-record-soc/vol28/pp117-129

OBP. *Ordinary of Newgate's Account*, www.oldbaileyonline.org, version 8.0, 17 May 2023

Scotland's Places. *Female Servant Tax Rolls, 1785–1792*, E326/6, https://scotlandsplaces.gov.uk/digital-volumes/historical-tax-rolls/female-servant-tax-rolls-1785-1792/female-servant-tax-rolls-volume-03-1785-6-burghs-f (accessed 20 December 2023)

Scotland's Places. *Inhabited House Taxes*, https://scotlandsplaces.gov.uk/digital-volumes/historical-tax-rolls/inhabited-house-tax-1778-1798

British Governmental Records

Commission to Inquire Concerning Charities, Reports, 1819–37.

National Records of Scotland, Inhabited House Tax, vol. 2 (E326/63–64).

Parliamentary Papers, 1801, Population Returns, Population Act, 41 Geo. III, 2 vols., 1800.

Parliamentary Papers, 1816, vol. 16, Abstract of Answers and Returns of Charitable Donations for the Benefit of Poor Persons, 1787–88.

Parliamentary Papers, 1819, vol. 9, Report from the Select Committee on the Education of the Lower Orders in the Metropolis (Brougham), 5 vols., 1816–1819.

Poor Law Commissioners. Reports of Special Assistant Poor Law Commissioners on the Statutes, 27 Henry VIII, c. 25; 14 Eliz. I, c. 5 (1572); 39 Eliz. I, c. 3 (1597); Eliz. I, c. 2 (1601); Eliz. I, c. 4.; 21 Jac. 1 c. 27 An Act to Prevent the Destroying and Murthering of Bastard Children; 27 Geo. 2.c33, or The Act for Better Preventing Clandestine Marriage 17 George II c. 5; Geo. III, c. 39 and 18 Geo. III, c. 47.

Statutes. The Acts of the Parliaments of Scotland, vol. IX: A.D. M.DC.LXXXIX—MDCXCV, 1822.

Primary

Aikin, John. *A General Description of the Country from Thirty to Forty Miles Around Manchester*. Manchester, 1795.

Anon. *Hints to Masters and Mistresses, Respecting Female Servants*. London, 1800.

Anon. *A Lady's Woman, the Maid-Servants Modest Defence: In Answer to a Pamphlet, Entitul'd Every-Body's Business Is No-Body's Business*. London, 1725.

Anon. *The New Art and Mystery of Gossiping: Being a Genuine Account of All the Women's Clubs in and About . . .* London, 1760.

Anon. *On the Institution of Working-Schools for Poor Girls, and of Sunday Schools for Poor Boys and Girls in Chester*. Chester, 1800.
Anon. *The Polite Lady, or a Course Female Education; in a Series of Letters from a Mother to Her Daughter*, 3rd ed. London, 1775.
Ashbridge, Elizabeth. *Life of Elizabeth Ashbridge*. London, 1886.
Ashton, John. *Chapbooks of the Eighteenth Century*. 1882, reprint ed., Seven Dials Press, 1969.
Bailey, W. and G. Culley. *General View of the Agriculture of Northumberland Cumberland and Westmoreland*. Board of Agriculture, 1794.
Baillie, Grissell. *The Household Book of Lady Grisell Baillie, 1692–1733*. Edited by Robert Scott-Moncrieff. Scottish History Society, 1911.
Bamford, Samuel. *The Autobiography of Samuel Bamford. Vol. 1: Early Days*. 1849, Routledge, 1967.
Barrington, Jonah. *Personal Sketches of His Own Times*, 3rd ed., 2 vols. London, 1869.
Beattie, James. *James Beattie's Day Book, 1773–1798*. Edited by Ralph S. Walker. Spalding Club, 1948.
Bird, James Barry. *A Present for Servants, from Their Ministers, Masters or Other Friends*, 10th ed. J. F. C. Rivington for the SPCK, 1787.
Black Kalendar of Aberdeen, 3rd ed. Geo. Clark and Son, 1845.
Blackstone, William. *Commentaries on the Laws of England*. Edited by Edward Christian, 4 vols., 13th ed. A. Strahan, 1800.
Book of Trades, or Library of the Useful Arts. Tabart & Co., 1806.
Boos, Florence. 'Mary Ann Ashford'. In *Memoirs of Victorian Working-Class Women: The Hard Way Up*. Palgrave, 2017.
Bristow, Amelia. *Faithful Servant; or, the History of Elizabeth Allen*, 2nd ed. London, 1837.
Brown, John. *On the Female Character and Education, a Sermon Preached at the Anniversary Meeting of the Guardians of the Asylum for Deserted Female Orphans*, London, 16 May 1765.
Brown, John. *Sermons on Various Subjects*. L. Davis and C. Reymers, 1764.
Burney, Fanny. *The Early Journals and Letters of Fanny Burney, vol. 2: 1774–1777*. McGill-Queen's University Press, 1991.
Burton, John. *Lectures on Female Education and Manners*, 2 vols. London, 1793.
Burton, John. *Religious Education of Poor Children Recommended, a Sermon Preached at the Parish Church of Christ-Church*. London, 17 May 1759.
Cadogan, William. *An Essay upon Nursing and the Management of Children*. London, 1748.
Campbell, Robert. *The London Tradesman*. London, 1747.
Cappe, Catherine. *An Account of Two Charity Schools for the Education of Girls and of a Female Friendly Society in York*. York, 1800.
Cappe, Catherine. *Observations on Charity Schools, Female Friendly Societies and Other Subjects*. J. Hatchard, 1805.
Cappe, Catherine. 'On Parish Apprentices'. *The Monthly Magazine* 12 (1801): 7–8.
Capper, Mary. 'A Memoir of Mary Capper'. Edited by Katherine Backhouse. *The Friends' Library* 12 (1848): 1–45.
Chapman, John. *The Ends and Uses of Charity Schools for Poor Children, a Sermon Preached at the Parish Church of Christ-Church*. London, 30 April 1752.
Collier Mary. *The Woman's Labour, an Epistle to Mr. Stephen Duck; in Answer to His Late Poem, Called the Thresher's Labour*. London, 1739.
Collyer, Joseph. *The Parents' and Guardians' Directory*. London, 1761.
Cripplegate Society. *Rules and Orders to Be Observed by a Friendly Society of Women*. 1774.

Darwin, Erasmus. *A Plan for the Conduct of Female Education, in Boarding Schools, Private Families, and Public*. London, 1797.
Davies, David. *The Case of Labourers in Husbandry Stated and Considered*. G. G. and J. Robinson, 1795.
Defoe, Daniel. *The Complete English Tradesman*. London, 1726.
Defoe, Daniel. *Essay Upon Projects*. 1697.
Defoe, Daniel. 'Everybody's Business Is Nobody's Business', 1725. In *The Novels and Miscellaneous Works of Daniel Defoe*, vol. 19. D. A. Talboys, 1841.
Defoe, Daniel. *The Great Law of Subordination Consider'd; or, the Insolence and Insufferable Behaviour of Servants in England Duly Enquir'd into*. London, 1724.
Defoe, Daniel. *Review*, 25 June 1709, 142.
Drury Lane Society. *Rules and Orders to Be Observed and Kept by a Friendly Society of Women*. London, 1788.
Eden, Frederick Morton. *The State of the Poor*, 3 vols. 1797.
Erskine, John. *An Institute of the Law of Scotland*, 4 vols. 1824.
Fielding, Henry. *Amelia*. 1751. Edited by David Blewett. Penguin, 1987.
Follows, Ruth. 'Journal of Ruth Follows'. *Friends Library*, n.d.
Fox, Eliza. *Memoir of Mrs. Eliza Fox*. Edited by Franklin Fox. N. Trübner and Co, 1869.
Fry, K. and R.E. Cresswell. *Memoir of the Life of Elizabeth Fry with Extracts from Her Journal and Letters*, 2 vols., 2nd ed. John Hatchard and Son, 1848.
Gibbons, Hannah. 'Journal of Hannah Gibbons'. *Friends Library*, n.d.
Gilbert, Ann Taylor. *Autobiography and other Memorials of Mrs. Gilbert, formerly Ann Taylor*, 2 vols. Edited by Josiah Gilbert. Henry S. King and Co., 1874.
Gisborne, Thomas. *An Inquiry into the Duties of Men in the Higher and Middle Classes of Society in Great Britain*, 2nd ed., 2 vols. 1795.
Granger, Joseph. *General View of the Agriculture of the County of Durham*. 1794.
Grubb, Sarah. 'Life and Letters of Sarah Grubb'. *Friends Library*, n.d.
Grubb, Sarah. 'Some Account of the Life and Religious Labours of Sarah Grubb.' *The Friends' Library* 12 (1848): 255–367.
Ham, Elizabeth. *Elizabeth Ham, by Herself, 1783–1820*. Edited by Eric Gillet. Faber and Faber Limited, 1945.
Hanway, Jonas. *Virtue in Humble Life, Containing Reflections on Relative Duties, Particularly Those of Masters and Servants*. 1774.
Hardyment, Christina, ed. *The Housekeeping Book of Susannah Whatman*. National Trust, 1987.
Hayley, William. *A Philosophical, Historical, and Moral Essay on Old Maids*, 3 vols. 1785.
Haywood, Eliza. *A Present for a Servant Maid*. 1743.
Herbert, Dorothea. *Retrospections of Dorothea Herbert, 1770–1806*. Town House, 1988.
Hogarth, William. *Anecdotes of William Hogarth, Written by Himself*. J.B. Nichols & Son, 1833.
Horne, George. *Reflections on the Importance of Forming the Female Character by Education*. Dublin, 1796.
Howard, John. *The State of the Prisons in England and Wales*. Warrington, 1777.
Humble Petition of the Poor Spinners. Leicester, 1788. British Museum Tracts, B. 544 (10).
Hurst, Sarah. *The Diaries of Sarah Hurst, 1759–1762: Life and Love in 18th Century Horsham*. Edited by Susan Djabri. Amberley, 2009.
The Infants Lawyer: Or the Laws (Both Ancient and Modern) Relating to Infants. London, 1697.
Ingram, Richard Acklom. *An Essay on the Importance of Schools of Industry and Religious Instruction*. London, 1800.

Kenrick, *Whole Duty of Woman*, 13th ed. 1792.
Knapp, Andrew and William Baldwin, eds. *The Newgate Calendar*. J. Robins and Co., 1824.
Locke, John. *Some Thoughts Concerning Education*. Harvard Classics, 1909–14.
Lonsdale, Roger, ed. *The New Oxford Book of Eighteenth-Century Verse*. Oxford University Press, 1984.
Lucas, Margaret. 'An Account of the Convincement and Call to the Ministry of Margaret Lucas'. *The Friends' Library* 13 (1849): 179–201.
Lucas, Margaret. *The Life of Margaret Lucas*. Friends Library Publishing, 2023.
Malthus, Thomas. *An Essay on Population*, 2 vols. 1798. Edited by Michael P. Fogarty. Everyman's Library. J. M. Dent and Sons Ltd., 1958.
Mandeville, Bernard. *The Fable of the Bees, or Private Vices, Public Benefits. With an Essay on Charity and Charity Schools*. London, 1723.
Marshall, William. *The Rural Economy of the Southern Counties*. London, 1798.
Marshall, William. *The Rural Economy West of England*. London, 1796.
McParlan, James. *Statistical Survey of the Country of Donegal*. Dublin, 1802.
Moir, John. *Female Tuition, or an Address to Mothers on the Education of Daughters*. London, 1784.
More, Hannah. *Cheap Repository Tracts: Entertaining, Moral, and Religious*, vol. 4. American Tract Society, 185-?.
More, Hannah. *Essays on Various Subjects, Principally Designed for Young Ladies*. London, 1777.
More, Hannah. *Strictures on the Modern System of Female Education*. London, 1799.
Möser, Justus. *Anwalt des Vaterlands*. Berlin, 1786.
Neale, Henry St. John. *Practical Essays and Remarks on That Species of Consumption Incident to Youth*. London, 1800.
A New Song of Mallinger or, the Female-Dear-Joy Tricked of her Maiden-Head, 1700, National Library of Scotland, https://digital.nls.uk/broadsides/view/?id=14542
Paine, Thomas. *Rights of Man*. Edited by Henry Collins. London, 1791.
Purefoy Letters, 1735–53. Edited by G. Eland, 2 vol. Sidgwick and Jackson, 1931.
Radcliffe, William. *Origin of the New System of Manufacture*. James Lomax, 1828.
Raper, Elizabeth. *Receipt Book of Elizabeth Raper*. Edited by Bartle Grant. The Nonesuch Press, 1924.
Richardson, Samuel. *Pamela*, 2 vols. 1740. J. M. Dent and Sons Ltd., 1914.
Rousseau, Jean Jacques. *Émile*. Translated by Barbara Foxley. J.M. Dent and Sons Ltd., 1974.
Rules, Orders and Regulations for the Original Female Friendly Society, Held at Vicar's Hall, Lichfield, 9 September 1794. Birmingham Reference Library 540458.
Saxby, Mary. *Memoirs of a Female Vagrant, Written by Herself*. J. Burdett, 1806.
Shaw, Benjamin. *The Family Records of Benjamin Shaw, Mechanic of Dent, Dolphinholme and Preston, 1772–1841*. Edited by Alan G. Crosby. The Record Society of Lancashire and Cheshire, 1991.
Sheridan, Richard Brinsley. 'The Rivals: A Comedy'. 1775.
Sinclair, Sir John. *The Statistical Account of Scotland (OSA)*, 21 vols. William Creech, 1791–1799.
Smith, Adam. *An Inquiry into the Nature and Causes of the Wealth of Nations*, Everyman ed. 1910.
Society for the Promotion of Christian Knowledge. *Account of Charity Schools in Great Britain and Ireland*. Annual. 1724, 1759.
Stephenson, Sarah. 'Life of Sarah Stephenson'. *Friends Library*, n.d.
Steuart, James. *Considerations on the Interest of the County of Lanark*. 1769.
Stewart, David of Garth. *Sketches of the Character, Manners, and Present State of the Highlanders of Scotland*. Constable, 1825.
Talbot, James. *The Christian Schoolmaster*. 1707.

Thrale, Hester. *Thraliana: The Diary of Mrs Hester Lynch Thrale (Later Mrs. Piozzi) 1776–1809*. Edited by Katherine C. Balderston. Clarendon Press, 1951.
Trimmer, Sarah. *The Charity Spelling Book: The Teacher's Assistant, Consisting of Lectures in the Catechitical Form*, 4th ed. London, 1798.
Trimmer, Sarah. *The Oeconomy of Charity: Or an Address to Ladies Concerning Sunday Schools*. London, 1787.
Trimmer, Sarah. *Reflections on the Education of Children in Charity Schools*. London, 1792.
Tyson, Moses and Henry Guppy, eds. *The French Journals of Mrs Thrale and Dr Johnson*. Manchester University Press, 1932.
Wakefield, Priscilla. *Reflections on the Present Condition of the Female Sex with Suggestions for Its Improvement*. London, 1798.
Wilkes, Wetenhall. *A Letter of Genteel and Moral Advice to a Young Lady*. London, 1740.
Wilson, John J. *The Annals of Penicuik; Being a History of the Parish and of the Village*. Privately Printed, 1795.
Wollstonecraft, Mary. *Vindication of the Rights of Woman*. London, 1792.
Woodforde, James. *The Diary of a Country Parson, 1758–1802*. Selected and edited by John Beresford. Canterbury Press, 1999.
Wray, Mary. *The Ladies Library*. London, 1714.
Young, Arthur. *The Farmer's Kalendar, or, a Monthly Directory for All Sorts of Country Business*. London, 1771.
Young, Arthur. *General View of the Agriculture of Suffolk*. London, 1797.
Young, Arthur. *A Six Months' Tour Through the North of England*. London, 1770.
Young, Arthur. *A Six Weeks' Tour Through the Southern Counties of England and Wales*. London, 1768, 1772.

Secondary

Abbott, Mary. 'Life Cycle', 111–28. In *A Cultural History of Childhood and Family in the Age of Enlightenment*. Edited by Elizabeth Foyster and James Marten. Bloomsbury Academic, 2010.
Abrams, Lynn. 'At Home in the Family: Women and Familial Relationships', 14–53. In *The Routledge History of Women in Europe from 1700*. Edited by Deborah Simonton. Routledge, 2006.
Abrams, Lynn. 'From Demon to Victim: The Infanticidal Mother in Shetland, 1699–1899', 156–80. In *Twisted Sisters: Women, Crime and Deviance in Scotland Since 1400*. Edited by Yvonne Galloway Brown and Rona Ferguson. Tuckwell Press, 2002.
Adair, Richard. *Courtship, Illegitimacy and Marriage in Early Modern England*. Manchester University Press, 1996.
Altick, Richard D. *The English Common Reader, a Social History of the Mass Reading Public, 1800–1900*. University of Chicago Press, 1957.
Anderson, R.D. *Education and the Scottish People*. Clarendon Press, 1995.
Andrew, Donna. *Philanthropy and Police: London Charity in the Eighteenth Century*. Princeton University Press, 1989.
Ariès, Philippe. *Centuries of Childhood*. Penguin Books, 1973.
Bailey, Joanne. 'Family Relationships', 13–32. In *A Cultural History of Childhood and the Family in the Enlightenment*. Edited by Elizabeth Foyster and James Marten. Bloomsbury Academic, 2010.
Bain, Ebenezer. *Merchant and Craft Guilds, a History of the Aberdeen Incorporated Trades*. Aberdeen, 1887.

Barclay, Katie. *Caritas, Neighbourly Love and the Early Modern Self*. Oxford University Press, 2021.
Barclay, Katie. 'The Early Modern Family', 16–32. In *Early Modern Childhood: An Introduction*. Edited by Anna French. Routledge, 2020.
Barclay, Katie. 'Love and Courtship in Eighteenth-Century Scotland', 37–54. In *Women in Eighteenth-Century Scotland*. Edited by Katie Barclay and Deborah Simonton. Ashgate/Routledge, 2013.
Barclay, Katie. 'Love, Care and the Illegitimate Child in Eighteenth-Century Scotland'. *Transactions of the RHS* 29 (2019): 105–25.
Barclay, Katie. *Love, Intimacy and Power: Marriage and Patriarchy in Scotland, 1650–1850*. Manchester, 2013.
Barclay, Katie. 'Marriage, Sex, and the Church of Scotland: Exploring Non-Conformity Amongst the Lower Orders'. *Journal of Religious History* 43, 2 (June 2019): 163–79.
Barty, Alexander B. 'Kilbryde in the Olden Days'. In *Stirling Natural History and Archaeological Society Transactions*. 1924–25.
Beattie, J.M. *Crime and the Courts in Early Modern England 1600–1800*. Princeton University Press, 1986.
Bellaigue, Christina de. 'Home Education 1750–1900: Domestic Pedagogies in England and Wales in Historical Perspective'. *Oxford Review of Education* 41, 4 (2015): 421–9.
Ben-Amos, Ilana Krausman. *Adolescence and Youth in Early Modern England*. Yale University Press, 1994.
Bennett, Judith M. and Amy M. Froide, eds. *Singlewomen in the European Past, 1250–1800*. University of Pennsylvania Press, 1999.
Benninghaus, Christina, Mary Jo Maynes and Brigitte Söland, eds. *Secret Gardens, Satanic Mills: Placing Girls in Modern European History*. Indiana University Press, 2004.
Berg, Maxine. *The Age of Manufactures, Industry, Innovation and Work in Britain, 1700–1820*. Routledge, 1994.
Berg, Maxine. 'What Difference Did Women's Work Make to the Industrial Revolution?'. *History Workshop* 35 (Spring 1993): 22–44.
Berry, Helen. *Orphans of Empire, the Fate of London's Foundlings*. Oxford University Press, 2019.
Bloch, Ruth H. 'Changing Conceptions of Sexuality and Romance in Eighteenth-Century America'. *William and Mary Quarterly* 60, 1 (2003): 13–42.
Brewer, John. *The Pleasures of the Imagination: English Culture in the Eighteenth Century*. Taylor & Francis Group, 2013.
Brown, A.F.J. *Essex at Work, 1770–1815*. Essex Record Office, 1969.
Buck, Ann. *Dress in Eighteenth-Century England*. Holmes & Meierk, 1979.
Bullock, Audrea Michelle. *Child Testimony and The Legal Definition of Childhood in Eighteenth-Century London*. MA Thesis, Miami University, 2004.
Burley, K.H. 'An Essex Clothier of the Eighteenth Century'. *Economic History Review*, New series, 11, 2 (1958): 289–301.
Burnette, Joyce. 'Laborers at the Oakes: Changes in the Demand for Female Day-Laborers at a Farm Near Sheffield During the Agricultural Revolution'. *Journal of Epidemiology and Community Health* 39 (1999): 41–67.
Burnette, Joyce. 'Testing for Occupational Crowding in Eighteenth-Century British Agriculture'. *Explorations in Economic History* 3, 3 (July 1996): 319–45.
Burnette, Joyce. 'The Wages and Employment of Female Day Labourers in English Agriculture, 1740–1850'. *The Economic History Review* 57, 4 (November 2004): 664–90.
Bushaway, Bob. *By Rite: Custom, Ceremony and Community in England 1700–1880*. Junction Books, 1982.

Calvi, Giulia and Carolina Blutrach-Jelín. 'Sibling Relations in Family History: Conflicts, Co-Operation and Gender Roles in the Sixteenth to Nineteenth Centuries: An Introduction'. *European Review of History: Revue européenne d'histoire* 17, 5 (2010): 695–704.

Cameron, Anne. 'Female Birthing Customs and Beliefs', 17–36. In *Women in Eighteenth-Century Scotland.* Edited by Katie Barclay and Deborah Simonton. Ashgate/Routledge, 2013.

Campbell, Stuart. 'Work and Play: The Material Culture of Childhood in Early Modern Scotland', 65–86. In *Children and Youth in Pre Modern Scotland.* Edited by Janay Nugent and Elizabeth Ewan. Boydell and Brewer, 2015.

Chapman, Stanley. *The Early Factory Masters: The Transition to the Factory System in the Midlands Textile Industry.* David & Charles, 1967; reprinted Gregg Revivals, 1992.

Cipolla, C. *Literacy and Development in the West.* Penguin Books Ltd., 1969.

Clark, Anna. 'Heterosexuality: Europe and North America'. In *A Cultural History of Sexuality in the Enlightenment.* Edited by Julie Peakman. Bloomsbury Academic, 2011.

Clark, Anna. *The Struggle for the Breeches: Gender and the Making of the British Working Class.* Rivers Oram Press, 1995.

Cohen, Elizabeth Storr and Margaret Louise Reeves, eds. *The Youth of Early Modern Women.* Amsterdam University Press, 2018.

Cohen, Michèle. 'The Pedagogy of Conversation in the Home: "Familiar Conversation" as a Pedagogical Tool in Eighteenth and Nineteenth-Century England'. *Oxford Review of Education* 41, 4 (July 2015): 447–63.

Coster, Will. *Family and Kinship in England 1450–1800.* Routledge, 2016.

Cranfield, G.A. *The Development of the Provincial Newspaper, 1700–60.* Oxford University Press, 1962.

Crawford, Patricia. *Parents of Poor Children in England, 1580–1800.* Oxford University Press, 2010.

Cressy, David. 'Levels of Illiteracy in England, 1530–1730'. *Historical Journal* 20, 1 (1977): 1–23.

Crosbie, Barbara. *Age Relations and Cultural Change in Eighteenth Century England.* Boydell and Brewer, 2020.

Crowston, Clare. *Fabricating Women, the Seamstresses of Old Regime France, 1675–1791.* Duke University Press, 2001.

Cunningham, Hugh. *Children and Childhood in Western Society.* Longman, 1995.

Cunningham, Hugh. *Time, Work and Leisure: Life Changes in England Since 1700.* Manchester University Press, 2016.

Davidoff, Leonore. *Thicker Than Water: Siblings and Their Relations, 1780–1920.* Oxford University Press, 2012.

Davies, C. Stella. *The Agricultural History of Cheshire, 1750–1850.* Chetham Society, 3rd series, 1960.

D'Cruze, Shani, ed. *Colchester People: The John Bensusan Butt Biographical Dictionary of Eighteenth-Century Colchester*, 2nd ed. Privately Published, 2010.

Dennison, Patricia, David Ditchburn and Michael Lynch, eds. *Aberdeen Before 1800, a New History.* Tuckwell Press Ltd., 2002.

Diack, Lesley. 'Motherhood and Poverty in Aberdeen', 172–85. In *Gendering Scottish History: An International Perspective.* Edited by Terry Brotherstone, Deborah Simonton and Oonagh Walsh. Cruithne Press, 1999.

Dunlop, O.J. and R.D. Denman. *English Apprenticeship and Child Labour—A History.* Fisher Unwin, 1912.

Durie, Alastair J., ed. *The British Linen Company 1745–1775.* Scottish History Society and Pillans & Wilson Ltd., 1996.

Durie, Alastair J. *The Scottish Linen Industry in the Eighteenth Century*. Edinburgh University Press, 1979.

Durston, Gregory. *Victims and Viragos: Metropolitan Women, Crime and the Eighteenth-Century Justice System*. Abramis, 2007.

Earle, Peter. *A City Full of People, Men and Women of London, 1650–1750*. Methuen, 1994.

Earle, Peter. 'The Female Labour Market in London in the Late Seventeenth and Early Eighteenth Centuries'. *Economic History Review* 42, 3, (1989): 328–53.

Emsley, Clive. *Crime and Society in England, 1750–1900*. Longman, 2010.

Emsley, Clive. 'Gender in the Proceedings of the Old Bailey'. *OBP*, https://www.oldbaileyonline.org/about/gender

Erickson, Amy Louise. 'Eleanor Mosley and Other Milliners in the City of London Companies 1700–1750'. *History Workshop Journal* 71, 1 (Spring 2011): 147–72.

Erickson, Amy Lousie. 'Married Women's Occupations in Eighteenth-Century London'. *Continuity and Change* 23, 2 (2008): 267–307.

Evans, Tanya. '". . . Overwhelmed with Shame and Destitute of Friends . . ."? Re-Presentations of London's Unmarried Mothers in the Eighteenth-Century'. Unpublished manuscript.

Evans, Tanya. '"Unfortunate Objects": London's Unmarried Mothers in the Eighteenth Century'. *Gender and History* 17, 1 (2005): 127–53.

Evans, Tanya. *Unfortunate Objects: Lone Mothers in Eighteenth-Century London*. Palgrave Macmillan, 2005.

Fairchilds, Cissy. 'The Production and Marketing of Populuxe Goods in Eighteenth-Century Paris', 228–48. In *Consumption and the World of Goods*. Edited by John Brewer and Roy Porter. Routledge, 1993.

Feeley, Malcolm and Deborah Little. 'The Vanishing Female: The Decline of Women in Criminal Process, 1687–1912'. *Law and Society Review* 25, 4 (1991): 719–57.

Field, Jacob. 'Domestic Service, Gender, and Wages in Rural England, c. 1700–1860'. *The Economic History Review* 66, 1 (Feb. 2013): 249–72.

Fildes, Valerie, ed. *Women as Mothers in Pre-Industrial England*. Routledge, 1990.

Fontaine, Laurence. 'In the 18th Century, Poverty Was More a Risk Than a State', Interview with Nicolas Gastineau. *Philonomist*, https://www.philonomist.com/en/interview/18th-century-poverty-was-more-risk-state (accessed 4 October 2024).

Fontaine, Laurence. *Vivre pauvre: Quelques enseignements tirés de l'Europe des Lumières* [Living Poor: Some Lessons Learned from the Europe of the Enlightenment]. Gallimard, 2022.

Formark, Bodil, Heta Mulari and Myry Voipio, eds. *Nordic Girlhoods: New Perspectives and Outlooks*. Palgrave, 2017.

French, Anna. *Early Modern Childhood: an Introduction*. Routledge, 2020.

Froide, Amy M. *Never Married: Singlewomen in Early Modern England*. Oxford University Press, 2005.

Froide, Amy M. *Silent Partners, Women as Public Investors During Britain's Financial Revolution, 1690–1750*. Oxford University Press, 2016.

Fryer, Peter. *Staying Power, the History of Black People in Britain*. Pluto Press, 1974.

George, M. Dorothy. *England in Transition*. 1931; reprint ed. Penguin Books, 1953.

George, M. Dorothy. *London Life in the Eighteenth Century*. 1965; reprint ed. Penguin Books, 1973.

Gillis, John R. 'Affective Individualism and the English Poor'. *Journal of Interdisciplinary History* 10, 1 (Summer 1979): 121–8.

Gillis, John R. *For Better, for Worse: British Marriages, 1600–Present*. Oxford University Press, 1986.

Gillis, John R. 'Resort to Common Law Marriage in England and Wales, 1700–1850'. Unpublished paper.

Gillis, John R. '"A Triumph of Hope over Experience": Chance and Choice in the History of Marriage'. *International Review of Social History* 4 (1999): 47–54.
Gillis, John R. *A World of Their Own Making: A History of Myth and Ritual in Family Life*. Oxford University Press, 1997.
Gillis, John R. *Youth and History, Tradition and Change in European Age Relations*. Academic Press, 1974.
Gleadle, Kathryn. 'The Imagined Communities of Women's History: Current Debates and Emerging Themes, a Rhizomatic Approach'. *Women's History Review* 22, 4 (2013): 524–40.
Golby, J.M. and A.W. Purdue. *The Civilisation of the Crowd: Popular Culture in England: 1750–1900*. Batsford, 1984.
Goldsmith, Sarah. 'Imagining Youth: Epistolary Representations of the Adolescent and Youthful Body', 40–63. In *Letters and the Body, 1700–1830: Writing and Embodiment*. Edited by Sarah Goldsmith, Sheryllyne Haggerty and Karen Harvey. Routledge, 2023.
Gottlieb, Beatrice. *The Family in the Western World*. Oxford University Press, 1993.
Gowing, Laura. *Common Bodies, Women, Touch, and Power in the Eighteenth Century*. Yale University Press, 2003.
Gowing, Laura. 'Giving Birth at the Magistrate's Gate: Single Mothers in the Early Modern City', 137–50. In *Women, Identities and Communities in Early Modern Europe*. Edited by Stephanie Tarbin and Susan Broomhall. Ashgate, 2008.
Gowing, Laura. 'Girls on Forms: Apprenticing Young Women in Seventeenth-Century London'. *Journal of British Studies* 55 (July 2016): 447–73.
Gowing, Laura. *Ingenious Trade: Women and Work in Seventeenth-Century London*. Cambridge University Press, 2021.
Gowing, Laura. 'Marked Bodies and Social Meanings', 133–54. In *A Cultural History of the Human Body in the Age of Enlightenment*. Edited by Carole Reeves. Bloomsbury Academic, 2010.
Green, Eileen, Sandra Hebron and Diana Woodward. *Women's Leisure, What Leisure?* Macmillan, 1990.
Griffin, Emma. 'Sex, Illegitimacy and Social Change in Industrializing Britain'. *Social History* 38, 2 (2013): 139–61.
Guttmann, Allen. *Women's Sports: A History*. Columbia University Press, 1991.
Guttormsson, Loftur. 'Parent-Child Relations', 251–82. In *Family Life in the Long Nineteenth Century*. Edited by M. Barbagli and D.I. Kertzer. Yale University Press, 2003.
Hammond, J.L. and Barbara Hammond. *The Village Labourer*. 1911; reprint ed. Longman, 1978.
Hanawalt, Barbara A. 'Childrearing Among the Lower Classes of Late Medieval England'. *Journal of Interdisciplinary History* 8, 1 (Summer 1977): 1–22.
Hans, Nicholas. *New Trends in Education in the Eighteenth Century*. Routledge and Kegan Paul Ltd, 1951.
Harris, Amy. *Siblinghood and Social Relations in Georgian England: Share and Share Alike*. Manchester University Press, 2012.
Harvey, Karen. *Reading Sex in the Eighteenth Century: Bodies and Gender in English Erotic Culture*. Cambridge University Press, 2004.
Hecht, J. Jean. *The Domestic Servant in Eighteenth-Century England*. Routledge and Kegan Paul, 1956; reprint ed. 1980.
Helgren, J. and C.A. Vasconcellos, eds. *Girlhood: A Global History*. Rutgers University Press, 2010.
Hendrick, Harry. 'The History of Childhood and Youth'. *Social History* 9, 1 (January 1984): 87–96.
Heywood, Colin. *Childhood in Modern Europe*. Cambridge University Press, 2018.

Heywood, Colin. 'Children's Work in Countryside and City', 125–41. In *The Routledge History of Childhood in the Western World*. Edited by Paula Fass. Routledge, 2013.
Higginbotham, Jennifer. *Fair Maids and Golden Girls: Early Modern Girlhood and the Production of Femininity*. PhD Dissertation, University of Pennsylvania, 2007.
Hill, Bridget. *Servants: English Domestics in the Eighteenth Century*. Oxford University Press, 1996.
Hill, Bridget. *Women, Work and Sexual Politics in Eighteenth-Century England*. Basil Blackwell, 1989.
Hindle, Steve. 'Representing Rural Society: Labor, Leisure, and the Landscape in an Eighteenth-Century Conversation Piece'. *Critical Inquiry* 41 (Spring 2015): 615–54.
Hitchcock, Tim. 'Reformulation of Sexual Knowledge'. *Signs: Journal of Women in Culture and Society* 55, 1 (2012): 823–32.
Hitchcock, Tim. '"Unlawfully Begotten on Her Body": Illegitimacy and the Parish Poor in St Luke's Chelsea', 70–86. In *Chronicling Poverty: The Voices and Strategies of the English Poor, 1640–1840*. Edited by Tim Hitchcock, Peter King and Pamela Sharpe. Palgrave, 1997.
Hitchcock, Tim and Robert Shoemaker. *London Lives, Poverty, Crime and the Making of a Modern City, 1690–1800*. Cambridge University Press, 2016.
Holloway, Sally. *The Game of Love in Georgian England: Courtship, Emotions and Material Culture*. Oxford University Press, 2018.
Honeyman, Katrina. *Child Workers in England, 1780–1820: Parish Apprentices and the Making of the Early Industrial Labour Force*. Taylor & Francis Group, 2007.
Horrell, Sara and Jane Humphries. '"The Exploitation of Little Children": Child Labor and the Family Economy in the Industrial Revolution'. *Explorations in Economic History* 73 (2019): 101–72.
Horrell, Sarah, Jane Humphries and Joachim Voth. 'Destined for Deprivation: Human Capital Formation and Intergenerational Poverty in Nineteenth-Century England'. *Explorations in Economic History* 38 (2001): 339–65.
Horrell, Sara, Jane Humphries and Jacob Weisdorf. 'Women and Children, Forgotten Family . . ., 1260–1860'. *Journal of Medieval and Early Modern Studies* 54, 3 (1 September 2024): 529–58.
Horrocks, Hilary and Sheonagh Martin. *The Georgian House*. National Trust for Scotland, 2013.
Houston, R.A. 'Age at Marriage of Scottish Women, Circa, 1660–1770'. *Local Population Studies* 43 (1989): 63–6.
Houston, R.A. 'The Demographic Regime', 1–18. In *People and Society in Scotland, vol. 1, 1760–1830*. Edited by Thomas M. Devine and Rosalind Mitchison. Edinburgh University Press, 1988.
Houston, R.A. *Literacy in Early Modern Europe, Culture and Education, 1500–1800*. Longman, 1988.
Houston, R. A. *Scottish Literacy and the Scottish Identity: Illiteracy and Society in Scotland and Northern England 1600–1800*. Cambridge University Press, 1985.
Humphries, Jane. *Childhood and Child Labour in the British Industrial Revolution*. Cambridge University Press, 2010.
Humphries, Jane. 'English Apprenticeship: A Neglected Factor in the First Industrial Revolution', 72–102. In *The Economic Future in Historical Perspective*. Edited by Paul A. David and Mark Thomas. Oxford University Press, 2006.
Humphries, Jane and Jacob Weisdorf. 'The Wages of Women in England, 1260–1850'. *Journal of Economic History* 75, 2 (June 2015): 405–47.
Hunt, Karen. 'Women as Citizens: Changing the Polity', 216–58. In *The Routledge History of Women in Europe Since 1700*. Edited by Deborah Simonton. Routledge, 2005.

Hunt, Margaret. 'Time-Management, Writing, and Accounting in the Eighteenth-Century Trading Family: A Bourgeois Enlightenment'. *Business and Economic History*, 2nd series, 18 (1989): 150–9.

Jones, Bernard. 'Ham, Elizabeth (1783–1859)'. *ODNB*, https://doi.org/10.1093/ref:odnb/45850

Jones, Mary G. *The Charity School Movement, a Study of Eighteenth Century Puritanism in Action*. Cambridge University Press, 1938; reprint ed., Frank Cass and Co Ltd, 1964.

Kelly, Thomas. *A History of Adult Education in Great Britain*. Liverpool University Press, 1970.

Kennedy, Líam and Martin W. Dowling. 'Prices and Wages in Ireland, 1700–1850'. *Irish Economic and Social History* 24 (1997): 62–104.

Kent, David. 'Ubiquitous but Invisible: Female Domestic Servants in Mid-Eighteenth-Century London'. *History Workshop Journal* 28 (1989): 111–28.

Kett, Joseph F. 'The Stages of Life', 166–91. In *The Family in Social-Historical Perspective*. Edited by Michael Gordon. St Martins Press, 1978.

Kilday, Anne-Marie. *A History of Infanticide in Britain, c. 1600 to the Present*. Palgrave Macmillan, 2013.

Kilday, Anne-Marie. 'Maternal Monsters: Murdering Mothers in Southwest Scotland, 1750–1815', 156–79. In *Twisted Sisters: Women, Crime and Deviance in Scotland Since 1400*. Edited by Yvonne Galloway Brown and Rona Ferguson. Tuckwell Press, 2002.

Kilday, Anne-Marie. 'Women and Crime', 174–93. In *Women's History: Britain 1700–1850, an Introduction*. Edited by Hannah Barker and Elaine Chalus. Routledge, 2005.

King, Peter. 'Gender, Crime and Justice in Late Eighteenth- and Early Nineteenth England', 44–74. In *Gender and Crime in Modern Europe*. Edited by Margaret Arnot and Cornelie Usborne. UCL Press, 1999.

King, Steven. 'Chance Encounters? Paths to Household Formation in Early Modern England'. *International Review of Social History* 44 (1999): 23–46.

Kittredge, Katharine. '"For the Benefit of Young Women Going into Service": Late Eighteenth-Century Proto-Young Adult Novels for Labouring-Class Girls'. *Women's Writing* 23, 1 (2016): 106–26.

Kussmaul, Ann. 'The Ambiguous Mobility of Farm Servants'. *Economic History Review* 34, 2 (May 1981): 222–35.

Kussmaul, Ann. *Servants in Husbandry in Early Modern England*. Cambridge University Press, 1981.

Lane, Joan. *Apprenticeship in England, 1600–1914*. Routledge, 1996.

Lane, Penelope, Neil Raven and K.D.M. Snell, eds. *Women, Work and Wages in England, 1600–1850*. Boydell, 2004.

Laqueur, Thomas W. 'The Cultural Origins of Popular Literacy in England, 1500–1850'. *Oxford Review of Education* 2, 3 (1976): 255–75.

Laqueur, Thomas W. 'Working-Class Demand and the Growth of English Elementary Education, 1750–1850', 192–205. In *Schooling and Society, Studies in the History of Education*. Edited by Lawrence Stone. The Johns Hopkins University Press, 1976.

Laslett, Peter. 'The Bastardy Prone Sub-Society', 217–46. In *Bastardy and Its Comparative History*. Edited by Peter Laslett, Karla Oosterveen and Richard M. Smith. Cambridge University Press, 1980.

Laslett, Peter. *Family Life and Illicit Love in Earlier Generations*. Cambridge University Press, 1977.

Laslett, Peter. 'Mean Household in England Since the Sixteenth Century', 125–59. In *Household and Family in Past Time*. Edited by Peter Laslett and Richard Wall. Cambridge University Press, 1972.

Laslett, Peter. *The World We Have Lost*. Charles Scribners' Sons, 1965.
Lawson, John and Harold Silver. *A Social History of Education in England*. Methuen and Co. Ltd, 1973.
Lemire, Beverly. *The Business of Everyday Life: Gender, Practice and Social Politics in England, c. 1600–1900*. Manchester University Press, 2005.
Leneman, Leah. *Promises, Promises: Marriage Litigation in Scotland, 1698–1830*. National Museums of Scotland, 2006.
Leneman, Leah and Rosalind Mitchison. 'Scottish Illegitimacy Ratios in the Early Modern Period'. *The Economic History Review*, 2nd series, 60 (1987): 41–63.
Leneman, Leah and Rosalind Mitchison. *Sexuality and Social Control: Scotland 1660–1780*. Basil Blackwell, 1989.
Levene, Alysa. *Childcare, Health and Mortality at the London Foundling Hospital: 'Left to the Mercy of the World'*. Manchester University Press, 2012.
Levene, Alysa. 'Children, Childhood and the Workhouse: St Marylebone, 1769–1781'. *The London Journal* 33, 1 (2008): 41–59.
Levene, Alysa. 'Parish Apprenticeship and the Old Poor Law in London'. *The Economic History Review* 63, 4 (2010): 915–41.
Levine, David. 'For Their Own Reasons: Individual Marriage Decisions and Family Life'. *Journal of Family History* 7 (1982): 255–64.
Logue, Kenneth. *Popular Disturbances in Scotland, 1780–1815*. Edinburgh University Press, 1979.
Lord, Evelyn. '"Weighed in the Balance and Found Wanting": Female Friendly Societies, Self Help and Economic Virtue in the East Midlands in the Eighteenth and Nineteenth Centuries'. *Midland History* 22, 1 (1997): 100–12.
Luddy, Maria and Mary O'Dowd. *Marriage in Ireland, 1660–1925*. Cambridge University Press, 2020.
Macfarlane, Alan. *The Family Life of Ralph Josselin, a Seventeenth-Century Clergyman*. Cambridge University Press, 1970.
Mackay, Theresa. 'Women at Work: Innkeeping in the Highlands and Islands of Scotland, 1790–1840'. *Journal of Scottish Historical Studies* 37, 2 (2017): 155–76.
Magrath, Jane. 'Mis-Reading the Bloody Body: The Case of Sarah Malcolm'. *Women's Writing* 11, 2 (2004): 223–36.
Malcolmson, Robert W. *Life and Labour in England, 1700–1800*. Hutchinson, 1981.
Malcolmson, Robert W. *Popular Recreations in English Society, 1700–1850*. Cambridge University Press, 1973.
Marshall, Dorothy. *The English Poor in the Eighteenth Century, a Study in Administrative History*. George Routledge and Sons Ltd., 1926.
Martin, Joanna. *Wives and Daughters, Women and Children of the Georgian Country House*. Hambledon, 2004.
Martin, Paula. *Cupar: The History of a Small Scottish Town*. Birlinn, 2006.
Mathias, Peter. 'Labour and the Process of Industrialisation in the First Phases of British Industrialisation'. In *Enterprise and Labour from the Eighteenth Century to the Present*. Edited by Peter Mathias and J.A. Davis. Blackwell, 1996.
Maudlin, Daniel. 'The Urban Inn: Gathering Space, Hierarchy and Material Culture in the Eighteenth-Century British Town'. *Urban History* 46, 4 (2019): 617–48.
Maynes, Mary Jo. 'Age as a Category of Historical Analysis: History, Agency, and Narratives of Childhood'. *Journal of the History of Childhood and Youth* 1, 1 (2008): 114–24.
Maynes, Mary Jo. 'Girlhood in Modern European History: (Proto-)Industrialisation, Consumption, Marriage, and Selfhood, ca. 1750–1900'. In *Themenportal Europäische Geschichte*, 2009, www.europa.clio-online.de/essay/id/fdae-1501
Maynes, Mary Jo. *Schooling in Western Europe, a Social History*. SUNY Press, 1985.

McKendrick, Neil. 'Home Demand and Economic Growth, a New View of the Role of Women and Children in the Industrial Revolution', 152–210. In *Historical Perspectives, Studies in English Thought and Society*. Edited by Neil McKendrick. Europa Publications, 1974.

McKendrick, Neil, John Brewer and J.H. Plumb. *The Birth of a Consumer Society; the Commercialization of Eighteenth-Century England*. Hutchinson, 1983.

Medick, Hans. 'The Protoindustrial Family Economy: The Structural Function of Household and Family During the Transition from Peasant Society to Industrial Capitalism'. *Social History* 3 (October 1976): 291–315.

Medick, Hans. 'Village Spinning Bees: Sexual Culture and Free Time Among Rural Youth in Early Modern Germany', 317–39. In *Interest and Emotion: Essays on the Study of Family and Kinship*. Edited by Hans Medick and David Warren Sabean. Cambridge University Press, 1984.

Meldrum, Tim. *Domestic Service and Gender*. Pearson, 2000.

Menis, Susanna. *A History of Women's Prisons in England: The Myth of Prisoner Reformation*. Cambridge Scholars Publishing, 2019.

Mikalachki, Jodi. 'Women's Networks and the Female Vagrant: A Hard Case', 52–69. In *Maids and Mistresses, Cousins and Queens: Women's Alliances in Early Modern England*. Edited by Susan Frye and Karen Robertson. Oxford University Press, 1999.

Mitchell, B.R. *European Historical Statistics, 1750–1970*, abridged ed. Macmillan, 1978.

Mitchell, C. and C. Rentschler, eds. *Girlhood and the Politics of Place*. Berghahn Books, 2016.

Mitchell, C., J. Reid-Walsh and J. Kirk. 'Editorial'. *Girlhood Studies* 1, 1 (Summer 2008).

Moore, Lindy. 'Education and Learning', 111–39. In *Gender in Scottish History*. Edited by Lynn Abrams, Eleanor Gordon, Deborah Simonton and Eileen Yeo. Edinburgh University Press, 2006.

Moore, Lindy. 'Urban Schooling in Seventeenth and Eighteenth-century Scotland', 79–96. In *Edinburgh History of Education in Scotland*. Edited by Robert Anderson, Mark Freeman and Lindsay Paterson. Edinburgh, 2015.

Muir, Angela Joy. 'Courtship, Sex and Poverty: Illegitimacy in Eighteenth-Century Wales'. *Social History* 43, 1 (2018): 56–80.

Muldrew, Craig. *The Economy of Obligation: The Culture of Credit and Social Relations in Early Modern England*. St Martin's Press, 1998.

Muldrew, Craig. 'From Credit to Savings? An Examination of Debt and Credit in Relation to Increasing Consumption in England (c.1650 To 1770)'. *Quaderni Storici, Nuova Serie*, 46, 137, 2 (2011): 391–413.

Muurling Sanne and Marion Pluskota. 'The Gendered Geography of Violence in Bologna, Seventeenth to Nineteenth Centuries'. In *The Routledge History Handbook of Gender and the Urban Experience*. Edited by Deborah Simonton, Anne Montenach, Elaine Chalus, Nina Javette Koefoed, Marjo Kaartinen, Katie Barclay and Nigel Worden. London: Routledge, 2017, 153–64

Neale, R.S. *Writing Marxist History: British Society, Economy and Culture Since 1700*. Blackwell, 1988.

Neave, D. *Friendly Societies in the Rural East Riding 1830–1912*. PhD thesis, University of Hull, 1985.

Nejedly, Mary. 'Earning Their Keep: Child Workers at the Birmingham Asylum for the Infant Poor, 1797–1852'. *Family and Community History* 20, 3 (2017): 206–17.

Nenadic, Stana. 'Necessities: Food and Clothing in the Long Eighteenth Century', 137–63. In *A History of Everyday Life in Scotland, 1600 to 1800*. Edited by Elizabeth Foyster and Christopher A. Whatley. Edinburgh University Press, 2010.

Neuberg, Victor E. *Popular Education in Eighteenth Century England.* Woburn Books Limited, 1971.
Newby, Howard. *Country Life: A Social History of Rural England.* Weidenfeld and Nicolson, 1987.
O'Connell, Lisa. *The Origins of the English Marriage Plot: Literature, Politics and Religion in the Eighteenth Century.* Cambridge, 2019.
O'Dowd, Mary and June Purvis. *A History of the Girl: Formation, Education and Identity.* Palgrave, 2018.
Ogilvie, Sheilagh. *A Bitter Living: Women, Markets, and Social Capital in Early Modern Germany.* Oxford University Press, 2003.
O'Hara, Diana. *Courtship and Constraint: Rethinking the Making of Marriage in Tudor England.* Manchester University Press, 2000.
O'Sullivan, Ellis. *Ascendancy: Women and Elementary Education.* Palgrave, 2017.
Oxford Review of Education, Special Issue: *Home Education 1750–1900: Domestic Pedagogies in England and Wales in Historical Perspective* 41, 4 (August 2015).
Parratt, Catriona M. *'More Than Mere Amusement': Working-Class Women's Leisure in England, 1750–1914.* Northeastern University Press, 2001.
Payne, Dianne Elizabeth. *Children of the Poor in London 1700–1780.* PhD Thesis, University of Hertfordshire, February 2008.
Perkin, Harold. *The Origins of Modern English Society, 1780–1880.* Routledge and Kegan Paul Ltd, 1972.
Phillips, Nicola. *Women in Business, 1700–1850.* Boydell, 2006.
Phillips, Pamela, F., ed. *Enlightened Nightscapes: Critical Essays on the Long Eighteenth-Century Night.* Routledge, 2023.
Pinchbeck, Ivy. *Women Workers and the Industrial Revolution, 1750–1850.* G. Routledge and Sons, 1930; reprint ed. Virago Press, 1981.
Pinchbeck, Ivy and Margaret Hewitt. *Children in English Society*, vol. 1. Routledge and Kegan Paul, 1969.
Plumb, J.H. 'The New World of Children in Eighteenth-Century England'. *Past and Present* 67 (May 1975): 64–93.
Pluskota, Marion. *Prostitution and Social Control in Eighteenth-Century Ports.* London: Routledge, 2016.
Probert, Rebecca. 'Control Over Marriage in England and Wales, 1753–1823: The Clandestine Marriages Act of 1753 in Context'. *Law and History Review* 27, 2 (2009): 413–50.
Proctor, Tammy. 'Home and Away: Women, Popular Culture and Leisure', 299–340. In *The Routledge History of Women in Europe Since 1700.* Edited by Deborah Simonton. Routledge, 2006.
Pullin, Nicola. *'Business Is Just Life': The Practice, Prescription and Legal Position of Women in Business, 1700–1850.* PhD thesis, Royal Holloway, University of London, 2001.
Radford, Peter. 'Women's Foot Races in the 18th and 19th Centuries: A Popular and Widespread Practice'. *Canadian Journal of History of Sport* 25, 1 (1994): 50–61.
Ramdin, Ron. *Remaining British, 500 Years of Black and Asian History in Britain.* Pluto Press, 1999.
Randall, Adrian. *Riotous Assemblies: Popular Protest in Hanoverian England.* Oxford University Press, 2006.
Razzell, Peter. 'The Growth of Population in Eighteenth-Century England: A Conundrum Resolved'. *Past & Present* 98 (February 1983): 121–50.
Razzell, Peter and Christine Spence. 'The History of Infant, Child and Adult Mortality in London, 1550–1850'. *The London Journal* 32, 3 (November 2007): 271–92.
Rendall, Jane. *The Origins of Modern Feminism Women in Britain, France and the United States, 1780–1860.* Macmillan, 1985.

Rendall, Jane. '"The Principle of Mutual Support": Female Friendly Societies in Scotland, c. 1789'. *Journal of Scottish Historical Studies* 40, 1 (2020): 17–39.

Rendall, Jane. 'Women's Associations in Scotland, 1797–1825', 206–28. In *Association and Enlightenment: Scottish Clubs and Societies 1700–1830*. Edited by M. Wallace and J. Rendall. Bucknell University Press, 2021.

Rizzo, Betty. 'Equivocations of Gender and Rank: Eighteenth-Century Sporting Women'. *Eighteenth-Century Life* 26, 1 (Winter 2002): 70–118.

Roche, Daniel. *The People of Paris, an Essay in Popular Culture in the 18th Century*. Berg, 1987.

Rule, John. *Experience of Labour in Eighteenth-Century Industry*. Croom Helm, 1981.

Rule, John. *The Labouring Classes in Early Industrial England, 1750–1850*. Longman Group Limited, 1986.

Rushton, Peter. 'The Matter in Variance: Adolescents and Domestic Conflict in the Pre-Industrial Economy of Northeast England, 1600–1800'. *Journal of Social History* 25, 1 (Autumn 1991): 89–107.

Sarti, Raphaella. 'All masters discourage the marrying of their male servants, and admit not by any means the marriage of the female': Domestic Service and Celibacy in Western Europe from the Sixteenth to the Nineteenth *Century', European History Quarterly* 38, 3: 417-49.

Sanderson, Elizabeth. *Women and Work in Eighteenth-Century Edinburgh*. Macmillan, 1996.

Schofield, Roger S. 'Dimensions of Illiteracy, 1750–1850'. *Explorations in Economic History* 10 (1972–73): 437–54.

Schofield, Roger S. 'The Measurement of Literacy in Preindustrial England', 311–25. In *Literacy in Traditional Societies*. Edited by Jack Goody. Cambridge University Press, 1968.

Sellman, Roger R. *Devon Village Schools in the Nineteenth Century*. David and Charles, 1967.

Sharpe, J.A. *Crime in Early Modern England 1550–1750*. Longman, 1984.

Sharpe, Pam. 'Literally Spinsters: A New Interpretation of the Local Economy and Demography in Colyton in the Seventeenth and Eighteenth Centuries'. *The Economic History Review* 44, 1 (1991): 46–65.

Sharpe, Pamela. *Adapting to Capitalism: Working Women in the English Economy, 1700–1850*. Longman, 1996.

Sharpe, Pamela. 'The Female Labour Market in English Agriculture During the Industrial Revolution: Expansion or Contraction?' *Agricultural History Review* 47, 2 (1999): 161–81.

Shepard, Alexandra. 'Crediting Women in the Early Modern English Economy'. *History Workshop Journal* 79, 1 (2015): 1–24.

Shoemaker, Robert B. *Prosecution and Punishment: Petty Crime and the Law in London and Rural Middlesex, c.1660–1725*. Cambridge University Press, 1991.

Shoemaker, Robert B. *Gender in English Society, 1650–1850*. Longman, 1998.

Shoemaker, Robert B. *Patterns of Crime and Prosecution*, https://www.oldbaileyonline.org/about/patterns-of-crime-and-prosecution

Simon, Joan. 'Was There a Charity School Movement? The Leicestershire Evidence', 55–100. In *Education in Leicestershire, 1540–1940, a Regional Study*. Edited by Brian Simon. Leicester University Press, 1968.

Simonton, Deborah. '"Birds of Passage" or "Career" Women? Thoughts on the Life-cycle of the European Servant'. *Women's History Review* 20, 2 (Spring 2011): 207–25.

Simonton, Deborah. 'Bringing Up Girls: Work in Pre-Industrial Europe', 23–37. In *Secret Gardens, Satanic Mills*. Edited by Christing Benninghaus, Mary Jo Maynes and Brigitte Sjöland. Indiana University Press, 2004.

Simonton, Deborah. 'Community of Goods, Coverture and Capability in Britain: Scotland Versus England', 31–47. In *Gender, Law and Economic Well-Being in Europe from the Fifteenth to the Nineteenth Century: North Versus South?* Edited by Anna Bellavitas and Beatrice Zucca Micheletto. Routledge, 2019.

Simonton, Deborah. *The Education and Training of Eighteenth-Century English Girls*. PhD Thesis, University of Essex, 1988.

Simonton, Deborah. *Gender in the European Town, Ancien to Modern*. Routledge, 2024.

Simonton, Deborah. *A History of European Women's Work, 1700 to the Present*. Routledge, 1998.

Simonton, Deborah. 'Inscribing the Town on Women's Bodies: Disorderly Behaviour in Aberdeen, 1747–1800'. In *Cultures of Sickness, Health and the Body in Medieval and Early Modern Europe*. Edited by Anni Hella and Anu Korhonen. Routledge, 2026.

Simonton, Deborah. 'Milliners and Marchandes de Modes: Gender, Skill and Creativity in the Workplace', 19–38. In *Luxury and Gender, c. 1700–1914*. Edited by Deborah Simonton, Marjo Kaartinen and Anne Montenach. Routledge, 2014.

Simonton, Deborah. 'Schooling the Poor: Gender and Class in Eighteenth-Century England'. *British Journal for Eighteenth-Century Studies* 23 (Autumn 2000): 183–202.

Simonton, Deborah. '"Sister to the Tailor": Guilds, Gender and the Needle Trades in Eighteenth-Century Europe', 135–58. In *Early Professional Women in Northern Europe, c. 1650 to the 1850s*. Edited by Johanna Ilmakunnas, Marjatta Rahikainen and Kirsi Vainio-Korhonen. Routledge, 2017.

Simonton, Deborah. '". . . to Merit the Countenance of the Magistrates": Gender and Civic Identity in Eighteenth-Century Aberdeen', 17–32. In *Gender in Urban Europe: Sites of Political Activity and Citizenship, 1750–1900*. Edited by Krista Cowman, Nina Javette Koefoed and Åsa Karlsson Sjögren. Routledge, 2014.

Simonton, Deborah. *Women in European Culture and Society: A Source Book*. Routledge, 2013.

Simonton, Deborah and Anne Montenach, eds. *Female Agency in the Urban Economy: Gender in European Towns, 1640–1830*. Routledge, 2013.

Simpson, Anthony E. 'Age of Consent', 181–205. In *Sexual Underworlds of the Enlightenment*. Edited by G.S. Rousseau and Roy Porter. Manchester University Press, 1987.

Skinner, Basil. 'Scots Fairs and Markets'. *Scotland's Magazine*, February 1962, http://www.basilskinner.com/scots-fairs-and-markets.html

Smith, Chloe Wigston. '"Callico Madams": Servants, Consumption, and the Calico Crisis'. *Eighteenth-Century Life* 31, 2 (2007): 29–55.

Smith, Richard. 'Some Issues Concerning Families and Their Property in rural England, 1200–1800', 133–96. In *Land, Kinship and Life-Cycle*. Edited by R.M. Smith. Cambridge University Press, 1984.

Smout, T.C. and A.J.S. Gibson. *Scotland, Prices, Food and Wages in Scotland, 1550–1780*. Cambridge University Press, 1994.

Snell, Keith D.M. 'Belonging and Community: Understandings of 'Home' and 'Friends' Among the English Poor, 1750–1850'. *The Economic History Review* 65, 1 (2012): 1–25.

Snell, Keith D.M. 'Agricultural Seasonal Unemployment, the Standard of Living and Women's Work in the South and East'. *The Economic History Review* 34 (August 1981): 407–37.

Snell, Keith D.M. *Annals of the Labouring Poor, Social Change and Agrarian England, 1660–1900*. Cambridge University Press, 1985.

Spence, Cathryn. *Women, Credit, and Debt in Early Modern Scotland*. Manchester University Press, 2016.

Stearns, Peter N. *Childhood in World History*. Routledge, 2006.

Stearns, Peter N. 'Defining Happy Childhoods: Assessing A Recent Change'. *Journal of the History of Childhood and Youth* 3, 2 (2010): 165–86.
Steedman, Carolyn. *Labours Lost: Domestic Service and the Making of Modern England*. Cambridge University Press, 2009.
Steedman, Carolyn. *Master and Servant: Love and Labour in the English Industrial Age*. Cambridge University Press, 2007.
Steedman, Carolyn. 'The Servant's Labour: The Business of Life, England, 1760–1820'. *Social History* 29, 1 (2004): 2–29.
Stone, Lawrence. *The Family, Sex and Marriage in England, 1500–1800*. Weidenfeld and Nicholson, 1977.
Stone, Lawrence. 'Literacy and Education in England, 1640–1900'. *Past and Present* 42 (February 1969): 69–139.
Strutt, Frederick. *Jedidiah Strutt Biography: 'Memorials of Old Derbyshire'*, https://belper-research.com/strutts_mills/memorials.html
Styles, John. 'Custom or Consumption? Plebeian Fashion in Eighteenth-Century England', 103–15. In *Luxury in the Eighteenth Century: Debates, Desires and Delectable Goods*. Edited by Maxine Berg and Elizabeth Eger. Palgrave Macmillan, 2003.
Styles, John. *The Dress of the People: Everyday Fashion in Eighteenth-Century England*. Yale University Press, 2008.
Styles, John. *Threads of Feeling: The London Foundling Hospital's Textile Tokens, 1740–1770*. The Foundling Museum, 2010.
Sweet, Rosemary. *The Writing of Urban Histories in Eighteenth-Century England*. Oxford University Press, 1997.
Thomas, Keith. 'Children in Early Modern England', 45–77. In *Children and Their Books*. Edited by Gillian Avery and Julia Briggs. Clarendon Press, 1989.
Thomis, Malcolm I. and Jennifer Grimmett. *Women in Protest, 1800–1850*. Croom Helm, 1982.
Thompson, E.P. *Customs in Common, Studies in English Popular Culture*. Merlin Press, 1991.
Thompson, E.P. 'Eighteenth-Century English Society: Class Struggle Without Class?' *Social History* 3, 2 (1978): 133–65.
Thompson, E.P. *The Making of the English Working Class*. Victor Gollancz, 1963.
Thompson, E.P. 'The Moral Economy of the English Crowd in the Eighteenth Century'. *Past and Present* 50 (February 1971): 76–136.
Thompson, E.P. 'Patrician Society, Plebeian Culture'. *Journal of Social History* 7, 4 (Summer 1974): 382–405.
Thompson, E.P. 'Time, Work Discipline, and Industrial Capitalism'. *Past and Present* 38 (1967): 56–97.
Thwaites, Wendy. 'Women in the Market Place: Oxfordshire, c. 1690–1800'. *Midland History* 9 (1984): 32–42.
Tilly, Louise and Joan Scott. *Women, Work and Family*. Routledge, 1987.
Tillyard, Stella. *Aristocrats: Caroline, Emily, Louisa and Sarah Lennox, 1750–1832*. Vintage, 1995.
Toulalan, Sarah. '"Age to Great, or to Little, Doeth Let Conception": Bodies, Sex and the Life Cycle, 1500–1750', 279–83. In *The Routledge History of Sex and the Body 1500 to the Present*. Edited by Sarah Toulalan and Kate Fisher. Routledge, 2013.
Toulalan, Sarah. 'Bodies, Sex and Sexuality', 29–52. In *The Routledge History of Women in Early Modern Europe*. Edited by Amanda Capern. Routledge, 2020.
Toulalan, Sarah. 'Child Sexual Abuse in Late Seventeenth and Eighteenth-Century London: Rape, Sexual Assault and the Denial of Agency', 23–44. In *Childhood and Child Labour in Industrial England: Diversity and Agency, 1750–1914*. Edited by Katrina Honeyman and Nigel Goose. Taylor and Francis, 2013.

Toulalan, Sarah. '"Unripe' Bodies": Children and Sex in Early Modern England', 131–50. In *Bodies, Sex and Desire from the Renaissance to the Present*. Edited by Kate Fisher and Sarah Toulalan. Palgrave Macmillan, 2011.

Vickery, Amanda. *The Gentleman's Daughter, Women's Lives in Georgian England*. Yale University Press, 1998.

Vincent, David. *Literacy and Popular Culture: England 1750–1914*. Cambridge University Press, 1989.

Voth, Hans-Joachim. 'Time and Work in Eighteenth-Century London'. *Journal of Economic History* 58 (1998): 29–58.

Wall, Richard. 'The Age at Leaving Home'. *Journal of Family History* 3 (1978): 181–202.

Wall, Richard. 'Inferring Differential Neglect of Females from Mortality Data'. *Annales de démographie historique* (1981): 119–40.

Wall, Richard. 'Mean Family Size in England Since the Sixteenth Century', 159–204. In *Household and Family in Past Time*. Edited by Peter Laslett and Richard Wall. Cambridge University Press, 1972.

Wallis, Patrick. 'Between Apprenticeship and Skill: Acquiring Knowledge outside the Academy in Early Modern England'. *Science in Context* 32, 2 (2019): 155–70.

Wallis, Patrick. *The Market for Skill, Apprenticeship and Economic Growth in Early Modern England*. Princeton University Press, 2025.

Wallis, Patrick and Marten Prak, eds. *Apprenticeship in Early Modern Europe*. Cambridge University Press, 2019.

Wallis, Patrick, Cliff Webb and Chris J. Minns. 'Leaving Home and Entering Service: The Age of Apprenticeship in Early Modern London'. *Continuity and Change* 25, 3 (December 2010): 377–404.

Webb, Robert K. *The British Working Class Reader, 1790–1848, Literacy and Social Tension*. Allen and Unwin, 1955.

White, Eryn. 'Women, Religion and Education in Eighteenth-Century Wales', 210–33. In *Women and Gender in Early Modern Wales*. Edited by Michael Roberts and Simone Clarke. University of Wales Press, 2000.

Whyte, Ian D. 'Protoindustrialisation in Scotland', 228–51. In *Regions and Industries: A Perspective on the Industrial Revolution in Britain*. Edited by Pat Hudson. Cambridge University Press, 1989.

Whyte, Ian D. and Kathleen A. Whyte. 'The Geographical Mobility of Women in Early Modern Scotland', 83–106. In *Perspectives in Scottish Social History*. Edited by Leah Leneman. Aberdeen University Press, 1988.

Wiesner, Merry E. *Women and Gender in Early Modern Europe*. Cambridge University Press, 1993.

Withrington, D.J. 'The S.P.C.K. and Highland Schools in Mid-Eighteenth Century'. *The Scottish Historical Review* 41, 132, Part 2 (October 1962): 89–99.

Woodward, Nick. 'Infanticide in Wales, 1730–1830'. *Welsh Historical Review* 23 (2007): 94–125.

Wright, Rebecca. *The Georgian Theatre Audience: Manners and Morals in the Age of Politeness, 1737–1810*. MA Thesis, Institute of Historical Research, 2014.

Wrightson, Keith. 'Infanticide in Earlier Seventeenth-Century England'. *Local Population Studies* 15 (1975): 10–22.

Wrigley, E.A., R.S. Davies, J.E. Oeppen and R.S. Schofield. *English Population History from Family Reconstitution*. Cambridge University Press, 1997.

Wrigley, E.A. and Roger S. Schofield. 'English Population History from Family Reconstitution: Summary Results, 1600–1799'. *Population Studies* 37 (1983): 157–84.

Wrigley, E.A. and Roger S. Schofield. *The Population History of England, 1541–1871*. Cambridge University Press, 1981.

Wunder, Heide. *He Is the Sun, She Is the Moon*. Harvard University Press, 1998.

INDEX

Note: Inevitably, many of the girls who flit through this book are not indexed, though a selection is listed under 'girls'.

For Product Safety Concerns and Information please contact our EU representative GPSR@taylorandfrancis.com Taylor & Francis Verlag GmbH, Kaufingerstraße 24, 80331 München, Germany

Printed and bound by CPI Group (UK) Ltd, Croydon, CR0 4YY
28/11/2025
02007808-0015